Photographer's Guide to the Leica D-Lux 6

Photographer's Guide to the Leica D-Lux 6

Getting the Most from Leica's Advanced Compact Camera

Alexander S. White

White Knight Press
Henrico, Virginia

Published by
White Knight Press
9704 Old Club Trace
Henrico, Virginia 23238
www.whiteknightpress.com
contact@whiteknightpress.com

ISBN: 978-1-937986-12-4 (paperback)
       978-1-937986-13-1 (e-book)

Printed in the United States of America

This book is dedicated to my wife, Clenise.

Contents

Author's Note

In October 2009, I published my first camera guide book, *Photographer's Guide to the Leica D-Lux 4*, which I followed in December 2010 with a similar book about the Leica D-Lux 5. Now that Leica has released its newest model in this series of advanced compact cameras, I have turned my attention to the D-lux 6.

All of the photographs illustrating the features of the D-Lux 6 are ones that I took with my D-Lux 6; the photographs showing the D-Lux 6 itself were taken with my Sony Alpha SLT-A99.

As always, my most supportive and encouraging partner in this endeavor has been my wife, Clenise, who provides inspiration, both photographic and personal, every single day.

Introduction

This book is a guide to the operation, features, and capabilities of the Leica D-Lux 6, one of the most capable and versatile "point-and-shoot" digital compact cameras available today. I chose this camera to write about partly because of my experience with its predecessors, the D-Lux 4 and D-Lux 5, but also because this camera stands out from the broad run of compact cameras for several reasons.

Consider the list of features you don't find every day in a compact camera that is not a DSLR (digital single-lens reflex): RAW image format; complete manual control of exposure and focus; burst capability for continuous shooting; a large, 3-inch (7.5 cm) diagonal and very sharp (920,000 pixels) LCD screen; a high-quality Leica lens with a wide 24mm equivalent focal length and a much brighter than ordinary f/1.4 - f/2.3 maximum aperture; HD (high-definition) motion picture recording with advanced features; excellent overall image quality, owing in part to the high quality of the camera's "intelligent" exposure and focus controls and image processing; and excellent performance in low light, owing in part to its fine performance at high ISO (light sensitivity) levels.

Moreover, the D-Lux 6 has an advanced MOS (metal-oxide semiconductor) light sensor considerably larger than those of many other compact cameras, resulting in greater image quality.

The D-Lux 6 also has a solid feel, partly because of its metal body and classic appearance. Many photographers will welcome the inclusion of physical switches to control many functions, so they don't have to navigate through menus to change the aspect ratio, focus mode, ISO, white balance, and other settings. And in addition to its useful pop-up flash, the camera is equipped with a hot shoe. The hot shoe can accept either an external flash unit or a high resolution electronic viewfinder. An external flash installed in this shoe can communicate with the camera for automatic flash control. The electronic viewfinder allows you to compose images through a shaded window rather than peering at an LCD display that can be washed out in sunlight.

Also, the D-Lux 6 includes basic functions and features similar to those of other cameras in its class: self-timer, macro (closeup shooting) mode, a wide range of shutter speeds (1/4000 second to 250 seconds), many different "scene" modes (such as portrait, night scenery, sunset, scenery, food, pet, and baby), and a full shooting mode with "creative" settings for producing images with exotically altered appearances.

Is anything lacking in the D-Lux 6? Some people would prefer a lens that goes beyond the 90mm equivalent of its maximum optical zoom; others would like a built-in optical viewfinder. Of course, the camera does not accept interchangeable lenses, and is equipped with a digital sensor which, although larger than average for a camera of this type, cannot provide the image quality of the larger sensors found on DSLRs. The camera could use better audio recording features, such as a jack for an external microphone, to support its excellent video capability.

But given that no camera can meet every possible need, the D-Lux 6 is an outstanding example of an advanced compact camera. It received an enthusiastic welcome by many photographers upon its release, sometimes to supplement a DSLR for occasions when it's inconvenient to carry a heavy load of gear, and sometimes as the photographer's only equipment to record vacation and family scenes. If you carry this camera with you, you will be ready to record a breaking news event (with still photos or movies), to capture a scenic view that catches your eye, to grab spontaneous "street photography" shots, or to experiment with the camera's many features to try new combinations of color effects, shutter speeds, and other settings from the D-Lux 6's wide array of possibilities.

This camera's quality and features have made it a winner by many measures. However, the documentation that comes with it does not always do justice to its capabilities. In addition, the documentation is split between a brief printed pamphlet and a much longer, but less convenient document that is provided on the CD-ROM that ships with the camera. I find it a lot easier to learn about a camera's features from a single guide, with illustrations, that takes the time to explain the features fully and clearly. That is the purpose of this book.

My goal is to provide a solid introduction to the D-Lux 6's controls and operation along with tips and advice as to when and how to use the various features. This book does not provide advanced technical information. If you already understand how to use every feature of the camera and when to use it and are looking for new insights, I have included some references in the Appendices that can provide more detailed information. This book is geared to the beginning to intermediate user who is not satisfied with the documentation provided with the camera, and who is looking for a reference guide that provides some additional help in mastering the camera's features.

One final note: There is a camera made by Panasonic, the Lumix DMC-LX7, that is very similar in operation and features to the Leica D-Lux 6. This book would be useful to owners of that camera as well, because of that similarity between the two cameras. However, I have published a separate book about that camera, *Photographer's Guide to the Panasonic Lumix LX7*, which includes photographs and screen shots illustrating the features of the Panasonic model specifically.

Chapter 1: Preliminary Setup

I will assume your Leica D-Lux 6 has just arrived at your home or office, perhaps purchased from an internet site. The box should contain the camera itself, lens cap, lens cap string, battery, battery charger, neck/shoulder strap, USB cable, audio-video cable, the user's manual on a CD, an abbreviated user's guide printed on paper, and one or two other pieces of paper, including a warranty card. That card includes a code that you can use to download Adobe Photoshop Lightroom software from the Leica internet site.

One of the first things you should do with your new camera is attach the lens cap string, a small loop supplied in a plastic envelope that is easy to overlook. Thread it through the small opening on the lens cap and then through the neck-strap bracket closest to the lens, as shown in Figure 1-1. Now your lens cap will be attached to the camera and can't be misplaced.

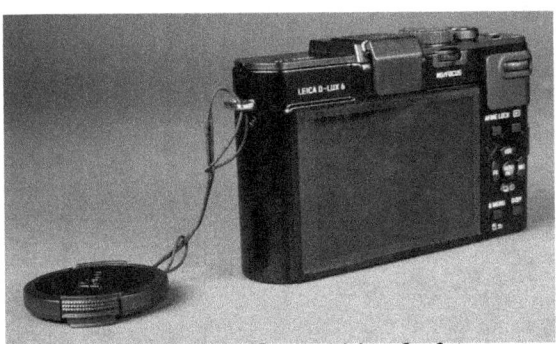

Fig. 1-1:   Lens Cap Attached to Camera with Lens Cap String

Some people don't like the removable lens cap provided with the D-Lux 6, because the cap has to be removed when you take a picture, may bother you as it dangles while you aim and focus, and has to be put back on the lens when you're done. I haven't found the cap to be a problem, because I'm used to cameras with removable lens caps. I see the point, though, because many other small cameras have built-in lens covers that automatically open up when you turn on the camera and close back down when the camera is turned off.

Some users of this camera deal with the lens cap situation by attaching the lens cap string to the right-side neck strap bracket rather than the left, so it's easy to hold the cap in the right hand while shooting, to keep it from flapping around.

If the lens cap situation really bothers you, there are "automatic" lens caps available for the D-Lux 6, as there were for earlier models, the D-Lux 4 and D-Lux 5. This sort of cap has leaves that open up as the lens extends, so the cap can stay on the camera and open and close as needed. I have tried one model, made by a company called JJC, that works quite well; you can find this item by searching on eBay or Amazon.com for "D-Lux 6 automatic lens cap." See Appendix A for further details.

As for the neck strap, it is quite useful when you're carrying the camera outside of its case, but I have found the strap to be a nuisance when placing the D-Lux 6 into a case, because of the strap's bulk. You might want to look for a wrist strap instead, which gives you a way to keep a tight grip on the camera but doesn't make it difficult to stow the camera safely in a case.

Charging and Inserting the Battery

The D-Lux 6 ships with a single rechargeable Lithium-ion battery, model number BP-DC-10U, the same battery as that used in the D-Lux 5. This battery has to be charged in an external charger; you can't charge it in the camera, even if you connect the camera to an optional AC adapter. So it's a very good idea to get an extra battery. I'll discuss batteries and other accessories in Appendix A. For now, let's get the battery charged.

You can only insert the battery into the charger one way; find the four goldish-colored metal contact strips on the battery, then look for the corresponding set of contacts (three, not four) inside the charger, and insert the battery so the two sets of contacts will connect up, as shown in Figures 1-2 and 1-3.

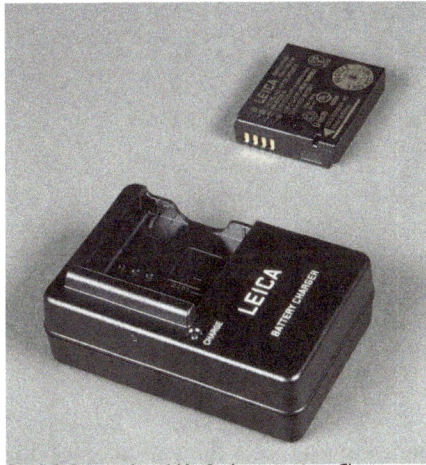

Fig. 1-2: Battery Lined Up for Inserting into Charger

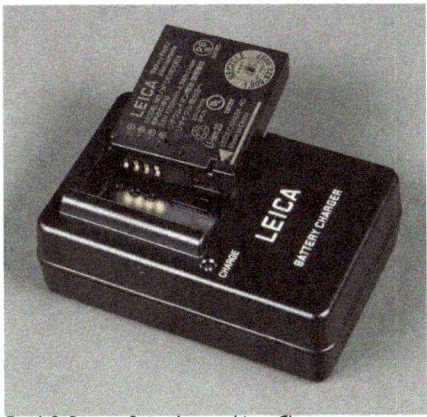

Fig. 1-3: Battery Being Inserted into Charger

With the battery inserted, plug the charger into any standard AC outlet or surge protector. The green light comes on to indicate that the battery is charging. When the green light turns off, after about two and a half hours, the battery is fully charged and ready to use. You shouldn't leave the battery in the charger indefinitely once it's charged, but I have often left it in the charger for 24 hours with no ill effects.

Once you have a charged battery, look for the small, light-gray, ridged latch on the memory card/battery door on the bottom of the camera, shown in Figure 1-4.

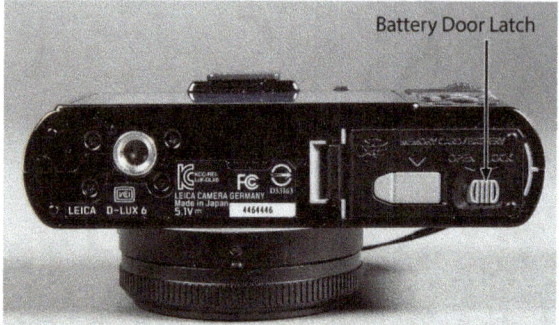

Fig. 1-4: Latch to Open Battery Compartment Door

Push the latch towards the center of the camera to release the door, and let the door open up. To insert the battery, look for the sets of metal contacts on the battery and inside the battery compartment, and guide the battery accordingly, as shown in Figures 1-5 and 1-6.

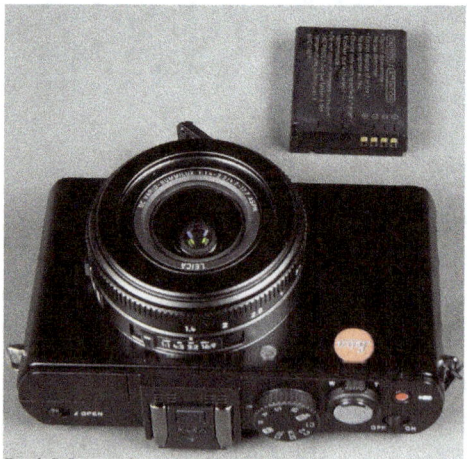

Fig. 1-5: Battery Lined Up for Insertion into Camera

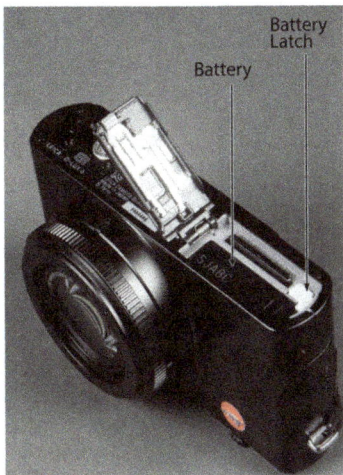

Fig. 1-6: Battery Secured by Battery Latch

You may need to use the right side of the battery to nudge the gray latching mechanism inside the battery compartment to the side, to allow the battery to slide in.

Slide the battery all the way in until the gray internal latch catches above the battery and locks it in place. Then close the battery compartment door, slide the external latch back to the right, and you're done.

Choosing and Inserting a Memory Card

The D-Lux 6 does not ship with a memory card. With this camera, unlike some others, this is not a fatal omission, because the D-Lux 6 has built-in memory that will let you take a few photographs even with no memory card inserted. The amount of built-in storage capacity is only about 70 megabytes (MB), which is pretty minuscule compared to storage cards of today that can hold up to 256 gigabytes (GB), or about 3600 times more. But if you're faced with a situation where you need to take a picture and don't have an available card, 70 MB is a lot better than nothing. (If you do record some images to the built-in memory, you can later copy them to a removable memory card; see the discussion of the Copy command at the end of Chapter 6.)

You shouldn't rely on the built-in memory if you don't have to, so you need to insert a separate memory card. The D-Lux 6 uses three varieties of card: Secure Digital (SD), Secure Digital High-Capacity (SDHC), and Secure Digital Extended Capacity (SDXC), as shown in Figure 1-7. There also is a special type of SD card, the Eye-Fi card, which I'll discuss a little later.

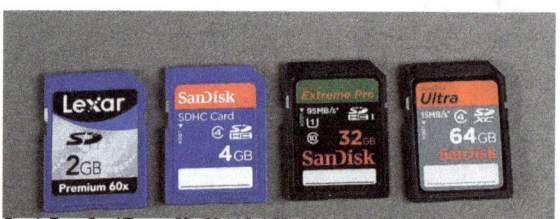

Fig. 1-7:   Card Types: SD, SDHC 4GB, SDHC 32GB, SDXC

All three types of SD card are small, about the size of a large postage stamp. The standard card, SD, comes in capacities from 8 MB to 2 GB. The high-capacity card, SDHC, comes in sizes from 4 GB to 32 GB. The newest type, SDXC, at this writing is available in a 48 GB, 64 GB, 128 GB, or 256 GB size. Larger sizes eventually should be available; the maximum capacity for SDXC theoretically is 2 terabytes, or about 2,000 GB.

What type and size of memory card you should use depends on your needs and intentions. If you're planning to record a good deal of high-definition (HD) video or many RAW photos, you need a card with a fairly large capacity. There are several variables to take into account in computing how many images or videos you can store on a particular size of card, such as the aspect ratio you're using (1:1, 3:2, 4:3, or 16:9), picture size, and quality.

Here are a few samples of what can be stored in the built-in memory or on a given card. If you're using the 4:3 aspect ratio and taking the highest-quality RAW and JPEG images together (recording two files for each image, as discussed in Chapter

4), you can store just 3 images in the built-in memory. If you record just JPEG images of the highest quality, you can store 16 pictures in the built-in memory. If you go to the other extreme and select the smallest size and lowest quality, you can store 656 images in the internal memory.

If you install an 8 GB SDHC card in the camera, you can store 460 of the highest-quality RAW plus JPEG images, 1800 of the highest-quality JPEG without RAW images, or more than 60,000 of the smallest size and lowest-quality still images.

If you're interested in video, here are some guidelines. With an 8 GB card, you can store a total of about 32 minutes of the highest-quality (PSH) AVCHD video footage, or about 56 minutes of the somewhat lower-quality FSH or SH formats. With the MP4 video format, you can store about 48 minutes of the highest-quality (FHD) format or about 90 minutes of the lower-quality HD format. If you use the lowest-quality VGA format, you can store a total of about 200 minutes of video.

If you are using the D-Lux 6's built-in memory, you can record and store only about 100 seconds of video in the lowest quality; you can't record in any other quality of video to the built-in memory.

Note, though, that there is an important caveat for video recording lengths with the D-Lux 6, as there is with most compact cameras that are designed primarily for still photography. There are built-in limitations on the length of continuous video recording in most formats. In most (but not all) cases, you can record only about 30 minutes of video in any one scene; you then have to stop and re-start your recording. Also, as you may expect, some video formats consume memory very rapidly, and so some of the smaller SD cards cannot record for the full amount of time that the camera would permit. There are some other considerations to be discussed with regard to recording limits; I will discuss video recording in more detail in Chapter 8.

One other consideration is the speed of the card. I often use a 16 GB SanDisk Extreme SDHC card, Class 10, rated at a transfer level of 30 MB/second, well beyond the minimum transfer speed for that class, which is 10 MB/second. That speed is more than enough to get good results for recording images and video with this camera. You should try to find a card of Class 6 or higher if you're going to record HD video.

Also, you need to realize that, if you have an older computer with a built-in card reader, or just an older external card reader, it may not read the newer SDHC cards. In that case, you would have to either get a new reader that will accept SDHC cards, or transfer images and videos from the camera to your computer using the camera's USB cable.

Using the newest variety of card, SDXC, also can be problematic with older computers. In mid-2010 I tried a 64GB SDXC card, and my MacBook Pro could not read it at all at first, even when I left it in the camera and connected the camera to the computer by USB cable.

Since my earlier experience with SDXC cards, though, the situation has improved. If you are using a computer with a relatively new version of the operating system, it will be able to read SDXC cards, provided you are using a compatible card reader. Specifically, the cards can be read by Windows 7 or 8; by Windows Vista with Service Pack 1 or 2; and by Windows XP with a software patch for reading the exFAT file system. That patch is available at http://www.microsoft.com/downloads. For Macintosh computers, you need to have Max OS X version 10.6.6 or later; otherwise, you need a patch such as one I found at www.sonnettech.com, a company that makes SDXC card readers.

As I write this, 64 GB SDXC cards cost about $50.00 and up, and prices are dropping. You can get a 128 GB SDXC card for about $130.00. So, if you don't mind the risk of losing a great many images or videos if you lose the card, you might want to choose an SDXC card with an enormous capacity of 64 GB, or even 128 GB. (SDXC cards with 256 GB capacity are very expensive at this writing.)

Finally, if you will have access to a wireless (Wi-Fi) network where you use your camera, you may want to consider getting an Eye-Fi card, two varieties of which are shown in Figure 1-8.

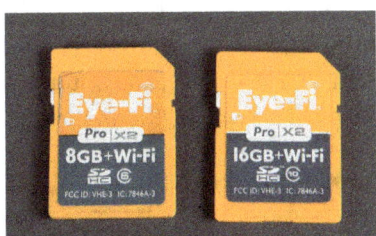

Fig. 1-8: 8 GB and 16 GB Eye-Fi Cards

This special type of storage device looks very much like an ordinary SDHC card, but it includes a tiny transmitter that lets it connect to a wireless network and send your images to your computer on that network as soon as the images have been recorded by the camera. The card also can send images directly to your mobile device with the appropriate Eye-Fi app such as those for the iPhone, iPad, and others.

I have tested both the 8 GB and 16 GB versions of the Eye-Fi card's Pro X2 model with the D-Lux 6, and they both work well. With either card, soon after I snap a picture, a little thumbnail image appears in the upper right corner of my computer's screen showing the progress of the upload. When all images are uploaded, they are available in the Pictures/Eye-Fi folder on my computer. The Pro X2 model can handle RAW files and video files as well as the smaller JPEG files. (At this writing, the Pro X2 is the only variety of Eye-Fi card that can handle RAW files. The 16 GB version of this card not only has greater storage capacity but also has higher writing speed, so you should look for the 16 GB card.) An Eye-Fi card is not a necessity, but I enjoy the convenience of having my images sent straight to my computer without having to put the card into a card reader or to connect the camera to the computer with a USB cable. As I write this, other manufacturers have begun introducing SD cards with WiFi capability, including the FlashAir card from Toshiba. Also, Transcend has announced a 32 GB card with WiFi abilities. I have tested only the Eye-Fi cards in the D-Lux 6.

Whatever type of SD card you get, once you have the card, open the same little door on the bottom of the camera that covers the battery compartment and slide the card in until it catches. The card goes in with its label facing the battery, as shown in Figure 1-9.

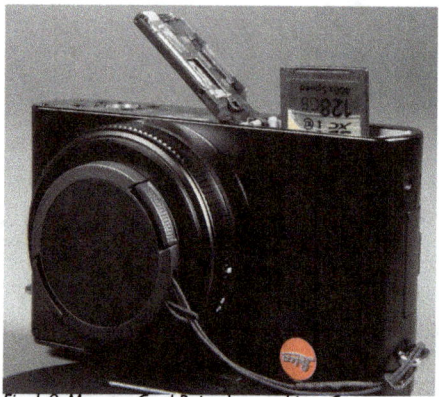

Fig. 1-9: Memory Card Being Inserted into Camera

Once the card has been pushed down until it catches, close the compartment door and push the latch back to the locking position. To remove the card, you push down on it until it releases and springs up so you can grab it.

When the D-Lux 6 is recording images or videos to an SD card, a red icon appears on the left side of the screen showing an arrow pointing to the right inside a little box representing the SD card, as shown in Figure 1-10.

If no SD card is in the camera, the red card icon flashes with the word "IN" added, showing that the camera is recording to the built-in memory instead of to a memory card, as shown in Figure 1-11.

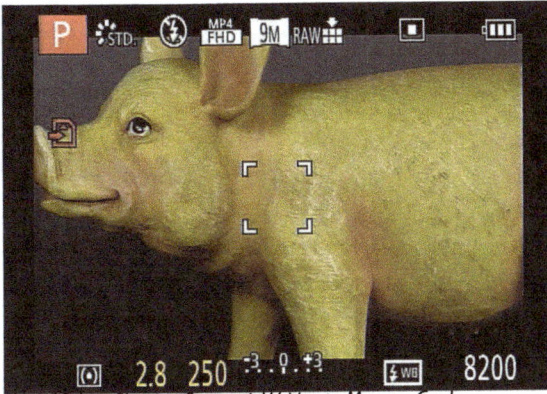

Fig. 1-10: Icon Showing Camera is Writing to Memory Card

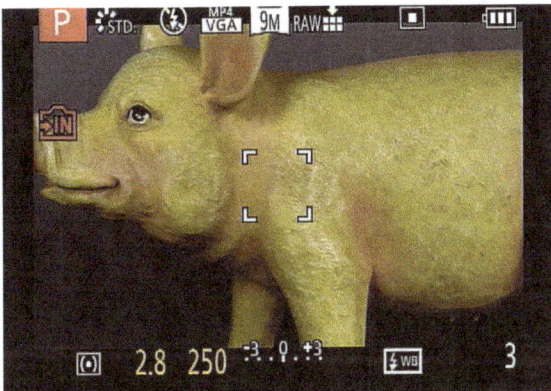

Fig. 1-11: Icon Showing Camera is Writing to Internal Memory

When either of those indicators is visible on the camera's display, it's important not to turn off the camera or otherwise interrupt its functioning, such as by taking out the battery or disconnecting an AC power adapter. You need to let the card complete its recording process in peace.

27

Introduction to Main Controls

Before I discuss some of the basic options for setting up the camera using the menu system and controls, it may be helpful to introduce the main controls, so you'll have a better idea of which button or dial is which. I won't discuss all of the controls here; they will be covered in some detail in Chapter 5. For now, I'm including below a series of images that show the major controls. As I come to each item for the first time in the text, I will describe its position and function; you may want to refer back to these images for a reminder about each control.

Top of Camera

On top of the camera are some of the more important controls and dials, as well as the accessory shoe, which can accommodate either an external flash or an optical or electronic viewfinder, and the two openings for the stereo microphone that records sound for videos, as shown in Figure 1-12. Controls such as the on/off switch and shutter button have functions that are self-explanatory. The mode dial is used to set the camera's shooting mode (Program, Aperture Priority, etc.). The zoom lever is used to change the focal length between wide-angle and telephoto; the aspect ratio switch determines the shape of your images, by setting the ratio of their width to their height (1:1, 4:3, 3:2, or 16:9). The movie button is used to start and stop the recording of a video.

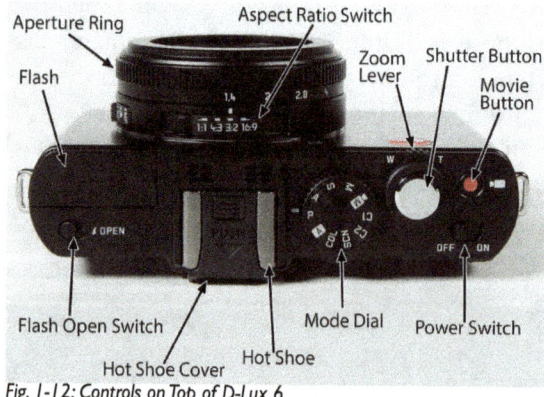

Fig. 1-12: Controls on Top of D-Lux 6

Back of Camera

Figure 1-13 shows the major controls on the camera's back. The rear dial is used to navigate menus, control items such as shutter speed and exposure compensation, and for other purposes. The ND/Focus lever is used to adjust manual focus and to activate the ND Filter, which reduces the light reaching the lens. The arrangement of five buttons on the right of the camera's back includes the four cursor buttons for navigating menus, which also control things such as white balance and ISO (light sensitivity). The Fn (Function) button can be assigned a single operation, to serve as a shortcut for carrying out that function. The drive mode button controls continuous or "burst" shooting as well as the self-timer, and the Display button selects the display screen used by the camera.

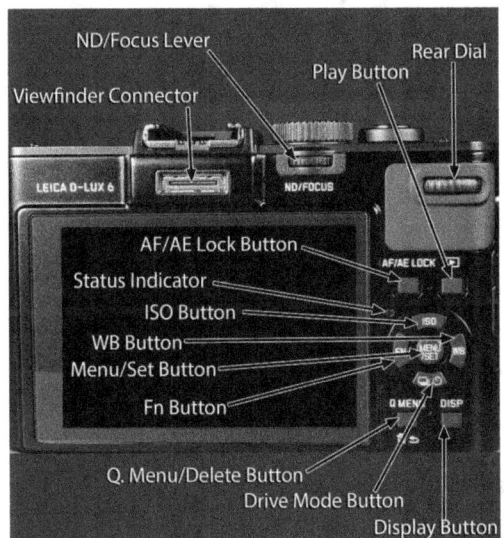

Fig. 1-13: Controls on Back of D-Lux 6

Front of Camera

There are only a few items to point out on the camera's front, shown in Figure 1-14. The AF assist lamp lights up to help with focusing in dark areas and as an indicator for the self-timer.

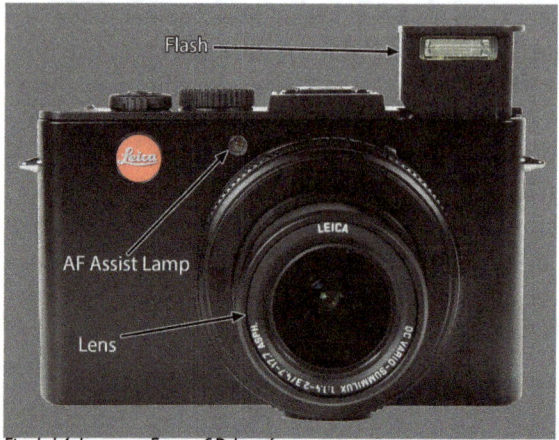

Fig. 1-14: Items on Front of D-Lux 6

Right Side of Camera

Inside the door on the right side of the camera are the USB/AV port and the HDMI port, as seen in Figure 1-15.

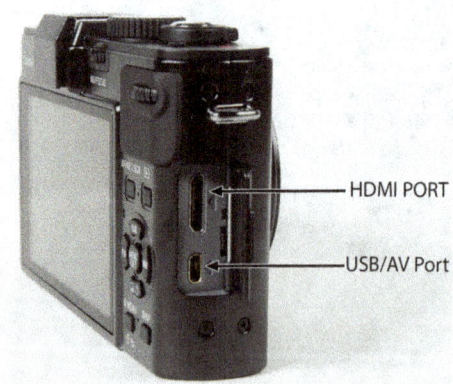

Fig. 1-15: Ports on Right Side of D-Lux 6

The upper port is where you insert an optional HDMI cable to connect the camera to an HDTV to view your images and videos. The lower one is where you connect the USB cable to connect the D-Lux 6 to a computer to manage images, or to a printer to print images directly from the camera. You also can connect an optional audio-video cable here to view images on a standard TV set.

Bottom of Camera

Finally, as shown in Figure 1-16, on the bottom of the camera are the tripod socket, the door for the battery and memory card compartment, and the small flap that is used to accommodate the cable for the AC adapter when it is connected to the camera, as discussed in Appendix A.

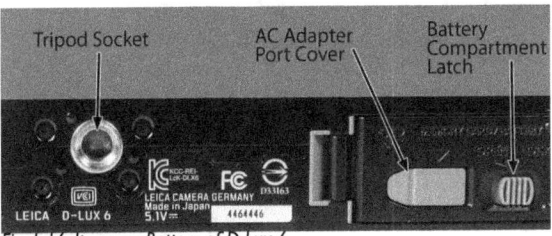
Fig. 1-16: Items on Bottom of D-Lux 6

Setting the Language, Date, and Time

It's important to make sure the date and time are set correctly before you start taking pictures, because the camera records that information (sometimes known as "metadata," meaning data beyond the data in the picture) invisibly with each image, and displays it later if you want. Someday you may be very glad to have the date (and even the time of day) correctly recorded with your archives of digital images.

To get these basic items set correctly, remove the lens cap and slide the camera's power switch, on the top right of the camera, to the On position. Then press the Menu/Set button (in the center of the array of five buttons on the camera's back). Push the left cursor button to move the selection into the column for selecting the menu type (Recording, Motion Picture, Scene, Play, or Setup, depending on the mode the camera is in). Red arrows will appear at the sides of the red frame surrounding the selected menu icon, as shown in Figure 1-17.

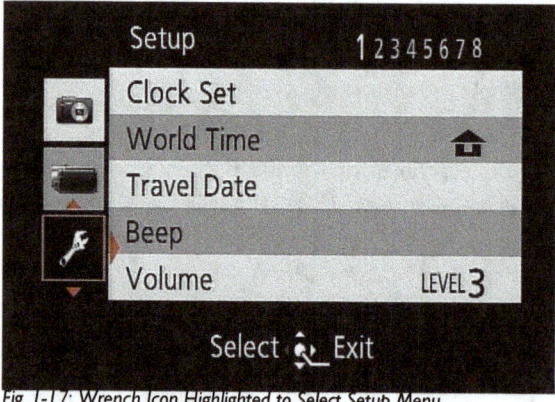

Fig. 1-17: Wrench Icon Highlighted to Select Setup Menu

Push the down button to highlight the wrench icon that represents the Setup menu, then push the right button to place the black selection rectangle in the list of Setup menu items.

Highlight Clock Set, then press the right button to get access to the clock and date settings, as shown in Figure 1-18.

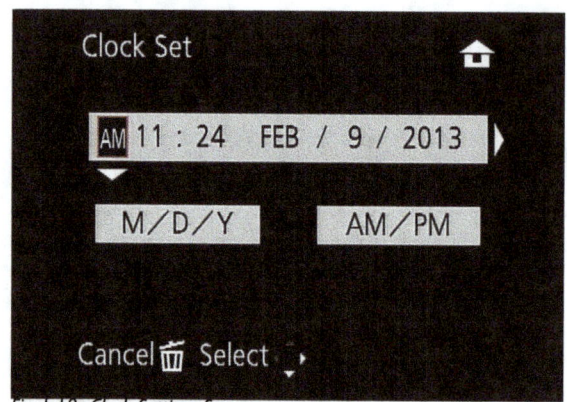

Fig. 1-18: Clock Settings Screen

Navigate by pressing the left and right cursor buttons or by turning the rear dial (at the upper right of the camera's back), and select values with the up and down cursor buttons. When you're done, press Menu/Set to save the settings. Then, using a similar procedure, navigate to the Language option on the final screen of the Setup menu, if necessary, and change the language that the camera uses for menus and messages.

Chapter 2: Basic Operations

Taking Pictures

Now the D-Lux 6 camera has the correct time and date set and has a fully charged battery inserted, along with an SD, SDHC, or SDXC memory card. Let's look at some scenarios for basic picture-taking. For now, I won't get into discussions of what the various options are and why you might choose one over another. I'll just describe a reasonable set of steps that will get you and your camera into action and will deposit a decent image on your memory card.

Fully Automatic: Snapshot Mode

Here's a set of steps to follow if you want to set the camera to its most automatic mode and let it make most of the decisions for you. This is a good way to proceed if you're in a hurry and need to grab a quick shot without fiddling with settings, or if you're new at this and would like to get started taking pictures without having to provide much input.

1. Look on the top of the lens barrel for the slide switch that selects among the four possible aspect ratios: 1:1, 4:3, 3:2, and 16:9, shown in Figure 2-1. Unless you know you want one of the other three aspect ratios, slide the switch over to the third position from the left to select the 3:2 aspect ratio for now. That aspect ratio is similar to that of standard 35mm film, and produces an image the same shape as the camera's LCD screen. It also is the best choice if you're going to take

34

your memory card to a photo lab for standard-sized prints of 6 inches by 4 inches (15 by 10 cm) in the U.S.

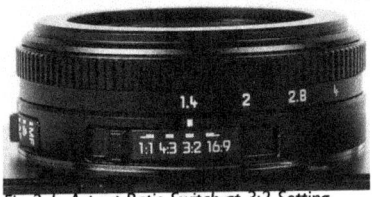

Fig. 2-1: Aspect Ratio Switch at 3:2 Setting

2. Remove the lens cap and let it dangle by its string (or cup it in your hand to keep it from flapping around).

3. Move the power switch at the right side of the camera's top to the On position. The camera makes a whirring sound, the lens extends outward to its open position, and the LCD screen lights up.

4. Turn the black, ridged dial on the camera's top (the mode dial) so the "A" inside a light-colored rectangle is next to the white dot to the left of the dial, as shown in Figure 2-2. This sets the camera to the Snapshot mode of shooting.

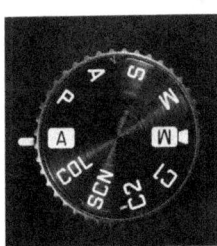

Fig. 2-2: Snapshot Mode

5. Find the slide switch on the left side of the lens barrel and notice it has three settings, reading from bottom to top: AF, AF Macro (with image of flower), and MF. Slide the switch to its uppermost position, selecting AF, for autofocus, as shown in Figure 2-3. With this setting, the camera will do its best to focus the lens to take a sharp picture within the normal (non-macro) focus range, which is from 1.6 feet (50 centimeters) to infinity.

35

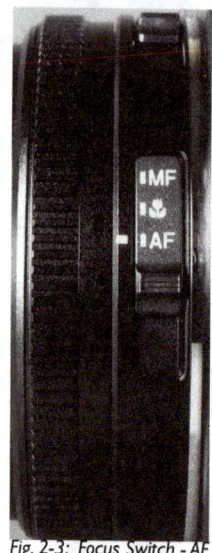

Fig. 2-3: Focus Switch - AF

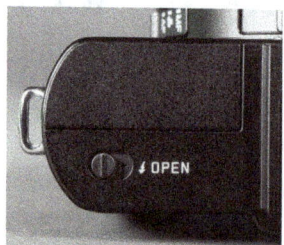

Fig. 2-4: Flash Open Switch

6. If you're taking a picture indoors, or it's dark enough that you think you might need the camera's built-in flash, find the little slide switch next to the word "Open" and the little lightning bolt on the far left side of the top of the camera, as shown in Figure 2-4. Push that switch to the right, and the flash will pop open. The camera will decide later whether the flash needs to be fired or not.

7. Aim the camera toward the subject and look at the screen to compose the picture as you want it. Locate the zoom lever on the ring that surrounds the shutter button on the top right of the camera, shown in Figure 2-5.

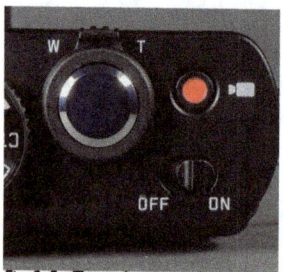

Fig. 2-5: Zoom Lever

Push that lever to the left, toward the W, to get a wider-angle shot (including more of the scene in the picture), or to the right, toward the T, to get a telephoto, zoomed-in shot.

8. Once the picture looks good on the LCD screen, push the shutter button halfway down. You should hear a beep and see a steady (not blinking) green dot in the upper right corner of the screen, indicating that the picture will be in focus, as shown in Figure 2-6. (The green rectangle in this image shows the focus point chosen by the camera in this focus mode.)

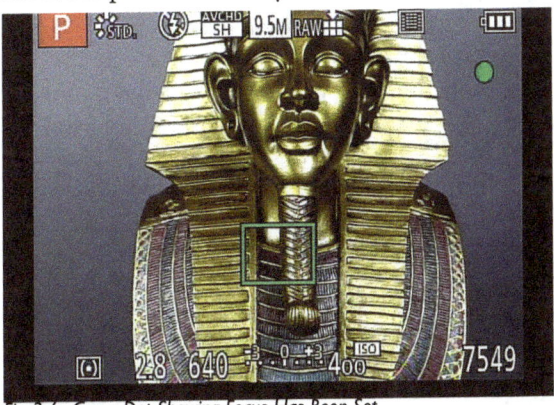

Fig. 2-6: Green Dot Showing Focus Has Been Set

If you hear a series of 4 quick beeps and see a blinking green dot, that means the picture is not in focus. Try moving to a slightly different angle and then test the focus again by pushing the shutter button halfway down.

9. Push the shutter button all the way down to take the picture.

Basic Variations from Fully Automatic

At this point I won't say much about the various still-picture shooting modes, except to name them. Besides Snapshot, which I just described, there are Program, Aperture Priority, Shutter Priority, Manual, and Scene. There are also two Custom modes, C1 and C2, which you can set up yourself, and the Creative Control mode, which gives you some special options for the look of your images. I'll discuss all of those shooting modes in Chapter 3, and I'll discuss Creative Video mode in Chapter 8. For now, I'm going to discuss some of the functions and features of the D-Lux 6 that you can adjust to suit whatever picture-taking situation you may be faced with. Not all of the settings can be adjusted in Snapshot mode, so we'll set the camera down to a lower level of automation, to the Program mode. In that mode, you'll be able to control most of the camera's functions for taking still pictures, but the camera will still adjust the exposure for you.

I'm not going to repeat the initial steps for taking a picture, because those were pretty basic. If you need a refresher on those steps, see the list in the above discussion of Snapshot mode.

Start by setting the mode dial on top of the camera to P, for Program, as shown in Figure 2-7.

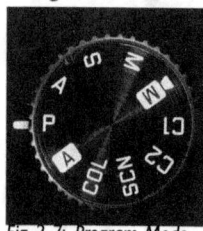

Fig. 2-7: Program Mode

You will immediately see some different indications on the LCD screen. These items show that some of the Snapshot mode settings have changed, because you now have more control over matters such as picture size and quality, white balance, and others. Using the Program mode setting, the camera will determine the proper exposure, both the aperture (size of opening to let in light) and the shutter speed (how long the shutter is open to let in light). In this mode you won't be making decisions about those settings; you will have control over those decisions in other modes, which I'll discuss later. That still leaves lots of choices you can make, though, so let's talk about the various settings you can adjust in Program mode.

Focus

Now that you're not using Snapshot mode, you have more control over focus than you did in that mode. Your first choice is between manual focus and autofocus. In other words, you have the option of setting the focus switch on the left side of the lens barrel to the MF setting, for manual focus. (If you try that in Snapshot mode, you'll get an error message on the LCD screen.) You also can select which of several types of autofocus operation you want the camera to use.

I'll discuss the various autofocus modes later, in Chapter 4, in some detail. Here we'll use the camera's menu system to make sure a standard autofocus mode is selected.

To enter the menu system, locate the circular group of five buttons to the right of the LCD screen.

The center button is marked Menu/Set. Press in on that button and you will see the menus. You navigate through the menus with the five buttons, as well as one of the buttons at the lower right of the camera's back. The button above the trash can icon, in this context, acts as a "cancel" button.

When the menu system first appears on the LCD, you should see the Photo Style setting on the top line of the Recording menu, as shown in Figure 2-8.

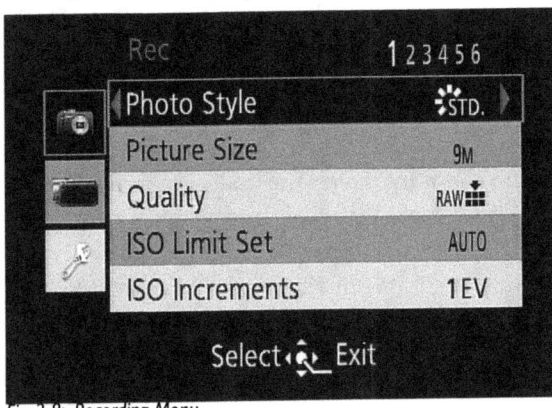

Fig. 2-8: Recording Menu

Press the down cursor button (the one directly below the Menu/Set button) several times to navigate down to the line on the second menu screen that says AF Mode. Press the right cursor button (the one directly to the right of the Menu/Set button) to navigate to a sub-menu that shows an array of the various autofocus modes, as shown in Figure 2-9. You navigate among those modes by using the up and down cursor buttons.

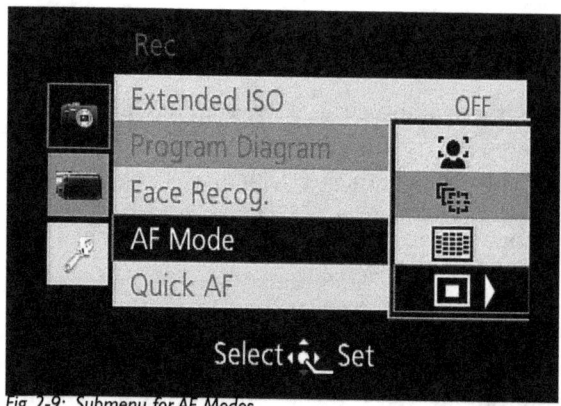

Fig. 2-9: Submenu for AF Modes

Go ahead and select the bottom icon in the vertical array of autofocus modes. This icon is a rectangle with a smaller rectangle inside it. I'll provide more details about these icons and the modes they stand for in Chapter 4; this one means "1-Area." With that setting, the camera will autofocus based on whatever is shown in the one area in the center of the screen. If you want to get a bit fancier, once you have highlighted this icon, you can press the right cursor button, which will take you to a screen where you can move the focusing box around and place it where you want it over the image, as shown in Figure 2-10. If you don't want to do that, then go ahead and press the Menu/Set button to select the "1-Area" autofocus mode and exit the menu system. While the focus frame is active, you can also change its size by turning the rear dial, at the top right of the camera's back, to one of four positions, producing a focus block from very small to extra large.

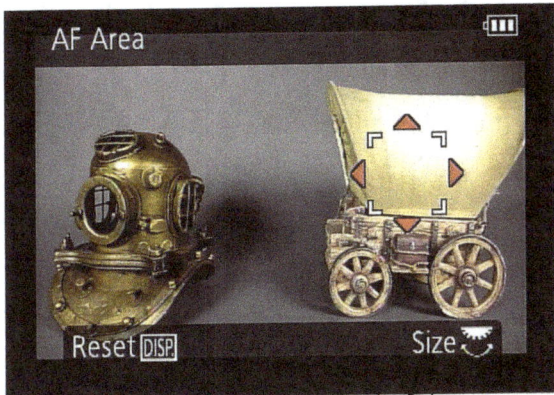

Fig. 2-10: 1-Area Focus Frame with Focus Moved to Right

Now you have selected the autofocus mode, which, in this case, will display a focusing bracket in the center of the screen, unless you have moved it to a different position. (In some other focus modes, no bracket is displayed until after focus is achieved.)When you aim the camera at a subject, be sure that the focus bracket, outlined by four white corners, is over the part of the picture that needs to be in the sharpest focus. When you press halfway down on the shutter button, if the camera is able to focus successfully, you will hear a beep, the white brackets will turn green, and a large green dot will appear, unblinking, at the upper right of the screen, as shown in Figure 2-11.

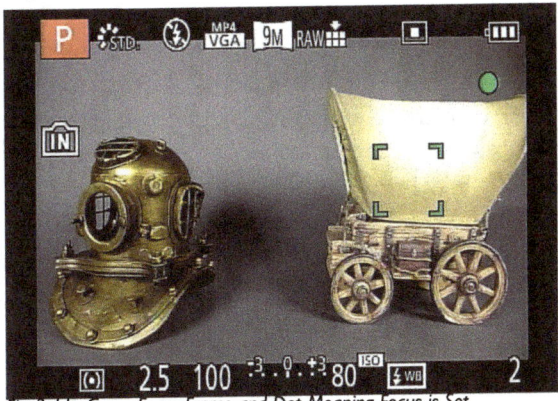

Fig. 2-11: Green Focus Frame and Dot Meaning Focus is Set

If you see a blinking green dot, that means the camera was not able to focus, either because the subject was outside of the focus range, or, perhaps, the subject was too difficult to focus on, as can happen with a subject that is too bright or too fast, lacks contrast, is behind glass, or is too dark. If everything looks okay to you, go ahead and press the shutter button all the way down to take the picture.

Suppose you want to take a picture in which your main subject is not in the center of the screen. Maybe your shot is set up so that a person is standing off to the right of center, and there is some attractive scenery to the left in the scene. One way to focus on the person on the right is to use the technique described above: that is, to go into the menu system, select this autofocus mode, and then press the right cursor button to move the focus frame over the subject. Once you have the focus area located where you want it and at your chosen size, go ahead and snap the picture.

There's one other way to focus on a different area of the screen, and this one is probably the easier of the two. Do not move the focus frame around the screen, but move the camera so that the focus frame is over the area that needs to be in focus. Then press the shutter button halfway down until the camera focuses and beeps. Keep the button pressed halfway while you move the camera back to create your desired composition, with the person off to the right. Then take the picture, and the area you originally focused on will be in focus. With this method, though, you need to realize that the half-press of the shutter button locks the exposure as well as the focus. If the exposure is different at the point where you locked focus from what it is at the location where you will take the picture, you may need to use exposure compensation to adjust your final image.

Manual Focus

There are several other autofocus modes available through the Recording menu, but I won't discuss those at this point; I'll discuss them in Chapter 4. For now, I will talk instead about manual focus, the other major option for focusing. Why would you want to use manual focus when the camera will focus for you automatically? Many photographers like the amount of control that comes from being able to set the focus exactly how they want it. And, in some situations, such as when you're shooting in dark areas or areas behind glass, where there are objects at various distances from the camera, or when you're shooting a small object at a very close distance, and only a narrow range of the subject can be in sharp focus, it may be useful for you to control exactly where the point of sharpest focus lies.

To take advantage of this capability, go to the focus slide switch on the side of the lens and push it all the way down to the MF position, as shown in Figure 2-12, which puts the camera into manual focus mode.

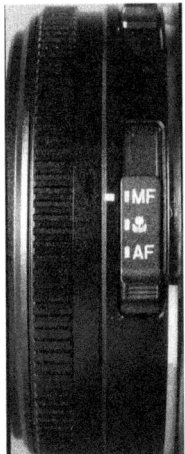

Fig. 2-12: Manual Focus

Instead of relying on the camera to focus automatically, you now need to use the ND/Focus lever to adjust the focus manually. You can also use the left and right cursor buttons to fine-

43

tune the focus to its optimal sharpness.

After you have set the focus switch to the MF position, the letters MF will appear in the upper right corner of the screen. In order to adjust the focus, use the ND/Focus lever, located at the top of the camera's back just below the mode dial, as shown in Figure 2-13.

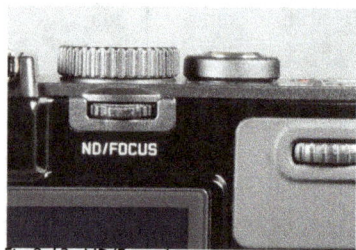

Fig. 2-13: ND/Focus Lever

Press that little switch to the left to focus on closer objects or to the right to focus on objects farther from the camera. Depending on your menu settings, when you move the focus lever you will immediately see either an enlarged image of the screen or just a normal-sized image. (You can control this function using the MF Assist option on the fourth screen of the Setup menu, as discussed in Chapter 7.) You also will see a focus scale near the bottom of the display, as shown in Figure 2-14.

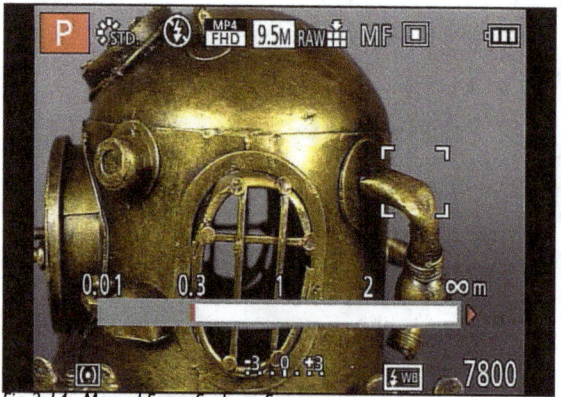

Fig. 2-14: Manual Focus Scale on Screen

Whether or not the image is enlarged, press the ND/Focus lever left or right until the image is in focus, then stop. At this point, you don't have to do anything else. You can just press the shutter button all the way down to take the picture. If you would like to tweak the focus a bit further, though, just to make sure you have it as sharp as you can at your selected focus point, you can use the left and right cursor buttons for some final adjustments. You need to press them quickly, before the focus scale disappears from the screen. You can hold either of those buttons down for continuous adjustments.

If you are using the enlarged screen of the MF Assist option, you can choose what part of the image is enlarged. To do so, while the enlarged area is on the screen, press the Menu/Set button, and a white frame will appear on the screen with red triangles pointing in four directions, as shown in Figure 2-15.

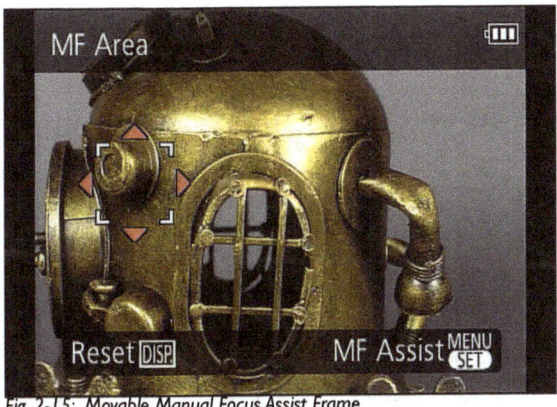

Fig. 2-15: Movable Manual Focus Assist Frame

Use the cursor buttons to move that box around the screen, then press Menu/Set again to set a new location for the enlarged focusing area. To reset the enlarged area back to the center of the screen, press the Display button while the movable box is on the screen. While the enlarged display is active, you can press in on the ND/Focus lever to change the magnification, including one display that magnifies only the center of the screen. Also, as I'll discuss in Chapters 5 and 7, you can

45

set the Function (Fn) button to an option called 1 Shot AF, in which case pressing the Function button will cause the camera to use its autofocus when the camera is in manual focus mode.

Exposure

Next, I'll discuss some possibilities for controlling exposure, beyond just letting the camera make the decisions. In the Snapshot mode, the D-Lux 6 is very good at choosing the right exposure, and the same is true of the Program mode. But there are going to be some situations in which you want to override the camera's automation.

Exposure Compensation

First, let's look at the control for adjusting exposure to account for an unusual, or non-optimal, lighting situation. Suppose you have the D-Lux 6 set to Program mode and you are pho-tographing a dark object, such as a figurine of a dark horse in front of a white background, as shown in Figure 2-16.

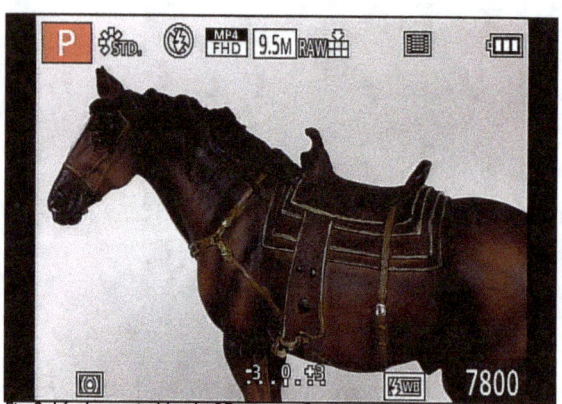

Fig. 2-16: Image in Need of Exposure Compensation

The camera will do a good job of averaging the amount of light coming into the lens, and will expose the picture accordingly. The problem is, the very light background will likely "fool" the camera into closing down the aperture, because the overall picture will seem quite bright. But your subject, which is not nearly as light in color, will seem too dark in the picture.

One solution here, which the D-Lux 6 makes very easy to carry out, is to use the exposure compensation control. You might not realize this without reading the manual, but the rear dial (located at the upper right of the camera's back) is also a button you can press in. It has various functions, both as a dial and as a button; one of its button functions is to activate the exposure compensation control.

Set up your picture in Program mode, and aim at your subject. Now press in firmly on the rear dial (it may take a strong push), and look at the small white scale in the bottom center of the screen, with tick marks extending to -3 to the left and +3 to the right. When you press in and release the rear dial, that scale will turn yellow, as seen in Figure 2-17.

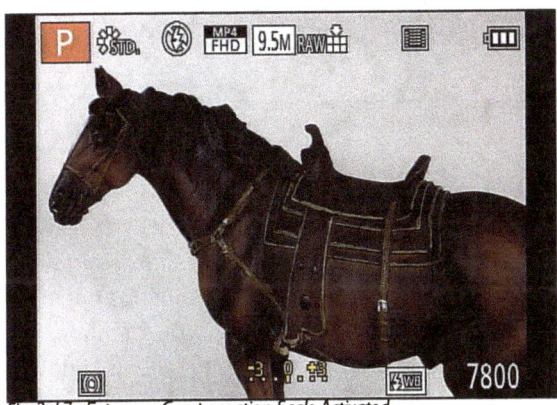
Fig. 2-17: Exposure Compensation Scale Activated

The change of color means that the exposure compensation control is now active. Now, when you turn the rear dial (rather than pressing in on it), you will see yellow tick marks appear on the scale, indicating a value ranging from -3 to +3 in increments of one-third EV.

The EV stands for Exposure Value, which is a standard measure of brightness. If you move the value down to -3, the picture will be considerably darker than the automatic exposure would produce. If you move it to +3, the picture will be noticeably brighter. The camera's screen shows you how the exposure is changing, before you take the picture. After 1 2/3 EV of exposure compensation is added, the image becomes brighter, and the figure can be seen more clearly, as shown in Figure 2-18.

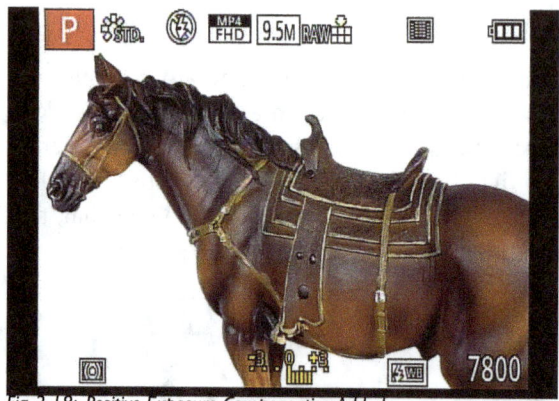

Fig. 2-18: Positive Exposure Compensation Added

Once you've taken the picture, you should reset the EV compensation back to zero, with no yellow tick marks extending to the left or right of the mid-point on the scale, so you don't unintentionally affect the pictures you take later. You need to be careful about this, because the camera will maintain any EV value you set, even when the camera is turned off and then on again.

To cancel the use of the exposure compensation control, press in on the rear dial until the scale at the bottom of the screen turns white. (This action does not cancel any exposure compensation setting that was made; it just cancels the rear dial's ability to adjust exposure compensation.)

Flash

Later on, in Chapters 3 and 4, I'll discuss other topics dealing with exposure, such as Manual exposure mode, Aperture Priority mode, the Intelligent Dynamic setting, and others. For now I'm going to discuss the basics of using the D-Lux 6's built-in flash unit, because that is something you may need to use on a regular basis. Later, I'll discuss using other flash units, and other options for using the built-in flash, such as controlling its output and preventing "red-eye."

Here is one fundamental point that you need to be aware of: The built-in flash on the D-Lux 6 will not pop up by itself, as such units do on some cameras. If you are in a situation in which you think flash may be needed or desirable, you need to take the first step of popping up the flash unit. To do so, use the flash open switch on the far left of the camera's top, as discussed earlier and shown in Figure 2-4.

Even though you have popped up the flash unit, in some shooting situations the flash will never fire. In the situations in which you're likely to want it to, though, it will be ready and willing to illuminate your subject as well as it can.

Let's explore a common scenario to see how the flash works. Turn on the camera and set the shooting mode to Snapshot with the mode dial on top of the camera and pop up the flash unit.

You will see the Auto Flash icon, indicated by an A, appear at the top of the LCD screen, as shown in Figure 2-19, to the right of the icon for the shooting mode setting, which, in this case, is the letter A in a red rectangle, indicating Snapshot mode.

The appearance of the flash icon will vary depending on several settings, which you can choose in some shooting modes, but not others. Since you're now using Snapshot mode, your choices of most functions, including flash, are limited.

If the flash unit is popped up, the camera will select what it believes to be the appropriate flash mode for the current conditions and will display an icon to announce that mode. If the flash is stowed away in its compartment, you'll see the "flash off" icon at the top of the screen. That icon is a lightning bolt inside the universal negative sign, a circle with a diagonal line through it, as shown in Figure 2-20.

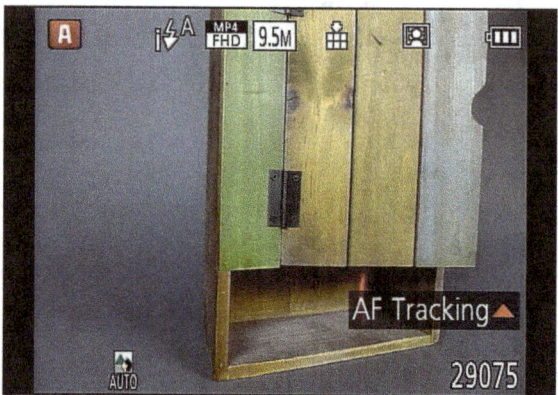

Fig. 2-19: Auto Flash Icon to Right of Recording Mode Icon

There is no way to make any other flash settings in this situation. You don't have any choice, but that's presumably what you wanted when you chose Snapshot mode.

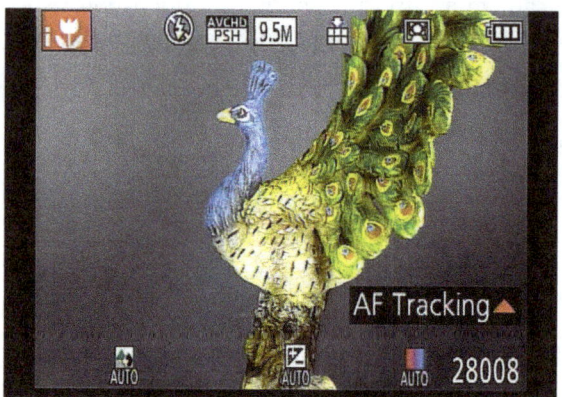

Fig. 2-20: Flash Off Icon to Right of Recording Mode Icon

Next, try setting the Mode dial to P, for Program mode. Now, if you go into the Recording menu and select the Flash item on the fifth screen, you will find several options available: Auto, Auto/Red-Eye, Forced Flash On, and Slow Sync/Red-Eye, as shown in Figure 2-21. I will discuss the use of those modes later, in Chapters 4 and 9.

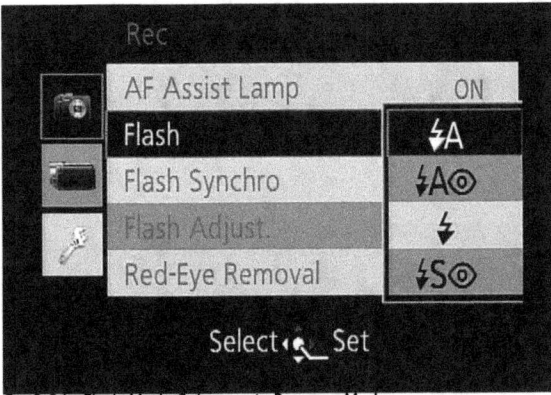

Fig. 2-21: Flash Mode Submenu in Program Mode

Motion Picture Recording

Let's try recording a short video sequence with the D-Lux 6. Later, I'll discuss some of the other options for video recording, but for now, let's stick to the basics. Once the camera is turned on, set the mode dial to Snapshot, press the Menu/Set button to enter the menu system, and then press the left cursor button followed by the down button, to activate the Motion Picture menu, symbolized by the icon of a movie camera, as shown in Figure 2-22.

Press the right button to go to the list of menu options. At the top of the screen, highlight Rec Mode and press the right button, giving the choices of AVCHD and MP4, as shown in Figure 2-23. (AVCHD stands for Advanced Video Coding High Definition; it and MP4 are video encoding formats.)

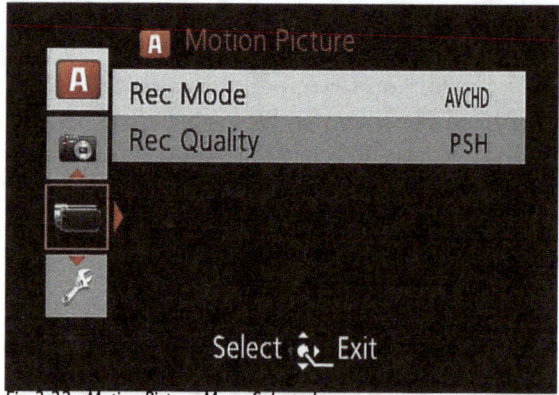

Fig. 2-22: Motion Picture Menu Selected

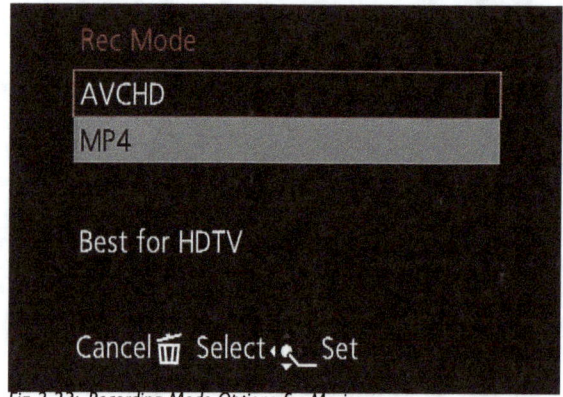

Fig. 2-23: Recording Mode Options for Movies

Highlight AVCHD and press the Menu/Set button to select it. Then go back to the menu screen and highlight the next option down, Rec Quality, and select PSH, for Progressive Super High. Then press the Menu/Set button to exit the menu system.

Be sure the slide switch on the left of the lens barrel is set to AF for autofocus, unless you want to use manual focus.

Now compose the shot the way you want it, and when you're ready, press the red Movie button on top of the camera, to the right of the shutter button.

You don't need to hold the button down; just press and release it. The LCD screen will show a blinking red dot as a recording indicator along with a countdown of recording time remaining, as seen in Figure 2-24, and the camera will keep recording until it reaches a limit of time or storage space, or until you press the Movie button again to stop the recording.

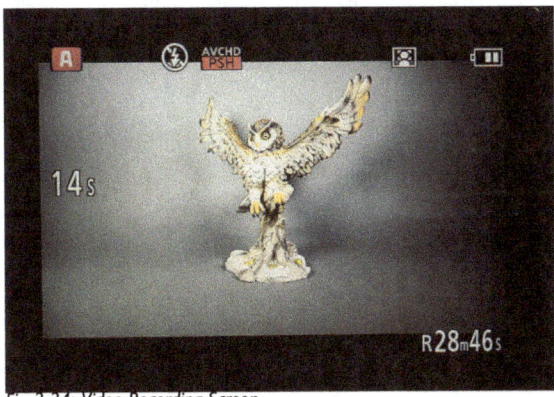

Fig. 2-24: Video Recording Screen

Don't be concerned about the level of the sound that is being recorded, because you have no control over the audio volume during the recording process. Note, though, that the D-Lux 6 does a very nice job of changing its focus and exposure automatically as necessary, and you are free to zoom in and out as the movie is recording.

This leads to a point that's not specific to the D-Lux 6: Unless you have a good reason to do otherwise, I recommend that you refrain from zooming during your shots and that you try to hold the camera as steady as possible, and move it only in very smooth, slow motions, such as a pan (side-to-side motion) to take in a wide scene gradually. Video from a jerkily moving or zooming camera can be very disconcerting to the viewer.

Viewing Pictures

Before we delve into more advanced settings for taking still pictures and movies, as well as other matters of interest, I'll talk about the basics of viewing your images in the camera.

Basic Playback

Playback is activated by pressing the Play button, the button at the top right on the back of the camera under a green triangle, below the rear dial, as shown in Figure 2-25.

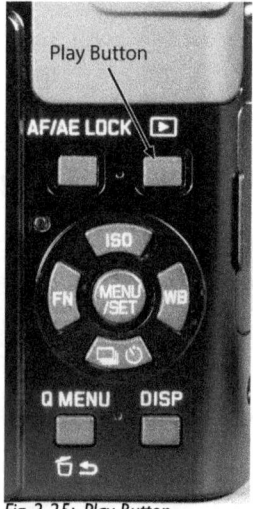

Fig. 2-25: Play Button

When you press that button, if you have any pictures in the camera's built-in memory or on the SD card, you will see one of the pictures displayed. It will be whatever image you last displayed; the camera remembers which picture was most recently on display even after being turned off and then back on.

To move to the next picture, press the right button; to move back one picture, press the left button. You can hold either of those buttons down to move quickly through the images. If you prefer, you can move through the pictures with left or right turns of the rear dial. The display on the screen will tell you the number of the picture being displayed. (If it doesn't, press the Display button until it does.) This number will have a three-digit prefix, followed by a dash and then a sequence number. For example, the card in my camera right now is showing picture number 101-0714; the next one is 101-0715.

If you would rather see an index view of multiple pictures, use the zoom lever on the top of the camera. Move it to the left, toward the W, one time, and the display changes to show twelve images in three rows of four, as shown in Figure 2-26.

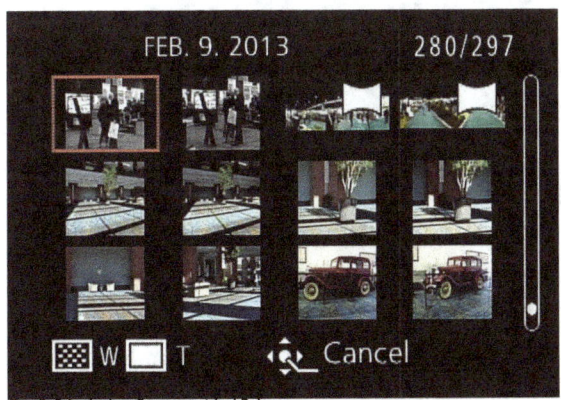

Fig. 2-26: Index Screen with 12 Images

Move it to the left once more, and it shows thirty pictures at a time, as shown in Figure 2-27.

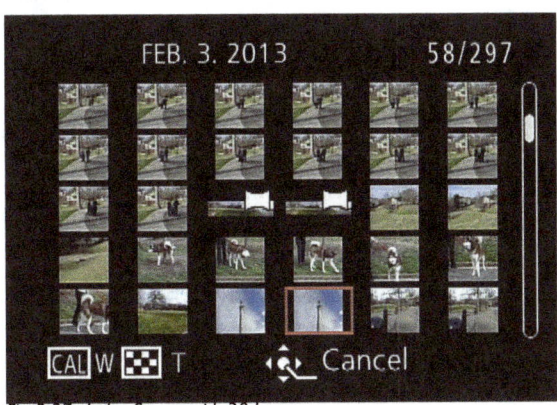

Fig. 2-27: Index Screen with 30 Images

Give it one final leftward push and a calendar screen appears, as seen in Figure 2-28. On that screen, navigate to a date and press the Menu/Set button to see all images taken on that date.

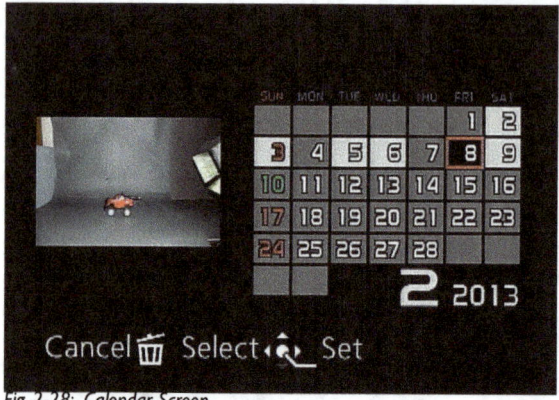

Fig. 2-28: Calendar Screen

You can also move the zoom lever to the right to retrace your steps through the options for multi-image viewing and back to viewing single images.

Move the zoom lever once to the left to see the twelve-picture screen. The right and left buttons will now move you through the pictures on this screen one at a time, while the top and bottom buttons move you up and down through the rows. If you move to the last row or the last image, the proper button will move you to the next screen of images. Once you've moved the selector to the image you want to view, press the Menu/Set button, and that image is chosen for individual viewing.

Once you have the single image you want displayed on the screen, you have more options. Press the zoom lever once to the right, toward the T, to zoom the image to twice its normal size, as shown in Figure 2-29. Press the lever repeatedly to zoom up to sixteen times normal size. Press the zoom lever back to the left to shrink the image down in the same increments. Or, you can press the Menu/Set button to return the image immediately to normal size.

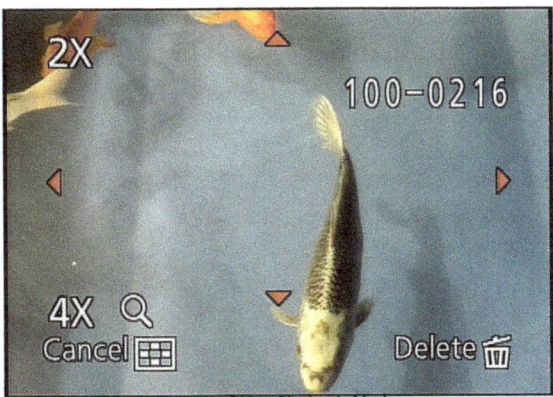

Fig. 2-29: Image Enlarged to 2X in Playback Mode

While the zoomed picture is displayed, you can scroll it in any direction with the cursor buttons. Also, you can review other images at the same zoom level by using the rear dial to navigate to the next or prior image, while the image is still zoomed.

Playing Movies

To play back movies, navigate through the images by the methods described above until you find an image for which the screen shows the motion-picture format information at the upper left. The bottom of the screen will display the message, Play Motion Picture, as shown in Figure 2-30.

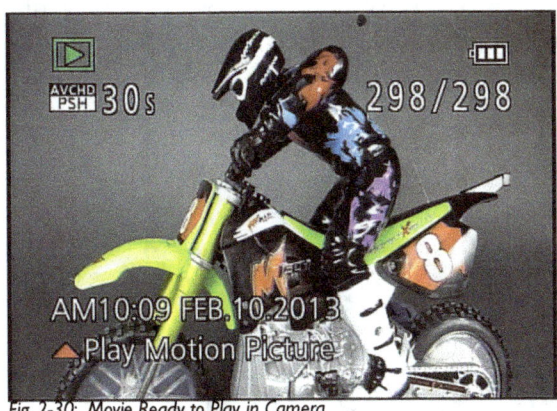

Fig. 2-30: Movie Ready to Play in Camera

With the first frame of the motion picture displayed on the screen, press the up button (the top button in the five-button array) to start playback.

The movie will start to play. You can now use the five-button array as a set of VCR controls; the camera displays an icon showing those controls, as seen in Figure 2-31.

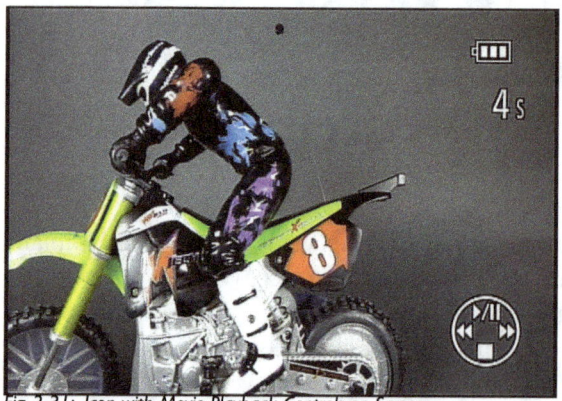

Fig. 2-31: Icon with Movie Playback Controls on Screen

The top button is Play/Pause; the right button is Fast Forward (or frame advance when paused); the bottom button is Stop; the left button is Rewind (or frame reverse when paused).

You can raise or lower the volume of the audio by pressing the zoom lever on top of the camera to the right or left. You will see a little window open up on the screen with a volume display when you activate this control, as shown in Figure 2-32.

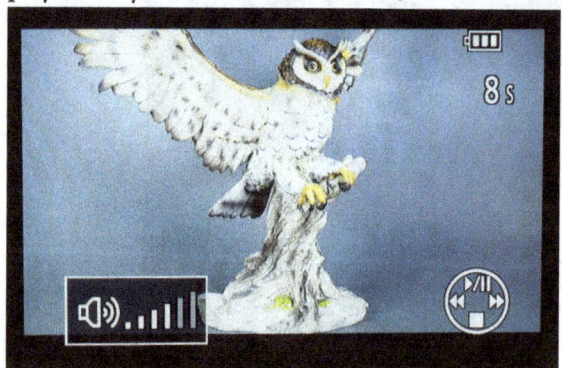

Fig. 2-32: Icon Showing Movie Volume Control on Screen

(This volume control will not appear when the camera is connected to a TV set, because the volume is controlled by the TV's controls in that situation.)

If you want to play your MP4 movies on a computer or edit them with video-editing software, they will import nicely into software such as iMovie for the Macintosh, or into any other Mac or Windows program that can deal with video files with the extension .mp4. This is a file extension used by Apple Computer's QuickTime video software; QuickTime itself can be downloaded from Apple's web site. For some Windows-based video editing software, you may need to convert the D-Lux 6's movie files to the more commonly used .avi format before importing them into the software. You can do so with a program such as mp4cam2avi, which is available at www.mp4cam2avi. sourceforge.net. There also is useful software at www.aunsoft. com. If you want to edit your AVCHD movies, there is software available that will let you do this, such as Adobe Premiere Pro Elements and others, though AVCHD is not as useful for editing as it is for playing directly on your HDTV.

To save a frame from a movie as a single image, play the movie to the approximate location of the image you want, then press the up button, which acts as the Play/Pause button in this context. Use the left and right buttons to maneuver to the exact frame you want.

Once you are viewing the single frame you want, press the Menu/Set button to select it, then, when prompted, as shown in Figure 2-33, highlight Yes and press Menu/Set to confirm, and you will have a new still image at the end of the current group of recorded images.

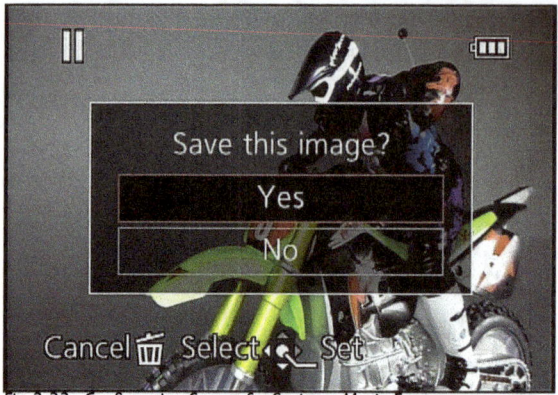

Fig. 2-33: Confirmation Screen for Saving a Movie Frame

Press the down button (Stop) to exit the motion picture Play-back mode. Note, though, that the saved still images will not be of high quality; each one will be of Standard quality and no larger than 2 MP in size.

Chapter 3: The Recording Modes

Up until now I have discussed the basics of how to set up the camera for quick shots, relying heavily on features such as Snapshot mode, in which settings are controlled mostly by the camera's automation. Like other sophisticated digital cameras, though, the D-Lux 6 has a large and potentially bewildering range of options available for setting up the camera to take pictures and movies. One of the main goals of this book is to remove the "bewildering" factor while extracting the essential usefulness from the broad range of features available. To do this, I will turn my attention to two subjects: In this chapter I will discuss the recording modes for still pictures and in Chapter 4 I will explain the Recording menu options. First, I will discuss the various recording modes.

Whenever you set out to record still images, you need to select one of the available recording modes on the mode dial: Snapshot, Program, Aperture Priority, Shutter Priority, Manual, Scene, Creative Control, C1, or C2. (The only other entry available on the mode dial is for Creative Video mode, which I will discuss in Chapter 8.) So far, we have worked with the Snapshot and Program modes. Now I will discuss the others, after a brief review of preliminary steps and some review of the first two recording modes.

Preliminary Steps Before Shooting Pictures

It can't hurt to recall the preliminary steps that you need to take for shooting still images, before discussing the various shooting modes. These steps don't have to be done in this exact order, but this is not a bad order to follow:

1. Check to be sure you have selected the aspect ratio you want: either 1:1, 4:3, 3:2, or 16:9, with the slide switch on top of the lens barrel. I generally use 3:2 or 4:3 for everyday shooting, but you may prefer one of the others.

2. Make sure you have selected the focus method you want: either AF for autofocus, AF Macro for autofocus with close-ups, or MF for manual focus. Use the slide switch on the left side of the lens barrel.

3. Remove the lens cap.

4. Turn on the camera.

Now you're ready to select a recording mode. I'll go over them all below.

Snapshot Mode

I've already talked about this mode. This is the one you probably want if you just need to have the camera ready for a quick shot, maybe in an environment with fast-paced events when you won't have much time to fuss with settings.

To make this setting, turn the mode dial, on top of the camera to the right of the flash shoe, to the light gray rectangle icon with the letter "A" inside it, as shown in Figure 3-1. (Be sure to distinguish this setting from the other capital "A" with no gray rectangle, which sets a different mode, Aperture Priority.)

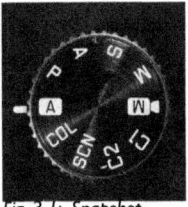
Fig. 3-1: Snapshot

When you select Snapshot mode, the camera makes quite a few decisions for you. Perhaps the most important decision the camera makes for you is the Quality setting, which is fixed at Fine, meaning your images will be saved as JPEG files, rather than files in the RAW format. As I'll discuss in Chapter 4, using the RAW format gives you a great deal of flexibility in processing your images on a computer, but it requires extra work. With the Snapshot shooting mode, you give up the option of using RAW.

Other settings made by the D-Lux 6 in this mode are less limiting. For example, the camera turns on Auto White Balance, scene detection, image stabilization, Quick Autofocus, backlight compensation, Intelligent ISO, Intelligent Resolution, and Intelligent Zoom, all of which are useful settings that will not unduly limit your options in most cases. I'll discuss all of those items in Chapter 4 in connection with Recording menu settings, except for scene detection and backlight compensation, which I will discuss here, because they are not options that are available on the Recording menu; they are available only in Snapshot mode.

With scene detection, the camera attempts to figure out if a particular scene type should be used for the current situation. It does not consider all of the scene settings that are available with Scene mode. Instead, the camera uses its programming to try to detect certain subjects or environments. Specifically, it looks for people; babies (if you have registered them using the Face Recognition menu option); night scenes; close-ups; sunsets; and scenes with motion. If it detects one of these factors, it displays an icon for that type of scene and adjusts its settings accordingly.

For example, in Figure 3-2, the camera detected a face and, in the upper left corner of the LCD screen, displayed the icon for intelligent detection of a portrait scene.

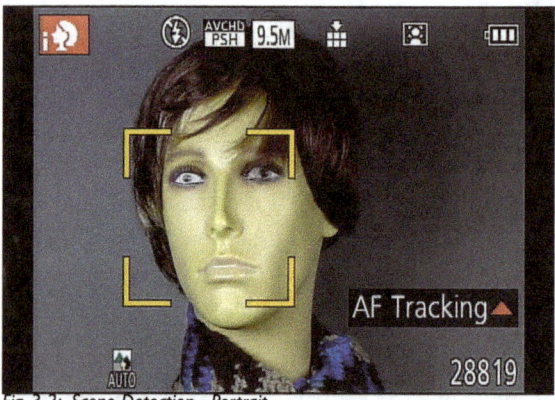

Fig. 3-2: Scene Detection - Portrait

In Figure 3-3, the camera realized that the subject was close to the camera, and displayed the flower icon, indicating a macro (close-up) scene.

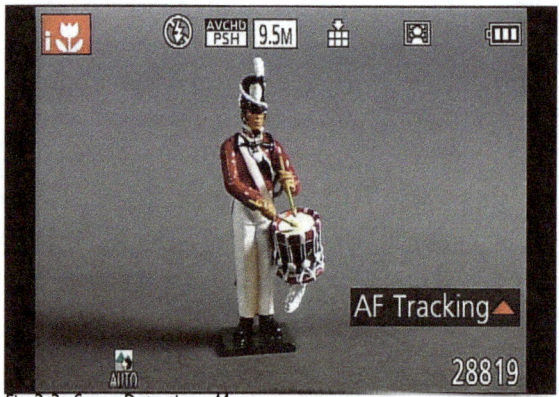

Fig. 3-3: Scene Detection - Macro

With backlight compensation, the camera will try to detect situations in which the subject of the photograph is lighted from behind. This sort of lighting can "fool" the camera's metering system into making the exposure too dark, because of the light shining toward the lens. Without backlight compensation, the result would be a subject that is too dark. With this setting, the camera automatically adjusts its exposure to be brighter, to overcome the effects of the backlighting. When the camera detects this situation, it displays the icon shown in Figure 3-4.

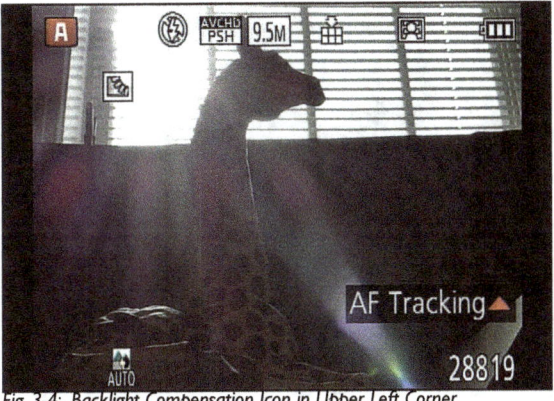

Fig. 3-4: Backlight Compensation Icon in Upper Left Corner

Even though the D-Lux 6 makes various automatic settings in Snapshot mode, there are still several options that you can adjust using the menu system and, to some extent, the physical control buttons.

First, you can use the Recording menu to select certain settings, although your choices are sharply limited compared to the many options that are available with this menu when the camera is set to the more advanced shooting modes (Program, Aperture Priority, Shutter Priority, and Manual). In those other modes, there are six screens of options available on the Recording menu; in Snapshot mode, there are only two screens of options. I will discuss those options below.

The first setting on the Recording menu in this mode, Picture Size, shown in Figure 3-5, allows you to select the resolution of your images. As noted above, you cannot use the RAW format in the Snapshot mode, only JPEG images, which, as I'll discuss in Chapter 4, are compressed to reduce the file size, leading to some reduction in quality.

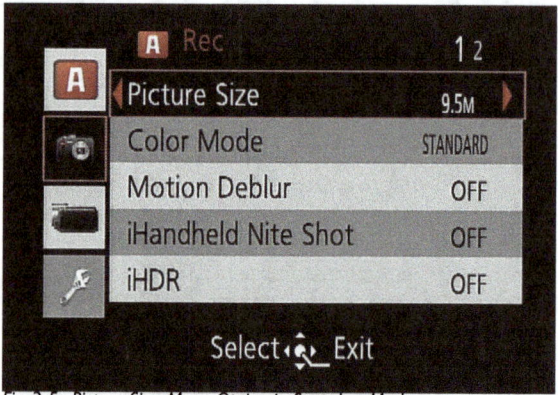

Fig. 3-5: Picture Size Menu Option in Snapshot Mode

I will discuss the Picture Size setting in more detail in that chapter. For most purposes, I recommend that you choose the largest size, which varies from 10 megapixels (displayed on the screen as 10M) to 7.5M, depending on the aspect ratio setting.

The second setting on the Recording menu in the Snapshot recording mode, Color Mode, shown in Figure 3-6, is a simplified version of the Photo Style setting, which is available in the more advanced recording modes.

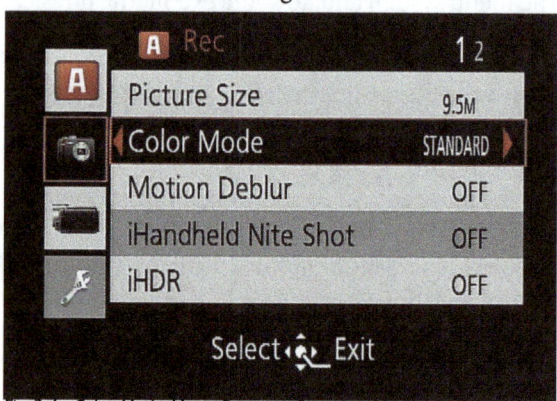

Fig. 3-6: Color Mode Menu Option in Snapshot Mode

The Color Mode setting is available on the Recording menu only when the camera is set to Snapshot mode. This setting has just four options: Standard, Happy, B/W, for Black and White, and Sepia. The Happy setting is similar to the Vivid option of the Photo Style menu item; it increases the saturation, or intensity, of the colors in the image. The other settings are self-explanatory.

The third setting on the menu, Motion Deblur, shown in Figure 3-7, is available only in Snapshot mode.

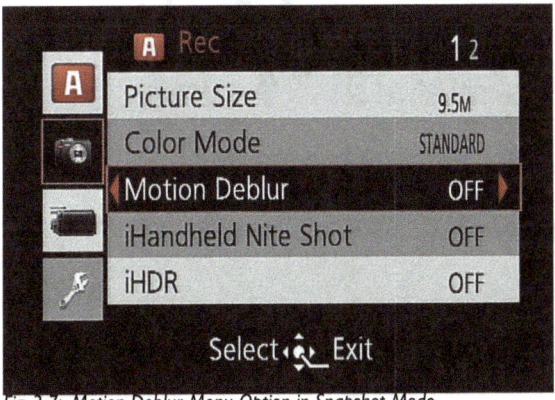

Fig. 3-7: Motion Deblur Menu Option in Snapshot Mode

With this setting, the camera will set the ISO level (sensitivity to light) higher so it can use a faster shutter speed and freeze the motion of the subject as much as possible. If you are photographing children, pets, or any other subject that is moving or likely to move, this setting can be quite useful. It does bring with it one clear limitation: When Motion Deblur is turned on, the camera's Intelligent Zoom function, which is automatically set in Snapshot mode, is disabled. As is discussed in Chapter 4, Intelligent Zoom doubles the camera's zoom range without a major reduction in image quality. With Motion Deblur turned on, you will be limited to the normal range of the optical zoom (24mm to 90mm). In addition, the camera may reduce the resolution of the image as a result of the internal processing it carries out when taking this sort of shot.

The next available menu setting is called iHandheld Nite Shot, shown in Figure 3-8.

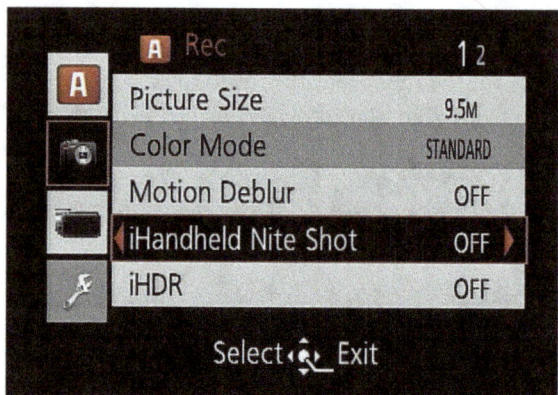

Fig. 3-8: iHandheld Nite Shot Option in Snapshot Mode

This special setting is designed to minimize the motion blur that can result from using a handheld camera at the slow shutter speed that is likely to be needed to get a sufficient exposure at night. If the camera detects darkness and senses that it is handheld, the camera will raise its ISO setting in order to permit the use of a faster than normal shutter speed. Also, because using a higher ISO can increase the visual "noise" or grainy look in an image, the camera will take a burst of several shots and combine them internally into a final image. By blending the contents of several images together, the camera can reduce the noise in the final, composite result. This setting is a very useful one to activate when shooting in low-light conditions without flash or a tripod.

The final option on the first screen of the Recording menu in Snapshot mode is iHDR, shown in Figure 3-9. With this setting, as with iHandheld Nite Shot, the D-Lux 6 will take a burst of shots and combine them internally to create a final result, if conditions call for that procedure. In this case, the conditions that will cause the camera to use the special processing are when there is strong contrast between the lightest and darkest parts of the scene, such as when one area is in deep shadow while another is in bright sunlight.

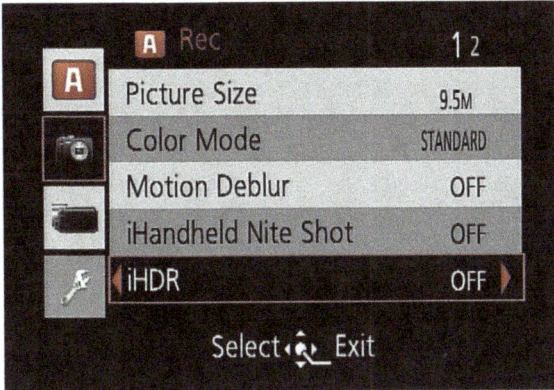

Fig. 3-9: iHDR Option in Snapshot Mode

I will discuss High Dynamic Range, or HDR photography, further in Chapter 9. Essentially, with HDR, the camera combines the most normally exposed parts of the multiple images in order to achieve a final result that appears to be properly exposed throughout most or all of its various areas. This setting can be very useful whenever you are taking photographs in highly contrasty conditions.

The first of the two menu options on the second and final screen of the Recording menu in this mode is Face Recognition, shown in Figure 3-10.

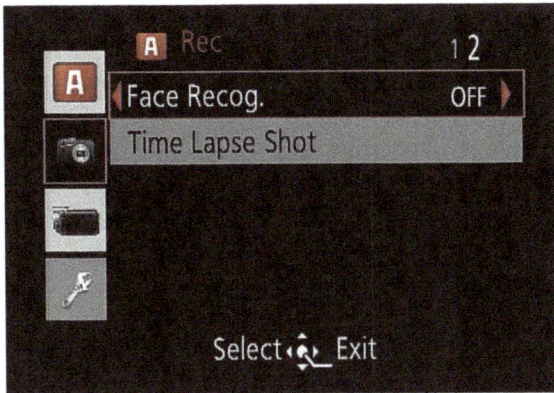

Fig. 3-10: Face Recognition Menu Option in Snapshot Mode

When this option is turned on, the camera will attempt to detect faces that you have registered using the procedure for storing names and faces. I will discuss the details of this menu option in Chapter 4.

The final option on the Recording menu in Snapshot mode, Time Lapse Shot, shown in Figure 3-11, lets you set the camera to take an evenly spaced series of shots of slowly unfolding actions, such as the opening of a flower. I will discuss this option in Chapter 4.

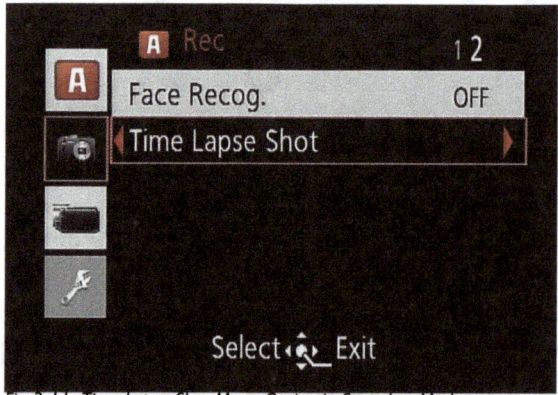

Fig. 3-11: Time Lapse Shot Menu Option in Snapshot Mode

Besides the settings mentioned above on the Recording menu and a few on the Setup and Motion Picture menus, as discussed in Chapter 2, there is one other item that you can adjust in Snapshot mode: AF Tracking. When the camera is set to Snapshot, you will see a message on the LCD, as shown in Figure 3-12, that you can press the up cursor button to activate AF Tracking.

Here is how this works. If you press the up button, a small set of white focus-tracking brackets will appear in the center of the screen, as shown in Figure 3-13, along with a message saying to press the AF/AE Lock button to lock in the tracking. Center those brackets over any subject you want to track, such as a child, pet, or other moving object. Then press the AF/AE

Lock button to lock the focus (and exposure) on that subject.

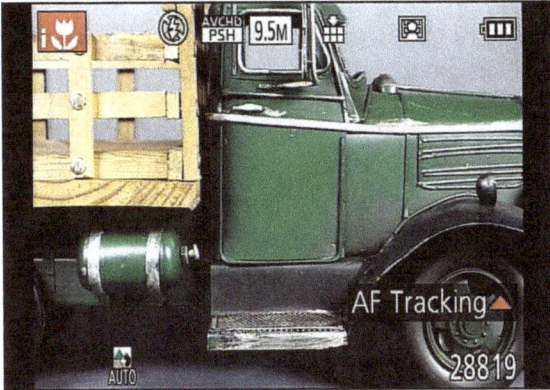

Fig. 3-12: AF Tracking Prompt on Screen

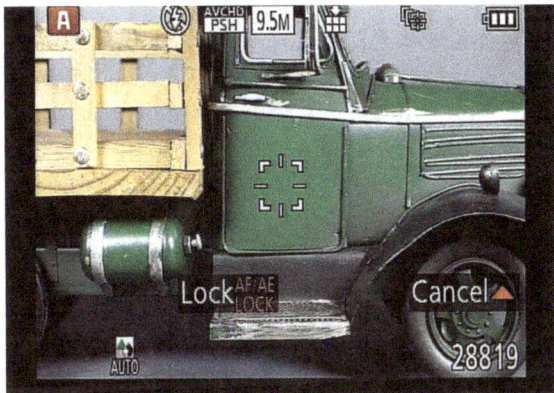

Fig. 3-13: AF Tracking Focus Frame on Screen

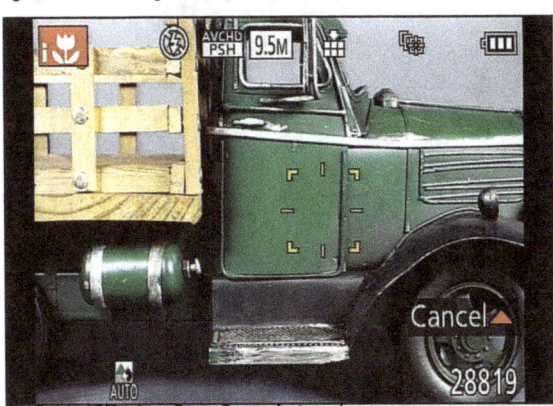

Fig. 3-14: AF Tracking Focus Frame Activated

The brackets will turn yellow, as shown in Figure 3-14, and the camera will try to keep that subject centered in the brackets, and will try to adjust the focus and exposure for that subject. To cancel this focus mode, press the up cursor button again.

Another option that is available in Snapshot mode is a special technique for taking an image with a blurred background, sometimes called the "bokeh" effect. Later in this chapter, in the discussion of Aperture Priority mode, I will discuss this process in more detail. Essentially, the wider open the aperture (the camera's opening to let in light), the more the background will be blurred, if other conditions are equal. In Snapshot mode, the camera provides you with a special control to blur the background.

To use the background defocus feature, press in on the rear dial, using it as a button. You will then see a display like that shown in Figure 3-15, with an icon representing the feature at the far right of the screen, and, at the bottom of the screen, a scale that has an icon with a blurred background at the far left and an icon with a sharp background at the far right.

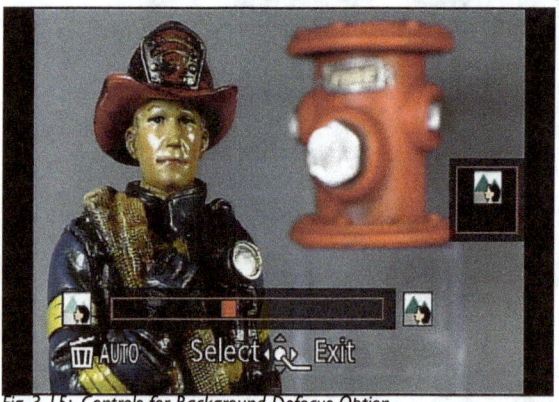

Fig. 3-15: Controls for Background Defocus Option

Turn the rear dial to the left to blur the background more or to the right to make it increasingly sharper. When you are done, press in on the rear dial or the Menu/Set button to lock in the setting; the camera will then display the chosen aperture setting in the lower left corner, as shown in Figure 3-16.

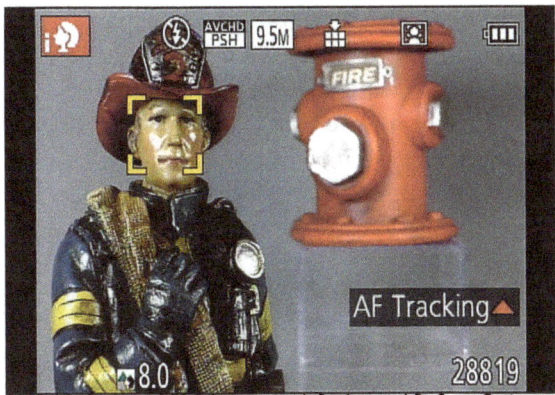

Fig. 3-16: Display of f/8.0 Aperture with Background Defocus Option

Snapshot Plus

There is one more menu setting you can make in Snapshot mode that is not available in other recording modes. This setting, called Snapshot Plus, is not really a different recording mode; it just adds two additional settings to those available in the standard Snapshot mode.

To activate Snapshot Plus mode, you use the menu system, but, instead of using the Recording menu, you move on the main menu screen to the icon above the camera icon that represents the recording menu, and select the A icon that represents Snapshot mode, as shown in Figure 3-17.

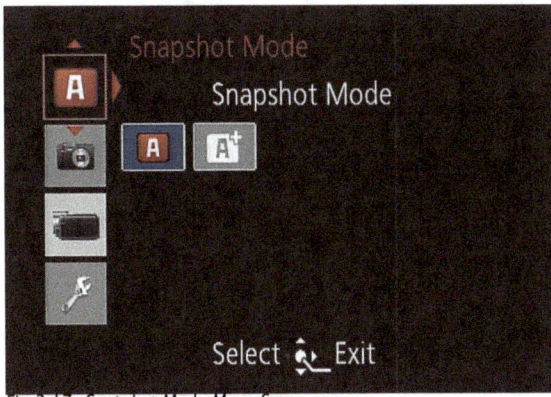

Fig. 3-17: Snapshot Mode Menu Screen

Then press the right cursor button to move the highlight into the right side of the menu screen, press it to the right one more time to highlight the A+ icon, as shown in Figure 3-18, and press the Menu/Set button to select that mode and return to the main recording screen.

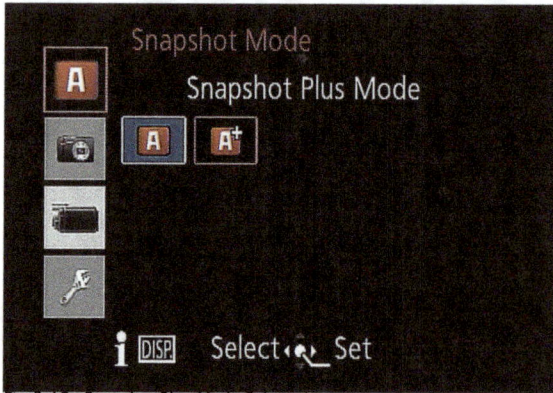

Fig. 3-18: Snapshot Plus Mode Selected

When you exit the menu and are back at the live view, you select the options for Snapshot Plus mode in the same way as you used the background defocusing option, discussed above. That is, you press in on the rear dial, using it as a button rather than as a dial. The difference in this mode is that you will see three new icons on the screen, as shown in Figure 3-19, rather than the single icon for background defocusing.

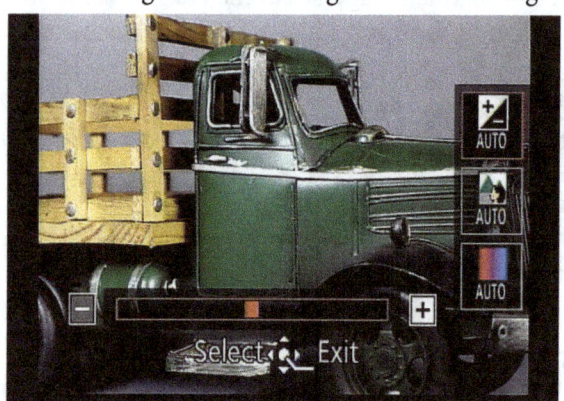

Fig. 3-19: Controls for Special Options in Snapshot Plus Mode

The defocusing icon will be in the center, and there will be two others: on top will be the icon for brightness, and on the bottom will be the icon for color adjustments.

To select one of the three icons, use the up and down cursor buttons to move from one to the other. When the icon for the feature you want to use is highlighted by a red frame, just turn the rear dial to the left or right or press the left and right cursor buttons to make adjustments. With the brightness option, turn the dial to the left to make the image darker, or right to make it brighter. With the color option, turning the dial to the left adjusts the camera's white balance to make the colors appear more reddish, or "warmer"; turning to the right makes the colors look more bluish, or "cooler."

When you have finished adjusting brightness, background defocusing, and color as you want them, press in on the rear dial again to exit from the adjustment screen. Note: Here is another way to activate the three icons for these settings. Instead of pressing in on the rear dial, just press the right button, which is labeled WB, for white balance, and the three icons will appear on the screen, ready for your adjustments.

Besides the options I have just discussed, there is another very useful item that you can control in Snapshot mode by pressing a button. If you press the down cursor button, which is marked with icons of a timer and a stack of frames, you get access to the D-Lux 6's burst-shooting and self-timer options. I will discuss these options in more detail in Chapter 5. For now, I will discuss basic information about these functions.

When you first press the down button, you will see three icons on the screen, as shown in Figure 3-20. The single rectangle at the left represents single-shot mode. Selecting this icon essentially turns off burst shooting and the self-timer. The middle icon represents burst shooting. When you highlight that icon, a set of six more icons appears below it. You can press the down button to reach that line of icons and navigate through them using the left and right buttons. As you progress to the right through this line, the choices represent faster shooting but

75

with some limitations as you reach the icons at the far right.

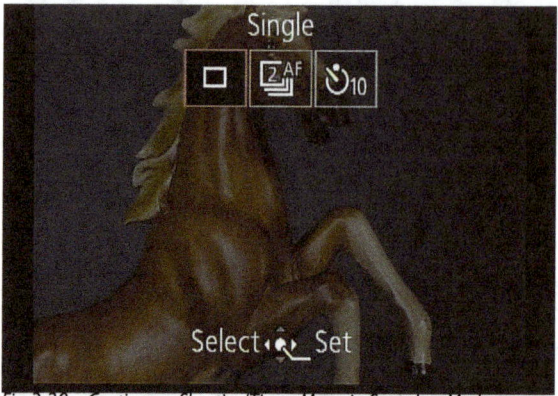

Fig. 3-20: Continuous Shooting/Timer Menu in Snapshot Mode

Once you have highlighted your chosen mode of burst shooting, press the Menu/Set button to exit back to the shooting screen. Now, when you hold down the shutter button, the camera will take a continuous burst of shots at a speed ranging from 2 to 11 shots per second.

If you select the icon at the far right among the initial group of 3 icons, as shown in Figure 3-20, you will activate the camera's self-timer. When this icon is highlighted, press the down button to activate the pair of icons below it, which represent the 10-second and 2-second timers. Highlight the one you want and press Menu/Set to exit to the shooting screen. The self-timer icon will appear on the screen, as shown in Figure 3-21.

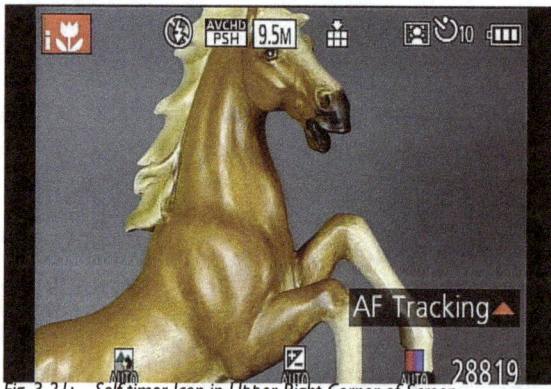

Fig. 3-21: Self-timer Icon in Upper Right Corner of Screen

When you have set the 10-second self-timer, once you press the shutter button the camera will beep and the reddish lamp on the front of the camera will flash slowly for the first 8 seconds, and more rapidly after that until the shutter is released. This setting is good for group photos when the camera is on a tripod. The 2-second timer is useful when you want to have a small delay after pressing the shutter button, so the camera will not be moved by the force of the shutter press. I will discuss the self-timer further in Chapter 5.

In summary, when you choose Snapshot mode, the D-Lux 6 still lets you make quite a few choices for your settings, but the extent of those choices is limited by comparison to the choices that are available in the more advanced recording modes. One of the limitations I don't like is that this mode reduces your Picture Size choices to just three or four, depending on what aspect ratio you have set, instead of the five or six that are available in Program mode. More importantly, in Snapshot mode you can't select RAW for the Quality setting, which is set automatically to Fine. I'll discuss RAW in Chapters 4 and 9, but if you want to have the highest possible quality of images or intend to process them using one of the more sophisticated photo editing programs, like Adobe Photoshop, you won't like having to do without the RAW Quality setting.

There are several other limitations imposed by Snapshot mode. When you choose this shooting mode, the Recording menu is limited to 7 choices: Picture Size, Color Mode, Motion Deblur, iHandheld Nite Shot, iHDR, Face Recognition, and Time Lapse Shot. It may not be such a bad thing to do without a lot of menu options, though, because, after all, the purpose of Snapshot mode is for the camera to make quick, reasonably good decisions for you so you can spring into action with the shutter button on a split second's notice. And, being able to turn on burst shooting or the self-timer by pressing the down button is quite useful.

Although the Snapshot shooting mode lets the camera make

most of the technical decisions, you still have a fair amount of involvement in taking photographs (and movies). Especially when you're just starting out to use the D-Lux 6, don't shy away from using Snapshot as you explore the camera's capabilities. The automation in this mode is very sophisticated and will often produce excellent results; the drawback is that you don't have as much creative control as you might like. But for ordinary picture-taking opportunities, vacation photos, and quick shots when you don't have much time to decide on particular settings, Snapshot is a wonderful tool to have at your fingertips.

Program Mode

Choose this mode by turning the mode dial to the P setting, as shown in Figure 3-22.

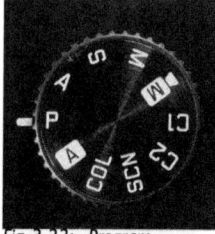

Fig. 3-22: Program

In Program mode, as with Snapshot mode, the camera automatically selects a combination of aperture and shutter speed that results in a suitable exposure for the current lighting conditions. However, this shooting mode lets you control more of the available settings than is possible in Snapshot mode. You still can override the camera's automatic exposure to a fair extent, though, by using exposure compensation, Program Shift, and exposure bracketing, also known as Auto Bracket. You don't have to make a lot of decisions if you don't want to, because the camera will make reasonable choices for you as defaults.

One way to look at Program mode is that it greatly expands the choices available to you through the Recording menu. You will be able to make choices involving picture quality, image stabilization, ISO sensitivity, metering method, and others. I won't discuss all of those choices here; if you want to explore that topic, go to the discussion of the Recording menu in Chapter 4 and check out all of the different selections that are available to you.

It is worth mentioning that Program mode has the great advantage of letting you choose RAW quality for your still images. To do that, activate the Recording menu by pressing the Menu/Set button (the center button in the five-button array). Navigate down to the Quality setting, then press the right button to pop up the sub-menu with the five Quality settings: Fine, Standard, RAW plus Fine, RAW plus Standard, and RAW, as shown in Figure 3-23.

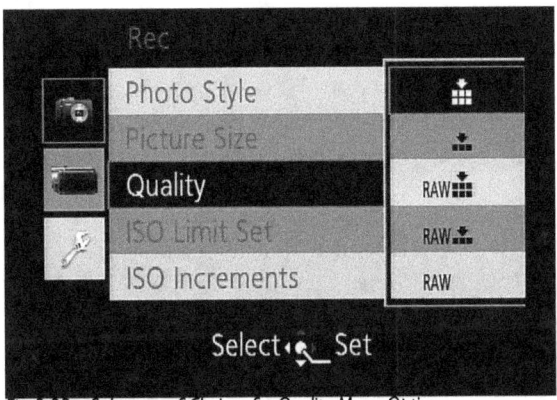

Fig. 3-23: Submenu of Choices for Quality Menu Option

The Fine and Standard settings produce normal JPEG images. (JPEG stands for Joint Photographic Experts Group, an industry group that sets standards for photographic file formats.) With the RAW plus Fine and RAW plus Standard settings, the camera actually records two images as noted, so you will have both the RAW and the non-RAW image available. This choice can be useful if you won't have immediate access to software for editing the RAW images, and want to be able to use the lesser-quality images quickly.

Besides unlocking the many options in the Recording menu, choosing Program mode also provides you with access to many options in the Setup menu that are not available in Snapshot Mode, such as various settings for the LCD screen display, the histogram, manual focus assist, and highlight, which I will discuss later.

Are there any drawbacks to using Program mode? As with any choice of this sort, there are some tradeoffs. The most obvious issue is that you don't have complete control over the camera's settings. You can choose many options, such as Photo Style, Quality, Picture Size, and ISO, but you can't directly control the aperture or shutter speed, which are set according to the camera's programming. You can exercise a good deal of control through exposure compensation, Program Shift, and auto bracketing (see later discussion), but that's not quite the same as selecting a particular aperture or shutter speed at the outset. If you need that degree of control, you'll need to select Aperture Priority, Shutter Priority, or Manual exposure for your shooting mode.

There is one specific issue to be aware of that is related to the lack of control over aperture and shutter speed when you're using Program mode. When that shooting mode is set, the Minimum Shutter Speed setting will be activated; you cannot turn it off. The slowest minimum shutter speed you can set in that situation is one second. So if you are trying to take a time exposure in a dark area (using a tripod, presumably), where the correct shutter speed would be, say, five seconds, the camera will not expose the picture properly. The minimum shutter speed setting of one second will be the longest exposure possible. If you expect to have exposures longer than one second, you need to select a shooting mode other than Program—namely, Manual, Aperture Priority, or Shutter Priority.

Aperture Priority Mode

You set this shooting mode by turning the Mode dial to the capital A that stands alone, as shown in Figure 3-24, not the "A" that is inside the light gray rectangle.

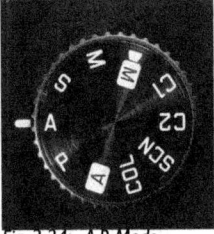

Fig. 3-24: A.P. Mode

This mode is similar to Program mode in the functions that are available for you to control, but, as the name implies, it also gives you, the photographer, more control over the camera's aperture.

Before discussing the nuts and bolts of the settings for this mode, let's talk about what aperture is and why you would want to control it. The camera's aperture is a measure of how wide its opening is to let in light. The aperture's size is measured numerically in f-stops. For the D-Lux 6, the range of f-stops is from f/1.4 (wide open) to f/8.0 (most narrow). The amount of light that is let into the camera to create an image on the camera's sensor is controlled by the combination of aperture (how wide open the lens is) and shutter speed (how long the shutter remains open to let in the light).

For some purposes, you may want to have control over how wide open the aperture is, but still let the camera choose the corresponding shutter speed. Here is an example involving depth of field. Depth of field is a measure of how well a camera is able to keep multiple objects or subjects in focus at different distances (focal lengths). For example, say you have three friends lined up so you can see all of them, but they are standing at different distances—five, seven, and nine feet (1.5, 2.1, and 2.7 meters)—from the camera. If the camera's depth of field is quite narrow at a particular focal length, such as five

81

feet (1.5 meters), then, in this case, if you focus on the friend at that distance, the other two will be out of focus and blurry. But if the camera's depth of field when focused at five feet (1.5 meters) is broad, then it may be possible for all three friends to be in sharp focus in your photograph, even if the focus is set for the friend at five feet (1.5 meters).

What does all of that have to do with aperture? One of the principles of photography is that the wider open the camera's aperture is, the narrower its depth of field is at a given focal length. So in our example above, if you have the camera's aperture set to its widest opening, f/1.4, the depth of field will be shallow, and it will be possible to keep fewer items in focus at varying distances from the camera. If the aperture is set to the narrowest opening possible, f/8.0, the depth of field will be greater, and it will be possible to have more items in focus at varying distances.

With a camera like the D-Lux 6, with its relatively small sensor and wide-angle lens, the effects of aperture on depth of field are not as pronounced as with some other cameras. However, the following two images generally illustrate the effects of aperture settings on depth of field, using an orchid at an indoor home and garden show, where the background included a variety of people and objects some distance away.

In these photos, the flower was quite close to the D-Lux 6's lens—within about 6 to 8 inches (15 to 20 cm). For Figure 3-25, the aperture of the camera's lens was set to f/2.0, the widest possible at that zoom range. (I'll discuss how zoom range affects aperture later in this chapter.) With this setting, because the depth of field at this aperture is quite shallow, the background is quite blurry, and therefore less distracting than it otherwise would be. In fact, as you may be able to see, even some parts of the orchid plant are slightly blurry, and only the central portion in the foreground is in the sharpest focus.

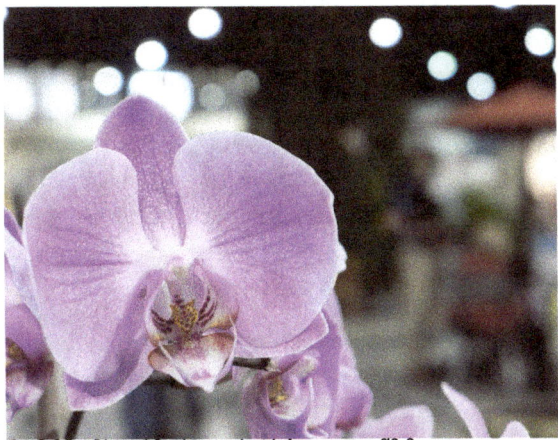

Fig. 3-25: Blurred Background with Aperture at f/2.0

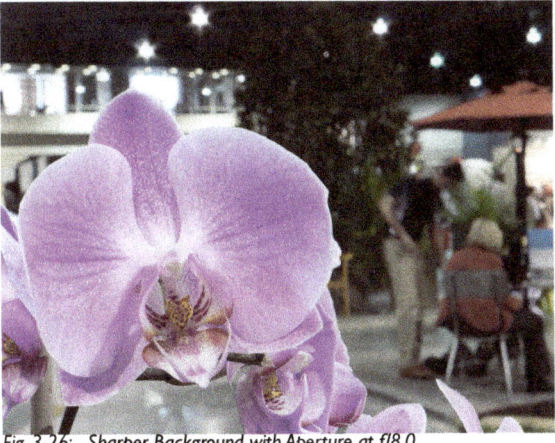

Fig. 3-26: Sharper Background with Aperture at f/8.0

Figure 3-26 was taken with the aperture set to f/8.0, the most closed-down aperture setting, resulting in a broader depth of field, and consequently keeping more of the orchid plant in focus and making the background considerably sharper.

These photos illustrate the effects of varying your aperture by setting it wide (low numbers) when you want to blur the background and narrow (high numbers) when you want to enjoy a broad depth of field and keep subjects at varying distances in sharp focus.

In practical terms, if you want to have the sharpest picture possible, especially when you have subjects at varying distances from the lens and you want them to be in focus to the greatest extent possible, then you may want to control the aperture, and make sure it is set to the highest number (narrowest opening) possible.

On the other hand, there are occasions when photographers prize a shallow depth of field. This situation arises often in the case of outdoor portraits. For example, you may want to take a photo of a person standing outdoors with a background of trees and bushes, and possibly some other, more distracting objects, such as a swing set or a tool shed. If you can achieve a shallow depth of field, you can have the person's face in sharp focus, but leave the background quite blurry and indistinct. This effect is sometimes called "bokeh," a Japanese term describing an aesthetically pleasing blurriness of the background. In this situation, the blurriness of the background can be a great asset, reducing the distraction factor of unwanted objects and highlighting the sharply focused portrait of your subject.

So with our awareness of the virtues of selecting an aperture, on to the technical steps involved. Once you have moved the mode dial to the A setting, the next step is quite simple. Use the aperture ring (surrounding the lens, in front of the aspect ratio switch) to change the aperture. One of the very nice features of the D-Lux 6 is that it has this physical control with which to adjust your settings. As you turn this ring, it clicks into place for each successive f-stop, and you can see the setting on the physical ring. If you have turned on the Exposure Meter option on the fourth screen of the Setup menu, you also can see the aperture (and shutter speed) in a graphic display on the camera's screen, as shown in Figure 3-27, in which the aperture is set to f/4.5.

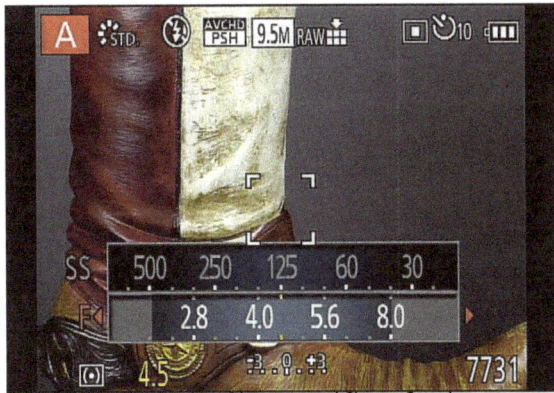

Fig. 3-27: Graphic Display of Aperture and Shutter Speed

Even without the graphic display, the f-stop value will appear at the bottom left of the screen, as in Figure 3-28.

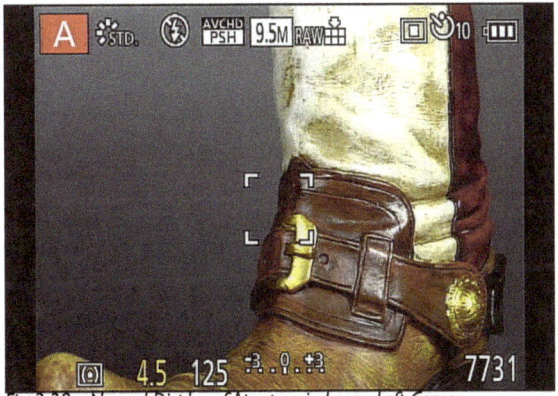

Fig. 3-28: Normal Display of Aperture in Lower Left Corner

The shutter speed will be displayed also, but not until you have pressed the shutter button halfway down to let the camera evaluate the lighting conditions.

Here is an important note about Aperture Priority mode that might not be immediately obvious and easily could lead to confusion: Not all apertures are available at all times. In particular, the widest-open aperture, f/1.4, is available only when

85

the lens is zoomed out to its wide-angle setting (moved toward the W indicator). At higher zoom levels, the widest aperture available changes steadily, until, when the lens is fully zoomed in to the 90mm level, the widest aperture available is f/2.3.

To see an illustration of this point, here is a quick test. Zoom the lens out by moving the zoom lever all the way to the left, toward the W. Then select Aperture Priority mode and set the aperture to f/1.4 by turning the aperture ring all the way to the 1.4 setting. Now zoom the lens in by moving the zoom lever to the right, toward the T. After the zoom indicator has appeared and then disappeared from the screen, you will see that the aperture has been changed to f/2.3, because that is the widest open the aperture can be at the maximum zoom level. (The aperture will change back to f/1.4 if you move the zoom lever back to the wide-angle setting; so you need to check your aperture after zooming out as well as after zooming in, to make sure you will not be surprised by an unexpected aperture setting.)

There may be some situations in which the camera cannot set a shutter speed that will result in a proper exposure for the aperture you have set. In that case, the aperture and shutter speed numbers on the display will turn red. You will need to adjust a setting, such as the aperture or ISO, or alter the lighting in order to expose the image normally. (You can still take the picture while the values are red, if you don't mind the inadequate exposure.) Also, there are some cases in which the range of shutter speeds available for setting is limited; the limiting factors include the ISO setting and the aperture setting. So, even though the camera has an overall range of shutter speeds from 250 seconds to 1/4000 second, not all of those speeds are available for any given shot in Aperture Priority mode. The slowest shutter speed available in this mode is 8 seconds and, in some cases, the fastest available is 1/2000 second.

Shutter Priority Mode

The next shooting mode is a complement to Aperture Priority mode. In Shutter Priority mode, you choose whatever shutter speed you want, and the camera will set the corresponding aperture in order to achieve a proper exposure of the image. In this case, the creative considerations are somewhat different than with Aperture Priority. The D-Lux 6 has a wide range of shutter speeds available in Shutter Priority mode (the range differs somewhat in some other modes). In this mode, you can set the shutter speed for a variety of intervals ranging from 8 full seconds to 1/4000 of a second. (The available shutter speed settings are different for motion pictures.) The camera will pick an aperture from its full range of f/1.4 to f/8.0, unless the lens is zoomed in. In that case, as discussed in connection with Aperture Priority mode, the widest aperture available is f/2.3.

If you are photographing fast action, such as a baseball swing or a hurdles event at a track meet, and you want to stop the action with a minimum of blur, you will want to select a fast shutter speed, such as 1/800 of a second. For Figure 3-29, I used that shutter speed to photograph a remote-controlled motorcycle as it flipped in the air after zooming up a ramp. The D-Lux 6 was able to freeze the model nicely in mid-air.

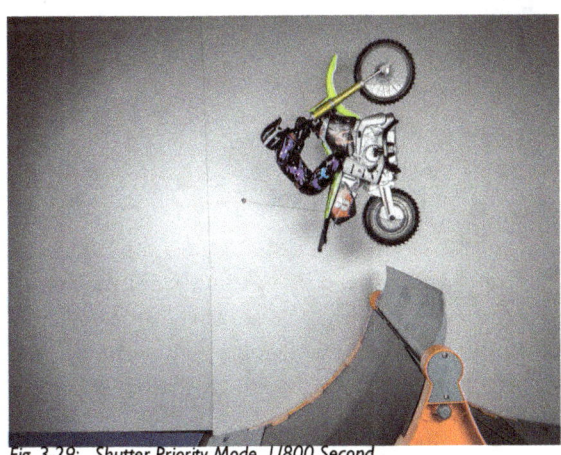

Fig. 3-29: Shutter Priority Mode, 1/800 Second

At other times, for creative purposes, you may want to select a slow shutter speed to achieve a certain effect, such as leaving the shutter open to capture a trail of automobiles' taillights at night. To illustrate, I took the image in Figure 3-30 by using a shutter speed of 4 full seconds to photograph a model of a Ferris wheel, which has a rotating bar with blinking lights. As the wheel spun around for this length of time, the lights traced the complete circular trails seen in this image.

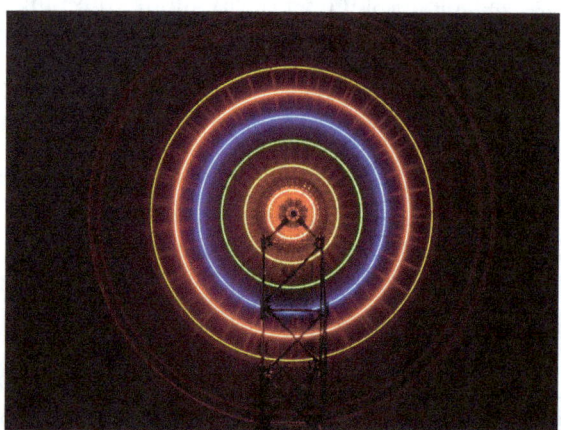

Fig. 3-30:   Shutter Priority Mode, 4 Seconds

You select Shutter Priority mode by setting the mode dial on top of the camera to the S indicator, as shown in Figure 3-31.

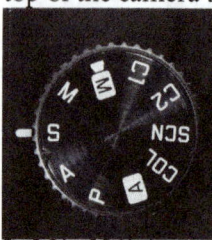

Fig. 3-31:   S.P. Mode

Then you select the shutter speed by left-and-right motion of the rear dial. Turn the dial to the right for faster (shorter) shutter speeds, and to the left for slower (longer) ones. The camera will then select the appropriate aperture to achieve a proper exposure, when you press the shutter button halfway down. There is one complication with Shutter Priority mode that is not present with Aperture Priority mode, though. With Aperture Priority mode, you control the aperture setting using the aperture ring, which does not control any other function. However, in Shutter Priority mode, you need to use the rear dial to set the shutter speed, and that dial can also control exposure compensation. So, you need to be careful to make sure that the shutter speed value (here, 40 for 1/40 sec) is highlighted in yellow on the camera's display, as shown in Figure 3-32.

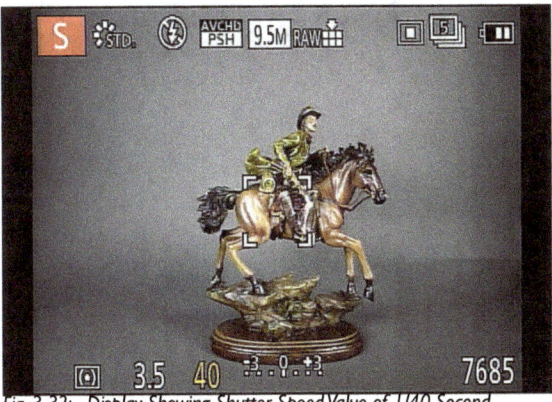

Fig. 3-32: Display Showing Shutter Speed Value of 1/40 Second

If that number appears in white, the rear dial will control exposure compensation. In that case, you need to press in on the dial to switch its function to controlling shutter speed.

Once you've pressed the shutter button halfway down, you need to watch the colors of the shutter speed number and the f-stop number on the screen. As with Aperture Priority mode, if the numbers turn red, that means that proper exposure at that shutter speed is not possible at any available aperture, according to the camera's calculations. For example, if you set the shutter speed to 1/8 of a second in a fairly dark indoor setting, the shutter speed number and the aperture number (which will be f/1.4, the widest setting, if the zoom is set to wide angle) may turn red, as shown in Figure 3-33, indicating that proper exposure is not possible. One good thing in this situation is that the camera will still let you take the picture,

89

despite having turned the numbers red to warn you. The camera is saying, in effect, "Look, you may not want to do this, but that's your business. If you want a dark picture for some reason, help yourself."

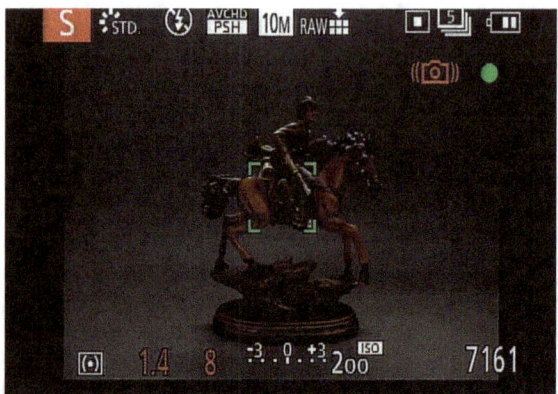

Fig. 3-33: Red Numbers for Settings Meaning Not Enough Light

(Note: This situation is less likely to take place when you're using Aperture Priority mode, because, unlike the situation with f-stops, there is a wide range of shutter speeds for the camera to choose from; a range from 8 seconds to 1/4000 second. So no matter what aperture you select, there is likely to be a shutter speed available that will result in proper exposure.)

On the shutter speed display, you should be careful to distinguish between the fractions of a second and the times that are one second or longer. The longer times are displayed with what looks like double quotation marks to the right, as in Figure 3-34, which shows a shutter speed of one second. For another example, when the display shows 3.2, that means 1/3.2, the first entry in the table on the next page. When the display shows 3.2", that means 3.2 seconds.

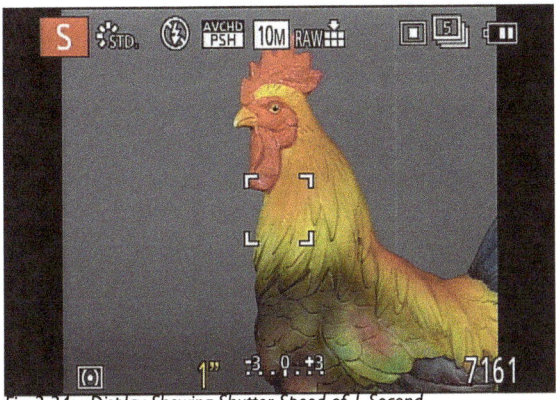

Fig. 3-34: Display Showing Shutter Speed of 1 Second

One aspect of the camera's display that can be somewhat confusing is that some of the times are displayed as a combination of fractions and decimals, such as 1/2.5 and 1/3.2. I find these numbers a bit hard to translate mentally into a time I can relate to. Here is a table that translates these numbers into a more understandable form:

Shutter Speed Equivalents	
3.2	1/3.2 = 0.31 or 5/16 second
2.5	1/2.5 = 0.4 = 2/5 second
1.6	1/1.6 = 0.625 = 5/8 second
1.3	1/1.3 = 0.77 = 10/13 second (approx. 0.8 sec)

Manual Exposure Mode

The D-Lux 6 has a fully manual mode for control of exposure, which lets you set both aperture and shutter speed yourself. Not all compact cameras have a manual exposure mode, which is a boon for photographers who want to exert full creative control over exposure decisions. For example, there may be times when you want to purposely underexpose or overexpose an image to convey a particular feeling or to produce a special effect, such as a silhouette. Or, there may be a tricky situation in which your most important subject is deeply shadowed and you prefer to use manual settings of aperture and shutter speed rather than relying on exposure compensation in order to expose the subject properly.

One situation where I find Manual exposure mode particularly useful is for taking individual shots to be combined in software to create HDR (High Dynamic Range) composite images. The HDR technique, which I will discuss more fully in Chapter 9, often is used in situations where the scene is partly in darkness and partly in bright light. To even out the contrast, you can take a series of shots of the scene, some considerably underexposed and others equally overexposed. You then combine these shots in special software that takes the best-exposed portions from several shots, resulting in a composite image that is well exposed through a wide range of lighting values.

The technique for using Manual exposure mode is not far removed from that for the Aperture Priority and Shutter Priority modes. To control exposure manually, set the mode dial to the M indicator, as shown in Figure 3-35.

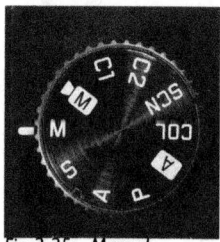

Fig. 3-35: Manual

Now the aperture ring will control aperture and the rear dial will control shutter speed. Earlier, we saw how the rear dial has two functions in Shutter Priority mode: controlling shutter speed and also controlling exposure compensation. In Manual exposure mode, you no longer can control exposure compensation, because that would be of no use when you're already adjusting the exposure manually. Therefore, there is no need to press in on the rear dial to make the dial control shutter speed; it has no other function available in Manual mode.

If you recall, with Aperture Priority mode, you cannot set the aperture to f/1.4 and other low numbers when the lens is fully zoomed in. The same situation is true with Manual mode; you cannot set the wide-open aperture of f/1.4 when the lens is zoomed all the way in to the 90mm equivalent setting.

With Manual exposure mode, the settings for aperture and shutter speed are independent of each other. When you change one value, the other one stays unchanged until you change it manually. The camera is leaving the creative decision about exposure entirely up to you, even if the resulting photograph would be washed out by excessive exposure or under-exposed to the point of near-blackness.

However, the camera is not going to abandon you completely, so you won't have to use a separate light meter or other external aids to gauge the correct exposure settings. Even though you have selected Manual exposure control, the camera will still provide help if you want it.

When the camera is set to Manual exposure mode, at the bottom center of the screen the D-Lux 6 displays a scale of tick marks ranging from -3 to +3 EV, with a zero at the mid-point, as shown in Figure 3-36. With this scale on the screen, you can adjust either aperture or shutter speed in turn, and additional tick marks will appear to the right or left of the zero point to indicate overexposure or underexposure. If you get the settings to a point where the exposure will be normal, the additional tick marks will disappear.

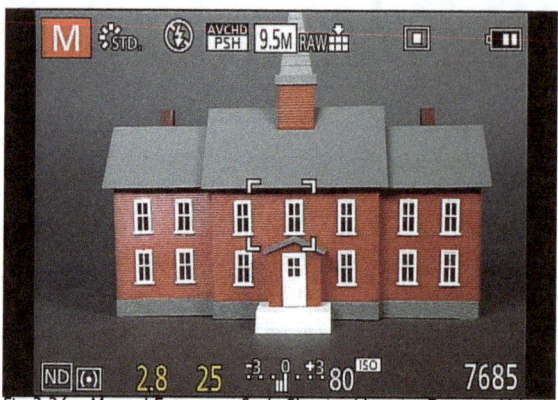

Fig. 3-36: Manual Exposure - Scale Showing Negative Exposure Value

Of course, you can adjust the settings however you want, leaving additional tick marks displaying to the right or left, as you please. But the camera is providing this display to show you what settings it would consider to yield a correct exposure given the lighting conditions in existence.

In Manual mode, you can set the shutter speed to as long as 250 seconds, a setting that is not available in any other recording mode. When the ISO is set above 1600, though, the longest shutter speed available is 30 seconds; above 3200 ISO, the longest available shutter speed is 8 seconds.

Scene Mode

Scene mode is quite different from the other shooting modes I have discussed so far. This mode does not have a single defining feature, such as permitting control over one or more aspects of exposure. Instead, when you select Scene mode and then choose a particular scene type within that mode, you are in effect telling the camera what sort of environment the picture is being taken in as well as what kind of image you are looking for, and you're letting the camera make a group of decisions as to what settings to use to produce that result.

I did not use Scene mode very much at first; however, after

using it for a while, I came to appreciate its usefulness, particularly in certain situations. I will discuss how it works and you can decide for yourself whether you might take advantage of it on some occasions.

Turning the mode dial to the SCN indicator, as shown in Figure 3-37, places the camera in Scene mode, but unless you want to settle for whatever scene setting is already in place, you now need to make another choice, and pick one from the fairly impressive list of possibilities.

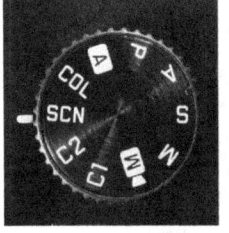

To make this choice, you need to use the menu system. When you select Scene mode, the menu system itself changes. In the generic exposure modes such as Program and Aperture Priority, the menu system has only three branches: Recording, Motion Picture, and Setup (unless

Fig. 3-37: Scene

the camera is in playback mode). When you use Scene mode, there is a fourth branch of the menu system, named Scene, as shown in Figure 3-38.

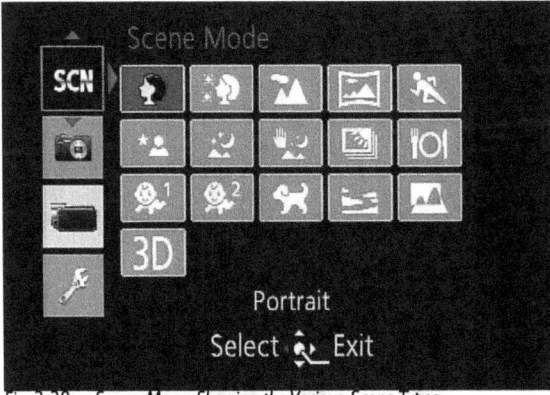

Fig. 3-38:   Scene Menu Showing the Various Scene Types

The Scene menu takes over as the first choice at the top of the menu system once you have pushed the Menu/Set button (the center button in the five-button array). (The Scene menu may appear automatically once you select SCN on the Mode dial; that option is controlled by the Scene Menu setting on the seventh screen of the Setup menu.)

Push the Menu/Set button, and you are faced with the Scene menu. Next, press the right button, and the selector (a black block surrounded by a red frame) moves onto the first choice of scene types, which is Portrait, as shown in Figure 3-39.

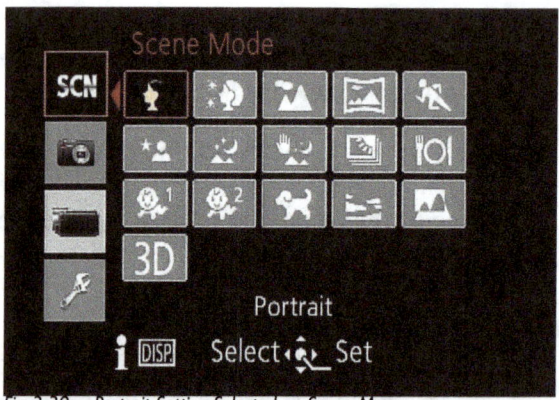

Fig. 3-39:   Portrait Setting Selected on Scene Menu

One good thing about the Scene menu system is that each scene type is labeled as you move the selector over it, so you are not left trying to puzzle out what each icon represents.

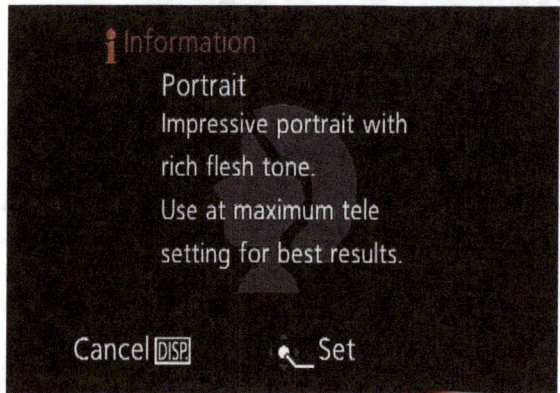

Fig. 3-40:   Information Display for Portrait Scene Setting

If you want a bit more information, press the Display button (the button in the lower right corner of the camera's back) while in the Scene menu, and the display will give you a brief description of the scene type that is selected in the menu, as shown in Figure 3-40. Press the Display button again to cancel the information screen and return to the Scene menu.

Keep pushing the right button to move the selector over the other scene types; when you reach the right edge of the screen, the selector moves to the far-left item in the next row down.

That's all there is to do to select a scene type. But there are numerous choices, and you need to know something about each to know whether it's one you would want to select. In general, each scene type carries with it a variety of settings, including things like focus mode, flash status, range of shutter speeds, sensitivity to various colors, and others.

There are some limitations on the settings you can make when you set the camera to Scene mode. No matter what scene type you select, you cannot adjust ISO, Metering Mode, Intelligent Dynamic, Minimum Shutter Speed, Intelligent Resolution, or Photo Style settings. However, with a few exceptions—namely, Panorama, Handheld Night Shot, HDR, and 3D—you can set the Quality to RAW, so you can take advantage of the special settings for the various scene types and still enjoy the flexibility of RAW shooting. With most of the settings you can use burst shooting, and with several you can use flash. (I am including a table later in this discussion of Scene mode that shows some of the major limitations on settings with the various scene types.) Now I will discuss some details about each of the scene settings, so you can make an informed choice.

Portrait

This setting is meant to yield rich skin tones. You should shoot close to the subject and set the zoom to full telephoto, to blur the background if possible, as shown in Figure 3-41. The camera uses a wide aperture if it can and initially sets the autofocus mode to Face Detection.

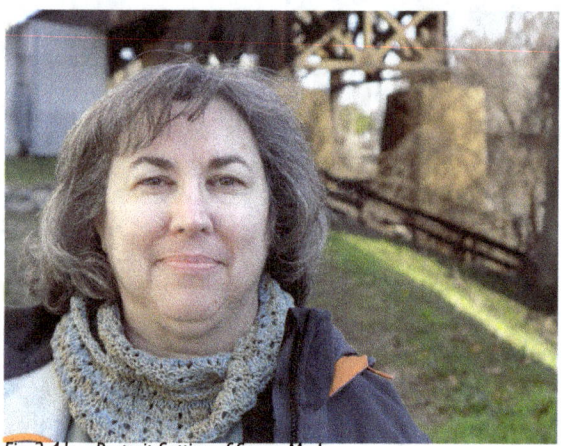

Fig. 3-41:   Portrait Setting of Scene Mode

The flash mode is initially set to Auto/Red-Eye Reduction. You can use RAW quality, burst shooting, and other flash modes, and you are able to change the white balance setting. (For the remaining scene types, I won't include details about these four items unless there is a particular reason to do so; see the table after the discussion of the various scene types for information about whether you can change those four settings.)

Soft Skin

This setting is similar to Portrait; it detects skin tones in faces and adds a "soft effect" to those areas. Flash mode is initially set to Auto/Red-Eye Reduction.

Scenery

This style is intended for photographs of landscapes and sub- jects other than individual people. It is useful for shots of buildings, gardens, and colorful scenery, as shown in Figure 3-42, in which I snapped an eye-catching work of art in an urban setting. The flash is forced off. (Even if you open up the flash unit, it will automatically be forced off, and will not fire. Ordinarily, there is no way for the user to force the built-in flash off when the unit is open, but the camera can do so au- tomatically when set to the Scenery setting and a few others.)

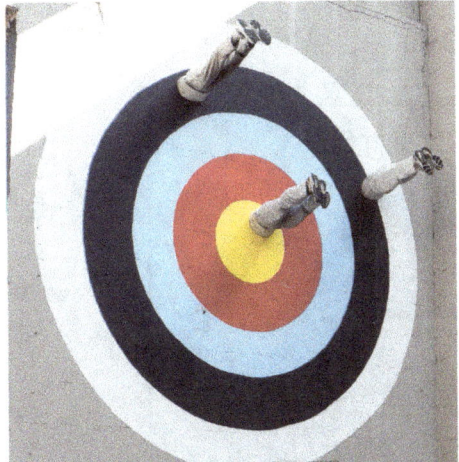

Fig. 3-42: Scenery Setting of Scene Mode

You cannot adjust the white balance, presumably because you will be shooting your outdoor vistas in daylight conditions.

Panorama Shot

The D-Lux 6 includes an excellent capability for automating the capture of panoramas. If you follow some fairly simple steps, the camera will stitch together a series of images internally and produce a high-quality result.

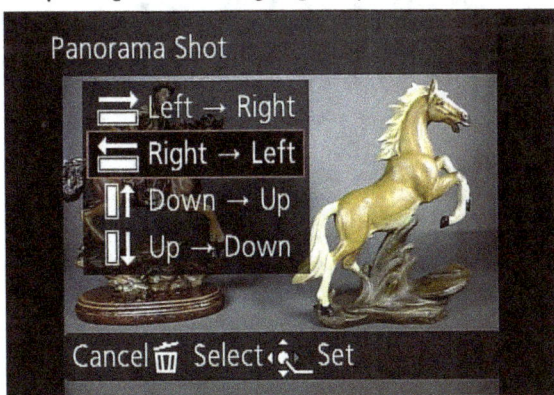

Fig. 3-43: Direction Options for Panorama Shot Setting

After selecting Panorama Shot from the Scene menu, press the Menu/Set button and you will see the display shown in Figure

3-43. On that screen, select the direction in which you want to move the camera to take the panoramic shot. Press Menu/Set again, and you will see the display shown in Figure 3-44.

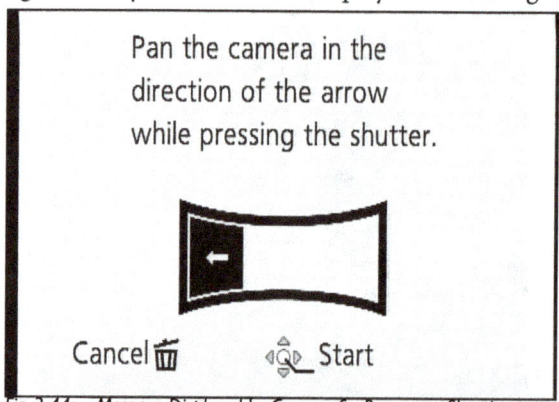

Fig. 3-44: Message Displayed by Camera for Panorama Shooting

At this point, press the Menu/Set button, and you will see the display shown in Figure 3-45, which provides guide lines for framing your panorama.

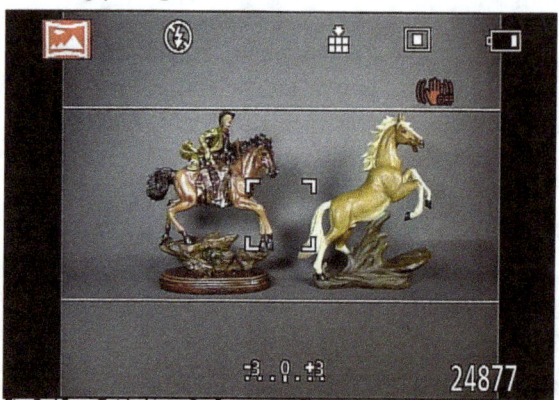

Fig. 3-45: Guide Lines for Panorama Shot

Now, when you are ready, press the shutter button all the way down and then release it, while starting to move the camera steadily in the direction you selected. (If you prefer, you can just press the shutter button without first pressing Menu/Set.) You will hear a continuous clicking sound as the camera takes multiple images. You should try to keep the camera steady in a single horizontal (or vertical) plane and move it at a steady rate, so that you would complete a full circle in about 8 seconds. You can keep moving the camera until the panorama ends of its own accord, or you can press the shutter button down again to stop the recording at any time.

A horizontal panorama will have a size of 8000 by 1080 pixels, resulting in a resolution of about 8.5 MP. A vertical panorama has a size of 1440 by 8000 pixels, or about 11.5 MP. Because of the different sizes with these two orientations, you can use the direction settings with horizontal or vertical orientations of the camera to achieve different results than usual. For example, if you set the direction to Down to Up and then hold the camera tilted vertically while you sweep it to the right, you will create a horizontal panorama that has 1440 pixels in its vertical dimension rather than the standard 1080.

I tend to shoot my panoramas moving the camera from left to right, but you may have a different preference. If you move the camera either too quickly or too slowly, the panorama will not succeed; if that happens, just try again. Generally speaking, panoramas work best when the scene does not contain moving objects such as cars or pedestrians, because, when items are in motion, the multiple shots are likely to pick up the same object more than once, in different positions.

It is advisable to use a tripod if possible, so you can keep the camera steady in a single plane as it moves. Note that focus, exposure, and white balance are fixed as soon as the first image is taken for the panorama.

When a panoramic shot is ready to be played back in the camera, the camera prompts you to press the up cursor button to start it playing back; it then scrolls across the screen so it can be viewed using the full area of the screen, rather than being squeezed so as to fit its full extent within the screen. (If you don't see the prompt, press the Display button until you do.)

Figures 3-46 and 3-47 are sample panoramas, both shot from left to right.

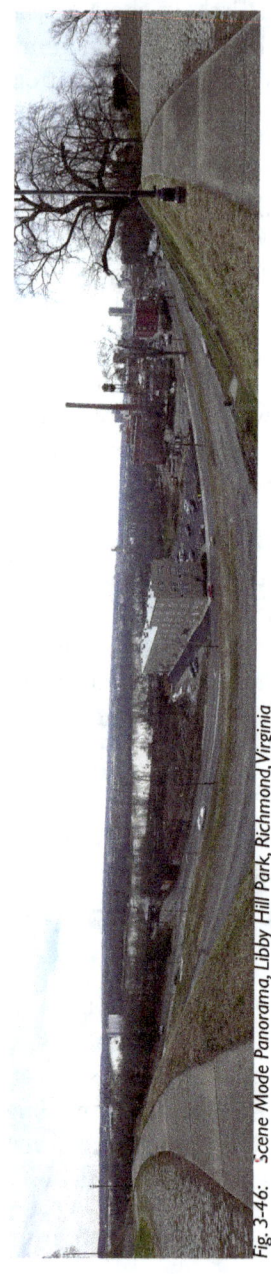

Fig. 3-46: Scene Mode Panorama, Libby Hill Park, Richmond, Virginia

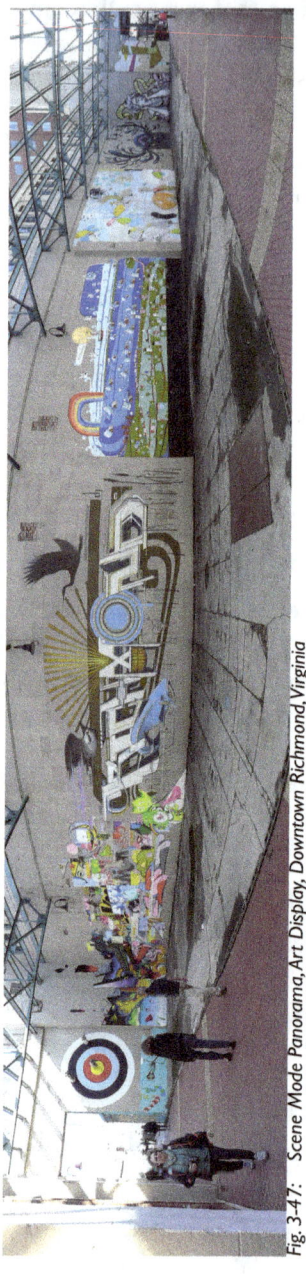

Fig. 3-47: Scene Mode Panorama, Art Display, Downtown Richmond, Virginia

Sports

This style is meant to stop action in bright daylight using fast shutter speeds at distances of 16 feet (4.9 meters) or more. The camera uses a relatively high ISO setting so it can use a fast shutter speed. (I'll discuss ISO, or sensitivity to light, later. Briefly, with a higher-numbered ISO, the camera is more sensitive to light, so it can use a faster shutter speed. The tradeoff is the possibility of more "noise" or grain of the image.) In Figure 3-48, I used the Sports setting to capture an image of kayakers as they suddenly came into view on the river.

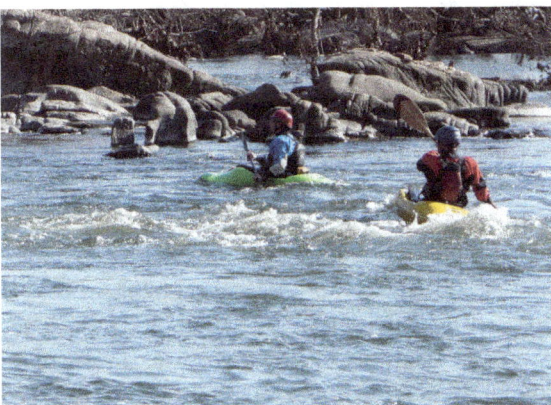

Fig. 3-48:   Sports Setting of Scene Mode, James River, Richmond, Virginia

Night Portrait

This style is designed for a portrait in low-light conditions, preferably with the camera on a tripod and possibly even using the self-timer to avoid shaking the camera. You should open the flash (or attach an external flash unit). If the built-in flash is used, the camera will set it to Slow Sync with Red-eye Reduction, and you cannot change that setting. If possible, the subject should be asked not to move for about a second while the image is being exposed. The purpose of the Slow Sync flash mode is to expose the main subject with the flash, but to keep the shutter open long enough to also expose the background with the ambient light, as seen in Figure 3-49.

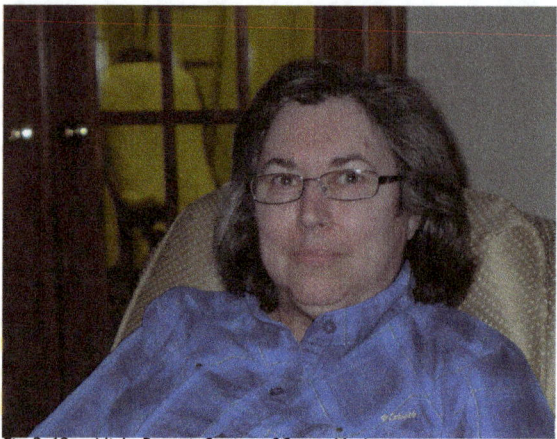

Fig. 3-49:   Night Portrait Setting of Scene Mode

Night Scenery

This style is meant for night-time scenes with the camera on a tripod, preferably using the self-timer to minimize camera shake. The shutter speed will be set for an exposure as long as 8 seconds, using only the available light. Because this style is for scenery and not portraits, the focus range will be from 16 feet (4.9 meters) to infinity. The flash will be forced off, and will not fire. In Figure 3-50, I used this setting to capture a view of an antique car that I happened across at an indoor exhibition. The camera used a shutter speed of 1.3 second to allow the scene to be exposed adequately.

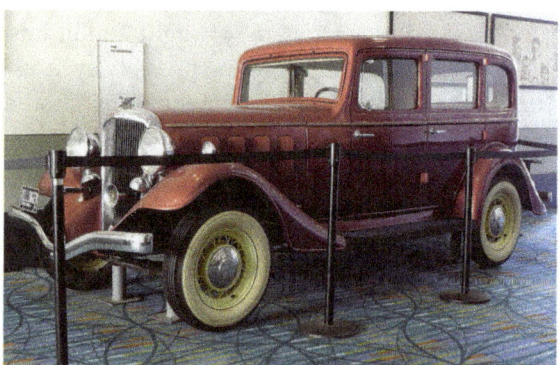

Fig. 3-50:   Night Scenery Setting of Scene Mode

Handheld Night Shot

With this setting, the D-Lux 6 uses a special process to take high-quality images in low light. It takes a rapid burst of shots and combines them internally into a single composite image. Because of this processing, the camera can use a high ISO setting and a fast shutter speed to minimize blur caused by camera motion. Although high-ISO shots often have visual noise or graininess, by combining several images the camera can reduce the noise in the final result. This setting is useful when you cannot use a tripod or flash and the lighting is dim. Of course, because multiple images are being taken, this setting works best for subjects that are not moving, or at least are not moving rapidly, such as the shot of a landscaping display at an indoor exhibition in Figure 3-51.

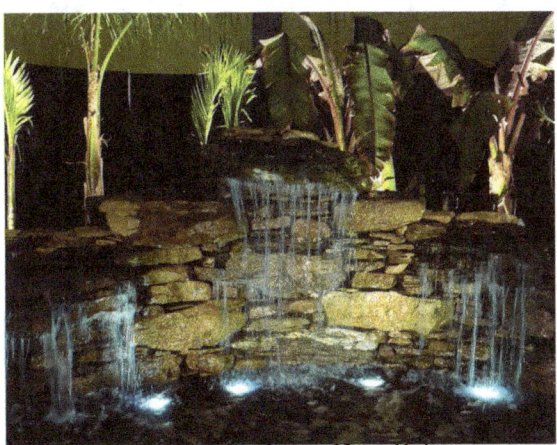

Fig. 3-51: Handheld Night Shot Setting of Scene Mode

HDR

HDR (High Dynamic Range), like Handheld Night Shot, involves a rapid volley of shots. In this case, the camera takes a burst of three shots and combines them internally to create the final image. The purpose of this setting is to even out the differences in brightness among various parts of a scene, such as when some areas are in dark shadows and others are in bright sunlight. The camera exposes the multiple shots with different exposure levels and then combines the most appropriately exposed portions for each part of the scene. I will discuss the general concept of HDR photography in more detail in Chapter 9. In Figure 3-52, I used the HDR setting to enhance a view of the downtown skyline.

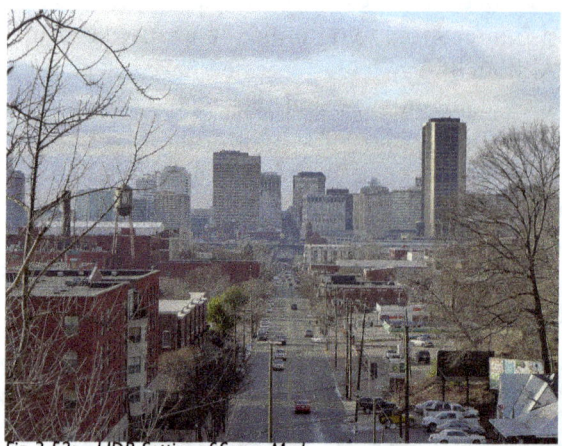

Fig. 3-52: HDR Setting of Scene Mode

This shot presented a situation in which there were shadows falling over parts of the roadway. The D-Lux 6 did a good job of preserving details even in some of the darker areas of the image.

Food

This scene is for those occasions when you're in a restaurant and are so impressed by the presentation of your meal that you want to photograph it, or for those people who are in the habit of documenting every meal they eat. Or you could use it for taking pictures for your cookbook. In any event, the idea here is to take a fairly close-up picture without flash, though the flash will be available if you want to use it. The autofocus range will be the same as for Autofocus Macro, or about two inches (5 cm) at wide angle, or two feet (61 cm) at telephoto, to infinity. With this setting, you cannot adjust the white balance. I used this setting in Figure 3-53 to record a Cajun shrimp sandwich just after it was served in a restaurant.

106

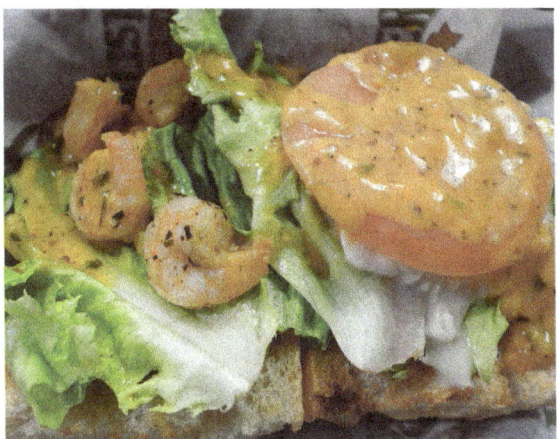

Fig. 3-53:   Food Setting of Scene Mode

Baby 1 and Baby 2

These settings are for baby pictures. The reason there are two different settings is to let you enter birth dates and names of two children, and have the child's name and age displayed along with the picture. In this way, the camera will keep track of what age the child is in each photo.

When you select one of these settings, the camera lets you enter name and age, as shown in Figure 3-54; you can leave either or both of these set to Off if you want, or enter the data.

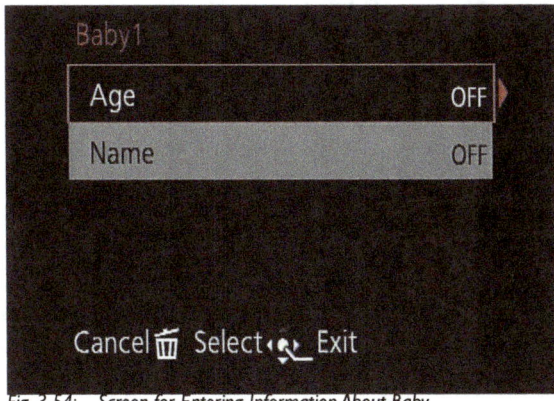

Fig. 3-54:   Screen for Entering Information About Baby

107

The camera gives you menus from which to choose the date, as shown in Figure 3-55, and letters for the names.

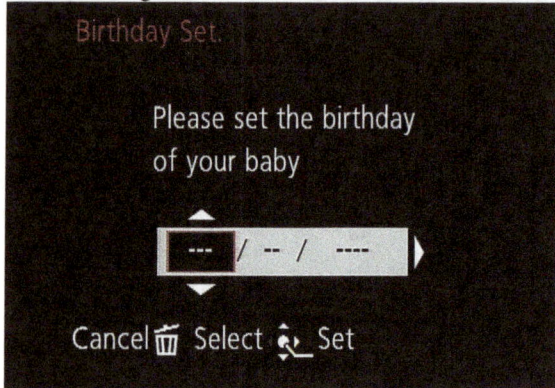

Fig. 3-55:   Screen for Entering Baby's Birth Date

Apart from the names and ages, the Baby 1 and Baby 2 scene types set the camera to use a weaker-than-normal flash output.

Pet

The Pet scene style is similar to Baby 1 and Baby 2 in that you can set your pet's name and age. The initial setting for the AF Assist Lamp menu option is Off, so your pet will not be startled by the reddish lamp that illuminates to assist with focusing. (You can turn the lamp back on using the AF Assist Lamp setting on the second screen of the Recording menu.)

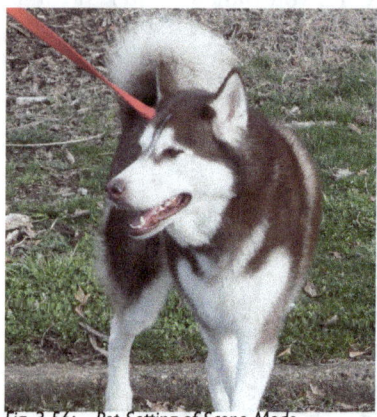

Fig. 3-56:   Pet Setting of Scene Mode

The camera turns AF Tracking on, with the idea that your subject is likely to be moving unpredictably. (You can change the autofocus mode using the AF Mode item on the first screen of the Recording menu.) In Figure 3-56, I used this setting to capture a shot of a Husky I encountered in a park.

Sunset

This scene style is designed to highlight the vivid reds and oranges of a sunset, as shown in Figure 3-57.

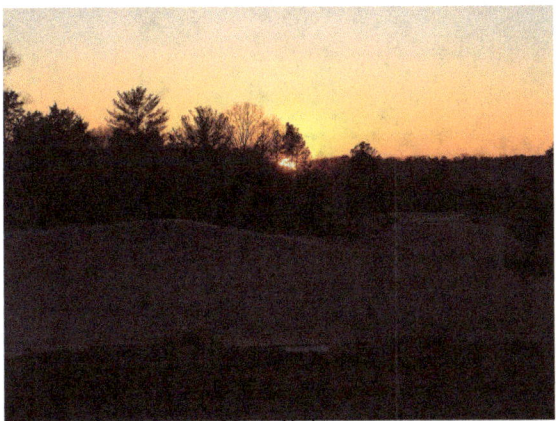

Fig. 3-57:   Sunset Setting of Scene Mode

The flash is forced off, and won't fire even if you open it up in dark conditions. Don't take the label "sunset" literally; you can use this mode for sunrise also, and, as a matter of fact, for any situation when you want to emphasize reddish or orange tones. You cannot adjust the white balance, because the camera uses special processing to emphasize the colors of sunsets.

Glass Through

This scene type, called Glass Through in the Leica user's guide and Through Window in the camera, is intended to make it easier to get good results when shooting images through glass, such as store windows or windows of vehicles or houses. It is not clear exactly what settings the camera adjusts in this mode; evidently it alters the contrast somewhat and adjusts the autofocus system to ignore close-up items, such as dirt or grime on the glass, that might distract the focusing mechanism. In Figure 3-58, I used this setting to shoot through the glass enclosing a collection of antique china. The resulting shot does show the items quite clearly.

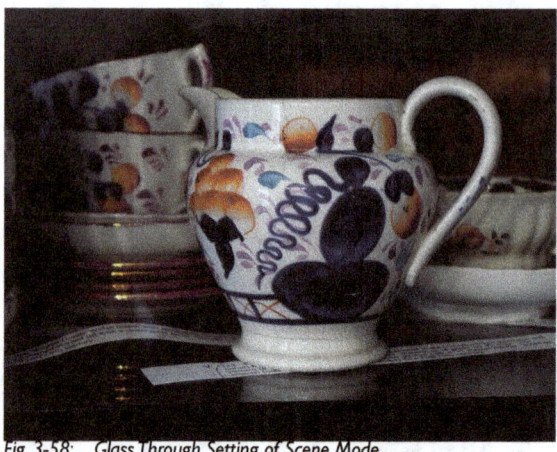

Fig. 3-58:   Glass Through Setting of Scene Mode

3D

This scene type lets you take 3D (stereoscopic) photos semi-automatically. What actually happens with this setting is that the camera guides you through the process of taking several shots of the same scene from slightly different angles. The camera then selects two of the resulting images and combines them internally into a single file with the .mpo extension. This file can be viewed in three dimensions on a 3D-capable television set, but it will be displayed only in two dimensions on the D-Lux 6's display screen. (Later in this discussion, though, I'll tell you how you can view it in 3D without a 3D TV set.)

Here is the procedure to follow. After selecting the 3D setting from the Scene menu, select an appropriate scene. Ideally, you should choose a stationary item or scene that has some interest in terms of depth as a 3D subject. The shot will work best in a well-lighted outdoor area. The process is most easily carried out without a tripod, though you have to hold the camera as steady as possible.

Frame the scene with the main part of the subject slightly to the right of the center of the image. Then, press and release the shutter button, and the camera will start clicking as it takes multiple shots. While the camera is clicking, hold it steady, and keep it pointed straight ahead, but move it directly to the right, about 4 inches (10 cm). If the process was successful, the camera will display the message, Creating 3D Photo. If not, it will display an error message and you can try again.

As noted above, the final result will be a single image that looks like any other 2D image on the camera's display; to view it in 3D, you can connect the camera to a 3D-capable TV set. Or, you can convert the file to a stereoscopic JPEG image that can be viewed with ordinary 3D glasses if you want to. Figure 3-59 is the result of converting a 3D image from the LX7 using special software. Here are the details for making this conversion.

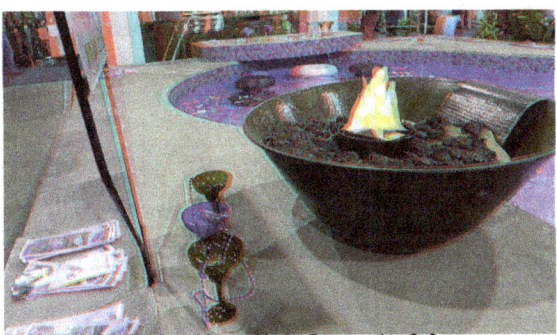

Fig. 3-59:   3D Setting of Scene Mode, Converted in Software

To do this, you can use a Windows program called Stereo Photo Maker, which can be downloaded free at http://stereo. jpn.org/eng/stphmkr. From the program's File menu, choose the command to Open Stereoscopic image. Using this command, open the camera's 3D image, with an .mpo extension. Then go to the Stereo menu and choose Color Anaglyph. On the sub-menu that appears, choose Dubois (red/cyan). You can then save that image as a single .jpg file like that shown in Figure 3-59, which looks blurry, with red and blue lines char-

111

acteristic of 3D images you may have seen in comic books or other printed materials. If you're using a Mac, there are other programs available, though I haven't used them. One possibility is Anabuilder, at http://anabuilder.free.fr. You also can use Photoshop or other general editing programs, but you'll need to experiment a bit, or find instructions on the web.

If you follow these steps with an .mpo image produced by the D-Lux 6, the final image should be ready for viewing, either on screen or on paper, using old-fashioned red/blue 3D glasses. (The red side goes over the left eye.) If it doesn't pop out as a 3D image when viewed through the glasses, go to the Adjustment menu and try various adjustments, including Auto Alignment, Easy Adjustment, and others, until it looks good.

Finally, as I promised earlier in this discussion of Scene mode, here is a table that shows which of several camera settings (RAW quality, burst shooting, flash, and white balance) are available with the different scene types:

Settings Available with Scene Types

Scene Type	RAW	Burst	Flash	WB
Portrait	yes	yes	yes	yes
Soft Skin	yes	yes	yes	yes
Scenery	yes	yes	no	no
Panorama	no	no	no	yes
Sports	yes	yes	yes	yes
N. Portrait	yes	yes	slow sync	no
N. Scenery	yes	yes	no	no
HH N. Shot	no	no	no	no
HDR	no	no	no	yes
Food	yes	yes	yes	no
Baby	yes	yes	yes	yes
Pet	yes	yes	yes	yes
Sunset	yes	yes	no	no

Settings Available with Scene Types				
Glass Through	yes	yes	no	yes
3D	no	no	no	yes

Creative Control Mode

Creative Control mode occupies its own place on the mode dial, so I will discuss it here in the context of the other shooting modes, even though it is a bit of a hybrid creature. It has some attributes of the Photo Style setting on the Recording menu, and some attributes of the Scene mode settings. For example, one of the Creative Control settings, Dynamic Monochrome, is similar to the Monochrome setting of the Photo Style menu option. Another Creative Control setting, High Dynamic, is similar in some ways to the HDR setting of Scene mode, and the Expressive setting of Creative Control mode is similar to the Vivid setting of the Photo Style option. However, there are significant differences among these various settings, and the Creative Control settings offer a range of adjustments that makes these options very useful for dramatic alteration of the colors and other attributes of your images.

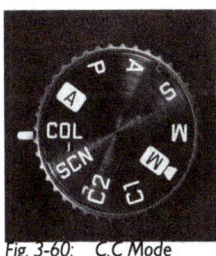

Fig. 3-60: C.C Mode

When you turn the mode dial to the COL setting, representing Creative Control, as shown in Figure 3-60, you will see a red square at the right of the display surrounding a sample image representing the selected setting; at the left of the screen is a larger square showing the effect that this setting would produce on the scene the camera is currently seeing. This display is extremely useful, because you can quickly scroll up and down through all 16 of the preset effects and see immediately how they would affect the current scene.

These various Creative Control choices provide different "looks" for your images, in some cases quite striking alterations of the normal color, texture, and brightness. It's impor-

113

tant to note that, because the Creative Control setting occupies its own slot on the mode dial, whatever selection you make for Creative Control is only in effect when the mode dial is set to that position. So, for example, if you switch the mode dial to Program or Aperture Priority mode, the Creative Control settings will no longer be in effect. If you later switch the dial back to Creative Control, though, whatever setting you previously made in that mode will once more take effect.

You also should note that, when you record a motion picture with the D-Lux 6, you don't need to move the mode dial; you only need to press the red Movie button on top of the camera. So, when you record a movie, you need to be sure the mode dial is set where you want it. For example, if you have just taken some still photos using an exotic setting from the Creative Control selections, that setting will still be in effect if you press the red button to record a movie. If you want a more ordinary look for your movie, be sure to set the mode dial back to Snapshot, Program, or some other standard mode, to avoid having the movie recorded using the Creative Control setting. On the other hand, being able to use Creative Control settings when shooting a movie can be a great advantage if you want to add a particular atmospheric look to your motion pictures. I'll discuss movie settings in more detail in Chapter 8.

Once you have selected a Creative Control setting, you can still make some additional settings from the Recording menu and with the camera's physical controls. For example, one feature of the Creative Control mode is that all of its selections can be used with the RAW setting for Quality, so you can have the flexibility of RAW images for post-processing if you want it.

Note, though, that, if you set Quality to RAW, your images will not retain the special features of the Creative Control settings, in most cases. For example, if you choose the Star Filter setting, the sparkling effect will not appear on the RAW image when it is displayed in software. However, the High Key effect will affect the RAW file. All of the effects will show up on RAW images when they are displayed in the camera, though. If you want to have the benefits of both RAW flexibility and the special processing from the Creative Control settings, you may want to set Quality to RAW + JPEG.

With the Creative Control mode, you also can set things such as Picture Size, AF Mode, and metering mode. However, several other settings are unavailable with the Creative Control shooting mode, including white balance, ISO, Intelligent Dynamic, Minimum Shutter Speed, and Photo Style. With some of the Creative Control options you can use burst shooting or flash; I will indicate those cases as I discuss the settings individually below.

In addition to the settings from the Recording menu and physical controls discussed above, with the Creative Control mode you can make several other adjustments, depending on which Creative Control setting is in effect. These adjustments are made using the icons at the right side of the display, in the same way as with the Snapshot Plus shooting mode, discussed earlier in this chapter. The numbers and subjects of the available adjustments vary according to the Creative Control setting.

For example, with the Expressive setting, there are three of these extra settings available, as shown in Figure 3-61.

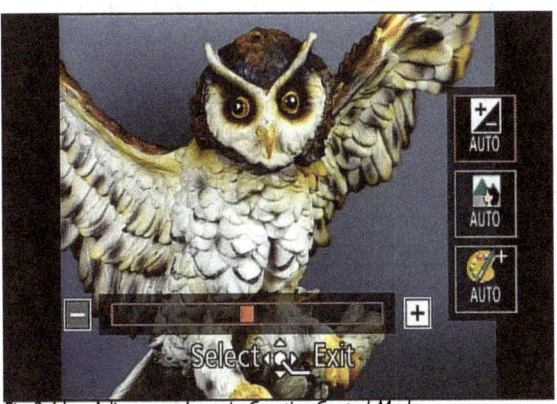

Fig. 3-61:   Adjustment Icons in Creative Control Mode

115

The three icons, from top to bottom, represent brightness, background defocusing, and the intensity of the selected effect itself. (With the Smooth Defocus and Radial defocus settings, there are only two icons; there is no need for a defocus adjustment with either of those settings.) As with the Snapshot Plus mode, you can activate this group of icons by pressing in on the rear dial, or, as an alternative, by pressing the right cursor button. As I discuss each Creative Control setting, I will mention what items can be controlled using the icons at the right of the screen, if those adjustments are different from the standard ones (brightness, background defocus, and intensity of the selected effect). Before I discuss the individual Creative Control settings, I am going to present two charts, each giving examples of how the 16 different settings affect the same scene. Later, I will provide individual examples using a few of the settings.

As you can see in the charts in Figures 3-62 and 3-63, there are some very dramatic effects and some more subtle ones. Some of these effects are best suited to a particular type of subject, and so they will not be presented in their best form in the charts. For example, the Miniature effect works best with a downward view on a busy road intersection, railroad, or some other large subject that might be reproduced in a miniature model. Similarly, the High key effect is not especially well suited for the outdoor scene shown here. The point of these charts is to show the basic differences among the various effects.

Note that all of the effects can be adjusted in some way, either as to strength or as to a particular attribute such as color. I have set all the strength adjustments to the middle range. For the Cross Process effect, I selected green as the color for processing.

Creative Control Sample Images - Chart 1

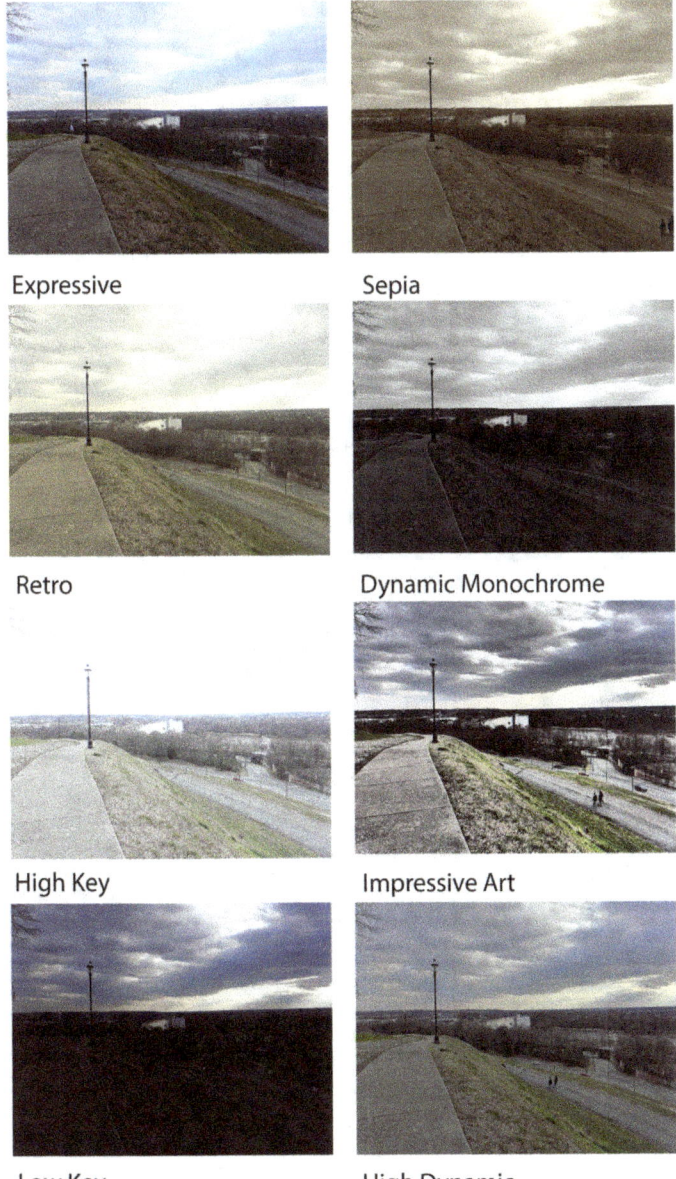

Expressive

Sepia

Retro

Dynamic Monochrome

High Key

Impressive Art

Low Key

High Dynamic

Fig. 3-62: Creative Control Mode Examples - I

Creative Control Sample Images - Chart 2

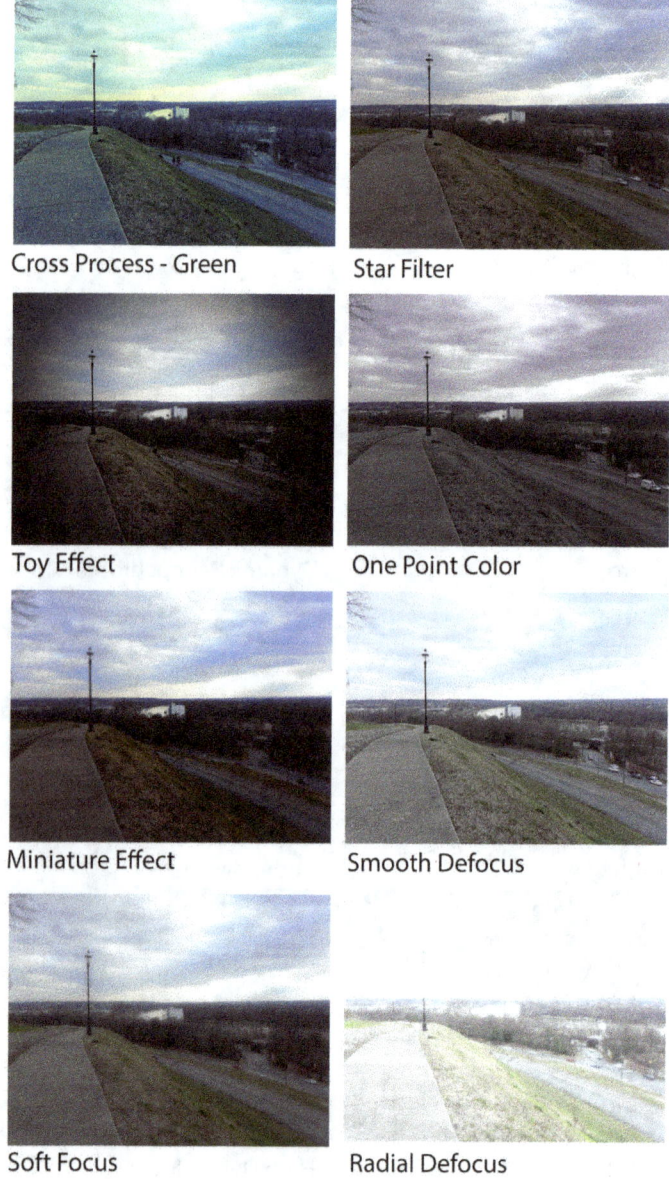

Cross Process - Green

Star Filter

Toy Effect

One Point Color

Miniature Effect

Smooth Defocus

Soft Focus

Radial Defocus

Fig. 3-63: Creative Control Mode Examples - 2

Here are some details about each of the 16 Creative Control choices. As I noted earlier, I will provide sample images for a few of the effects; the charts in Figures 3-62 and 3-63 give an overview of all of the settings.

Expressive

I would call this setting something like "super-vivid"; some people call it "pop art." When I aim the camera at my relatively mild-toned blond wooden desk, the Expressive style transforms that brownish hue to a screaming red and paints a bland blue covering for a printer with a garish, bright sky-blue color. If you like your colors with strong, wild saturation, this style is for you. However, don't overlook the fact that you can use the Vivid setting of the Photo Style menu option to achieve a similar result. That Photo Style setting is available in the more advanced shooting modes such as Program, Aperture Priority, and the like; therefore, you can use more menu and other settings in conjunction with that setting than you can with the more limiting Creative Control Expressive setting.

Retro

This style appears to me to be the opposite of Expressive; it paints the scene with subdued, somewhat yellowish tones, de-emphasizing the glaring qualities of Expressive. It evokes a gentle feeling of past times. In this case, adjusting the bottom icon's setting to the left increases yellowish tones, and adjusting it to the right increases reddish tones.

High Key

"High key" is a technique in which a studio photographer uses high-intensity lighting throughout the scene, striving for a very bright overall look with light colors and few shadows. This technique often is used in advertising photography. With the D-Lux 6, this single setting cannot necessarily remake your image to look like a traditional high key shot, but the camera does boost the exposure to produce a brighter-than-normal image. Moving the slider for the bottom icon to the left produces more pinkish tones, while setting it to the right yields bluer hues.

Low Key

"Low key" lighting, of course, is the opposite of "high key." With this option, the photographer welcomes shadows and dark areas in the image. Here again, the D-Lux 6 cannot produce a true "low key" image all by itself; what it does is reduce the exposure and otherwise process the photograph to look more dark and shadowy than normal. Here again, as with the High Key setting, the bottom icon's setting can be moved to the left for a redder look, or to the right for a bluer appearance.

Sepia

With the Sepia setting, the D-Lux 6 produces a monochrome image with a sepia (brownish) tone and softens the contrast somewhat to give the look of an antique photograph.

In this case, adjusting the setting of the bottom icon decreases the overall contrast of the image, while moving it to the right increases the contrast, producing a somewhat harsher, darker appearance.

Dynamic Monochrome

This setting converts the image to black and white, but with heightened contrast to produce a more dramatic effect. As with Sepia, you can use the left or right adjustments with the bottom icon to decrease or increase contrast. Note that, if you just want to shoot monochrome images, you can use the Photo Style setting on the Recording menu, which is available in the more advanced shooting modes such as Program, Aperture Priority, and the like; therefore, as with the Expressive setting, discussed above, you can use more menu and other settings in conjunction with the Photo Style setting than you can with the more limiting Creative Control setting.

Impressive Art

This setting has some similarities to the Expressive, Dynamic Monochrome, and High Dynamic settings. It produces images with high contrast and dramatic variations in color intensity. Using the bottom icon's settings, you can adjust the intensity all the way to the left to produce a monochrome image, or all the way to the right to produce an oversaturated image with exploding, vibrant colors. You can achieve some interesting effects with this setting, as seen in Figure 3-64, which adds a dramatic appearance to what is otherwise the fairly straight-forward view of a downtown area of office buildings and parking lots along a major thoroughfare.

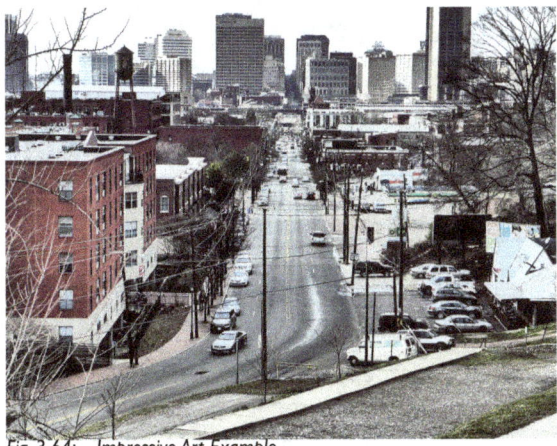

Fig. 3-64:   Impressive Art Example

High Dynamic

This setting is oriented less to altering the colors of the image than to leveling out the shadows and highlights. As you can see from the name, it is akin to the High Dynamic Range or HDR processing that is often done with software, and some-times, as here, through in-camera processing. In some cases, this type of processing is used to produce dramatic, even sur-realistic effects. However, you also can use the in-camera set-ting just to improve the quality of details in shadowed areas. In Figure 3-65, I used the High Dynamic setting from inside a

121

dimly lighted room to capture a view of the outdoors without having the image washed out in brightness from the scene.

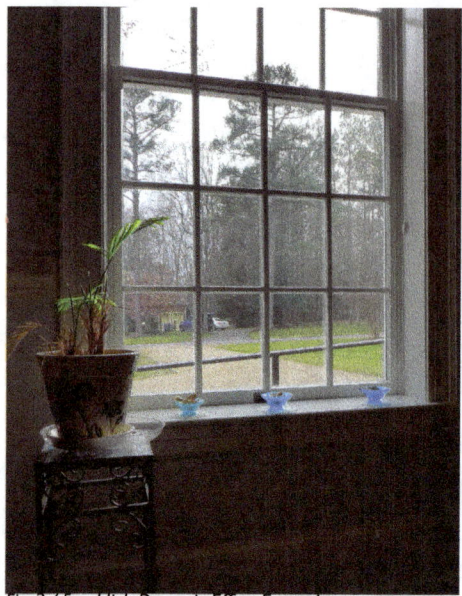

Fig. 3-65:   High Dynamic Effect Example

With a normal exposure, the indoor part of the image would be much darker, with no clear details visible. The High Dynamic setting altered the processing so more details are visible in the dark areas, while the bright areas are not washed out and overexposed. I will discuss High Dynamic Range (HDR) processing in general in Chapter 9. As with the Impressive Art setting, the bottom icon lets you adjust the image from monochrome at the left to oversaturated color at the right.

Cross Process

This setting gives you the ability to add a distinctive color tint to your images, in either green, blue, yellow, or red. In this case, you use the adjustment made available through the bottom icon at the right of the screen to select one of those colors, as shown in Figure 3-66. Once that selection has been made, your images will be tinted with the selected color.

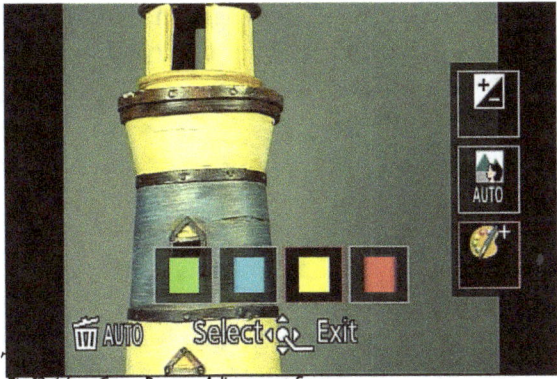

Fig. 3-66: Cross Process Adjustment Screen

As with some of the other Creative Control selections, this one is not strictly an example of color processing. Rather, this setting tries to reproduce the effects that are achieved with a primitive "toy" camera. There has been a popular movement for this sort of photography in recent years, using cameras like the Holga and Diana, which are purposely constructed to lack sharpness, and to suffer from vignetting at the corners. The photographs from such cameras can be quite appealing in their own way, and the Toy Camera setting lets you experiment with a good simulation of this sort of image.

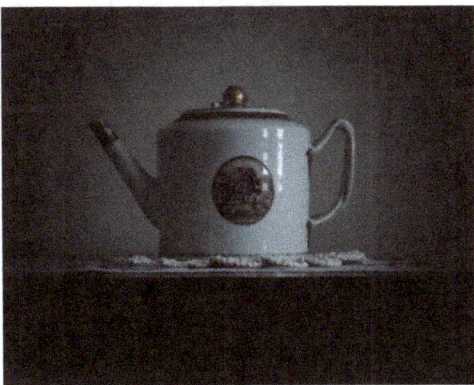

Fig. 3-67: Toy Camera Effect Example

Using this effect can be a pleasing way to highlight a single subject in the middle of the frame, such as the antique teapot shown in Figure 3-67. With this setting, the bottom icon's adjustment produces more reddish or orange tones to the left, and more bluish ones to the right. For this image, I moved the slider to the bluish side.

Miniature

The next Creative Control setting is called the Miniature effect. When you apply this option to an image, the camera adds blurring at one or more sides of an image or at the image's top or bottom, to simulate the appearance of a photograph of a tabletop model or miniature. Such images often appear blurred in one area, either because of the narrow depth of field of these close-up photos, or because of the use of a tilt-and-shift lens, which causes blurring at the edges. This is a rather odd and specialized effect, but I have seen it show up on television commercials and elsewhere, so it evidently is becoming increasingly popular.

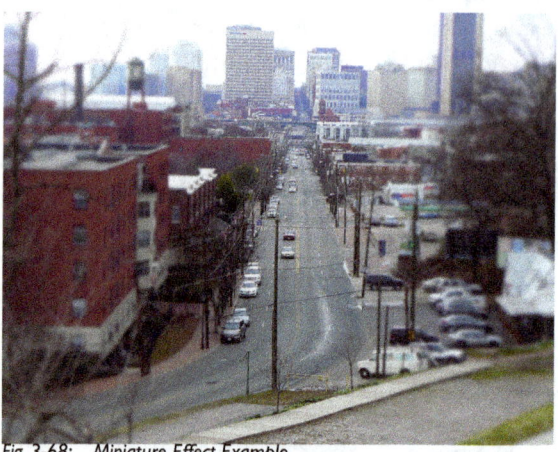

Fig. 3-68: Miniature Effect Example

For this feature to work well, you need to choose an appropriate subject. I have found that this effect looks interesting when applied to something like a street scene or a house, which might actually be reproduced in a tabletop model. For example, if you are able to get a high vantage point above a roadway, as in Figure 3-68, you may be able to get a photo of the traffic and adjacent buildings, letting this processing make it look as if you had photographed a high-quality tabletop setup with model cars and buildings.

With this setting, only two icons appear at the right side of the screen when you press in on the rear dial or press the right cursor button—the top icon adjusts brightness and the bottom one adjusts the intensity of the colors. In order to adjust the settings for the miniature effect itself, you need to use other controls, as discussed next.

When the Miniature setting has been selected, press the left cursor button (Fn button), and a long red frame will appear on the screen, as shown in Figure 3-69.

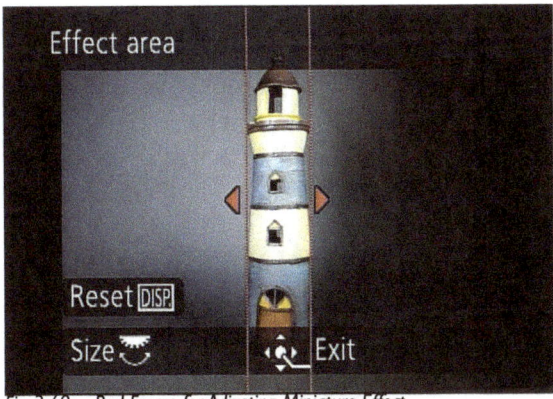

Fig. 3-69: *Red Frame for Adjusting Miniature Effect*

This frame represents the area of the image that will remain in sharp focus. The areas outside of that frame will be defocused and fuzzy, contributing to the overall effect. So, for example, if you are shooting from an overpass down towards a highway intersection, you may want to line up the red frame over the road that you want to remain in focus, leaving the areas outside the frame to be out of focus.

To move the red frame, use the four cursor buttons. When you see triangles on the frame, press the buttons corresponding to those triangles to move the frame in the direction of the triangle. Use the other two cursor buttons to flip the frame to a different orientation (horizontal or vertical). Then, turn the rear dial to change the size of the frame. When you have the frame oriented and sized as you want it, press the Menu/Set button to exit back to the shooting screen and take your picture.

With this setting, you cannot use burst shooting or the flash, although you can use RAW image quality. Also, note that you can use the Miniature setting when shooting movies. If you do so, no audio is recorded, and the action is speeded up to about ten times normal speed, which helps reinforce the illusion that you are filming a model scene rather than a life-sized one.

Soft Focus

With this setting, the camera defocuses the overall image to achieve a soft, hazy look. Somewhat oddly, you can still use the three icons at the right of the screen, to control brightness, background defocus, and the overall intensity of the general defocusing effect. You cannot use burst shooting or record movies with this setting in effect.

Star Filter

This setting lets you add cross-shaped "stars" of light to your images at bright points in the scene, producing a sparkling effect. This effect can be quite pleasing with a subject that lends itself to this look, like the collection of shiny theatrical masks in Figure 3-70. The bottom adjustment icon in this case controls the size of the rays of light; adjust to the left for shorter rays, and to the right for longer ones. You cannot use this effect with burst shooting or when recording movies.

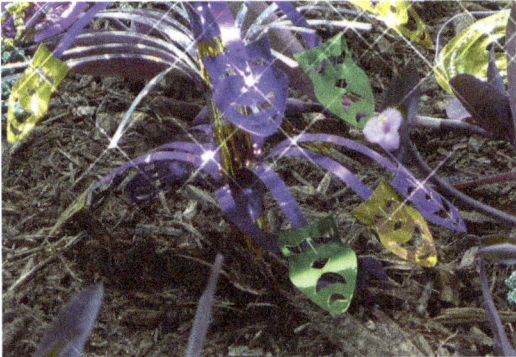

Fig. 3-70:   Star Filter Example

One Point Color

This is a setting that I enjoy quite a bit. It lets you select any one color in a scene for the camera to retain, while turning the rest of the image black and white. You can achieve a dramatic effect with this setting, by placing a clear emphasis on a small part of the scene that is in color. In this case, the bottom icon's adjustment is used to determine how closely an item must match the selected color in order to show up in color. Move the slider to the left to restrict the color selection to the minimum, and to the right to include a broader range of similar colors.

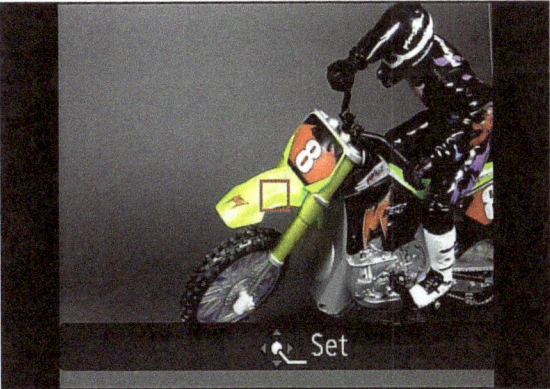

Fig. 3-71:   Screen to Select Color for One Point Color Effect

In order to select the color that is retained, press the left cursor button, and a small square will appear in the center of the screen, as shown in Figure 3-71. As prompted by the camera,

127

place that square over an area with the color you want to retain, and press the Menu/Set button to confirm the selection. Then, as shown in Figure 3-72, only objects matching that color will appear in color on the shooting screen and in the final image after you take the picture. You can use burst shooting with this setting and you also can shoot movies with it.

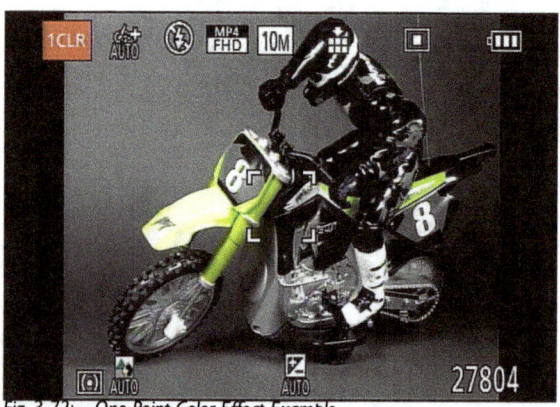

Fig. 3-72:   One Point Color Effect Example

Smooth Defocus

This setting is intended to enhance the smoothness of defocused areas in the background of an image. Normally, when a larger aperture is used, the background may appear out of focus, with the "bokeh" effect, as discussed earlier in this chapter and in Chapter 2. With this special effect, Leica says that the defocused areas will appear smoother than normal because of special processing that is used. This effect appears to be quite subtle, and I have had difficulty detecting any difference in shots taken with it and without it. However, it is worth trying it in situations when you especially want to have a smoothly defocused background. This is one of only two Creative Control settings that permit the use of flash. With this setting, if you pop up the built-in flash unit, the camera will turn it on, set to the Slow Sync with Red Eye Reduction mode, indicating that this setting can be used for portraits at night. The bottom adjustment icon is used for adjusting the intensity of colors.

128

This setting cannot be used for burst shooting or movies. It is advisable to use a tripod, because a slow shutter speed is likely to be used.

Radial Defocus

This final setting for the Creative Control mode provides a different approach to softening the focus of your images. In this case, the camera defocuses the entire image subtly. The effect is most apparent if there are lamps or other single-point light sources in the image. Using the adjustment provided by the bottom of two icons at the right of the screen, you can move the slider to the left for minimal defocusing, and to the right to maximize the effect. With this effect, as with the previous one, you cannot use burst shooting or shoot videos, but you can use the flash, set to Slow Sync with Red Eye Reduction.

Custom Modes: C1 and C2

Finally, I will briefly mention the C1 and C2 positions on the mode dial, seen in Figure 3-73. (I will discuss the Creative Video mode in Chapter 8.)

These two positions do not represent independent shooting modes. Instead, they are used in conjunction with the powerful and very useful Custom Set Memory menu item, which I will discuss in Chapter 7. Essentially, you can use these slots

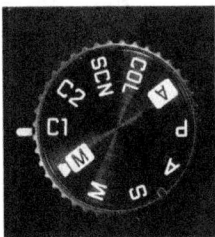

Fig. 3-73: C1 Mode

on the mode dial to recall complete sets of custom values for your important menu settings and some other settings. Once you have stored the settings, just turn the mode dial to the C1 position to recall your most important group of settings. With the C2 position, you have to take one further step, because that position has three sub-settings: C2-1, C2-2, and C2-3. See Chapter 7 for further details.

Chapter 4: The Recording Menu

Much of the power of the D-Lux 6 resides in the many options provided in the Recording menu, which gives the user control over the appearance of the images and the ways in which they are captured. Depending on your own preferences, you may not have to use this menu too much. You may prefer to use the various Scene mode settings, which choose many of the options for you, or you may prefer, at least on occasion, to use Snapshot mode, in which the camera makes its own choices. You also can use the Q.Menu button to get access to the Quick menu to change several of the more important settings. However, it's nice to know that you can have the degree of control that the Recording menu provides if you want it, and it is very useful to understand what types of items you can select from this comprehensive menu.

The Recording menu is quite easy to use once you have played around with it a bit. As I discussed earlier, the menu options can change depending on the setting of the mode dial on top of the camera. For example, if you're using Snapshot mode, the Recording menu options are very limited, because that mode is for a user who wants the camera to make most of the decisions without input. For the following discussion, I'm assuming you have the camera set to Program mode (mode dial turned to the P setting), because with that setting you have access to all of the power of the Recording menu. (Though some menu options will be unavailable in certain situations.)

So turn the mode dial on top of the camera to P for Program

mode, then enter the menu system by pressing the center button in the five-button array on the back of the camera—the one labeled Menu/Set.

In the menu system, besides the Recording menu, you will see the Motion Picture menu and the Setup menu. Also, when the camera is set to Snapshot mode, Scene mode or Creative Control mode, a menu specific to that mode appears, as I discussed earlier. If the camera is in playback mode, there are different menu options for controlling playback, as I'll discuss in Chapter 6. I'll discuss the Setup menu, which has options for controlling various camera functions such as LCD brightness and operational sounds, in Chapter 7. I'll discuss the Motion Picture menu in Chapter 8.

Once you press the Menu/Set button, you will initially see the Recording menu, as shown in Figure 4-1.

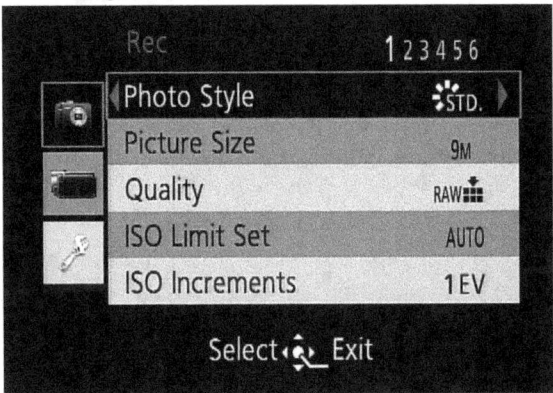

Fig. 4-1:   First Screen of Recording Menu

If you want to get access to the Setup or Motion Picture menu, you need to press the left cursor button. That action will move the highlight into the left column of the menu screen, as shown in Figure 4-2. In that column, you can navigate up and down with the cursor buttons to highlight the icons for the Motion Picture menu (movie camera icon) or for the Setup menu (wrench icon).

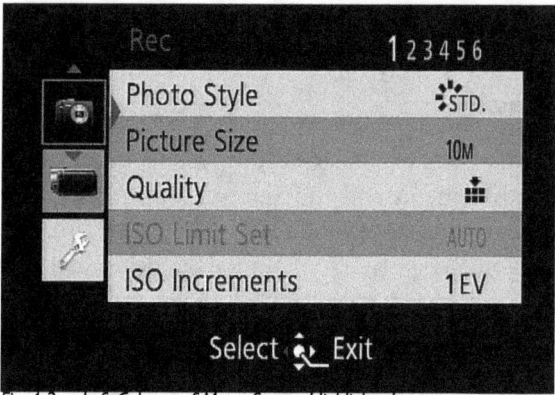

Fig. 4-2: Left Column of Menu Screen Highlighted

For now, we're working with the Recording menu, symbolized by the gray still-camera icon at the top of the left column. If you navigated over to the left column with the icons for the three menus, press the right cursor button to move back over to the main part of the screen, with the Recording menu items. The black highlight rectangle will highlight the first item on the first menu screen, which is Photo Style.

On the main section of the menu screen you will see a fairly long list of options, each occupying one line, with its name on the left and its current setting on the right. You have to scroll through several screens to see all of the options. If you find it tedious to scroll using the up and down cursor buttons, here's a tip for navigating any menu system on the D-Lux 6: You can use the zoom lever on top of the camera to speed through the menus one full screen at a time. You can tell which numbered screen you are on by noting which number is highlighted in the line of numbers at the top right of the screen.

Also, depending on the location of a particular menu option, you may be able to reach a menu item more quickly by reversing direction with the cursor buttons, and wrapping around to reach the option you want. For example, if you're on the top line of the first screen of the menu, you can scroll up to reach the bottom option on the last screen of the menu.

Some menu lines may have a dimmed, "grayed-out" appear-

132

ance at times, meaning they cannot be selected under the present settings.

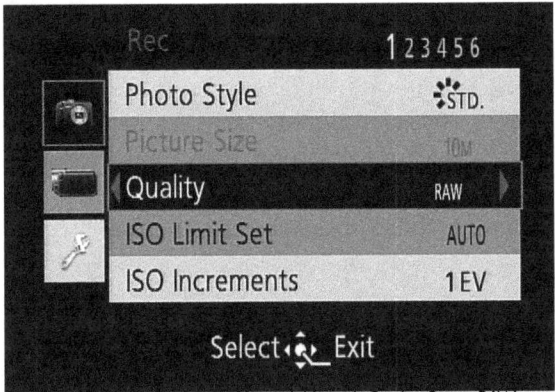

Fig. 4-3: Picture Size Option Unavailable with Quality Set to RAW

For example, as shown in Figure 4-3, if Quality is set to RAW, you cannot set Picture Size, which is automatically set to the maximum value when RAW is selected, so the Picture Size line is grayed out.

Also, if you have set Quality to RAW, you cannot set Intelligent Dynamic or Digital Zoom. If you want to follow along with the discussion of all of the options on the Recording menu, set Quality to Fine, which is the setting represented by the icon of an arrow pointing down onto two rows of bricks, as shown in Figure 4-4.

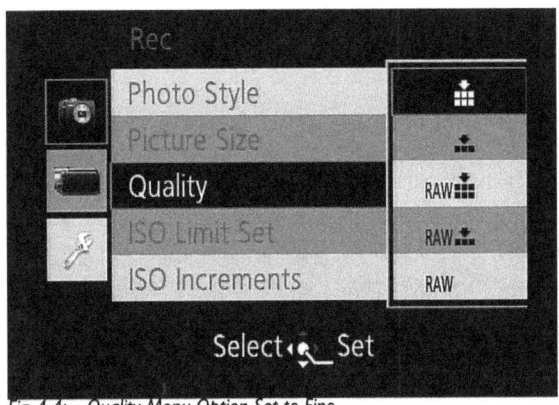

Fig. 4-4: Quality Menu Option Set to Fine

133

To do so, scroll down using the bottom button until the Quality line is highlighted, then press the right button to pop up the sub-menu. Scroll up or down as needed to highlight the icon with the six bricks, and then press the Menu/Set button to select that option.

With that setting, you should have access to every option on the Recording menu. I'll start at the top, and discuss each option on the list.

Photo Style

This top item on the Recording menu gives you several options for selecting a setting that determines the overall appearance of your images. These settings yield differing results in terms of warmth, color cast, and other attributes.

There are a few points you need to bear in mind about the Photo Style selections. First, they are not available in all recording modes. They are available only when the shooting mode is set to Program, Aperture Priority, Shutter Priority, Manual, or Custom. They also are available when you're recording a movie with the shooting mode set to one of the modes listed above. You cannot choose a Photo Style setting when you have set the camera to Snapshot mode, Creative Control mode, or Scene mode. In Snapshot mode, though, as discussed in Chapter 3, the camera provides an abridged version of Photo Style, called Color Mode, which offers just four choices: Standard, Happy, B&W, and Sepia.

To select a Photo Style setting, highlight the Photo Style line on the Recording menu, as shown in Figure 4-5. Press the right cursor button or turn the rear dial to scroll through the available settings: Standard, Vivid, Natural, Monochrome, Scenery, Portrait, and Custom. When your chosen setting is highlighted, you can press Menu/Set to select it and exit to the shooting screen.

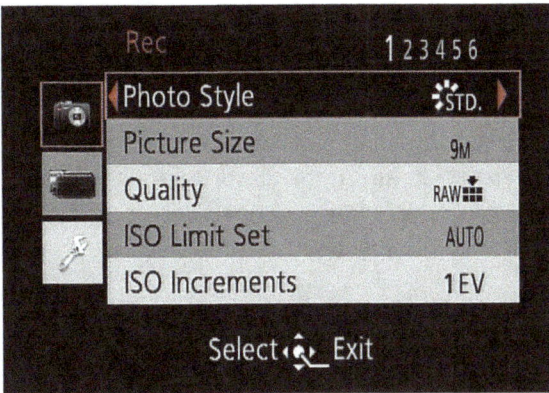

Fig. 4-5:   Photo Style Menu Option

If you want to go further and fine-tune the setting, the D-Lux 6's menu system provides you with the capability of adjusting the four parameters that are used to create the Photo Style settings: contrast, sharpness, saturation, and noise reduction. In order to make further adjustments to those parameters, press the down cursor button when the main setting (such as Vivid or Natural) is highlighted with a red frame. A new highlight frame will then appear in the block that contains the four adjustable parameters, as shown in Figure 4-6.

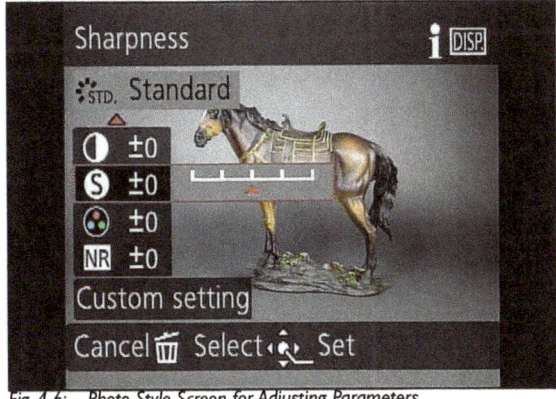

Fig. 4-6:   Photo Style Screen for Adjusting Parameters

In this case, the second line is highlighted, which means you

135

can alter the sharpness setting; the word Sharpness appears at the top left of the screen, indicating that that value can now be adjusted.

Once you have placed the highlight block on one of the four parameters, press the left and right cursor buttons to change the value of that parameter up to two levels, either positive or negative. The camera will remember those settings even when it is turned off.

There is one slightly unusual point to make about the Monochrome setting for Photo Style. Monochrome means there is no color in the image, only shades of black, white, and gray. Therefore, the saturation adjustment does not work to increase or decrease the saturation of colors for the Monochrome setting. However, with the D-Lux 6, you can, in fact, adjust the setting on the saturation line for that setting, and you will see a change in the appearance of your images. This adjustment is not actually saturation, though; the camera adjusts the color tone of the monochrome image from reddish for negative values to bluish for positive values.

Here's one point that's not mentioned in the user's manual, though it makes sense if you think about it. When you set Photo Style to Monochrome, if the Quality is set to RAW, the picture you take will show up as black-and-white on the camera's LCD screen, but, when you import the image file into software that reads RAW files, the image will show up in color. This happens because the RAW format allows you to manipulate the "raw" data seen by the camera's sensor, which includes the color information. You can convert these images back to black-and-white on your computer by moving the saturation slider to zero in your RAW software or by using another method of conversion (such as the Image—Adjustments—Black & White command in Photoshop).

Also, it's worthwhile to spend a little time making sure you grasp the differences between the Photo Style settings and the Creative Control shooting mode. Here are a few pointers to help distinguish between them. Creative Control is a shooting mode, with its own slot on the mode dial. When you select this mode on the dial, you are limiting some of your options, because some settings (including Photo Style) become unavailable. Also, the various Creative Control settings (Expressive, Retro, High Key, High Dynamic, etc.) cannot be fine-tuned by the user to a large degree, although the intensity of the setting or some other aspects can be controlled. The Photo Style settings, on the other hand (Standard, Vivid, Natural, Monochrome, etc.), all can be configured by the user with detailed further adjustments of four parameters.

Finally, although the settings in Creative Control mode, like the Photo Style settings, involve some adjustments to contrast, sharpness, and saturation, there is clearly considerably more processing going on inside the camera in the Creative Control mode, at least for certain settings, including High Dynamic, Toy Camera, and Miniature, which alter the image in fairly significant ways beyond those three parameters.

The bottom line, in my opinion, is that there is no neat way to categorize the Creative Control and Photo Style settings, which amount to a mixed bag of some very useful photographic tools. You really need to work with them until you discover which ones are most useful to you. Personally, in Creative Control I tend to use Dynamic Monochrome, Impressive Art, High Dynamic, Star Filter, and One Point Color, because of the distinctive looks they provide. I use Photo Style more often, though, because I prefer to shoot in Program, Aperture Priority, or Shutter Priority mode most of the time. I often just use the Standard setting and add effects, if needed, later through software; for street photography I often use the Monochrome Photo Style setting with some adjustments to sharpness and contrast. But there are many choices available, and I recommend that you explore them thoroughly.

Here are summaries of the Photo Style settings, along with example images of the same scene for purposes of comparison.

Standard

No change from the normal setting, as shown in Figure 4-7.

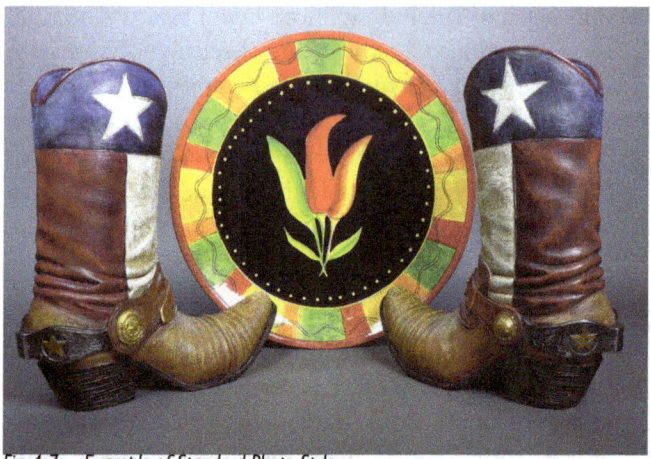

Fig. 4-7:   Example of Standard Photo Style

Vivid

The Vivid setting of Photo Style uses increased saturation (intensity or vividness) and contrast of the colors in the image to make the colors "pop" out in dramatic fashion, as shown in Figure 4-8.

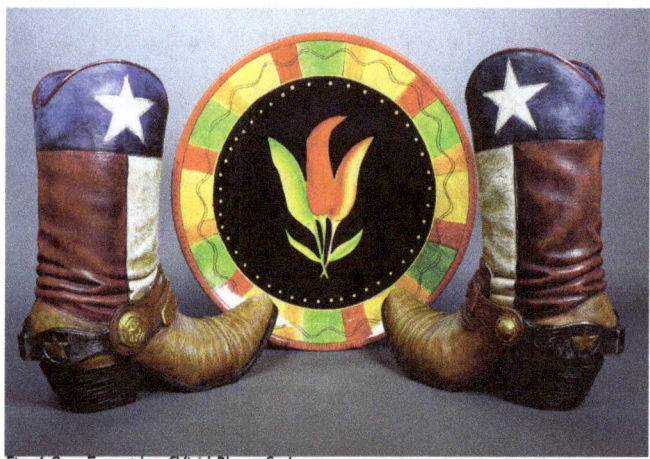

Fig. 4-8:   Example of Vivid Photo Style

Natural

With Natural, the D-Lux 6 reduces contrast to produce a softer, more subdued appearance, as shown in Figure 4-9.

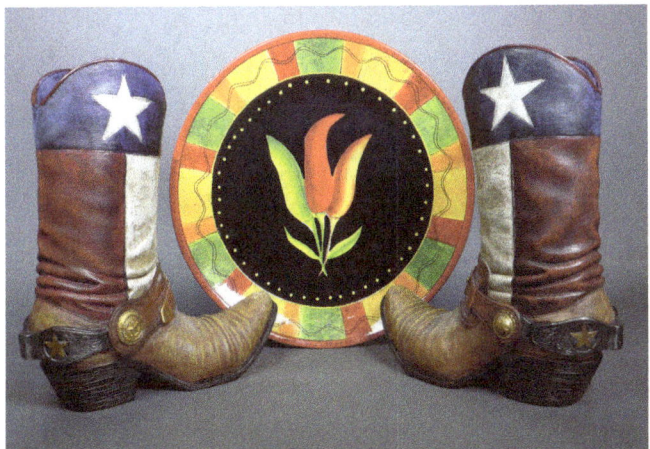

Fig. 4-9:   Example of Natural Photo Style

Monochrome

The Monochrome setting uses standard values for contrast and sharpness, but presents the image in black and white, with all color removed (that is, saturation reduced to zero), unless you use the saturation adjustment to add a red or blue tone. An example is shown in Figure 4-10.

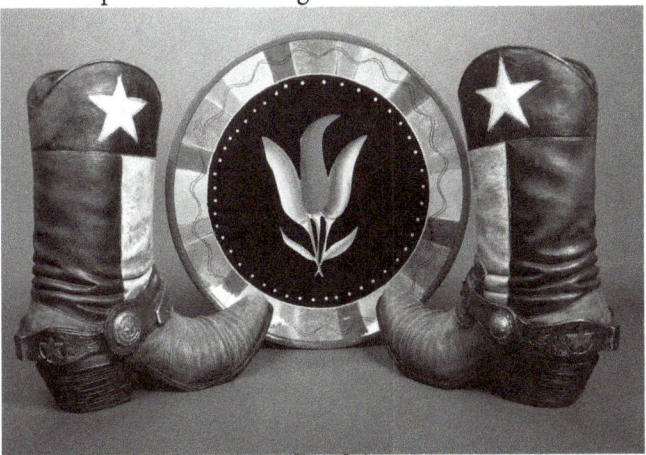

Fig. 4-10:   Example of Monochrome Photo Style

139

Scenery

The Scenery setting for Photo Style provides increased emphasis on the blues and greens of outdoor scenes, with additional saturation of those hues, as shown in Figure 4-11.

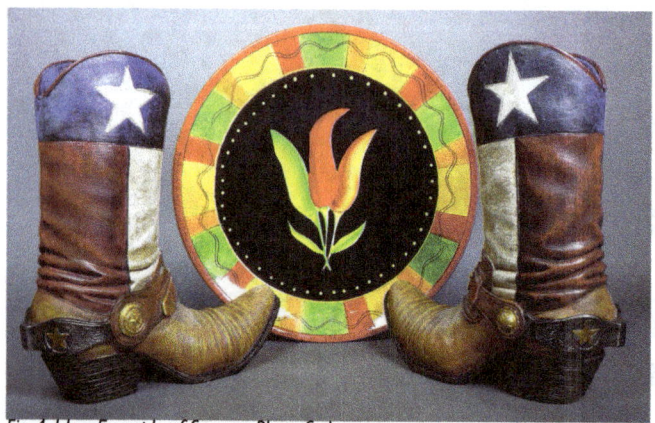

Fig. 4-11: Example of Scenery Photo Style

Portrait

The Portrait setting for Photo Style puts emphasis on flesh tones, as shown in Figure 4-12.

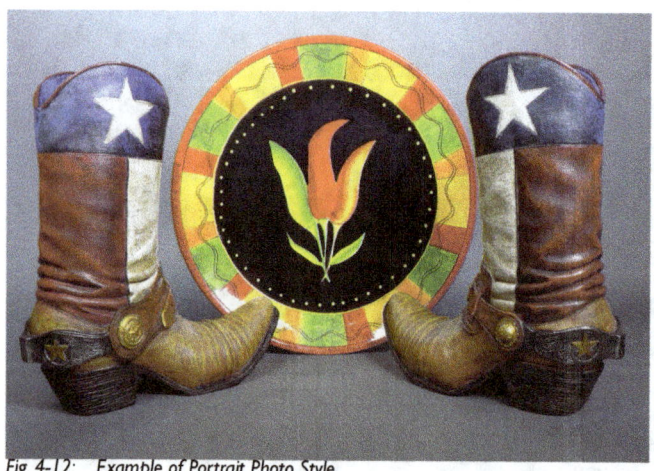

Fig. 4-12: Example of Portrait Photo Style

Custom

Finally, the Custom slot is available for you to create and store a setting that you have customized using your own preferred settings for the four parameters that can be adjusted individually (contrast, sharpness, saturation, and noise reduction). To use this slot, first select any one of the basic Photo Style settings (Standard, Vivid, Natural, Monochrome, Scenery, or Portrait), then press the down cursor button and proceed to adjust any or all of the four parameters for that setting as you want them. Next, move the cursor down one line below the four parameters to highlight the Custom setting label, as shown in Figure 4-13.

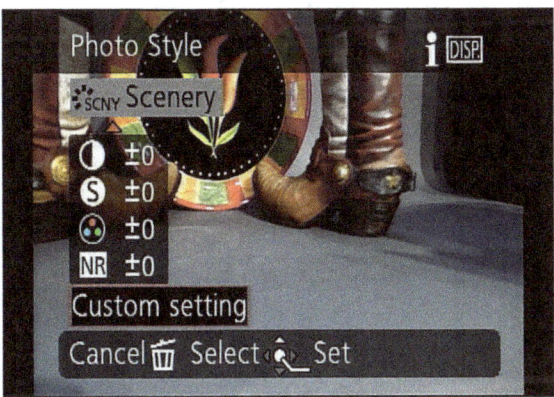

Fig. 4-13:   Custom Setting Line for Photo Style Option

If you then press Menu/Set, the settings you have made will be stored in the Custom slot of the Photo Style setting.

After you have stored the Custom setting, you can recall it at any time by selecting Custom for your setting. You can alter the Custom setting in the future by choosing a different set of settings and storing it to the Custom slot, overwriting the previous entry.

Picture Size

This second item on the Recording menu, shown in Figure 4-14, controls the number of megapixels (MP) in the images you record with the camera, up to and including its maximum of 10.1 MP. (The highest number shows up as simply 10 MP on the menu.)

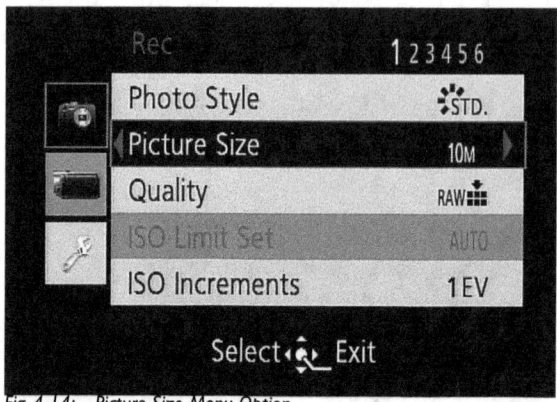

Fig. 4-14:   Picture Size Menu Option

The maximum MP setting is controlled by the aspect ratio that you have set. You can set the aspect ratio to one of four settings using the switch on top of the lens barrel: 1:1, 4:3, 3:2, or 16:9. If you set the aspect ratio to 4:3, the maximum MP setting is the full 10 MP. If you set the aspect ratio to 3:2, the camera achieves that image shape by cutting off some MP vertically but adding some horizontally, so the maximum setting for Picture Size is 9.5 MP. At the 16:9 setting, even more vertical MP are lost but horizontal ones are added, and the maximum Picture Size is 9 MP. At the 1:1 aspect ratio, pixels are lost in both directions, resulting in a maximum image size of 7.5 MP.

There are several points that you need to bear in mind about the MP settings. First, the higher the MP setting, the better the overall quality of the image, all other factors being equal. However, you can create a fuzzy and low-quality image with a high MP setting with no trouble at all; the MP setting does not guarantee a great image. But if all other factors are equal, a higher MP count should yield noticeably higher image quality. Also, when you have a large MP count in your image, you have some leeway for cropping it; you can select a portion of the image to enlarge to the full size of your print, and still retain acceptable image quality.

On the other hand, images with high MP counts eat up your storage space more quickly than those with low MP counts. If you are running low on space on your SD card and still have a lot of images to capture, you may need to reduce your Picture Size setting so you can fit more images on the card.

As noted earlier, the Picture Size setting is grayed out and unavailable when you have selected RAW for the Quality setting. However, if you select RAW + Fine or RAW + Standard, with which the camera records both a RAW and a JPEG image, the Picture Size option is available for setting the size of the JPEG image.

Extended Optical Zoom

Another point to consider for making the Picture Size setting is how much zoom range you need or want. You might not think that picture size is related to zoom, but with the D-Lux 6 it is.

The camera has a feature called Extended Optical Zoom, designated as EZ in the user's manual illustrations. When you set the Picture Size to 3 MP, for example (with aspect ratio of 4:3), you will find that you can zoom in farther than you can with Picture Size set to its maximum. If you try this, you will see an EZ designation appear on the menu screen to the right of the Picture Size setting, as shown in Figure 4-15.

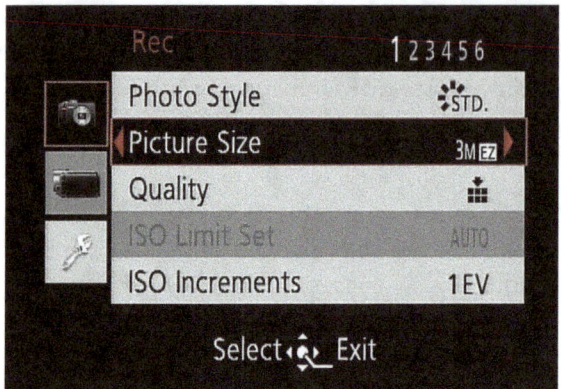

Fig. 4-15: EZ Indication for Smaller Picture Size Setting

You also will see the EZ icon on the LCD screen to the left of the zoom scale, as you move the zoom lever on top of the camera toward the T setting, for Telephoto, as shown in Figure 4-16.

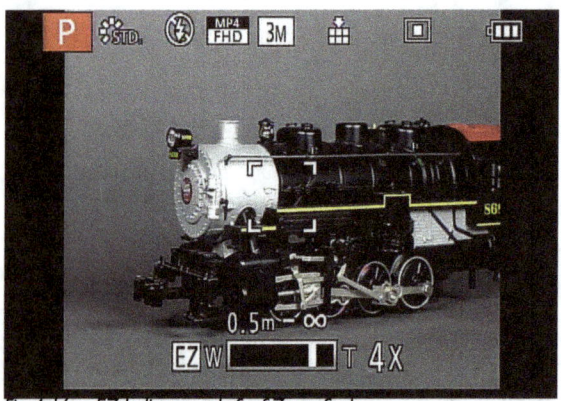

Fig. 4-16: EZ Indicator at Left of Zoom Scale

Depending on the Picture Size setting, the scale will extend to a zoom level of as much as 6.7X normal, or about an equivalent of 160mm, rather than the ordinary maximum zoom of 3.8X or about an equivalent of 90mm. (If you turn on Digital Zoom, discussed later in this chapter, the zoom range will extend even farther; for now, I am assuming that Digital Zoom is turned off.)

144

This feature needs further explanation. The lens of the D-Lux 6 has an actual, physical focal length range of 4.7 millimeters (mm) to 17.7 mm, which you can see engraved on the end of the lens casing, as shown in Figure 4-17.

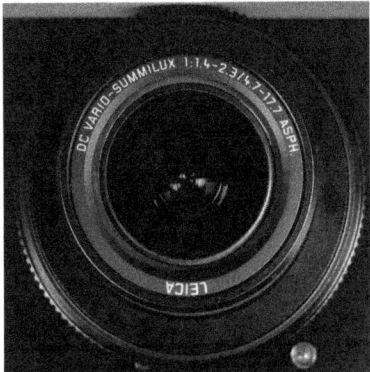

Fig. 4-17: Actual Focal Length Engraved on Lens

This means that, at its full wide-angle (unzoomed) setting, the lens's actual focal length is 4.7 mm. As with most digital cameras today, the camera's documentation converts this figure to the "35mm-equivalent," that is, to the focal length for the lens that would be the equivalent of this lens on a camera that uses 35mm film. In this case, that focal length is 24mm, which is still a very wide setting for a standard lens. The 35mm equivalent value for the fully zoomed setting of the D-Lux 6's lens (17.7mm) is 90mm. So the 35mm equivalent zoom range for this lens is 24mm to 90mm.

Normally, the maximum zoom value for the D-Lux 6's lens is 90mm, or 3.8 times the unzoomed setting of 24mm. However, when you set the Picture Size to a value lower than the maximum 10MP, such as 3MP, the camera lets you zoom in farther on the subject you are viewing using the zoom lever. What is actually happening is the camera takes the normal area that the optical zoom "sees," and then blows it up to a larger size, which is possible because the lower MP setting means the camera is using a lower resolution and can present a larger zoomed image. Extended Optical Zoom has a maximum power of 6.7

times the normal lens's magnification.

To sum up the situation with Extended Optical Zoom, whenever you set the Picture Quality to a level below 9MP, you get a bit of additional zoom power because of the reduced resolution. In reality, you could achieve the same result by taking the picture at the normal zoom range with the Picture Size set to the full 10MP or 9MP, and then cropping the image in your computer to enlarge just the part you want. But with Extended Optical Zoom, you do get the benefit of seeing a larger image on the LCD screen when you're composing the picture, and the benefit of having the camera perform its focus and exposure operations on the actual zoomed image that you want to capture, so the feature is not useless. You just need to decide whether it's of use to you in a particular situation.

Digital Zoom

One other note before we leave this subject: The D-Lux 6 has another zoom-related feature called Digital Zoom, and still another called Intelligent Zoom. Digital Zoom is activated through the Recording menu by scrolling down through the various options until you reach Digital Zoom on the fourth screen (assuming the camera is in Program mode). You then push the right cursor button to pop up the sub-menu, use the up or down button to select ON, and press the center button (Menu/Set) to activate the feature, as shown in Figure 4-18.

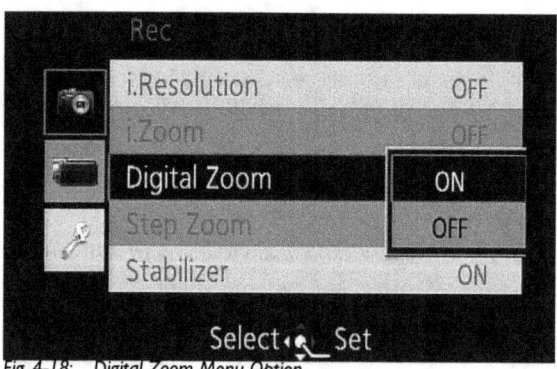

Fig. 4-18: Digital Zoom Menu Option

With Digital Zoom, unlike Extended Optical Zoom, you get what the Leica user's manual calls "deterioration" of the image. As with many digital cameras, Digital Zoom is available on the D-Lux 6 as a way of further enlarging the pixels that are displayed so the image appears larger; there is no additional resolution available, so the image can quickly begin to appear blocky and of low quality. Experts often recommend staying away from this sort of zoom feature. As with Extended Optical Zoom, it might occasionally be of use to help you in viewing a distant subject. Digital Zoom has a maximum power of 15.1 times the normal lens's magnification. When you combine all of the zoom options, including Digital Zoom, there is a maximum total zoom power of about 27 times normal. Digital Zoom is not available in Snapshot mode.

I'll discuss Intelligent Zoom later, as another one of the Recording Menu options.

Quality

The next setting on the Recording menu is Quality. I have already discussed the Quality setting briefly, in connection with basic picture-taking. I'll mention the main information again here, in order to provide a description of all of the features on the Recording menu.

It's important to distinguish the Quality setting from the Picture Size setting. As I discussed above, Picture Size concerns the image's resolution, or the number of megapixels in the image. Quality has to do with how the image's digital information is compressed for storage on the SD card and, later, on the computer's hard drive. There are three levels of quality available: RAW, Fine, and Standard, as shown in Figure 4-19. RAW is in a category by itself, and I'll spend some time discussing how to work with files of that type. Fine and Standard are two levels of compression for computer image files which use the JPEG standard. Images saved with Fine quality are subjected to less compression than those saved with Standard quality. In other words, Standard-quality images have their digital data "compressed" or "squeezed" down to a smaller size to allow more of the files to be stored on an SD card or computer drive, with a corresponding loss of image quality. The more compression an image is subjected to, the less clear detail it will contain. So unless you are running out of space on your storage medium, you probably want to leave the Quality setting at Fine to ensure the best quality. (Of course, you may prefer to shoot in the RAW format for maximum quality.)

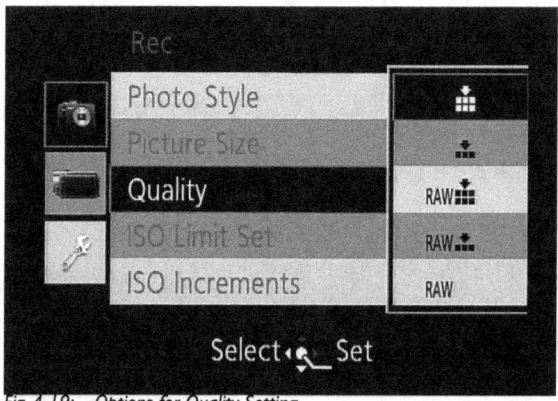

Fig. 4-19:   Options for Quality Setting

With the D-Lux 6, besides choosing one of the individual Quality settings (RAW, Fine, or Standard), you also have the option of setting the camera to record images in RAW plus either Fine or Standard. If you choose that option, the camera will record each image in two files—one RAW, and the other a JPEG file in either Fine or Standard quality, depending on your selection. If you then play the image back in the camera, you will see only one image, but if you copy the files to your computer, you will find two image files—one with a .jpg extension and one with an .rwl extension. The RAW file will be much larger than the JPEG one. In a few examples I just looked at on my computer, the RAW files were all about 11 MB and the corresponding JPEG files were between about 1.7 and 4 MB.

Why would you choose the option of recording images in

148

RAW and JPEG at the same time? Say you're taking pictures of a one-time event such as a wedding or graduation. You may want to preserve them in RAW for the highest quality and for later processing with photo-editing software, but also have them available for quick review on a computer that might not have software that reads RAW files, or you might want to be able to send them to friends quickly without having to first convert them from RAW to JPEG. Also, if you are shooting with special settings, such as those in Creative Control mode, you may want to have both the JPEG file that includes all of the special processing, and the RAW file that does not. Shooting with both quality settings simultaneously is an option that's open to you if space on your SD card is not a major consideration. If you have a high-capacity card, or multiple cards available, you may want to take advantage of both ways to record images.

One final note: When you select the 3D setting in Scene mode, the Quality item changes on the Recording menu. There is no RAW option; you can choose 3D plus Fine or 3D plus Standard.

ISO (Sensitivity)

The next three settings on the Recording menu—ISO Limit Set, ISO Increments, and Extended ISO—all have to do with sensitivity, or ISO, one of the more important settings on the D-Lux 6. ISO is a measure of how sensitive the camera's digital sensor is to light. With the D-Lux 6, the ISO setting itself is not made through the Recording menu. Instead, you use the up cursor button on the camera's back, which is labeled ISO, to make the actual setting of the ISO value. Then you can use the three settings on the Recording menu to control how the camera sets the ISO. Before I explain how those settings work, I will provide some background information about ISO.

ISO is an acronym for the International Organization for Standardization, which develops worldwide standards for many areas of industry, science, and other fields. When I first started

149

in film photography, this standard was called ASA, for American Standards Association. The ISO acronym reflects the more international nature of the modern photographic industry.

Originally the ISO/ASA standard designated the "speed," or light sensitivity, of film. So, for example, a "slow" film might be rated ISO 64, or even ISO 25, meaning it takes a considerable amount of exposure to light to create a usable image on the film. Slow films yield higher-quality, less-grainy images than faster films. There are "fast" films available, some black-and-white and some color, with ISO ratings of 400, or even higher (such as Ilford Delta 3200 Professional black-and-white film), that are designed to yield usable images in lower light. Such films often can be used indoors without flash, for example.

With digital technology, the industry has retained the ISO concept, but it applies not to film, but to the light sensitivity of the camera's sensor, because there is no film involved in a digital camera. The ISO ratings for digital cameras are supposed to be essentially equivalent to the ISO ratings for films. So if your camera is set to ISO 100, there will have to be a good deal of light to expose the image properly, but if the camera is set to ISO 1600, a reasonably well exposed (but "noisier" or "grainier") image can be made in very low light.

The upshot is that, generally speaking, you should shoot your images with the camera set to the lowest ISO possible that will allow the image to be exposed properly. (One exception to this rule is if you want, for creative purposes, the grainy look that comes from shooting at a high ISO value.) For example, if you are shooting indoors in low light, you may need to set the ISO to a high value (say, ISO 800) so you can expose the image with a reasonably fast shutter speed. If the camera were set to a lower ISO, it would need to use a slower shutter speed to take in enough light for a proper exposure, and the resulting image would likely be blurry and possibly unusable.

To summarize: Shoot with low ISO settings (around 100) when possible; shoot with high ISO settings (say 400 or higher, up to

1600 or even 3200) when necessary in dimmer light to allow a fast shutter speed to stop action and avoid blurriness, or when desired to achieve a creative effect with graininess.

Here are the details about the ISO sensitivity setting. As noted above, the ISO setting on the D-Lux 6 is not made through the Recording menu. However, because you need to know about this setting in order to understand the three ISO-related settings that are made through this menu, I will discuss ISO in this chapter, rather than in Chapter 5, which discusses settings made with the camera's physical controls.

The ISO setting is available only when the camera is set to one of the more advanced shooting modes: Program, Aperture Priority, Shutter Priority, Manual, or Creative Video. To make the setting, press the up button, marked ISO, and a small menu will appear on the display screen, as shown in Figure 4-20.

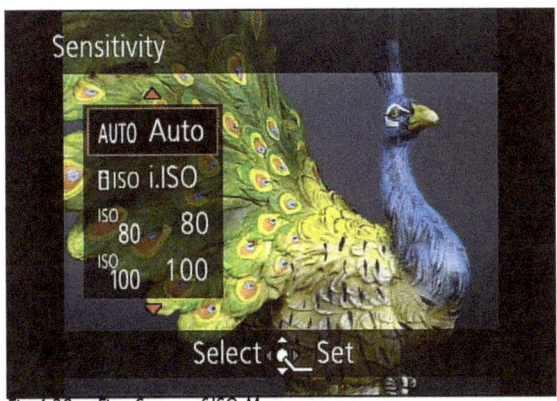

Fig. 4-20:   First Screen of ISO Menu

You can scroll through the values on this menu either by pressing the up and down buttons or by turning the rear dial. The possible numerical values are 80, 100, 200, 400, 800, 1600, 3200, and 6400, unless you change the ISO Increments setting, discussed below. There is one caveat, though: If you turn on Extended ISO (discussed below) and set the ISO to a value higher than 6400, the camera automatically reduces the resolution of the images that will be recorded to 2.5 MP or 3 MP, depending on the aspect ratio that is in effect. Also, with those high ISO settings, you cannot set the Quality to RAW, and you cannot use burst shooting with flash. So, although the very high ISO settings are available, they come with some tradeoffs in terms of image size and other functions. (And that's in addition to whatever loss in quality results from the noise that is introduced by the use of the high ISO value.)

When you set a numerical value for the ISO, you cannot then set ISO Limit (discussed below). When you set ISO Sensitivity to Auto, the camera automatically adjusts ISO to an appropriate value based on the brightness of the scene and your exposure settings, subject to the maximum value set with ISO Limit, if any has been set. When you use the Intelligent ISO setting, the camera adjusts the ISO based on the movement of the subject as well as the brightness, so you can use a higher shutter speed to stop the motion.

When would you want to use a numerical value for the ISO, rather than setting it to Auto ISO or Intelligent ISO? One example is if you want the highest quality for your image, and you aren't worried about camera movement, either because you are using a tripod so a slow shutter speed won't result in blur, or the lighting is bright enough to use a fast shutter speed. Then you could set the ISO to its lowest possible setting of 80 to achieve high quality. On the other hand, if you want a grainy, noisy look, you can set the ISO to 1600 or even higher to introduce noise into the image. You also might want a high ISO setting in order to use a fast shutter speed in low light. In many cases, though, you can just leave the setting at Auto or Intelligent and let the camera adjust the ISO as needed.

ISO Limit Set

ISO Limit Set, seen in Figure 4-21, is the first ISO-related selection on the Recording menu. This item lets you set an upper limit for the value the camera will choose for ISO, when you have set the ISO level to either Auto ISO or Intelligent ISO, as discussed above. The choices for this setting are Auto, 200, 400, 800, 1600, and 3200. When the ISO level is set to Auto ISO and ISO Limit is set to Auto, then the camera will set the ISO in a range up to 1600, depending on the available light.

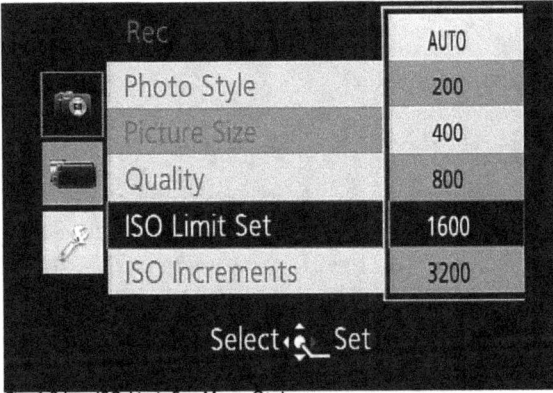

Fig. 4-21: ISO Limit Set Menu Option

ISO Increments

Using this option, illustrated in Image 4-22, you can expand the range of values available for the setting of ISO. Normally, ISO is set only at the numerical values noted above; if you select the increment of 1/3 EV instead of the normal 1 EV, then several interpolated values for ISO are added, such as 125, 160, 250, 320, 500, 640, and 5000. When this menu option is turned on, you can set these additional values from the menu that appears when you press the up (ISO) button.

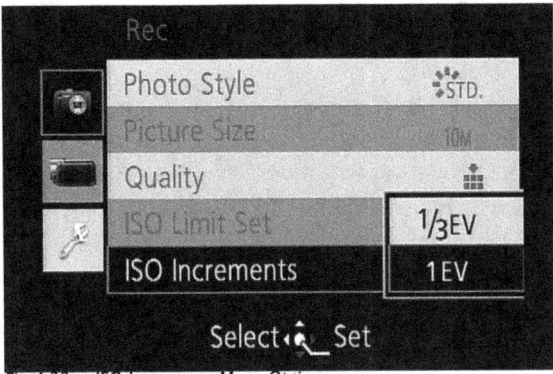

Fig. 4-22: ISO Increments Menu Option

Note that this menu option applies only to the settings you make yourself. Even if the ISO Increments option is set to 1 EV, the camera can still set intermediate ISO values when Auto ISO or Intelligent ISO is in effect and the camera is choosing the ISO value. I personally have never found a reason to use the 1/3 EV option, and I generally leave this setting at its default value of 1 EV.

Extended ISO

The third ISO-related option on the Recording menu, Extended ISO, shown in Figure 4-23, can be turned either on or off. When it is turned on through the menu item, you get access to the highest ISO level of 12800, which is not available otherwise. Also, if you have set the ISO Increments option, discussed above, to 1/3 EV, then you will also get access to the ISO settings of 8000 and 10000.

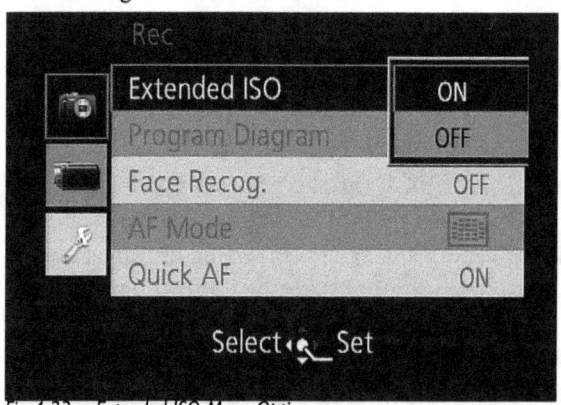

Fig. 4-23: Extended ISO Menu Option

However, much as with the Extended Optical Zoom function, discussed earlier in this chapter, Extended ISO works by limiting the Picture Size setting to a lower value, so the camera's sensor can devote its processing capacity to a smaller area but achieve greater low-light capability. So, if you select an ISO setting above 6400 (8000, 10000, or 12800), the Picture Size setting will be limited to either 2.5 MP or 3.0 MP, depending on the aspect ratio that is in use.

And there also are two other limitations imposed when you are using one of the high ISO settings available with this menu option: You cannot use RAW quality, and you cannot use burst shooting with flash.

In my experience, there are few occasions when I would want to use ISO values above 6400 with the D-Lux 6, because of the disadvantages that come when you make such a setting. For example, if I am faced with shooting in a dark environment, such as a dimly lighted room, I would prefer to use one of the special settings that is designed for such shots, such as the Night Scenery or Handheld Night Shot settings in Scene mode.

Or, as an alternative, I could shoot in Shutter Priority mode with RAW quality, setting the shutter speed to 1/30 second so I could hand-hold the camera without causing motion blur. With an ISO setting as high as 6400, the shot should be usable. Even if it is too dark, the chances are good that I could pull details out of the shadows by processing the RAW file in appropriate software. On the other hand, the quality of images shot at ISO 12800 is noticeably degraded because of the excessive noise.

To check the degree to which a very high ISO rating affects image quality, I took photographs of a model of a knight on horseback at ISO 100 and at ISO 12800, for comparison. As you can see in Figure 4-24, the low-ISO shot at the top is quite clear, but the noise level in the high-ISO shot is quite noticeable, and would make the shot unusable for many purposes.

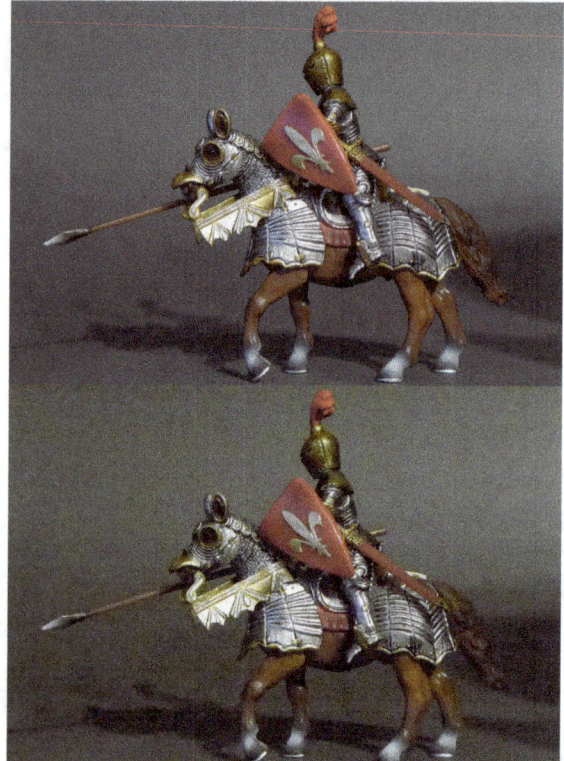

Fig. 4-24: ISO 100 at Top, ISO 12800 at Bottom

But, if you don't want to be involved with processing RAW images and you don't mind a reduced picture size and visual noise, having the ability to use super-high ISO settings is a good option to have available for dim-light shooting situations.

Program Diagram

This next option on the Recording menu is a special setting that is available only when the camera is set to Program mode; it does not even appear on the menu screen in any other mode. The Program Diagram menu option, shown in Figure 4-25, gives you a choice of three settings: STD (Standard), MAX

(Maximum Aperture), and MTF (Optimum Accuracy). This menu item actually is concerned largely with automatically controlling the use of the camera's built-in ND (neutral density) filter. I will discuss the ND filter further in Chapter 5, because it is controlled by a physical switch, the ND/Focus lever at the top center of the camera's back. Essentially, the ND filter cuts down the amount of light reaching the sensor, to enable the use of wider apertures or slower shutter speeds, or both, when you are shooting in a fair amount of light.

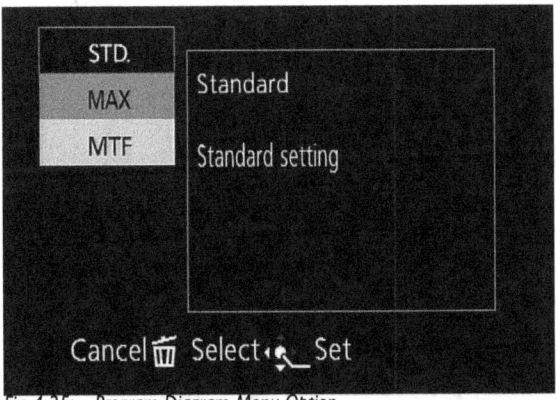

Fig. 4-25:   Program Diagram Menu Option

When Program Diagram is set to Standard, there is no effect on your shots; the ND filter is available for your use if you activate it manually. With the MAX setting, the camera will automatically turn on the ND filter if the lighting conditions call for it, so that you can use the widest possible aperture. The idea is that you can achieve a defocused background, as discussed in Chapter 3 in connection with Aperture Priority mode. Finally, with the MTF setting, the camera again will use the ND filter automatically if its programming calls for it, but in this case the goal is to find the combination of shutter speed and aperture that will yield the best overall results in terms of sharpness and clarity, based on the performance characteristics of the lens. In other words, the setting attempts to stop down the aperture to a narrow setting, but not so narrow as to cause the distortion that can be caused at the most narrow apertures.

My own preference is to leave this setting at STD and activate the ND filter using the ND/Focus lever when I see a need for it. If I want to have a wide aperture, I will use Aperture Priority mode.

Face Recognition

With the Face Recognition option, you have the capability of registering the faces of up to six people so that the camera will recognize them when Face Recognition is turned on. I will not discuss all of the many restrictions and options for this setting; the details are provided at pages 130 to 131 of the Leica user's guide.

Here are the essential steps to follow. First, go to the Face Recognition item on the second screen of the Recording menu and select the third option, Memory, as shown in Figure 4-26.

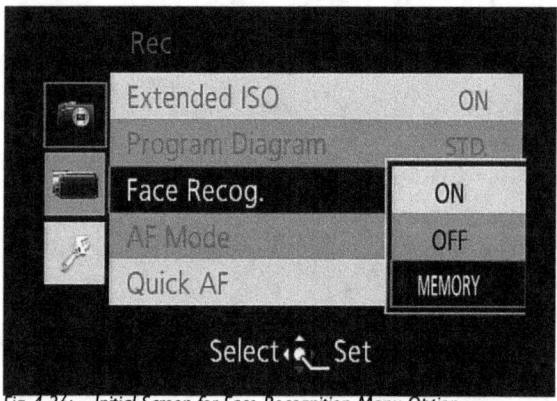

Fig. 4-26:   Initial Screen for Face Recognition Menu Option

Press Menu/Set, and you will be taken to the screen shown in Figure 4-27.

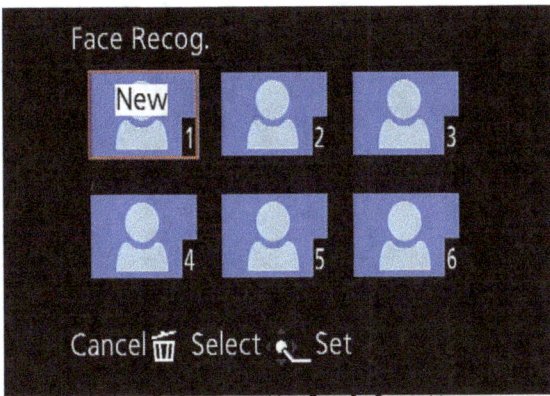

Fig. 4-27: *Screen for Registering New Face for Recognition*

Move the red highlight frame to the first available blue block that says New, and press Menu/Set; you will see the screen shown in Figure 4-28, which prompts you to position the face to be registered in the yellow frame. Then, when the face is properly positioned, press the shutter button to take a picture. If the registration fails, you will see an error message.

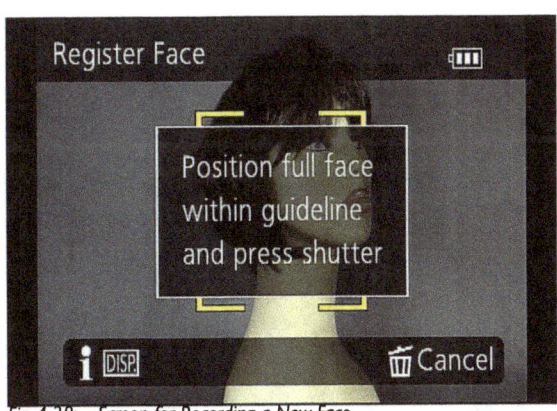

Fig. 4-28: *Screen for Recording a New Face*

If it succeeds, you will see a screen like Figure 4-29. You can then enter data for the face, including name and age.

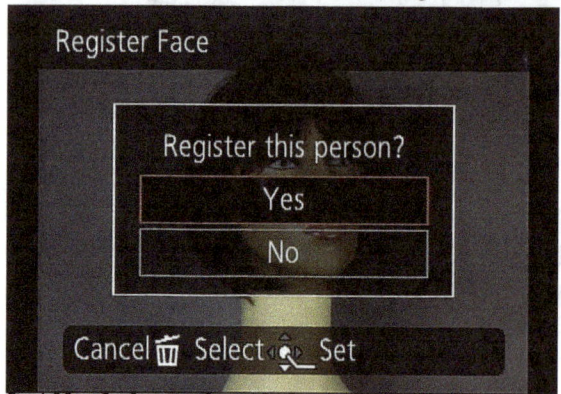

Fig. 4-29: Confirmation Screen for Face Recognition Option

Once you have one or more faces registered, you can turn Face Recognition on through the Recording menu whenever you want the camera to try to recognize those faces. When it does, it will place a frame over the face and display the name, if one was entered into the camera's memory, as shown in Figure 4-30. The camera will adjust its focus and exposure for the recognized face or faces.

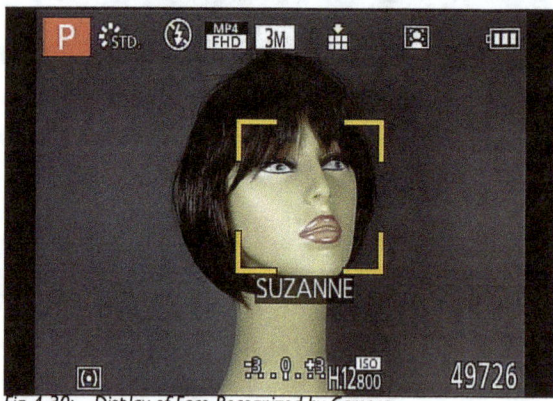

Fig. 4-30: Display of Face Recognized by Camera

This feature can be useful if you are taking photos at a school event and you want to make sure the camera focuses on your child when you are aiming at a group of children. However, it also can slow down camera performance, and the camera may have trouble recognizing faces unless you save them using multiple angles and types of lighting. If you don't want the camera to use its recognition, just turn this menu item off.

AF (Autofocus) Mode

When you set the slide switch on the left side of the lens to the AF position for autofocus, the camera uses its built-in programming to focus the lens automatically. When the camera is set to Snapshot mode or one of the other automatic shooting modes, the camera does not let you make any further choices about what autofocus mode to use; the camera will make automatic judgments about how to focus.

When the camera is in Program mode or one of the other more advanced shooting modes, you can select from the four menu options for AF Mode, which will instruct the camera on how you want it to choose the subject that it focuses on. This setting on the Recording menu lets you select among four different autofocus methods: Face Detection, AF Tracking, 23-Area, and 1-Area. Here is how they work.

Face Detection

When you select this setting, shown in Figure 4-31, the camera does not display any focusing brackets or rectangles until it detects a human face.

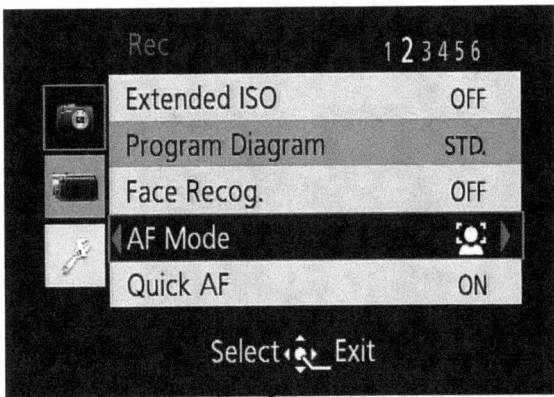

Fig. 4-31: Face Detection Menu Option

If it does, it outlines the general area of the face with a yellow rectangle, as shown in Figure 4-32.

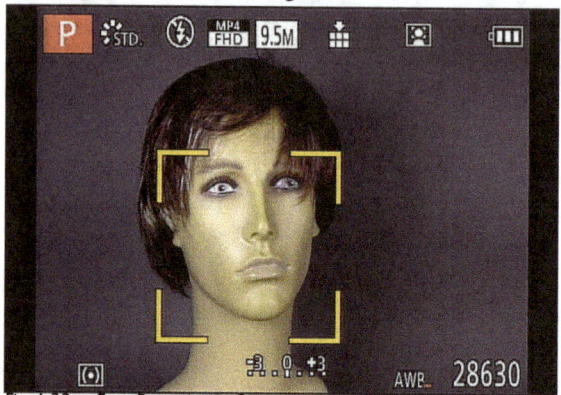

Fig. 4-32:   Face Detection in Operation

Then, when you press the shutter button halfway down, the rectangle turns green when the camera has focused on the face. If your subject moves after the yellow AF brackets have turned green, your shot will not be in focus, and you need to refocus. If the camera detects more than one face, it displays white rectangles for secondary faces, as shown in Figure 4-33. Any faces that are the same distance away from the camera as the face within the yellow rectangle will also be in focus, but the focus will be controlled by the face in the yellow rectangle.

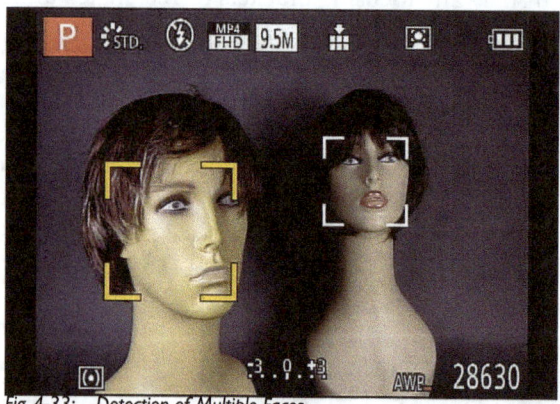

Fig. 4-33:   Detection of Multiple Faces

As you might expect, Face Detection is not a perfect system. If conditions do not permit the camera to properly detect a face or faces, it is best to switch to another autofocus mode to avoid confusion. Face Detection cannot be used in the following varieties of Scene mode: Panorama, Night Scenery, Hand-held Night Shot, and Food. It also is not available with the Soft Focus and Miniature settings of Creative Control mode. Face Detection is automatically activated in Snapshot mode. It is the initial setting for the following Scene types: Portrait, Soft Skin, Night Portrait, HDR, and Baby.

AF Tracking

This setting for AF Mode allows the camera to maintain its focus on a moving subject. As with other AF modes, you set this one using the Recording menu. Scroll down to AF Mode, press the right button to bring up the sub-menu, and then select the second icon, which is a group of offset focus frames, designed to look like a moving focus frame, as shown in Figure 4-34.

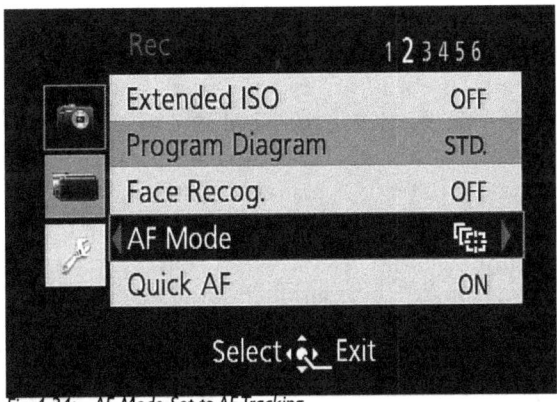

Fig. 4-34:   AF Mode Set to AF Tracking

The camera will then display a special white focus frame, with spokes sticking out of it, in the center of the display, as shown in Figure 4-35. Move the camera to place this focus frame over your subject and press the AF/AE Lock button, above and to the left of the array of five buttons on the back of the camera.

163

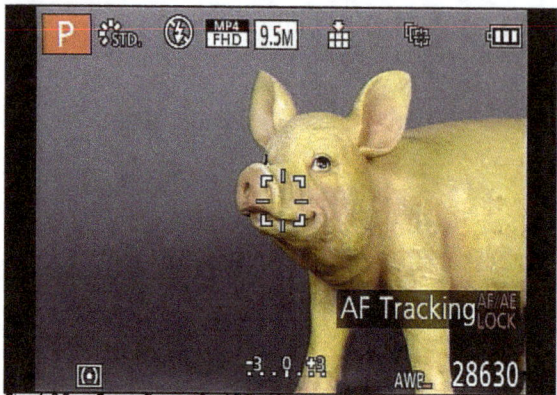

Fig. 4-35:   Focus Frame for AF Tracking

The camera will then do its best to keep that target in focus, even as it moves. The D-Lux 6 will display yellow brackets that should stay close to the subject on the LCD screen. When you are ready, press the shutter button to take the picture. If you want to cancel AF Tracking, press the AF/AE Lock button again.

If the camera is not able to maintain focus on the moving subject, the focus frame will turn red and then disappear. AF Tracking will not work when you're recording a movie; 1-Area mode will be used instead. AF Tracking also cannot be used with certain Scene mode and Creative Control mode types. However, it is available in Snapshot mode by pressing the up cursor button, and it is initially turned on for the Pet scene type, though you can switch to another autofocus method if you want.

When would you use AF Tracking? The idea here is to reduce the time it takes for you to be able to take a picture of a moving subject. If you are trying to snap a picture of your restless four-year-old or your fidgety Jack Russell Terrier, AF Tracking can give you a head start, so the camera's focus is close to being correct, and the focusing mechanism has less to do to achieve correct focus when you suddenly see the perfect moment to press the shutter button.

23-Area

This method of focusing causes the camera to focus on up to 23 smaller focus areas within the overall autofocus area, which is the same area as that of the current aspect ratio setting. You cannot select which of the 23 areas the camera focuses on; it selects however many areas it detects that are at the same distance from the camera and can be focused on.

To make this setting, select the third icon on the AF Mode menu, which looks like a screen with multiple focus points, as shown in Figure 4-36.

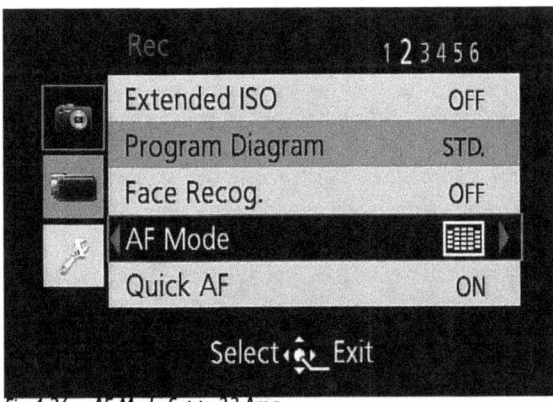

Fig. 4-36: AF Mode Set to 23-Area

When you use the 23-Area focusing method, once you push the shutter button down halfway, the camera will display green rectangles to show you which of the multiple focus areas it has selected to focus on, as shown in Figure 4-37.

The 23-Area method can be useful if your subject is not in the center of the screen and you don't want to be bothered moving the focus point around. With this method, the camera provides a broad range of focus areas, and, if it finds a subject to focus on within the area that has been defined for it, it establishes the focus on that subject. It is a good mode to use when you are shooting scenery or general scenes that do not require you to focus on faces or on any one particular object.

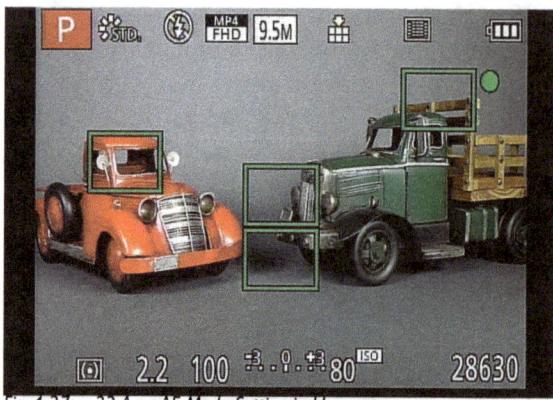

Fig. 4-37:   23-Area AF Mode Setting in Use

1-Area

This next AF Mode setting is made using the last icon on the AF Mode menu, as shown in Figure 4-38.

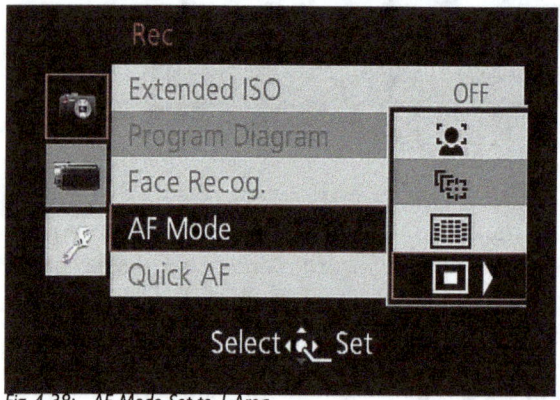

Fig. 4-38:   AF Mode Set to 1-Area

This method initially sets up the camera to focus on the subject in the center area of the screen, but you can change the position of the focus frame to focus on your chosen subject. The camera uses a single, small focusing rectangle that you can move around the screen as you wish. When you have high-

166

lighted the AF Mode icon on the menu, you can press the right button while the 1-Area selection is highlighted, to move directly to setting the location of the autofocus rectangle using the direction buttons, as shown in Figure 4-39.

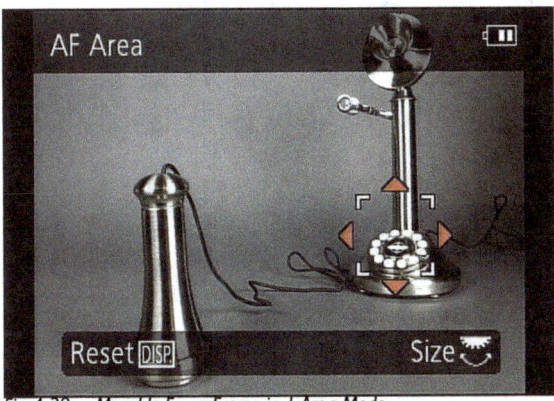

Fig. 4-39:   Movable Focus Frame in 1-Area Mode

When you have finished moving the focus frame, press the Menu/Set button to fix the frame in place. If you want to move the frame back to the default selection in the middle of the screen, press the Display button at the bottom right of the camera. The focus area will also move back to its starting position when the camera is switched to Snapshot mode, enters Sleep Mode, or is turned off.

In addition, whenever the focus rectangle is activated, as indicated by the presence of red triangles on each side of the rectangle, you can change the size of the rectangle by turning the rear dial to one of four positions, as shown in Figure 4-40, which shows the largest size.

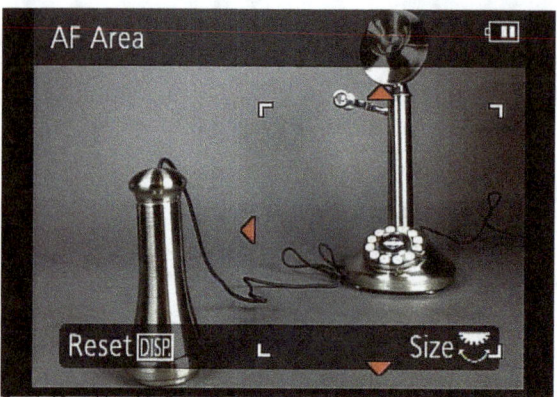

Fig. 4-40:   Movable Focus Frame Enlarged to its Largest Size

You can reset the size (as well as the position) of the rectangle to normal by pressing the Display button. The size will be reset to the default when you turn off the camera. Your chosen size cannot be saved as a custom setting.

Once you move the focus frame to a new location, in order to move it again you have to use the menu system and go back through the process of selecting this focus mode, and then moving to the screen that lets you reposition the focus frame. However, there is an easier way to move the frame, if you use the camera's ability to assign a particular operation to the Function button (left cursor button). As is discussed in Chapters 5 and 7, you can use the Function Button Set option on the second screen of the Setup menu to assign the Focus Area Set operation to that button. Then, whenever you want to move the focus frame again, just press the Function button, and the frame will be activated, ready to move to a new location. I like to assign that duty to the Function button, because it makes the 1-Area autofocus mode much more useful to me.

The 1-Area method is a very good one to use for general shooting, because it lets you quickly move the focus area to just where you want it. I prefer using this method to letting the camera choose from among 23 areas with no input from me.

Quick AF

This next function on the Recording menu, Quick AF, can be turned either on or off, as seen in Figure 4-41.

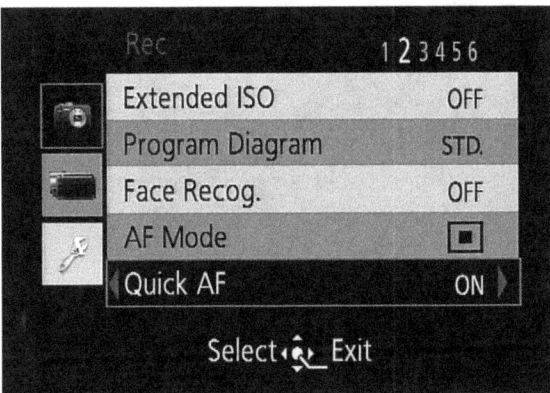

Fig. 4-41: Quick AF Menu Option

If you turn this option on, the camera will focus on the subject whenever the camera has settled down and is quite still, with only minor movement or shake. You do not need to press the shutter button halfway down to achieve focus; the camera focuses on its own.

The advantage of turning Quick AF on is that you will have a slight improvement in focusing time because the camera does not wait until you press the shutter button to start the focusing process. The disadvantage is that the battery will run down faster than usual. So, unless you believe that a split second for focusing time is critical, I would stay away from this setting, and leave this menu option set to Off. The camera will still focus automatically when you press the shutter button halfway down; it just will take a little bit longer.

AF/AE Lock

This setting lets you change the function of the AF/AE Lock button, which is located to the upper left of the array of five buttons on the back of the camera. You can use this menu item to set that button to lock both the autofocus and autoexposure settings by choosing the AF/AE setting, or just one or the other by choosing the AF or AE setting, as shown in Figure 4-42.

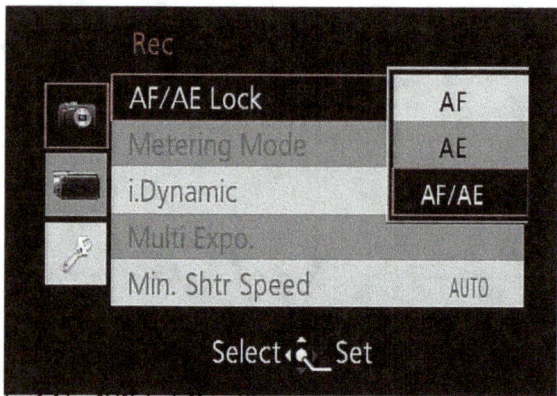

Fig. 4-42: AF/AE Lock Menu Option

The camera will indicate on the LCD display which of the two values are locked, once you press the AF/AE Lock button and the values are locked in. For example, Figure 4-43 shows the display when both values are locked, with the AFL icon at the upper right and the AEL icon at the lower left of the screen.

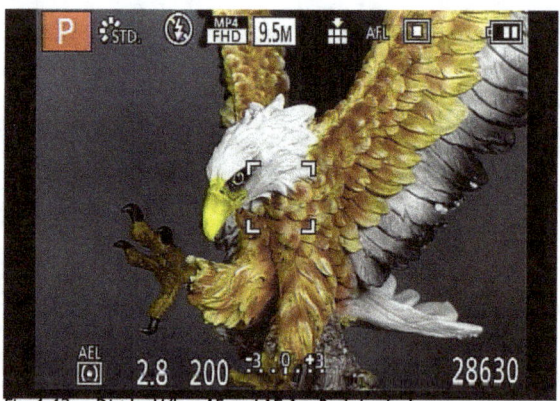

Fig. 4-43: Display When AF and AE Are Both Locked

It is not possible to lock exposure using the AF/AE button in

Manual shooting mode (unless ISO is set to Auto) or in Scene mode, even though the display will still show the AE indicator if the button is set to lock exposure. I will discuss the use of the AF/AE button itself in Chapter 5.

Metering Mode

The next option on the Recording menu lets you choose what method the camera uses to meter the light and determine the proper exposure. The D-Lux 6 gives you a choice of three methods: Multi metering, Center-weighted, and Spot. If you choose Multi, the camera evaluates the brightness at multiple spots in the image that is shown on the LCD screen, and calculates an exposure that takes into account all of the various values. With Center-weighted, the camera gives greater emphasis to the brightness of the subject(s) in the center of the screen, while still taking into account the brightness of other areas in the image. With Spot, the camera evaluates only the brightness of the subject(s) in the small spot-metering area.

The Leica user's manual recommends using Multi mode for general shooting, presumably on the theory that it produces a reasonable choice for exposure, based on evaluating the overall brightness of everything seen on the LCD screen. However, if you want to make sure that one particular item in the scene is properly exposed, you may want to use the Spot method, and aim the spot metering area at that object or person, then lock in the exposure.

Choosing your metering method is less complicated than some other choices. Just enter the Recording menu and scroll down to the line for Metering Mode, then press the right arrow to activate the sub-menu with the three choices, as shown in Figure 4-44.

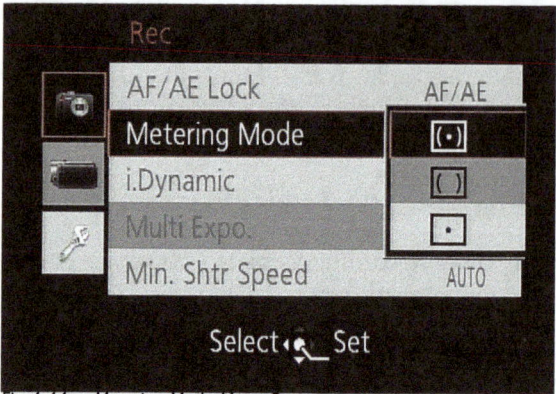

Fig. 4-44: Metering Mode Menu Option

The first icon, a rectangle with a pair of parentheses and a dot inside, represents Multi mode; the second, a rectangle with a pair of parentheses inside, represents Center-weighted; and the third, a rectangle with just a dot inside, represents Spot.

With Multi or Center-weighted, metering is quite simple: Point the camera at the subject(s) you want and let the camera compute the exposure. If you choose Spot as your metering technique, the process can be more involved. Presumably, you will have a fairly small area in mind as the most important area for having the correct exposure; perhaps it is a small object you are photographing for an online auction. The LCD screen will display a small + sign in the center of the screen, as shown in Figure 4-45, and you need to be sure that the + is over the most important object.

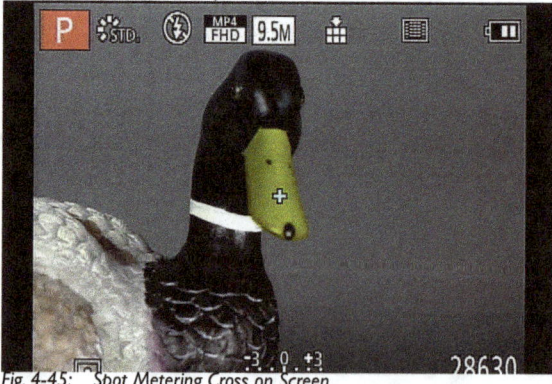

Fig. 4-45: Spot Metering Cross on Screen

If that object is not in the center of the screen, then you may need to use the AE Lock control, which is operated by the small button just to the right of the LCD on the back of the camera. If you want that button to lock only the exposure, as discussed above, you can set that limitation through the Recording menu, on the AF/AE Lock line. Just select AE Lock. Of course, the chances are pretty good that if you want to expose one object correctly you will also want to focus on that object, so it's often going to be okay to leave the AF/AE lock button set to lock both autofocus and autoexposure.

Aim the camera so the + in the middle of the screen touches the object to be exposed correctly, then press the AE Lock button. The LCD will show that AE-L (or AE-L and AF-L) has been engaged. You can now move the camera back to compose the picture as you want it, perhaps with the correctly exposed object off to one side. The exposure setting will not change as you recompose the image. Press the shutter button, and the image will be exposed as you wanted it. The AE-Lock stays in effect until you cancel it by pressing the AE-Lock button again.

Note that there is a sparsely-documented feature of the camera that lets you move the little + around the camera's screen so that you can place it right over the area of the picture that you want properly exposed. This will work only if, in addition to using the Spot metering mode, you are also using the 1-Area autofocus method. In that case, whenever you move the focusing target, the Spot-metering target moves along with it, so the target serves two purposes at once. For example, Figure 4-46 shows the display when both Spot metering and 1-Area autofocus are in effect.

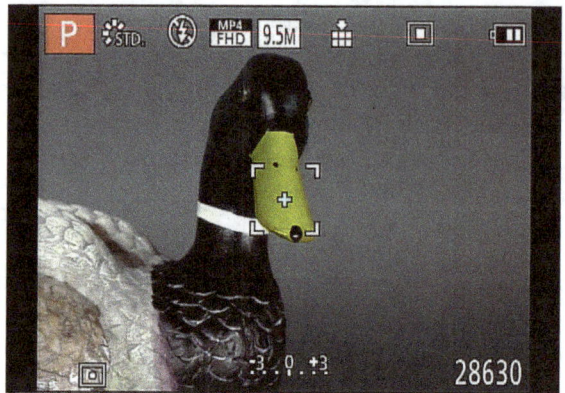

Fig. 4-46:   Display with Both Spot Metering and 1-Area Autofocus

The Metering Mode setting is not available in the Snapshot or Scene modes. When Multi metering is selected and the auto-focus mode is set to Face Detection, the camera will attempt to expose a person's face correctly, assuming a face has been de-tected. The current setting for Metering Mode is indicated by an icon in the lower left of the display, as shown in Figure 4-47.

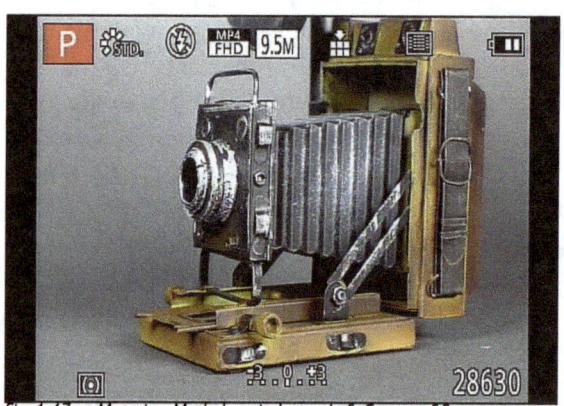

Fig. 4-47:   Metering Mode Icon in Lower Left Corner of Screen

Intelligent Dynamic

The Intelligent Dynamic, or i.Dynamic, setting causes the camera to adjust the exposure automatically to compensate for a situation in which there is a large difference in brightness between the background and the subject of the picture. It is not available when the Quality is set to RAW or RAW + JPEG, so you need to set Quality to Standard or Fine to use this feature. It also is not available in the Snapshot, Scene, or Creative Control shooting modes. As shown in Figure 4-48, this feature can be set to Off, Low, Standard, or High, depending on how dramatic an effect you wish to achieve.

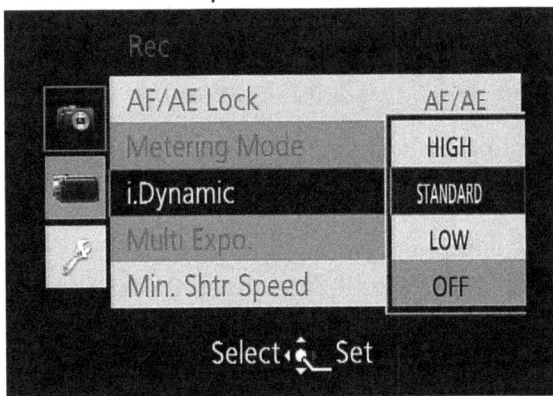

Fig. 4-48:   Intelligent Dynamic Menu Option

The function of this option is to boost the ISO setting slightly, in the shadowed areas of the image only, when there is so much contrast in the scene as to cause the loss of details in shadows. The ISO will be raised enough to bring out more details in the shadowed areas. Its particular value lies in the fact that it can selectively alter the ISO setting for only the part of the image where that alteration is called for. I generally leave this setting set to Standard.

Multiple Exposure

The Multiple Exposure option is more in the category of trick or creative photography than control of normal image-making. In a nutshell, it lets you create double or triple exposures in the camera. The steps to take are a bit unusual, because you actually carry out the picture-taking while in the Recording menu system.

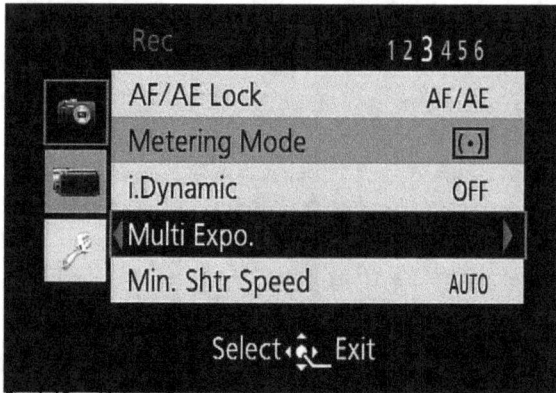

Fig. 4-49:   Multiple Exposure Menu Option

Enter the Recording menu and scroll down to Multi. Expo, as shown in Figure 4-49, then press the right button, which takes you to a screen with the word Start highlighted, as shown in Figure 4-50. Press the center button (Menu/Set) to select Start. The screen then has the word Cancel displayed, as shown in Figure 4-51; you can press the center button to end the process if you have had second thoughts.

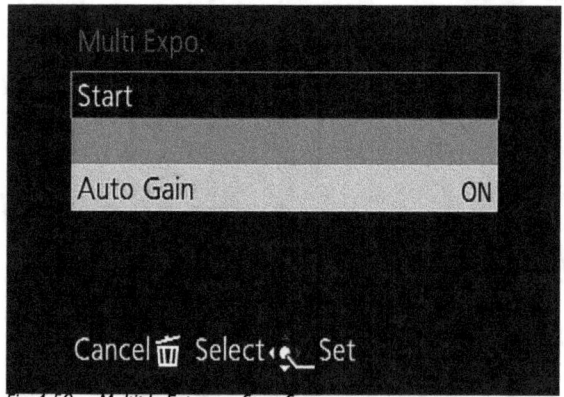

Fig. 4-50:   Multiple Exposure Start Screen

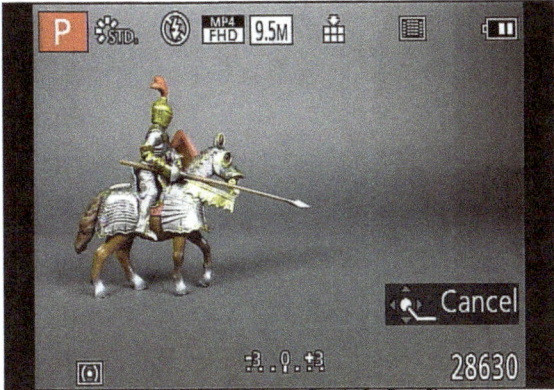

Fig. 4-51:   Multiple Exposure Option - Ready for First Shot

If you are going to proceed, then compose and take the first picture. At this point the screen will display the image you just took along with the choices Next, Retake, and Exit, as shown in Figure 4-52.

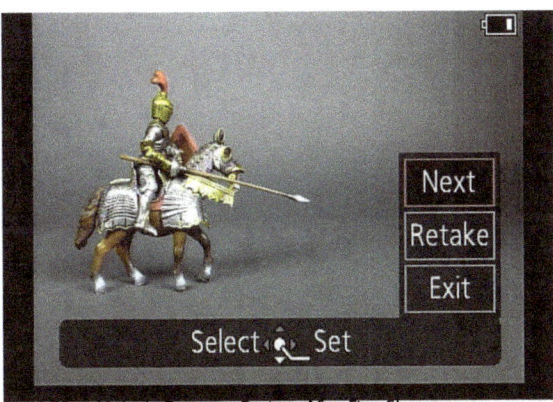

Fig. 4-52:   Multiple Exposure Option - After First Shot

If you're not satisfied with the first image, scroll to Retake and select that option with the center button, then retake the first image. If you're ready to proceed to taking a superimposed image, leave Next highlighted and press the shutter button halfway down, or, if you prefer, press the Menu/Set button. This action produces the interesting effect of leaving the first

177

image on the screen and making the screen live at the same time to take a new image, as shown in Figure 4-53.

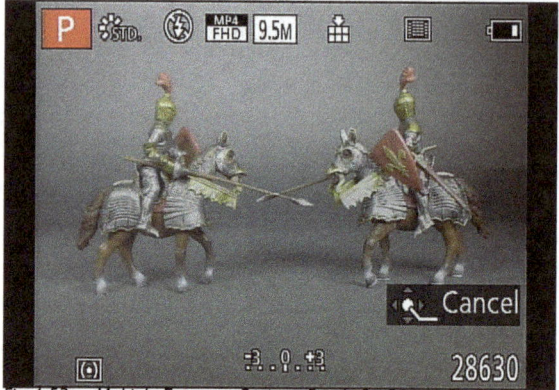

Fig. 4-53:   Multiple Exposure Option - Ready for Second Shot

Compose the second shot as you want it, while viewing the first one, and press the shutter button fully to record that image. You can then repeat this process to add a third image, retake the second image, or exit the whole process. When you are done, you will have a single image that combines the two or three superimposed images you recorded.

Before you take the images using the Multiple Exposure procedure, the menu gives you the option of setting Auto Gain on or off, as shown in Figure 4-54.

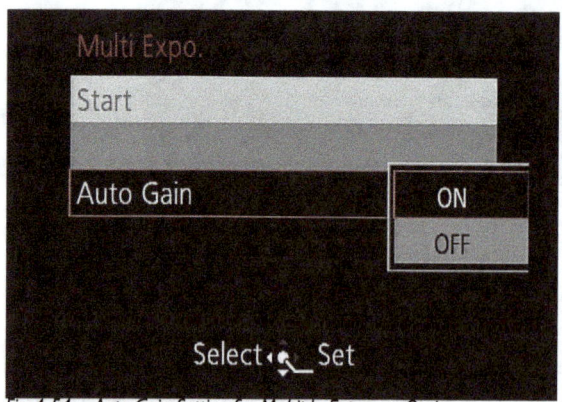

Fig. 4-54:   Auto Gain Setting for Multiple Exposure Option

If you set Auto Gain on, the camera adjusts the exposure based on the number of pictures taken; if you turn it off, the camera adjusts the exposure for the final superimposed image. In my experience, the On setting produces results with clearer images of the multiple scenes; Off produces fainter images.

The Multiple Exposure feature is not available in Snapshot, Scene, Creative Control, or Creative Video modes. In addition, you cannot use this feature with burst shooting, the Intelligent Dynamic setting, or any of the bracketing features.

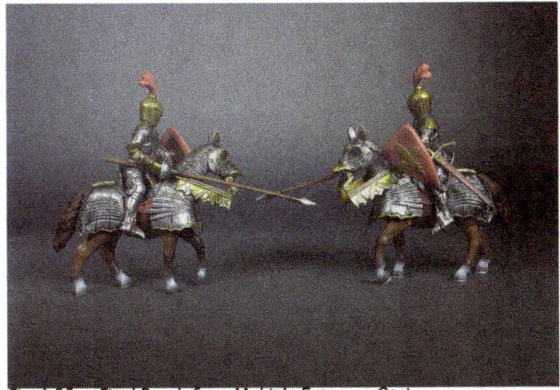

Fig. 4-55:   Final Result from Multiple Exposure Option

For the final image in Figure 4-55, I shot in RAW + JPEG and used the RAW file for editing. I used the Auto Contrast command in Photoshop to increase the overall contrast, which was a bit weak before that adjustment.

Minimum Shutter Speed

The setting for Minimum Shutter Speed, shown in Figure 4-56, lets you set the slowest shutter speed the camera will use, in a range from 1/250 second to one full second.

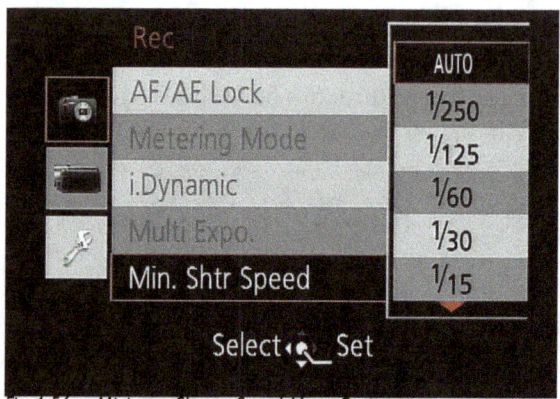

Fig. 4-56: Minimum Shutter Speed Menu Option

You can use this setting when you want to avoid the motion blur that is likely to result from a slow shutter speed, such as 1/4 second. When you select any setting other than the default, which is AUTO, the camera displays the indicator MIN along with the minimum shutter speed at the bottom of the LCD screen, to the left of center, as shown in Figure 4-57.

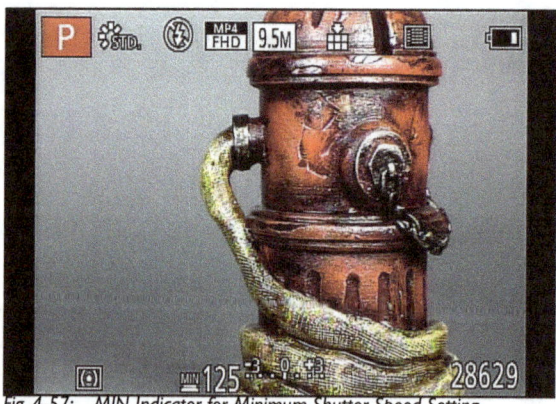

Fig. 4-57: MIN Indicator for Minimum Shutter Speed Setting

With the AUTO setting, the camera will use any shutter speed up to one full second, if the camera is steady or the Stabilizer is turned off. If camera shake is an issue, the camera will not use speeds slower than about ¼ second. If the camera cannot achieve a proper exposure using a specific setting, the MIN indicator flashes in red when you press the shutter button halfway, meaning there is not enough light available. The camera will still take the picture if you continue to press the shutter button fully down; it has warned you, but will follow your instructions. In effect, this setting is a low-light alarm that you can ignore if you want to. I always leave this setting on AUTO.

Note that this setting only has any effect when you are shooting in Program mode, either by setting the Mode dial to P or by setting it to C1 or C2, with a custom setting that includes Program mode. This makes sense, because there are likely to be times when you would be hampered by having a minimum shutter speed of one second, the slowest available with this setting. For example, if you're taking a long exposure in a dark area, or shooting infrared photos (see Chapter 9), you may need an exposure of several seconds. If you're in a situation like that, you have to remember not to set the camera to Program mode. You can choose Aperture Priority, Shutter Priority, Manual, or Scene mode. Note, though, that in Aperture Priority or Shutter Priority mode, the slowest shutter speed available is 8 seconds, whereas you can set it to a full 250 seconds in Manual mode.

Intelligent Resolution

The Intelligent Resolution, or i.Resolution, option can be set to Off, Low, Standard, or High, as shown in Figure 4-58. This setting increases the apparent resolution of images by providing additional sharpening through in-camera digital manipulation. It does seem to improve image quality somewhat in certain situations. I recommend that you try shooting with it turned on and off to see if it provides actual benefits for your shots. I do not use it myself, because I prefer to shoot with

RAW quality and add sharpening with my editing software.

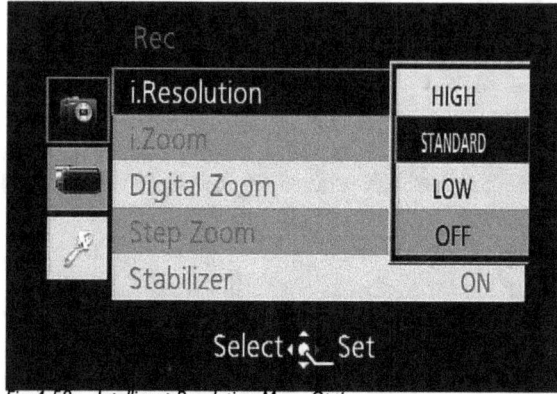

Fig. 4-58:   Intelligent Resolution Menu Option

Intelligent Zoom

The Intelligent Zoom, or i.Zoom, option, shown in Figure 4-59, is related to the i.Resolution feature, discussed above, although you do not have to turn on i.Resolution in order to take advantage of i.Zoom.

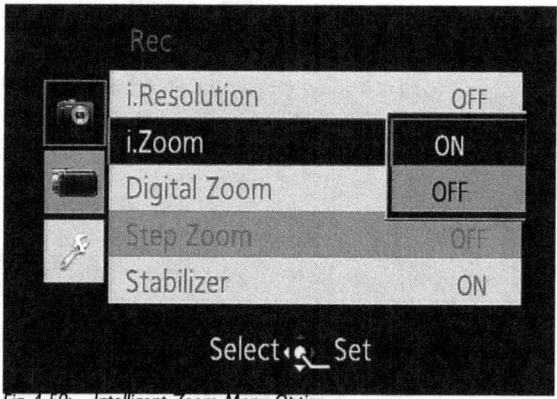

Fig. 4-59:   Intelligent Zoom Menu Option

When i.Zoom is turned on, the camera extends the zoom range up to two times normal, and automatically uses i.Resolution processing in the extended part of the zoom range in order to improve the appearance of the image, so you can zoom to the higher level of magnification without image deterioration, using either normal optical zoom or Extended Optical Zoom. For example, without the i.zoom setting, the limit for the optical zoom is 3.8X; with i.zoom turned on, the maximum is 7.5X. The question of image quality in this situation is a matter of judgment; as with i.resolution, I recommend that you try this setting to see if you are satisfied with the quality of the images. If so, you can then use an effective zoom range up to 180mm, rather than the 90mm of the optical zoom alone.

The i.Zoom feature is not available in conjunction with certain types of shooting that involve special processing, including Panorama shots, ISO settings above 6400, and several other situations, as detailed at page 94 of the Leica user's guide.

Digital Zoom

I discussed the Digital Zoom feature earlier in this chapter in connection with Picture Size and Extended Optical Zoom. I will discuss it here again briefly, because it is the next item on the Recording menu. First, note a few restrictions: Digital Zoom is not available if you have the camera set to Snapshot mode or if you have Quality set to RAW. It also is not available with some burst settings or with certain other shooting settings and features, as detailed at page 94 of the Leica user's guide. To recap briefly, you access Digital Zoom through the Recording Menu and turn it either on or off. Remember, this is really an artificial sort of zoom that does not give you any added "real" magnification; it just enlarges the existing image, making it increasingly fuzzy and blocky as you zoom in further. It's best avoided, except possibly for helping you view a distant object while composing your shot.

Step Zoom

This is a useful feature for helping you control how the zoom operates. When this function is turned on through the Recording menu, as shown in Figure 4-60, you can zoom the lens to specific focal lengths, rather than just zooming in a continuous range.

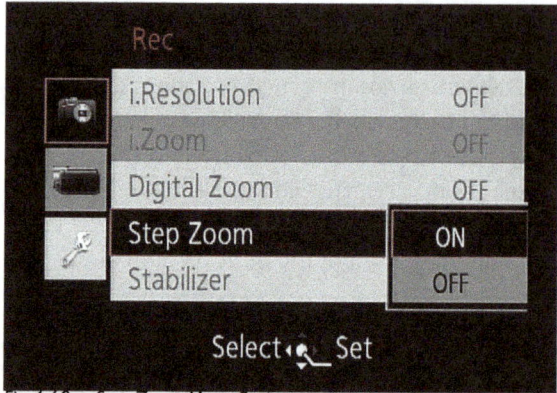

Fig. 4-60: Step Zoom Menu Option

Starting from the wide-angle setting of 24mm, you can zoom to settings of 28mm, 35mm, 50mm, 70mm, and 90mm, the full extent of the optical zoom. You will see a scale at the bottom of the display that shows the various choices as you zoom to each one, as shown in Figure 4-61.

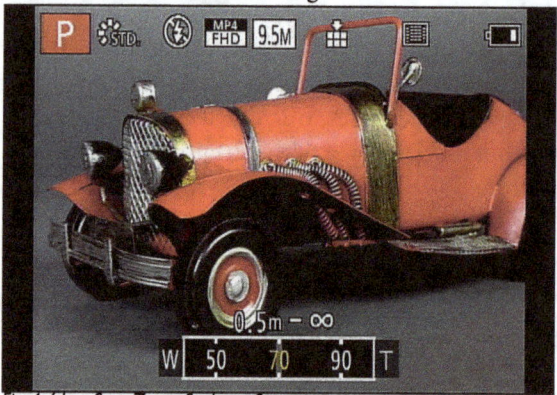

Fig. 4-61: Step Zoom Scale on Screen

(If the aspect ratio is set to 1:1, the zoom settings are somewhat different; the series starts with focal lengths of 29mm, 33mm, and 41mm.) If you have activated Intelligent Zoom, Extended Optical Zoom, or Digital Zoom, the available focal lengths increase accordingly, to 135mm, 200mm, 300mm, and 360mm.

184

To move to a particular zoom increment, give a short nudge to the zoom lever, and the zoom indicator will move to the next numbered setting and stop. This option can be of particular use if you happen to have an external optical viewfinder with a particular focal length setting, and want to set the camera's focal length to correspond to the viewfinder's frame lines.

One problem with using this feature is that, if Step Zoom is turned on, you cannot zoom to any focal length other than the specified ones. Therefore, you can't fine-tune your focal length to frame a subject; you can only zoom to one of the available settings. There is a trade-off between having complete control over your zoom range and having a repeatable, precise value for your zoom. It's good to be able to have this choice, though, for particular situations in which it is useful.

Step Zoom is not available in Snapshot mode or when recording movies.

Stabilizer

The D-Lux 6 has an optical image stabilization system, which helps minimize the effect of camera shake on the image.

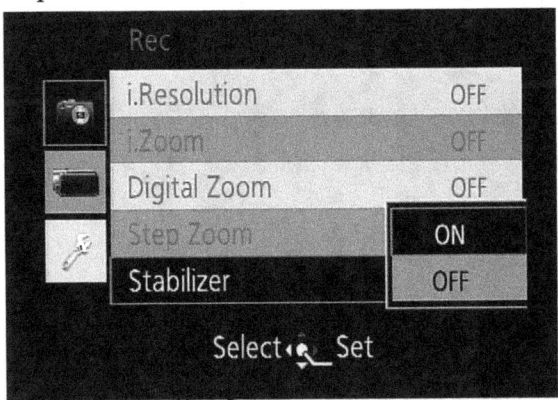

Fig. 4-62: Stabilizer Menu Option

This system, unlike the system used in the older D-Lux 5 model, does not have multiple modes; the Stabilizer setting can be set only to On or Off, as shown in Figure 4-62. I generally leave this setting turned on unless I have the camera on a tripod, in which case the setting is unnecessary and possibly could cause some distortion as the camera tries to correct for camera movement that does not exist.

The camera automatically turns stabilization off when you are shooting panoramas or 3D shots in Scene mode or high-speed videos in Creative Video mode. The setting is fixed on and cannot be turned off for the Handheld Night Shot setting in Scene mode.

Autofocus Assist Lamp

The autofocus (AF) assist lamp is the reddish light on the front of the camera, near the lens below the hot shoe and the mode dial. The lamp illuminates when the ambient lighting is dim, to help the autofocus mechanism achieve proper focus by providing enough light to define the shape of the subject. Ordinarily, this option is left turned on for normal shooting, because the light only activates when it is needed because of low-light conditions. However, you have the option of setting it to the off position using the AF Assist Lamp menu option, shown in Figure 4-63, so that it will never turn on.

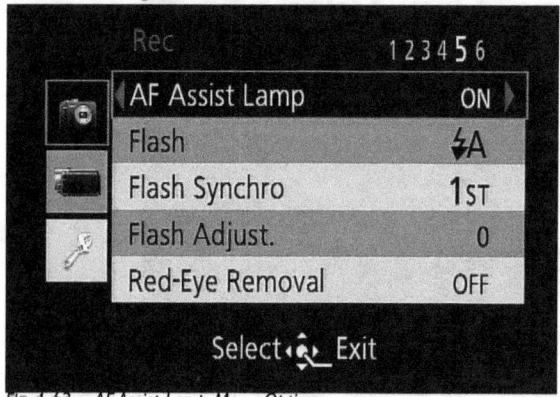

Fig. 4-63: AF Assist Lamp Menu Option

You might want to do this if you are trying to shoot your pictures without being detected, or without disturbing a subject such as a sleeping child or animal.

186

In Snapshot mode, you cannot turn off the AF assist lamp. With some of the Scene mode settings, such as Scenery, Night Scenery, Handheld Night Shot, and Sunset, the AF assist lamp cannot be turned on. The lamp does not illuminate when you are using manual focus (unless you have set up the Function button to use 1 Shot AF, and you press that button to cause the camera to autofocus).

Note that the AF assist lamp also serves as the self-timer lamp. Even if you set the AF Assist Lamp menu option to Off, the lamp will still light up when the self-timer is used; there is no way to disable the lamp for that function.

Flash

The available settings for the Flash item on the Recording menu vary somewhat according to the shooting mode. In most modes, the available settings for Flash are Auto Flash, Auto Flash with Red-Eye Reduction, Forced Flash On, and Slow Sync with Red-Eye Reduction, as shown in Figure 4-64.

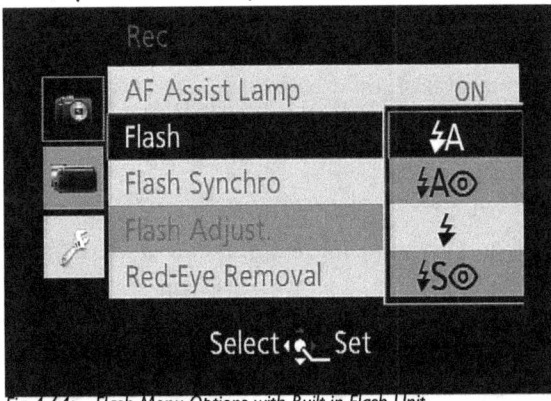

Fig. 4-64: Flash Menu Options with Built-in Flash Unit

Note that the list does not include Forced Flash Off, because you can choose that option by stowing the flash unit back inside the camera. In Snapshot mode, the flash is set to Auto Flash, and you have no control over that setting, although the camera will vary the automatic flash setting as needed.

If you place into the hot shoe a flash unit that communicates with the D-Lux 6 and turn it on, then the Flash menu item gives you up to five options, including Forced Flash Off, which is the last option at the bottom of the menu shown in Figure 4-65.

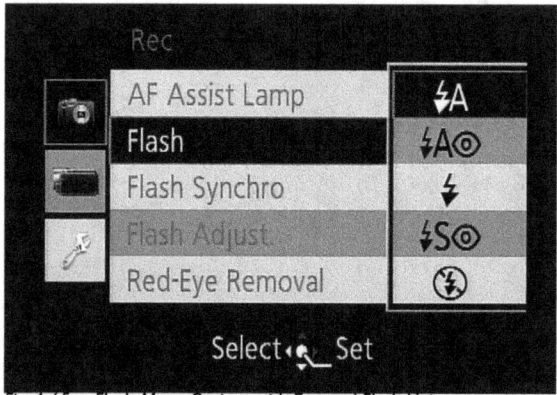

Fig. 4-65:   Flash Menu Options with External Flash Unit

You could turn off the external flash unit using its own power switch, but for some reason the camera is programmed to let you force the external flash off through software, even though you can't turn off the built-in flash unit in this way. You have to stuff the built-in flash unit back down into the camera to force it off.

In Chapter 9, I'll provide some more discussion of when to use the various Flash options.

Flash Synchro

This setting is one you may not have a lot of use for, unless you encounter the particular situation it is designed for. The Flash Synchro menu option, as shown in Figure 4-66, has two settings—1st and 2nd. Although the user's manual does not use this terminology, the 1st and 2nd are references to 1st-curtain sync and 2nd-curtain (also known as rear-curtain) sync.

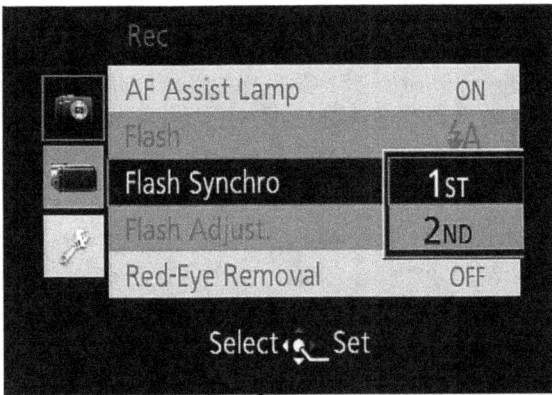

Fig. 4-66:   Flash Synchro Menu Option

The normal setting is 1st, which causes the flash to fire early in the process when the shutter opens to expose the image. If you set it to 2nd, the flash fires later, just before the shutter closes.

The reason for having the 2nd-curtain sync setting available is that it can help you avoid having a strange-looking result in some unusual situations. This issue arises when you are taking a relatively long exposure, such as one second, of a subject with taillights, like a car or motorcycle at night, that is moving across your field of view. With 1st-curtain sync, the flash will fire early in the process, freezing the vehicle in a clear image. However, as the shutter remains open while the vehicle keeps going, the camera will capture the moving taillights in a stream that appears to be extending in front of the vehicle. If, instead, you use 2nd-curtain sync, the initial part of the exposure will capture the lights in a trail that appears behind the vehicle, while the vehicle itself is not frozen by the flash until later in the exposure. Therefore, with 2nd-curtain sync in this particular situation, the final image is likely to look more natural than with 1st-curtain sync.

The images in Figures 4-67 and 4-68 illustrate this concept using a remote-controlled model car with a red tail light shining out of its rear end.

189

Both pictures were shot with the D-Lux 6's built-in flash, using an exposure of one-half second in Shutter Priority mode. In Figure 4-67, using the normal (1st) setting for Flash Synchro, the flash fired quickly, and the light beam continued on during the long exposure to make the streak of bright light appear in front of the car.

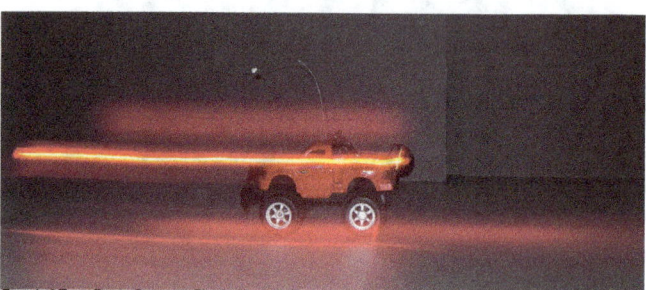

Fig. 4-67: First-Curtain Flash Example

In Figure 4-68, using the 2d setting, the flash did not fire until the car had traveled to the left, overtaking the place where the light had made its streak visible.

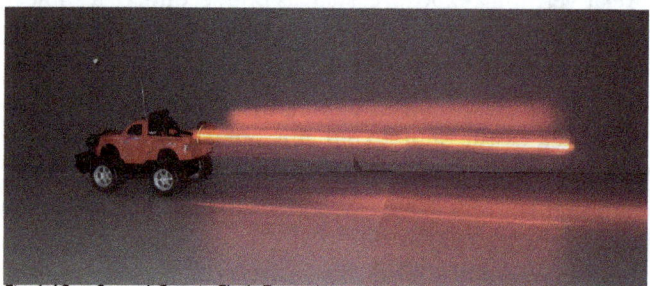

Fig. 4-68: Second-Curtain Flash Example

If you are trying to convey a sense of natural motion, the 2d setting for Flash Synchro, as seen here, is likely to give you better results than the default setting.

To sum up the situation with the 1st and 2nd Flash Synchro settings, a good general rule is to always use the 1st setting unless you are sure you have a real need for the 2nd setting. Using the 2nd setting makes it harder to compose and set up the shot, because you have to anticipate where the main subject will be when the flash finally fires late in the exposure process.

When the setting is 2nd, the indication "2nd" appears next to the flash icon when the flash is on.

The Flash Synchro setting is not available in Snapshot mode, Motion Picture mode, Creative Control mode, or with any of the Scene types.

Flash Adjustment

Flash Adjustment, the next option on the Recording menu, is a nice capability to have. This menu item lets you lower or raise the intensity of the flash, which can be useful in situations in which the subject is very small, or reflectivity is unusually high or low. I find it useful to reduce the flash intensity for portraits in many cases, to avoid putting a harsh glare on a face.

Navigate to this item, press the right button to pop up the sub-menu, and you are presented with the flash intensity screen, as shown in Figure 4-69.

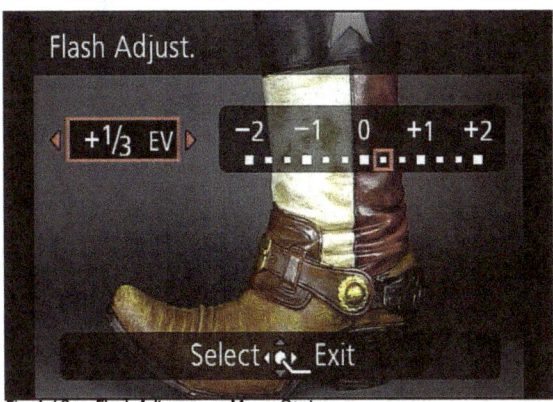

Fig. 4-69:   Flash Adjustment Menu Option

Use the right and left cursor buttons or turn the rear dial to increase or decrease the EV of the flash up to 2 full levels in either direction. This setting stays in place even when the camera is turned off and then back on. So, be careful to reset the flash output adjustment to zero (unchanged) when you are done with it, unless you want the adjustment to be used in the future. The LCD screen will help you remember the value that it's set on, by displaying a plus sign or minus sign next to the Flash mode icon to indicate a change in the flash output value, as shown in Figure 4-70. The flash output adjustment is not available in Snapshot mode or Creative Video mode.

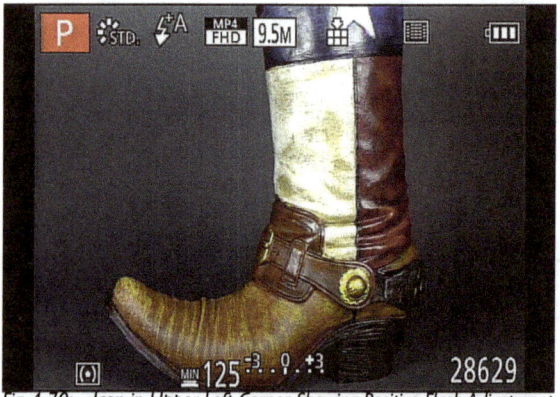

Fig. 4-70:   Icon in Upper Left Corner Showing Positive Flash Adjustment

The Flash Adjustment option works well with external flash units that are attached to the D-Lux 6's hot shoe, if they operate automatically in TTL (through-the-lens) mode and communicate properly with the camera. With such external flash units, you can raise or lower the output of the flash in exactly the same way as with the built-in flash unit. The two units that I have tested this operation with are Leica's own flash that works with the D-Lux 6, the CF22, and the Metz Mecablitz 36 AF-4. There undoubtedly are other external flash units that will also operate in this way.

Red-eye Removal

This setting on the Recording menu is not to be confused with Red-eye Reduction, which is an aspect of how the flash fires. "Red-eye" is the unpleasant phenomenon that crops up when a flash picture is taken of a person, and the light illuminates his or her retinas, causing an eerie red glow to appear in the eyes. One way the D-Lux 6 (like many cameras) deals with this problem is with the Red-eye Reduction setting for the flash, which causes the flash to fire twice: once to make the person's pupils contract, reducing the chance for the light to bounce off the retinas, and then a second time to take the picture.

The D-Lux 6 has a second line of defense against red-eye, called Red-eye Removal.

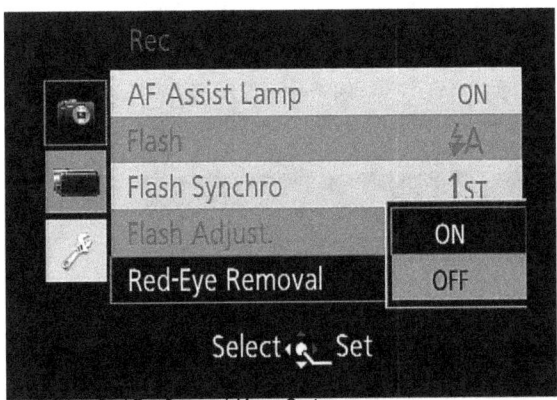

Fig. 4-71: Red-Eye Removal Menu Option

When you select this option, as shown in Figure 4-71, then, whenever the flash is fired and Red-eye Reduction is activated, the camera also uses a digital red-eye correction method, to actually remove from the image the red areas that appear to be near a person's eyes. This option operates only when the Face Detection setting is turned on.

Personally, I would not use this option, because I process my images using Photoshop or other software, and it's easy to fix red-eye at that stage. But this option could be convenient if you take lots of photos at a gathering and want to share them quickly, without doing post-processing on a computer.

Optional Viewfinder

This function can be set to either Off or On, as shown in Figure 4-72, depending on whether or not you have an optional external viewfinder attached to the camera.

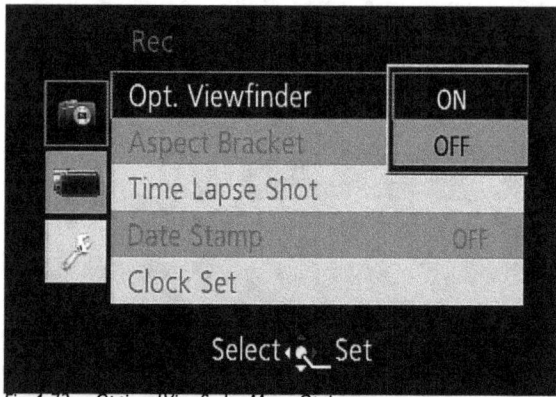

Fig. 4-72: *Optional Viewfinder Menu Option*

The D-Lux 6, like many compact digital cameras (as opposed to DSLRs), does not have a built-in viewfinder, but forces you to rely exclusively on its LCD screen to compose pictures. This system works quite well in normal lighting conditions, but in bright outdoor light or very dim light it can become difficult to see the screen. In addition, some photographers like to be able to hold the camera up to their eye rather than hold it out at arm's length to see the LCD screen. Therefore, as I will discuss in the section on accessories (Appendix A), you can obtain an optional external viewfinder that attaches to the camera's hot shoe and lets you compose photographs without the use of the LCD screen. If you attach an optical viewfinder, you may want to turn off the LCD display to conserve battery power.

The On setting of this option lets you turn the LCD screen off. Actually, it adds the turned-off-screen option to the cycle of options you get when you press the Display button on the back of the camera. With Optional Viewfinder set to On, pressing the Display button in Recording mode cycles through the following options: full display information; focus brackets only (if in a focus mode that uses brackets); information display and electronic level; focus brackets and electronic level; display off. With Optional Viewfinder set to Off, you get the same options, minus the display off option. When the display is turned off through this setting, the green status light to the left of the ISO button lights up, as shown in Figure 4-73, to let you know the display is off by choice, and that the camera is still powered up. And, although the LCD does not display the image that the camera sees, the screen displays a green dot to confirm focus, as well as the flash-status icon, when the shutter button is pressed halfway to confirm focus.

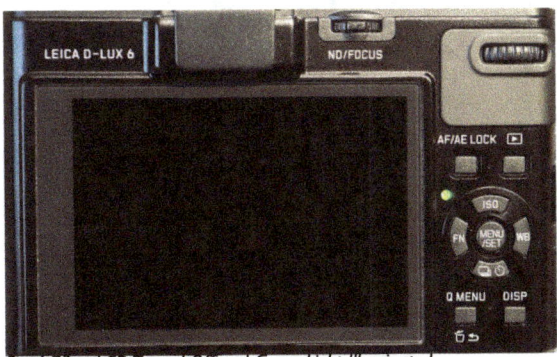

Fig. 4-73:   LCD Turned Off and Green Light Illuminated

At this writing, Leica offers an electronic viewfinder, Model No. EVF3. There are optical viewfinders available from other companies. Both types of viewfinder are discussed in Appendix A. This menu option is only needed when using an optical viewfinder; when the electronic one is attached, its controls can turn off the LCD display. Note that, if you want to, you can turn on this menu option even if you do not have an optical viewfinder attached, if you want to be able to turn off the LCD display to avoid attracting attention or distracting people around you with the light from the screen.

Aspect Bracket

This next option on the Recording menu lets you take multiple images with one press of the shutter button, all with different aspect ratios. You don't have to select anything other than the function itself. There are four aspect ratios available with the D-Lux 6—1:1, 4:3, 3:2, and 16:9—and the camera automatically records your image using all four of these settings.

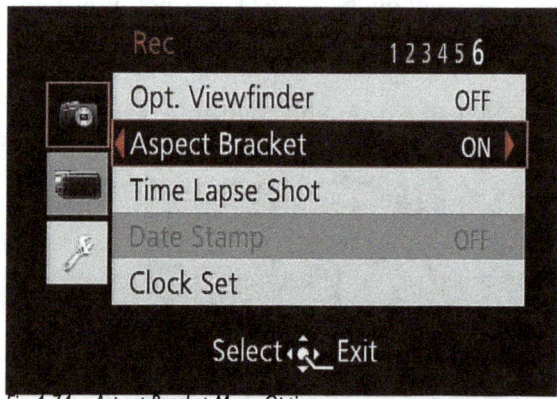

Fig. 4-74: Aspect Bracket Menu Option

To activate the Aspect Bracket procedure, select this menu option and press the right cursor button to reach the Aspect Bracket screen, shown in Figure 4-74. Then use the cursor buttons to change the setting for Aspect Bracket from Off to On, and press the Menu/Set button to exit.

You will see a screen like that shown in Figure 4-75, with four different colored rectangles outlining the frames for the four aspect ratios. The frame for the currently selected setting will be thicker than the others. When you press the shutter button, the camera will capture the image in all four aspect ratios.

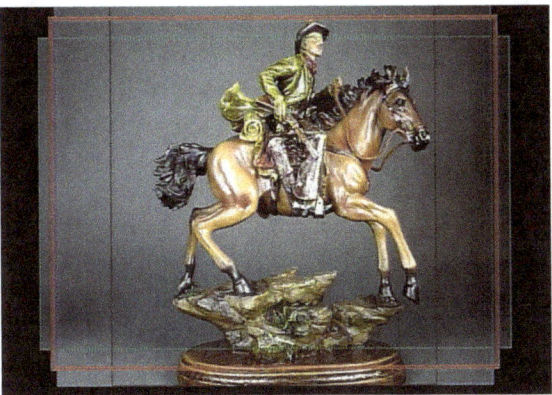

Fig. 4-75: Aspect Bracket Screen Display

One thing that can be a bit confusing about Aspect Bracket is that you will hear only one shutter activation, so it will sound as if only one picture is being taken, but the camera actually records four images at the same time despite the single shutter sound.

Aspect Bracket cannot be used at the same time as Auto Bracket or burst shooting, and Aspect Bracket is not available when you are shooting with RAW quality. (This can be confusing, because the camera will let you set both Aspect Bracket and RAW, but only one image will be recorded when you press the shutter button.) It also cannot be used with certain Scene or Creative Control mode settings or during video recording. Aspect Bracket, like Auto Bracket, is canceled when the camera is turned off.

Time Lapse Shot

The Time Lapse Shot option provides a fairly useful, although limited, capability for automatically shooting a time-lapse series of photographs. You undoubtedly have seen sequences in the movies or on television in which an event that takes a fair amount of time, such as a sunset, a flower opening, clouds moving across the sky, or a parking lot filling up with cars, is shown in a speeded-up series of images, so it appears to happen in a matter of a few seconds. Those sequences often are taken with specialized cameras that can record hundreds or thousands of images at a wide range of intervals. The D-Lux 6 can only record a relatively small number of images in this sort of sequence, but this capability still can be useful for studies of various natural phenomena, or just for producing an unusual and engaging series of shots. It is especially useful that the D-Lux 6 can use its time-lapse mechanism with any shooting mode (except for Creative Video mode, which involves recording video, not still images). Because you can use the more advanced shooting modes, you will have access to all of the major settings for the images, including RAW quality, white balance, ISO, and others.

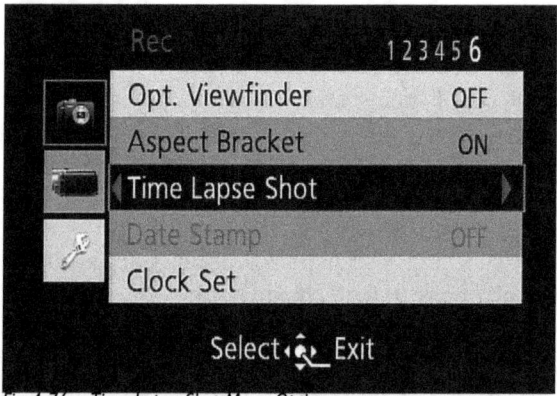

Fig. 4-76: Time Lapse Shot Menu Option

To set up the camera for time-lapse photography, highlight the Time Lapse Shot option on the Recording menu, shown in Figure 4-76, and press the right button to move to the setup screen, shown in Figure 4-77.

On that screen, use the cursor buttons to navigate through the various options. Select a start time, the interval between shots, and the total number of shots. You also can use the block containing a musical note icon to set whether or not the camera sounds an alert when it is about to take another picture in the series.

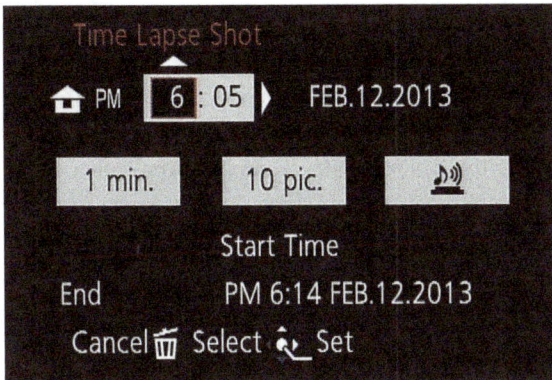

Fig. 4-77:   Time Lapse Shot Settings Screen

The interval can be set to any value from 1 to 30 minutes. One point to bear in mind when setting the interval is that, if the lighting is very dim, the camera may need to set a long shutter speed. For example, if the camera is set to use a shutter speed of 1 minute, which requires a long time for in-camera processing after the exposure is made, this system will not succeed if the interval between shots is set to less than 5 minutes. The total number of shots can be 10, 20, 30, 40, 50, or 60. You can turn on the flash if you want, and it will fire for each shot.

When you have made all of the settings as you want them, press the Menu/Set button, and the camera will display the screen shown in Figure 4-78, prompting you to press the shutter button when you're ready to start the sequence.

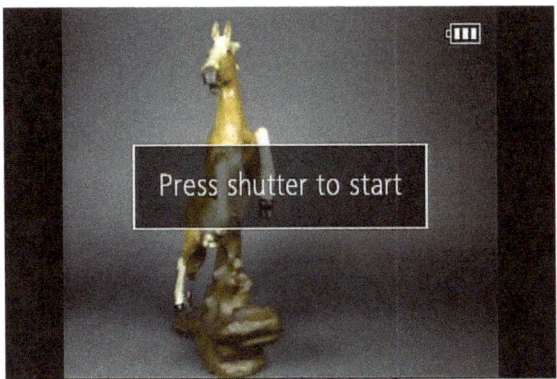

Fig. 4-78:   Time Lapse Shot - Prompt for Starting Sequence

When you press it, the camera will beep and flash the red lamp on its front with a 2-second countdown. It will repeat this process at the specified interval, until the total number of images has been recorded. Of course, if the battery runs down or the memory card fills up, the process will end prematurely.

When the sequence is complete, you will have the designated number of images saved to your memory card, ready for display in playback mode. (Time-lapse photography with the D-Lux 6 cannot be saved to the internal memory.) Assuming you have a detailed display screen selected in playback mode, the first image in the series will be displayed with indications like those in Figure 4-79, showing that you can press the up button to play back the sequence quickly, like a short movie.

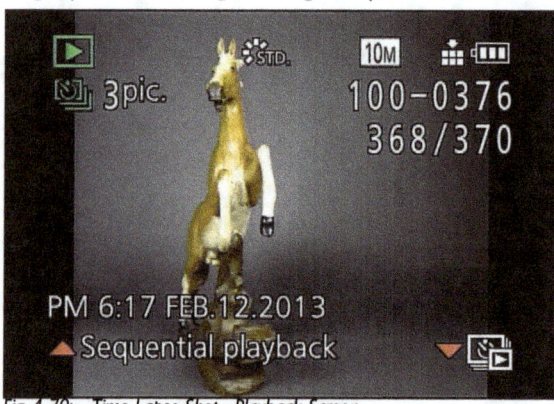

Fig. 4-79: Time Lapse Shot - Playback Screen

If you would prefer to view the images individually, you can press the down button. You can then press the right button repeatedly to view the time-lapse images one at a time.

Date Stamp

This option controls whether the camera places the current date, or date and time, on a recorded image, as shown in Figure 4-80. Note that this information is placed permanently on the image and cannot be deleted (unless you use Photoshop or similar software to edit it out). You might want to use this feature with images for a scientific experiment, but you ordinarily would not want to use it for general picture-taking, because the date (or date and time) information will mar the image.

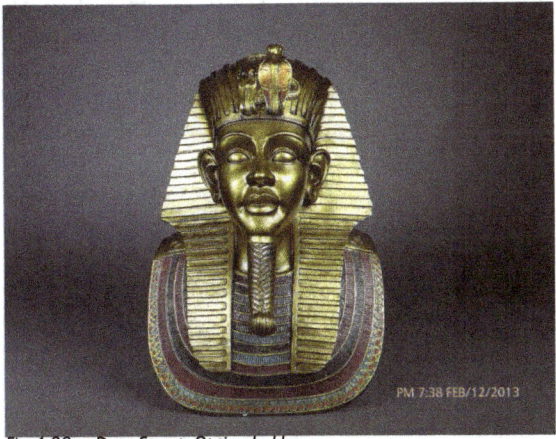

Fig. 4-80:   Date Stamp Option In Use

For ordinary images, you can always use editing software to retrieve the date and time information, which is recorded invisibly with the images (assuming the camera is set to the correct date and time).

To use this feature, go to the Date Stamp option on the Recording menu, as shown in Figure 4-81, then select either W/O Time, With Time, or turn the option off altogether. This feature cannot be used with burst shooting, bracketing, 3D shots, or panoramas.

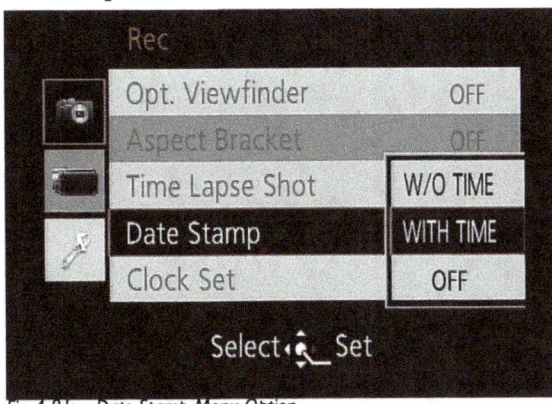

Fig. 4-81:   Date Stamp Menu Option

Clock Set

The final option on the D-Lux 6's Recording menu is Clock Set, which functions in the same way as the same item on the Setup menu, as discussed in Chapter 1 and Chapter 7. This option is also included on the Recording menu, presumably for convenience in case you find that the time and date settings need to be adjusted.

Chapter 5: Other Controls

Not all of the settings that affect the recording process are located on the Recording menu. Several important functions are controlled by physical buttons and switches on the camera. I have already discussed some of these, but in order to make sure all of the information about these controls is included in one place, I'll go through each physical control, some in greater detail than others. I'll start with the two controls that are visible on the top of the lens barrel, as shown in Figure 5-1.

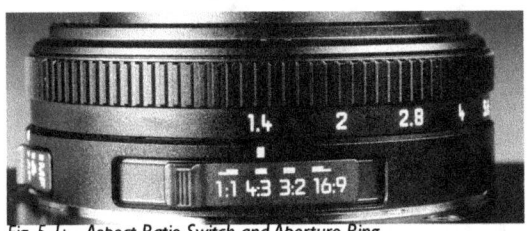

Fig. 5-1: Aspect Ratio Switch and Aperture Ring

Aspect Ratio Switch

This switch on top of the lens has four settings: 1:1, 4:3, 3:2, and 16:9, representing the ratio of the width of an image to its height. This setting does not affect just the shape of the image; it also determines how many megapixels an image can contain. When the aspect ratio is set to 4:3, the maximum resolution of 10 MP is available, because that is the aspect ratio of the image sensor; when the setting is 3:2, the greatest possible resolution is 9.5 MP; at 16:9, the highest possible resolution is 9 MP. At the 1:1 ratio, the largest resolution available is 7.5 MP. If you want your image to use the entire area of the LCD screen, choose 3:2, which is the aspect ratio of the screen.

With 4:3, there will be black bars at the sides of the screen as you compose your shot; with 16:9, there will be black bars at the top and bottom of the screen.

Figures 5-2 through 5-5 illustrate the different shapes that are produced for images that are taken with the D-Lux 6's various aspect ratio settings. I took all of these shots of a large mural from the same vantage point with the camera on a tripod, so you can see the different parts of the scene that are included with each setting.

In Figure 5-2, the aspect ratio was set to 3:2. This aspect ratio is useful if you want to use the entire area of the image in a print that is 4 by 6 inches (10 by 15 cm), the standard size for prints in the United States. As you can see, this image omits some of the top and bottom areas of the scene.

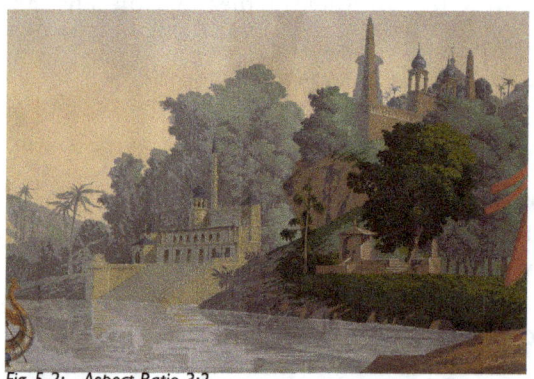

Fig. 5-2:   Aspect Ratio 3:2

Figure 5-3 illustrates the appearance of an image taken with the 4:3 setting, which represents the shape of a standard (non-widescreen) computer monitor, again, a standard shape, and one that has the advantage of using the full resolution of the sensor, although it does not include a few of the pixels at the left and right of the image.

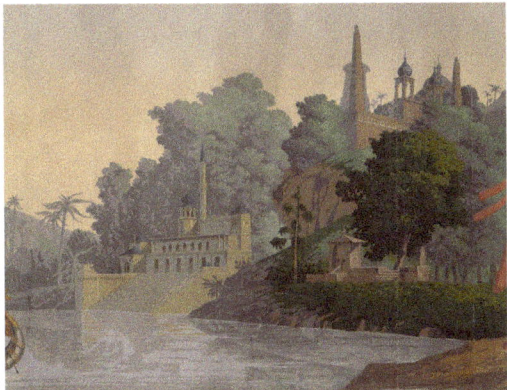

Fig. 5-3: Aspect Ratio 4:3

For Figure 5-4, the aspect ratio switch was set to the 16:9 position, which is commonly known as a widescreen setting. This is a good setting to use if you plan to view your images on a widescreen TV set. This setting omits pixels at the top and bottom of the image.

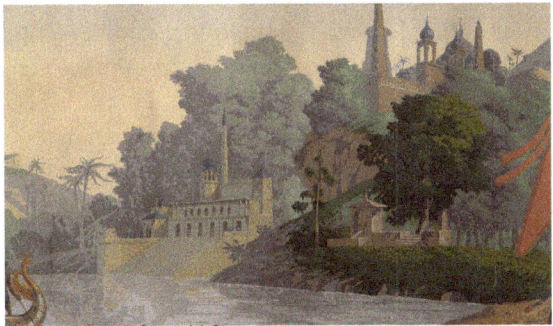

Fig. 5-4: Aspect Ratio 16:9

Finally, the 1:1 setting was used for Figure 5-5. This setting is popular with many photographers because of its symmetry and because the neutrality of the shape leaves open many possibilities for your compositions. With this aspect ratio, the image loses pixels at the left and right.

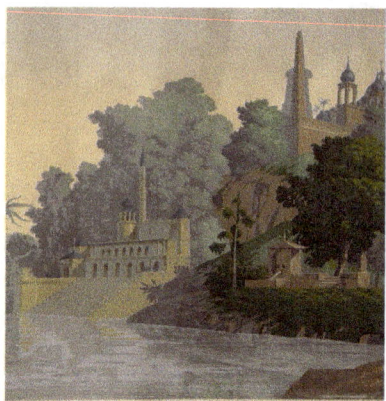

Fig. 5-5: Aspect Ratio 1:1

Aperture Ring

The aperture ring is the large ridged ring that surrounds the lens and is marked with aperture (f-stop) numbers from 1.4 (widest aperture) at the left to 8 (narrowest aperture) at the right. This ring is similar to the rings found on some tradition-al film cameras and their lenses. Its operation could hardly be more simple and intuitive: Just turn the ring until the selected aperture is next to the white selection dot in front of the aspect ratio scale. Besides the aperture values that are designated on the ring, you can turn the ring to intermediate values in 1/3-stop increments, such as f/1.6, f/3.5, and f/7.1. You can feel a gentle click as the ring stops at any of the values that can be selected.

The aperture ring functions only in the shooting modes in which you can select a specific aperture: Aperture Priority mode and Manual exposure mode. In other shooting modes, the ring has no function at all. Also, note that, as was discussed in Chapter 3, when the lens is zoomed in, the maximum ap-erture decreases. So, even if the aperture ring is set to the f/1.4 position, if the lens is then zoomed all the way in, the aperture value will change to f/2.3, and will not agree with the setting on the ring.

Next, I will discuss one very important control that sits by it-self on the left side of the lens barrel. This control, the focus switch, is seen in Figure 5-6.

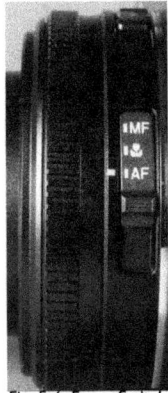

Fig. 5-6: Focus Switch

Focus Switch

The focus switch is located on the left side of the lens barrel as you hold the camera in shooting position. Its three selections are Autofocus, Autofocus Macro, and Manual Focus. I have previously discussed Autofocus and Manual Focus. The third setting, Autofocus Macro, needs some additional discussion. When you move the switch on the lens to select this mode, the focusing system changes to a macro range. So, instead of the normal focusing range of 1.64 feet (50 cm) to infinity at wide angle, the lens can focus down to as close as 0.4 inch (1 cm). It is a good idea to set the flash to Off when using macro mode, because the flash would not be useful at such a close range. I'll discuss macro shooting in more detail in Chapter 9.

Next, I will discuss the several controls on the top of the cam-era, as shown in Figure 5-7.

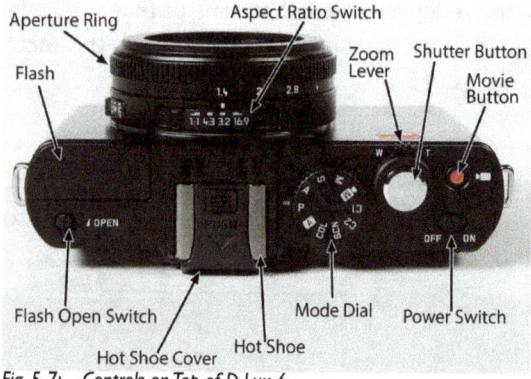

Fig. 5-7: Controls on Top of D-Lux 6

Flash Open Switch

The flash open switch is on top of the camera at the far left. It has only one function—to unlatch the flash mechanism so it can pop up and be available in case conditions call for its use. If you, the user, do not manually pop the flash unit up using this switch, it will not be available, because the camera cannot pop the unit up automatically. One good point about this system is that, if you want to make sure the flash does not fire, such as when you are in a museum or similar location, you can just keep the flash stowed away inside the camera and it cannot fire. Of course, this also means that you must remember to pop up the flash if you believe it may be needed. In some cases, such as with Scene mode settings like Night Portrait, the camera will prompt you to pop up the flash unit if you have not already done so before selecting that setting.

Mode Dial

The mode dial is on top of the camera to the right of the hot shoe when the camera is in shooting position. This dial switches the camera between the various modes of shooting: Snapshot, Program, Aperture Priority, Shutter Priority, Manual, Creative Video, Custom 1, Custom 2, Scene, and Creative Control. If you happen to leave it in a position that does not select one of those settings, the camera will display a message advising you that the dial is not in a proper position.

I have one recommendation about the use of the mode dial, though this is just a matter of personal preference. When I am finished with a shooting session, I like to turn the dial back to the Snapshot or Program position. That way, if I pick up the camera to grab images or video of a quickly-unfolding event, the camera will be in a mode that can take standard, usable shots. If I were to leave the dial set to the Creative Control position, for example, there would be a risk of getting shots that were distorted by special effects or some other setting that made it hard to see the subject clearly.

Shutter Button

This control is quite familiar by now. You press it down half-way to check focus and exposure, and press it the rest of the way to record the image. You can also press it to wake the camera up from Sleep Mode, and you can half-press it to exit to recording mode from a menu screen or from playback mode. The shutter button has a somewhat different use when you are using the Multiple Exposure option on the Recording menu. After the initial exposure is made, you can move to the next one by pressing the shutter button halfway down (or by pressing the Menu/Set button).

Also, you should note that, although you ordinarily record motion pictures by pressing the red Movie button, when the camera is set to Creative Video mode, you have the additional option of using the shutter button to start and stop a movie. In other shooting modes, if you press the shutter button while recording a video, you will take a still picture, but in Creative Video mode, you will start a video recording.

Zoom Lever

The zoom lever is the ring with a ridged handle that encircles the shutter button. The lever's basic function is to change the lens's focal length to various values ranging between wide-angle, by pushing it to the left, toward the W indicator, and tele-photo, by pushing it to the right, toward the T indicator. The lever also has other functions. When you are viewing pictures in playback mode, the lever enlarges the image on the LCD screen when pushed to the right, and selects different numbers and arrangements of thumbnail images to view when pushed to the left. In addition, when you are playing a motion picture taken by the camera, the zoom lever can be used to raise and lower the audio volume. Also, you can use this lever to speed through the menus a full page at a time.

Power Switch

The power switch is on the far right of the camera's top. Slide it right for On and left for Off. When you do either of these actions, the little green status light to the right of the LCD and to the left of the up (ISO) button blinks briefly.

If you leave the camera unattended for a period of time, it au-tomatically powers off, if the Sleep Mode option is turned on through the Economy option on the Setup menu. I'll discuss the Setup menu later, but this option can be set to be off alto-gether so the camera never turns off just to save power, or to turn the camera off after one, two, five, or ten minutes of in-activity. You can cancel the Sleep Mode shutdown by pressing the shutter button halfway.

Movie Button

The last control on the top of the camera to be discussed here is the red Movie button. You press this button once to start re-cording a movie, and press it again to stop the recording. You can use this button no matter what shooting mode the camera is set to. In Chapter 8, I will provide details about how the vari-ous menu and control settings affect the recording of movies.

Next, it's time to discuss the controls found on the back of the camera, as shown in Figure 5-8.

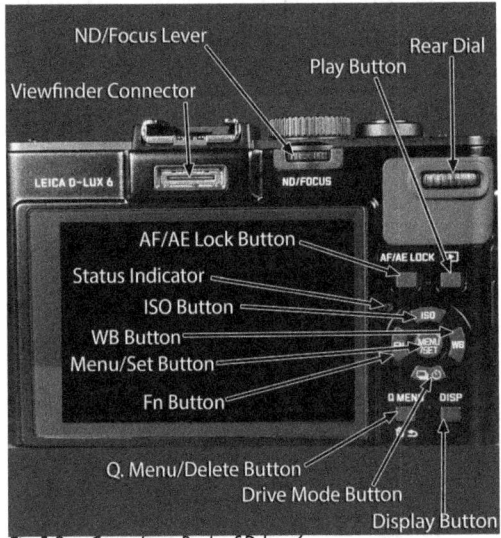

Fig. 5-8:   Controls on Back of D-Lux 6

Play Button

This button is located below the rear dial at the upper right of the camera's back, under a small gray triangle. You press this button to put the camera into playback mode. Press it again to switch back into recording mode. When the camera is in play-back mode, the menu options change; see the discussion of playback mode options in Chapter 6. If you don't like having to remove the lens cap before turning the camera on, you can hold down the Play button while moving the power switch to the On position; this procedure starts the camera in playback mode, and you won't get an error message if the lens cap is still on, as you do when starting the camera in recording mode. Also, you can press the Play button even after seeing the lens cap error message; pressing this button will cancel the message and put the camera into playback mode.

ND/Focus Lever

This small but important control at the top of the back of the D-Lux 6 is used to adjust focus manually, to control the camera's built-in neutral density (ND) filter, and to scroll through or enlarge images during playback.

When you turn on manual focus by moving the focus switch to the MF position, you can then adjust the focus by moving the ND/Focus lever to the left or right. A focus scale will appear at the bottom of the display, as shown in Figure 5-9.

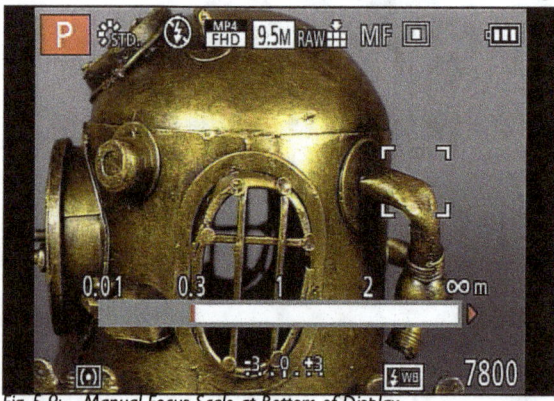

Fig. 5-9:   Manual Focus Scale at Bottom of Display

As noted on the screen, you can make fine adjustments to the focus by pressing the left and right cursor buttons.

To enlarge an area on the screen to help you adjust the focus, while the manual focus scale is visible, press the Menu/Set button, and the red and white MF Area box will appear, as seen in Figure 5-10. You can move that box around using the four direction buttons. When it is located where you want it, press Menu/Set again, and the area under the box will be magnified.

Also, there is one situation in which you can use the ND/Focus lever to adjust focus manually even in autofocus mode. To do this, use the AF/AE Lock button to lock the focus; you can then make adjustments to the focus using this lever.

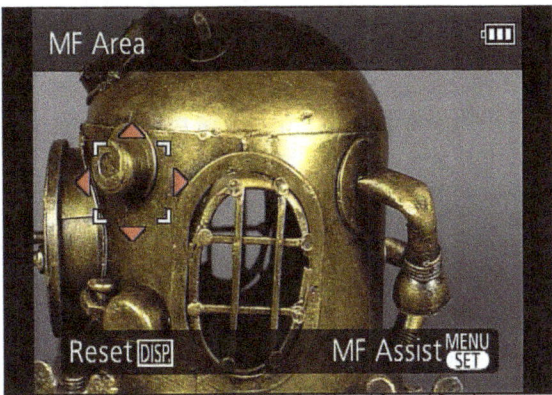

Fig. 5-10: MF Assist Frame Ready to be Moved Around Display

Another function of the lever is to operate the ND filter. This built-in filter blocks a substantial amount of light from reaching the camera's sensor, thereby letting the D-Lux 6 use a longer shutter speed or wider aperture, or both, than it could otherwise. This feature is useful if, for example, you want to photograph a waterfall using a long shutter speed to let the flowing waters blend together over a period of a second or more, but the light is so bright that you cannot use a slow shutter speed without drastically overexposing the image. The ND filter reduces the light by about 3 EV steps, which often will be enough to let you use the long shutter speed you want to use.

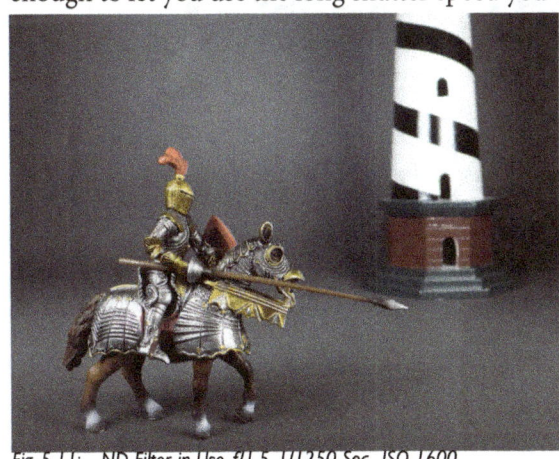

Fig. 5-11: ND Filter in Use, f/1.5, 1/1250 Sec., ISO 1600

213

In other cases, you may want to use a wide aperture. For example, in Figure 5-11, I wanted to use the widest aperture possible to blur the background, but I also wanted to use a high ISO to produce a grainy effect. Without the ND filter, the lighting was so bright that the camera's fastest available shutter speed of 1/2000 second was insufficient to expose the scene properly. With the ND filter activated, though, the camera was able to expose the scene with a shutter speed of 1/1250 second.

To activate the ND filter, press in on the ND/Focus lever, using it as a button rather than as a lever or switch to turn. You will hear a clicking sound as the filter is activated. To deactivate it, press the lever in one more time. An ND icon appears on the screen when the ND filter is in use, as shown in Figure 5-12.

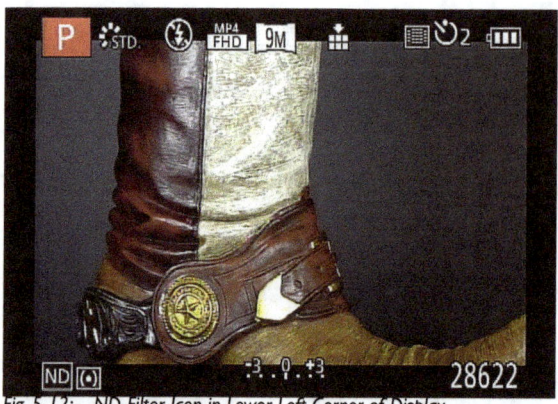

Fig. 5-12:   ND Filter Icon in Lower Left Corner of Display

The ND filter is not available in Snapshot or Scene mode, but it is in Snapshot Plus mode. It may be automatically activated when the Program Diagram option on the Recording menu is set to MAX or MTF, as discussed in Chapter 4.

Finally, in playback mode, you can press the ND/Focus lever to enlarge an image, centered at its focus point. Also, you can press the lever left and right to scroll through your images, as an alternative to using the cursor buttons or the rear dial.

214

Rear Dial

This ridged dial at the upper right of the back of the camera, just below the power switch, has several functions, some of which I have already discussed. One of its most important duties is to adjust shutter speed when the camera is in Shutter Priority or Manual exposure mode. In addition, you can turn the rear dial to navigate through the options on any menu screen and through items on some selection screens, such as the Clock Set setting screen. The dial also moves the selection left and right through the items on the Quick Menu, discussed below. In playback mode, you can turn this dial to navigate through the images and videos stored in memory. The dial also has other functions, described below.

Exposure Compensation with Rear Dial

One important use of the rear dial is to adjust exposure compensation, an option that is available in Program, Aperture Priority, Shutter Priority, Scene, and Creative Video modes. You start by pressing in on this dial, using it as a button, as prompted on the display. (See Figure 5-13 for an example of the prompting display.) When you press in on the dial, the exposure compensation scale at the bottom center of the display, which was white, will turn yellow to indicate that you can now adjust that value using the dial, as shown in Figure 5-14.

Turning the rear dial right and left now will raise and lower the level of exposure compensation, as shown in Figure 5-15. In Shutter Priority mode, if the rear dial is not adjusting exposure compensation, it will adjust shutter speed. In Aperture Priority and Program modes, if the dial is not adjusting exposure compensation, it will not adjust anything. In Manual mode, the rear dial can control only shutter speed; exposure compensation is not available. The situation is similar for the various exposure-mode settings within Creative Video mode, as discussed in Chapter 8.

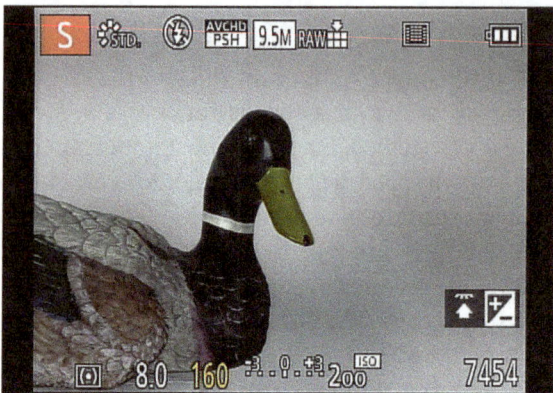

Fig. 5-13: Icons Prompting to Press Rear Dial for Exposure Compensation

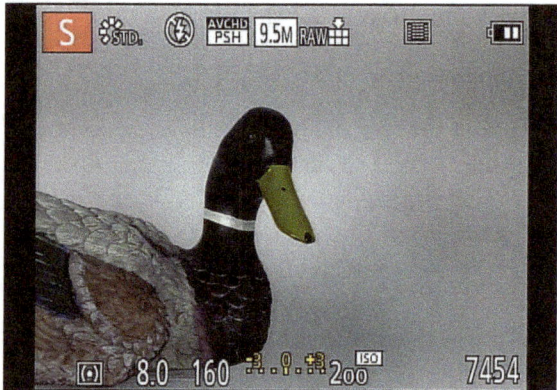

Fig. 5-14: Exposure Compensation Scale Turned Yellow

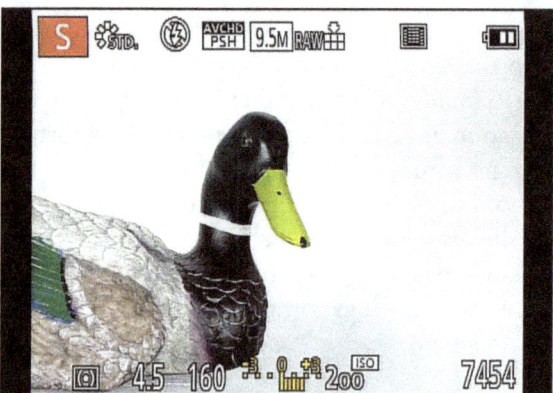

Fig. 5-15: Effect of Positive Exposure Compensation on Image

Program Shift with Rear Dial

Program Shift is a function of the rear dial that may not be obvious. This feature, which is available only when you're taking pictures in Program mode, lets you take the camera's automatic settings for aperture and shutter speed and reset them to a different combination that yields the same exposure. That is, you can "shift" both settings the same amount in opposite directions. For example, if the camera computes the correct settings as f/2.0 at 1/100 second, you can shift those settings to any equivalent pair, such as f/2.2 at 1/80 second, f/2.5 at 1/60 second, f/2.8 at 1/50 second, or f/3.2 at 1/40 second.

Why would you want to do this? You might want a slightly faster shutter speed to stop action better, or a wider aperture to blur the background more, or you might have some other creative reason. Of course, if you really are interested in setting a particular shutter speed or aperture, you probably are better off using Aperture Priority mode or Shutter Priority mode. However, having the Program Shift capability available is a good thing for a situation in which you're taking pictures rapidly using Program mode, and you want a quick way to tweak the settings somewhat.

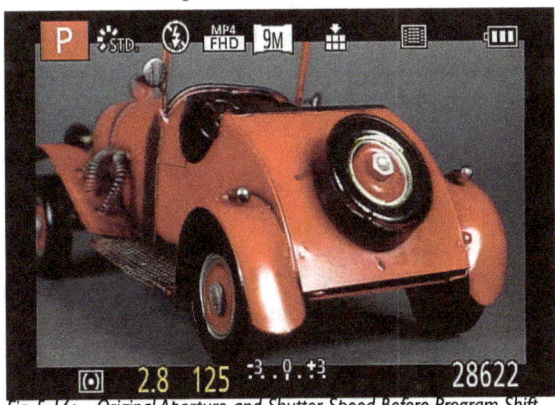

Fig. 5-16: Original Aperture and Shutter Speed Before Program Shift

Here's how to use Program Shift. When you're about ready to take the picture, press the shutter button down halfway to calculate the exposure. You will see the values chosen by the camera for shutter speed and aperture in yellow figures at the bottom left of the LCD screen, as shown in Figure 5-16. Within about ten seconds, turn the rear dial left or right to shift the values.

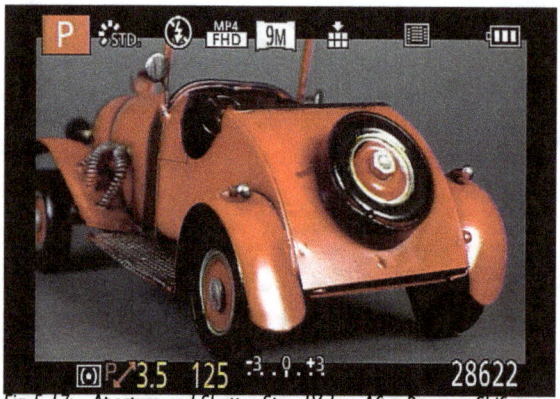

Fig. 5-17: Aperture and Shutter Speed Values After Program Shift

You will see the new values in the same location, and the Program Shift icon (a P next to a diagonal two-headed red arrow) will appear to the left of those values to indicate that Program Shift is in effect, as shown in Figure 5-17.

To cancel Program Shift, use the rear dial to change the settings until the Program Shift icon disappears. Also, turning off the camera will cancel Program Shift.

Quick Menu/Trash Button

Quick Menu Function

The next control to be discussed is the Q.Menu (Quick Menu)/ Trash button, located at the bottom left of the control area on the camera's back, below the array of five buttons. When you press the Q.Menu button while the camera is in recording mode, a mini-version of the camera's menu system opens up at the top of the screen, like a Windows or Macintosh computer program's main menu system, as shown in Figure 5-18.

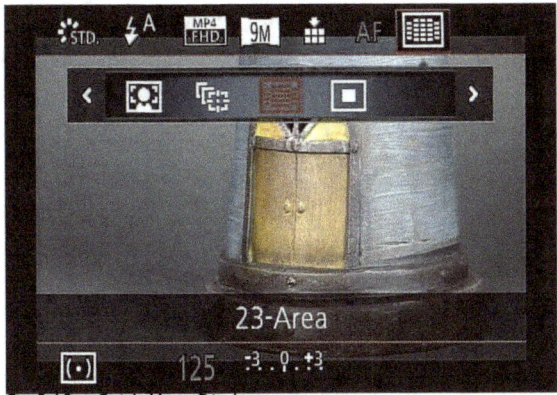

Fig. 5-18: Quick Menu Display

You navigate right and left across the menu options by pressing the cursor buttons or by turning the rear dial until you
find the category you want. You then navigate down one level
to the sub-menu by pressing the down button, and then again
move left and right through the sub-menu with the buttons or
dial. Finally, press the Menu/Set button or press in on the rear
dial to make your choice of the highlighted item. Note that the
selections wrap around in all directions, so if you navigate all
the way to the right of the menu headings and keep going, you
will reach the selections on the left. Similarly, if you navigate
all the way to the bottom of a menu category and keep going,
you will wrap around to the top. To exit from the Quick Menu,
press the Q.Menu button again.

The available menu options vary according to what mode the
camera is in; not surprisingly, the Quick Menu offers the largest variety of choices when the camera is in Program, Aperture
Priority, Shutter Priority, or Manual mode. It offers the smallest variety in Creative Control mode and Snapshot mode,
though it still offers several choices. There are moderate numbers of choices in Scene mode and Creative Video mode.

In my experience, the Quick Menu is a very useful alternative
to the Recording menu. This system is, in fact, quite quick, and
lets you make certain settings very efficiently that otherwise

would require a longer time, in part because you can see all of the available options at the same time on the screen as soon as you press the Q.Menu button.

For example, I find that the Quick Menu is an excellent way to get access to the Quality setting to select RAW or Fine quality for still images. Access to the feature is very fast this way, and, even better, when you later press the Q.Menu button again to go back to change the Quality setting, the Quality option is still highlighted, and it takes just one quick movement of the cursor button and one quick press of the Menu/Set button to change from RAW to Fine or vice-versa.

Cancel/Trash Function

The Q.Menu button also serves as a Cancel or Trash button in some situations. When you are viewing menu screens, you can press this button to cancel out of a selection or other event, such as the use of the Format command on the Setup menu to erase and re-format a memory card, as shown in Figure 5-19.

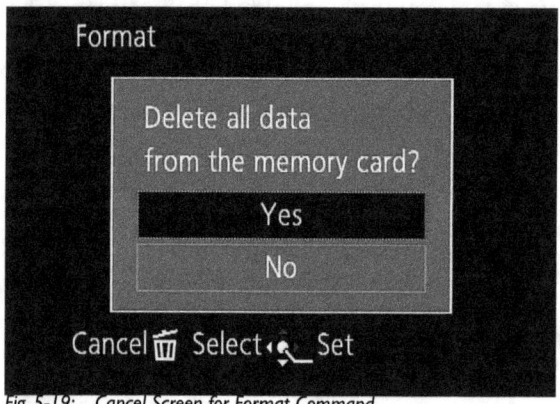

Fig. 5-19:   Cancel Screen for Format Command

When the camera is set to playback mode, the Q.Menu/Trash button takes on the identity of the trash can. Press the button while an image is displayed, and you are presented with several options on the LCD screen: Delete Single Yes/No; Delete

Multi; and Delete All, as shown in Figure 5-20.

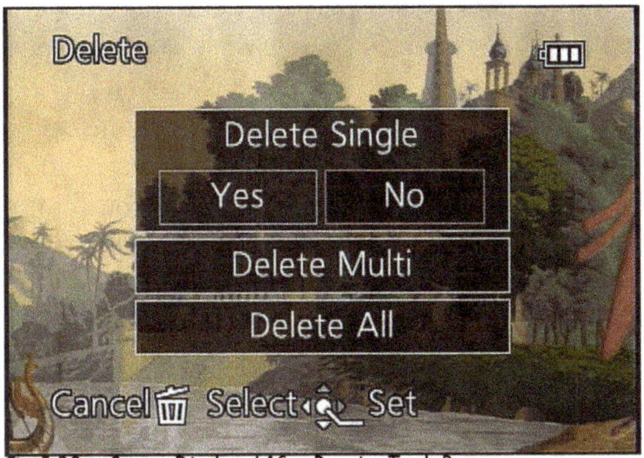

Fig. 5-20: *Screen Displayed After Pressing Trash Button*

Use the cursor buttons to navigate to your choice. If you select Delete Single Yes, then the camera will delete the image that is currently displayed on the screen (unless it is protected with the Protect function, as discussed in Chapter 6).

If you select Delete Multi, then the camera presents you with a display of recent pictures, up to six at a time per screen. You then move through them with the cursor buttons or the rear dial, and press the Display button to mark any picture you want to be included in the group for deletion. You can press Display a second time to unmark a picture for deletion. When you are finished marking pictures for deletion, press Menu/ Set to start the deletion process; the camera will ask you to confirm, and one more press of Menu/Set will carry out the deletion of all of the marked images. Delete All, of course, deletes all images, unless you have marked some as Favorites and choose the option to delete all except Favorites. (Favorites are images you have singled out for special treatment, as discussed in Chapter 6). You can interrupt a deletion process with the Menu/Set button, though some images may have been deleted before you press the button.

AF/AE Lock Button

The AF/AE Lock button is located at the upper left of the camera's back, next to the Play button. As I discussed in Chapter 4, using the Recording menu you can set whether this button locks both autofocus and autoexposure, or just one or the other. Then, you can just press this button to lock that single setting (or both settings). Press it again to unlock. You cannot lock exposure with the button when the camera is set to Manual exposure or Scene mode, and the button does not lock either value in Snapshot mode. When you lock focus using this button, you can then adjust the focus manually using the ND/Focus lever, even though the camera is in autofocus mode.

When you have set the AF Mode to AF Tracking through the Recording menu, the AF/AE Lock button has another function. In this context, when prompted on the screen, as shown in Figure 5-21, you center the tracking focus brackets over your moving subject, and press this button.

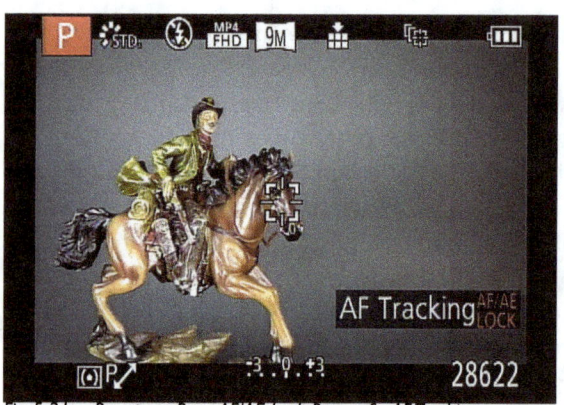

Fig. 5-21:   Prompt to Press AF/AE Lock Button for AF Tracking

At that point, the brackets will turn yellow, and the camera will do its best to keep them centered over the subject as it (or the camera) moves. If you want to cancel the current tracking, just press AF/AE Lock again. The button also serves this purpose when AF Tracking is used in Snapshot mode.

222

Five-Button Array

What I call the five-button array is the set of five buttons on the back of the camera, arranged in a pattern that looks a bit like the leaves of a clover, set on a circular platform. I generally refer to the four outer buttons as cursor buttons, and to the center button as the Menu/Set button.

These buttons act as cursor keys do on a computer keyboard, letting you navigate up and down and left and right through the various menu options. However, the buttons' functions do not stop there. Each of the four directional buttons performs at least one additional function, as shown by its icon or label. I will discuss all of those functions for each button in turn.

Up Button: ISO

The up cursor button doubles as the ISO button. Pressing this button when the D-Lux 6 is in recording mode gives you immediate access to the menu for selecting the ISO sensitivity value for your photography. I discussed the ISO setting in some detail in Chapter 4, in connection with the ISO-related items on the Recording menu—ISO Limit Set, ISO Increments, and Extended ISO. You cannot make the basic ISO setting using the menu system; you have to press the up button and then select a value from the menu that appears, as shown in Figure 5-22.

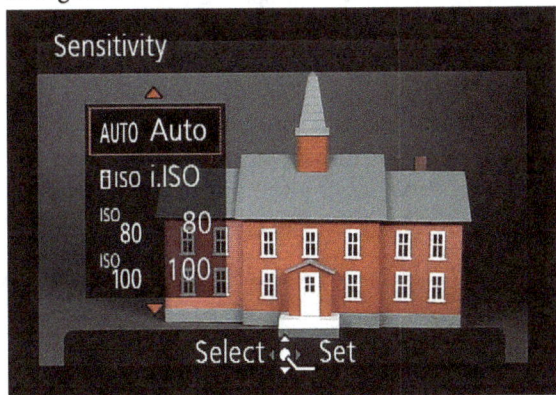

Fig. 5-22:   First Screen of ISO Menu

In Snapshot, Creative Control, and Scene shooting modes, ISO is set to Auto and the ISO button has no effect for controlling this setting. You also cannot adjust ISO when shooting movies, unless the camera is in Creative Video mode.

In Snapshot mode, the up button activates AF Tracking; if you press the button when the camera is ready to shoot in that mode, the camera will display the AF Tracking focus frame; you can cancel by pressing the up button again.

In the playback context, the up button is used to start playing a motion picture when the initial frame of the motion picture is displayed on the screen. That button also serves as a play/pause button once the movie has started playing. The button also starts playback for panoramas, time-lapse shots, and high-speed burst sequences. When a normal still image is displayed on the screen, if you press the up button, the camera will present you with options for using its Auto Retouch or Creative Retouch procedure to make adjustments to the image's processing. I will discuss that process in Chapter 6.

Right Button: White Balance

The right button is assigned the important duty of calling up the menu for selecting the camera's setting for white balance. I will provide some background about this concept before discussing the mechanics of making the setting.

One issue that arises in all photography is that film, or a digital camera's sensor, reacts differently to colors than the human eye does. When you or I see a scene in daylight or indoors under various types of artificial lighting, we generally do not notice a difference in the hues of the things we see depending on the light source. However, the camera's film or sensor does not have this auto-correcting ability. The camera "sees" colors differently depending on the "color temperature" of the light that illuminates the object or scene in question. The color temperature of light is a numerical value that is expressed in a unit known as kelvins (K). A light source with a lower kelvin rating produces a "warmer" or more reddish light. A light source with a higher kelvin rating produces a "cooler" or more bluish light. For example, candlelight is rated at about 1,800 K; indoor tungsten light (ordinary light bulb) is rated at about 3,000 K; outdoor sunlight and electronic flash are rated at about 5,500 K; and outdoor shade is rated at about 7,000 K.

What does this mean in practice? If you are using a film camera, you may need a colored filter in front of the lens to "correct" for the color temperature of the light source. Any given color film is rated to expose colors correctly at a particular color temperature (or, to put it another way, with a particular light source). So if you are using color film rated for daylight use, you can use it outdoors without a filter. But if you happen to be using that film indoors, you will need a color filter to correct the color temperature; otherwise, the resulting picture will look excessively reddish because of the imbalance between the film and the color temperature of the light source.

With a modern digital camera, you do not need to worry about filters, because the camera can adjust its electronic circuitry to correct the "white balance," which is the term used in the context of digital photography for balancing color temperature.

The D-Lux 6, like many digital cameras, has a setting for Auto White Balance, which lets the camera choose the proper color correction to account for any given light source. You get access to this setting by pressing the right button, which calls up the White Balance menu screen, shown in Figure 5-23. You then have the following choices for the White Balance setting, most of them represented by icons: Auto White Balance (AWB); Daylight; Cloudy; Shade; Flash; Incandescent; White Set 1; White Set 2; and Color Temperature. (Only the first four options are shown in Figure 5-23; you need to scroll down to reach the others.)

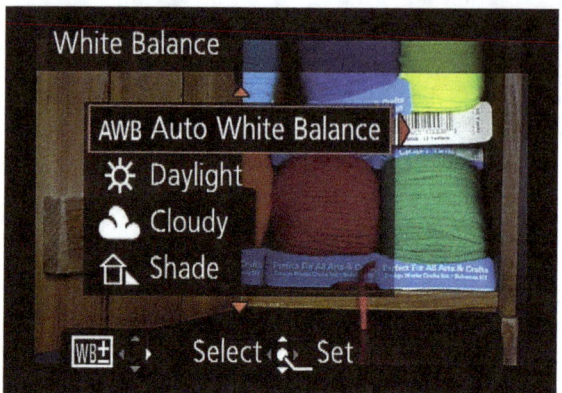

Fig. 5-23:   First Screen of White Balance Settings

Most of the settings are self-explanatory. You may want to experiment, though, and see if the specifically named settings (Daylight, Shade, Incandescent, etc.) produce the results you want. If not, you may be better off setting the white balance manually. That is, you can use either the White Set 1 or White Set 2 option, either of which lets you measure the white balance based on the light that is actually illuminating your subject, and save a custom setting to that slot in the camera's memory. Then, you can use that custom setting whenever you are faced with the same lighting situation in the future.

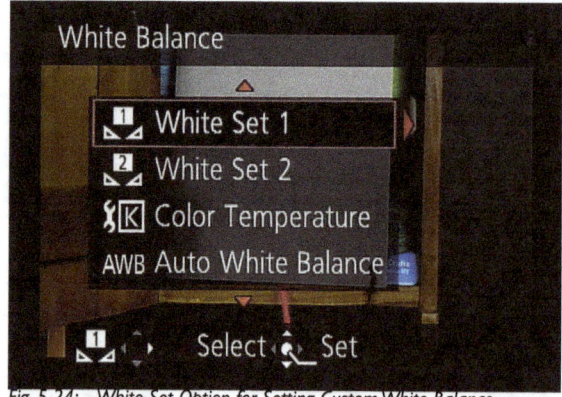

Fig. 5-24:   White Set Option for Setting Custom White Balance

To set white balance manually, press the right button to pop up the White Balance menu and scroll to select White Set 1 or

White Set 2, as shown in Figure 5-24.

Then press the right button, and a yellow rectangle will appear in the middle of the display, as shown in Figure 5-25.

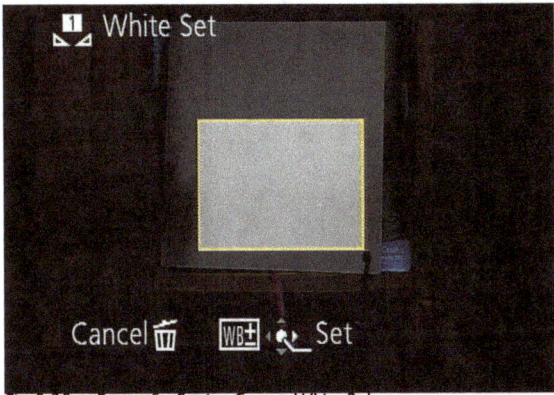

Fig. 5-25: Frame for Setting Custom White Balance

Aim the camera at a sheet of white or gray paper or other flat surface under the light source you will be using, and fill the rectangle with the image of that surface. Then press the Menu/Set button (not the shutter button) to lock in that white balance setting. Now, until you change that setting, whenever you select that preset value (White Set 1 or White Set 2, as the case may be), it will be set for the white balance you have just set. This system can be very useful if you often use a particular light source, and want to have the camera set to the appropriate white balance for that source.

To set the color temperature directly by number, choose the Color Temperature option from the White Balance menu, as shown in Figure 5-26. Press the right cursor button to pop up a screen with a color temperature value displayed, as shown in Figure 5-27. You then can press the up and down buttons or turn the rear dial to adjust that value, anywhere from 2500K up to 10000K in increments of 100K.

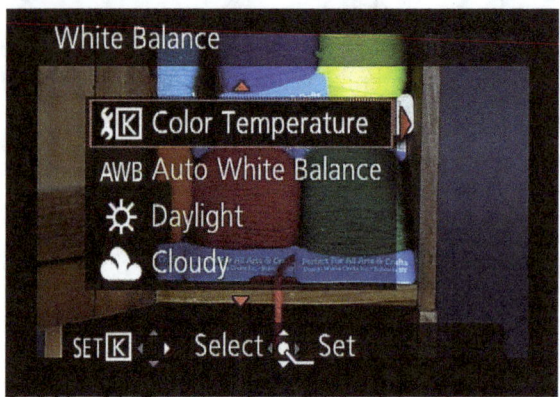

Fig. 5-26:   Color Temperature Option for White Balance Setting

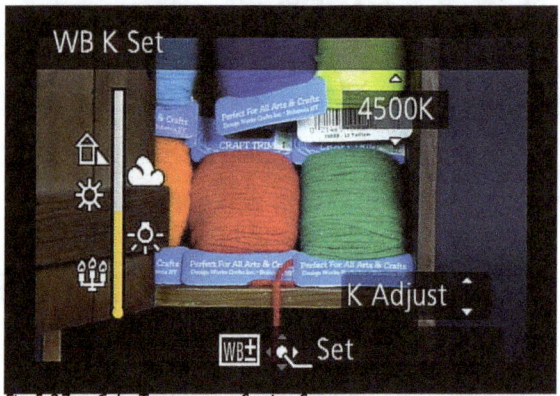

Fig. 5-27:   Color Temperature Setting Screen

One way to determine the appropriate numerical K value for a particular light source is to use a color temperature meter like the Sekonic Prodigi meter shown in Figure 5-28.

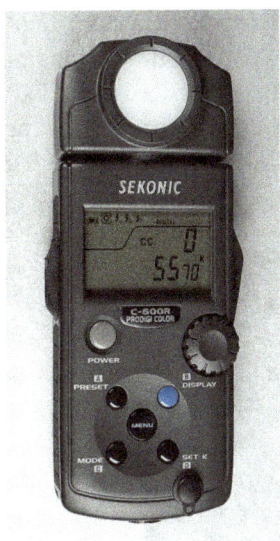

Fig. 5-28: Sekonic Prodigi

That meter works well, and I find it quite convenient to use it when I'm striving for accuracy in my white balance settings. This device is fairly expensive, though, and you may not want to use that option. In that case, you can still use the Color Temperature option, but you will have to do some guesswork or use your own sense of color. For example, if you are shooting under lighting that is largely from incandescent bulbs, you can use the value of 3,000 K as a starting point, because, as noted earlier in this discussion, that is an approximate value for the color temperature of that light source. Then you can try setting the color temperature figure higher or lower, and watch the camera's display to see how natural the colors look. As you lower the color temperature, the image will become more "cool" or bluish; as you raise it, the image will appear more "warm" or reddish. Once you have found the best setting, leave it in place and take your shots.

Once you have selected a White Balance setting, either using one of the preset values such as Daylight, Incandescent, or

229

Cloudy, or using a custom-measured setting or a color temperature value, you still have the option of fine-tuning the setting. To do so, after you have selected your desired white balance setting, before pressing the Menu/Set button, press the right button one more time, and you will be presented with a screen for fine adjustments, as shown in Figure 5-29.

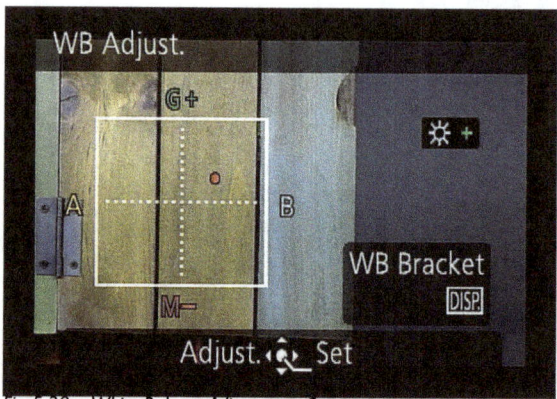

Fig. 5-29:   White Balance Adjustments Screen

You will see a box with a pair of axes that intersect at a zero point, marked by a red dot. The four ends of the axes are labeled G, B, M, and A, for Green, Blue, Magenta, and Amber.

You can now use all four directional buttons to move the red dot away from the center along any of the axes, to adjust these four values until you have the color balance exactly how you want it. The camera will remember this value whenever you select the white balance setting that you fine-tuned, so be sure to remove the adjustment by setting it back to the zero point when it is no longer needed. When you have altered the setting using this screen, the white balance icon on the camera's display changes color and/or includes a colored plus or minus sign to indicate what changes you have made along the color axes. For example, Figure 5-30 shows the icon, in the bottom right corner of the screen, after the White Balance setting of Daylight was adjusted toward the Green side of the axes.

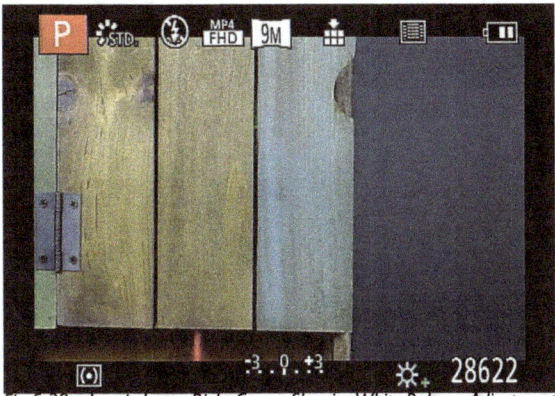

Fig. 5-30: Icon in Lower Right Corner Showing White Balance Adjustment

One more note: If you're shooting in RAW quality, you don't have to worry about white balance so much, because, once you import the RAW file into your software, you can change the white balance however you want. This is one of the marvels of RAW. If you had the camera's white balance setting at Incandescent while shooting under a bright sun, you can just change the white balance setting to Daylight in the RAW software, and the software will correct the image to look as if it had been shot with the white balance set to Daylight. No one need ever know about the error of your shooting.

Before I discuss white balance bracketing, I am going to include a chart (Figure 5-31) that shows how the white balance settings affect the images taken by the D-Lux 6.

Leica D-Lux 6 White Balance Chart

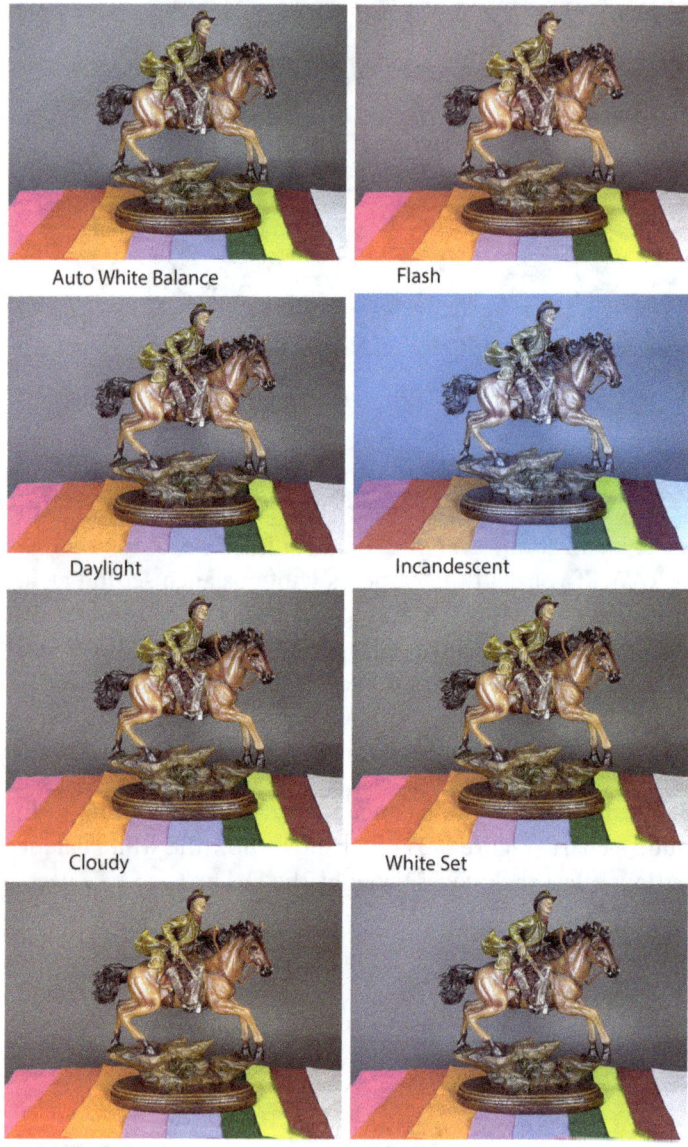

Fig. 5-31:   *White Balance Chart for Leica D-Lux 6 Camera*

The images in the chart were taken under artificial light balanced for daylight with the camera set for each available white balance setting, as indicated on the chart. As you can see, as might be expected, the best results were obtained with the Auto White Balance, Daylight, Color Temperature, and White Set settings. The only setting that is clearly far from accurate is the Incandescent setting. Note that the D-Lux 6 does not offer any settings for fluorescent lights. You may need to use the White Set or Color Temperature options when faced with that type of illumination.

There is still one more aspect of white balance to be discussed—white balance bracketing. Later in this chapter, I'll discuss exposure bracketing, also known as Auto Bracket, a feature with which the D-Lux 6 automatically takes three pictures at varying exposures so you can have three options to choose from. You can do something similar with white balance—set the camera to take three images at once with different white balances, giving you a better chance of having one image with a perfect color balance. I'm discussing this option here rather than in the section on Auto Bracket, because this option is accessed from the white balance setting screen.

Here is how to set up white balance bracketing. After pressing the right (WB) button to select white balance, select a main setting, such as Daylight, Incandescent, White Set 1, or any other choice. Then press the right button to access the fine adjustment screen, which I discussed above. Next, press the Display button to activate white balance bracketing, as prompted by the camera. See Figure 5-32 for an example of the prompting message.

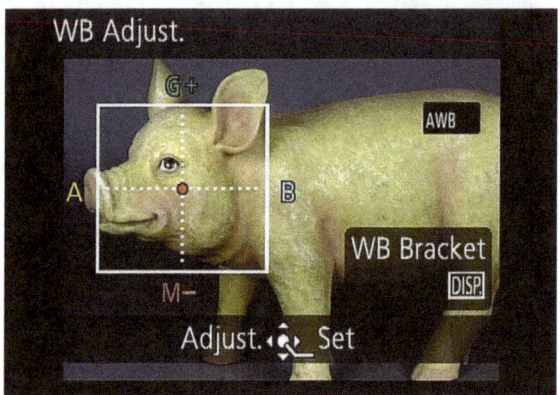

Fig. 5-32: Screen with Prompt to Press Display Button for WB Bracket

Then, you need to decide on which axis to set the bracketing: the Amber-Blue axis, or the Magenta-Green axis. The bracketing will not function unless you select one of those axes and then use the right button to set a bracket width on the Amber-Blue axis, or the up button to set a bracket width on the Magenta-Green axis. Press one of those buttons one, two, or three times, and you will see red dots appear on the chosen axis. Those dots indicate the differences among the three shots that the camera will take. Note that you can also set an adjustment to the white balance setting using the adjustment screen; if you do that, the white balance bracketing will take the adjustment into account and bracket the exposures with the adjustment factored in.

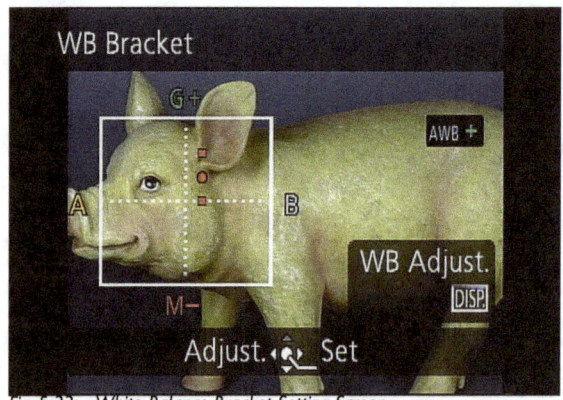

Fig. 5-33: White Balance Bracket Setting Screen

For example, Figure 5-33 shows how white balance bracketing is set up to take three shots with the greatest possible differences along the Magenta-Green axis, with an adjustment made toward the Blue side of the Amber-Blue axis. Once the dots are set up as shown in that figure, press the Menu/Set button, and the camera will return to the live view.

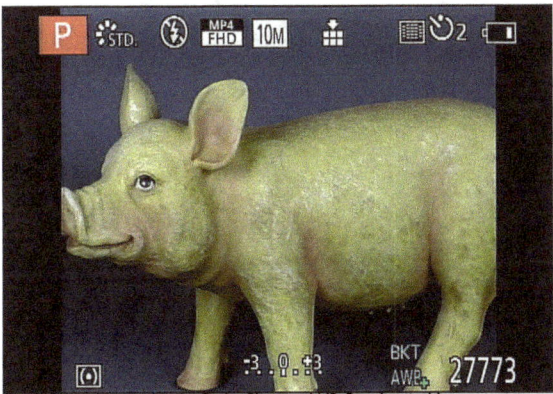

Fig. 5-34:   Icon in Lower Right Showing WB Bracket in Use

As shown in Figure 5-34, the display will then show the BKT icon just above the icon for the white balance setting, in the lower right corner of the display. Now, when you press the shutter button, the camera will take three pictures with three different white balance adjustments, from normal to more green, with an overall adjustment toward blue. You will only hear the sound of the shutter once, though; the camera alters the white balance settings electronically.

This function does not work in Snapshot, Creative Control, or Creative Video mode. It also does not work with RAW images, although it may seem as if it does. When you go through the steps of setting White Balance Bracket when Quality is set to RAW, the camera will complete the process, and will even place the icon for this function on the screen. However, it will place an X next to the icon, indicating that you have turned on this option, but it will not work, as shown in Figure 5-35.

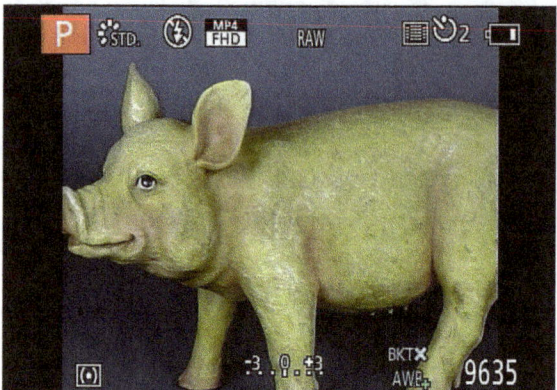

Fig. 5-35:   White Balance Bracket Icon with X Because of RAW Setting

The right button also has some miscellaneous functions. For example, in Snapshot Plus mode, you can press this button instead of pressing the rear dial, to get access to the adjustment screen for Brightness, Background Defocusing, and Color. When playing movies and slide shows, the right button acts as a navigation control to move through the images.

Left Button: Function (Fn)

The left button in this group of controls bears the label "Fn." To me, this is the "Function" button, though some people prefer to call it the Fn button without drawing conclusions about its meaning. In any event, this button provides a very useful service—it gives you, the photographer, the option of selecting any one of a number of camera settings with one press of this button, without having to go through the menu system.

The default (factory) setting for the Function button is to give you quick access to the Photo Style settings, but there are several other choices available. You can set the button to give you access to any one of several other options from the Recording menu or the Setup menu: Quality; Metering Mode; AF Mode; Focus Area Set; 1 Shot AF; i.Dynamic; Level Gauge; Guide Line; Video Recording Area; Remaining Display; Flash; Flash Adjustment; or Aspect Bracket. Just go into the Setup Menu, select Fn Button Set, and then make your choice from the list that appears. You cannot set the Function button's action while the camera is in Snapshot mode.

Several of the items that can be assigned to the Function button, namely, Photo Style, Quality, Metering Mode, AF Mode, i.Dynamic, Guide Line, Video Recording Area, Remaining Display, Flash, Flash Adjustment, and Aspect Bracket, are self-explanatory; these are items that also can be set from the Recording or Setup menu, or, in the case of Aspect Bracket, from the continuous-shooting menu, which is ordinarily reached by pressing the down button, as discussed below. Assigning one of these items to the Function button is just a shortcut that lets you avoid having to dig into the menu system.

However, three items in the list are ones that cannot readily be set in any other way than by being assigned to the Function button. I will discuss those here.

First, the Focus Area Set option, whose menu option is shown in Figure 5-36, gives you a way to move the autofocus frame around the screen when the AF Mode is set to 1-Area Focus.

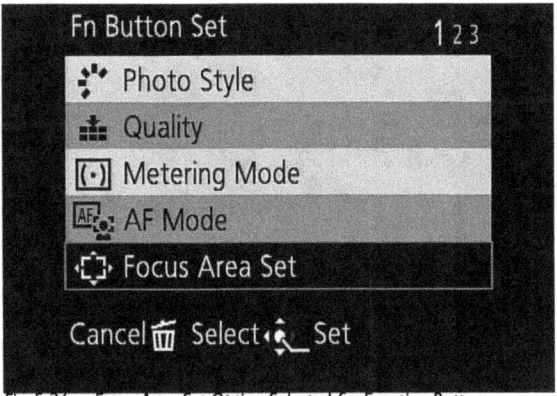

Fig. 5-36: Focus Area Set Option Selected for Function Button

As I discussed in Chapter 4, when you select 1-Area Focus for AF Mode from the Recording menu, you can press the right button to go to a further screen, where you can move the frame around using the four cursor buttons and change its size using the rear dial. However, once that setting has been made and the camera is back in recording mode, there is no easy way to get back to the screen for adjusting the location and size of the focus frame. You would have to go back to the Recording menu and work through the selection screens again to get to the adjustment screen. If you choose the Focus Area Set option, then you can just press the Function button whenever the camera is in recording mode, and you can then immediately adjust the location and size of the focus frame.

I find this to be one of the most useful settings for the Function button, because it is not that much use having a focus frame that is adjustable if you have to dig through the menu system every time you want to change its location or size.

Second, the 1 Shot AF option, shown in Figure 5-37, also is a very useful one.

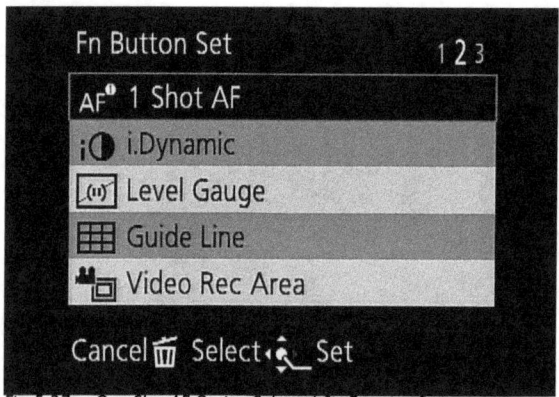

Fig. 5-37: One Shot AF Option Selected for Function Button

If you assign this feature to the Function button, then, when the camera is in manual focus mode, you can press the button at any time to force the camera to use its autofocus mechanism. You then are free to continue focusing manually. So, this option gives you the best of both worlds in a way, because you can see how well the camera can focus on your subject automatically, but continue to tweak the focusing manually.

Third, the Level Gauge option, shown in Figure 5-38, is not as important a feature as the two discussed previously, because you also can call up the level gauge using the Display button.

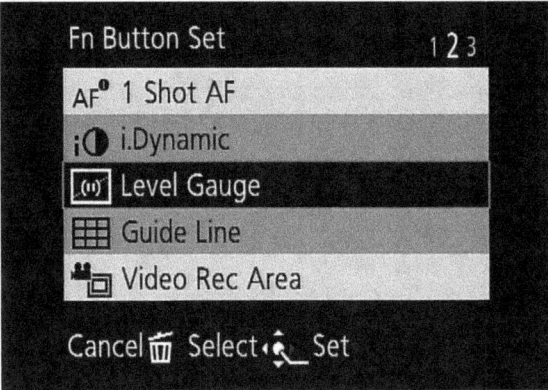

Fig. 5-38: Level Gauge Option Selected for Function Button

However, when you do that, you have to switch to a different display screen, whereas, if you use the Function button setting, you can just press the Function button whenever you want to turn the level display on (or off). So, if you find yourself using the level often but do not want to have to switch display screens to call it up, you might find that this setting for the Function button is a useful one for you.

The left button also has various miscellaneous duties. For example, in the One Point Color setting of Creative Control mode, you press this button to select the single color that will be retained in your image. In playback mode, this button acts as a navigation control to move through the images when you are playing movies or slide shows.

Down Button: Continuous Shooting/Self-Timer

The last of the cursor buttons to be discussed, the down button, provides access to the camera's continuous shooting and self-timer options. When the camera is set to a shooting mode in which burst shooting is available, this feature provides you with an impressive array of options. Before describing them, I will provide a brief introduction to the concept of burst, or continuous shooting.

Burst Shooting

With film cameras, burst shooting involves the use of a special motor to advance the film rapidly, and often the use of an oversized cassette to hold a large quantity of film. This sort of equipment is bulky and expensive, and, of course, shooting and developing large numbers of exposures is itself quite costly. With digital cameras like the Leica D-Lux 6, expense is no longer a factor. Continuous shooting is literally available at your fingertips whenever you want to take advantage of it.

The usefulness of rapid bursts of exposures is clearer in some contexts than in others. For example, when you're shooting sports, it's worthwhile to fire off a swift sequence of shots in order to catch the perfect instant when a baseball player tags a runner heading for home plate, or to catch a soccer ball as it bounces off a player's head towards the goal. But continuous shooting also can be helpful in more ordinary shooting, such as pictures of children at play. You have a better chance of capturing a fleeting smile or cute gesture if you keep the exposures rolling. And, even when your subject is not moving, it can be advantageous to take multiple shots. For example, when you're taking a portrait, there may be subtle changes in the subject's expression, or in the way sunlight falls on a cheek. Taking a series of shots gives you some insurance against coming away from the photo session with no winning images.

One great feature of the D-Lux 6 camera is that the burst-shooting options are available in every shooting mode for still images, including Snapshot, Creative Control, and Scene, although there are a few specific settings of Creative Control mode and Scene mode with which burst shooting cannot be used. (For all of the restrictions on burst shooting, see page 120 of the Leica user's guide.)

Now I will discuss how to select the various options for burst shooting and the differences in their features. For purposes of this discussion, I will assume the camera is set to Program mode and Quality is set to Fine. (You can shoot RAW quality images with burst options, but the speed and quantity of the shots are likely to be more limited than with Fine quality.)

To get to the burst options, press the down button, and the camera will display the screen shown in Figure 5-39.

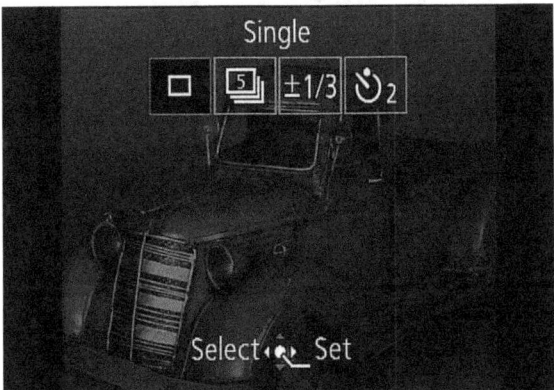

Fig. 5-39: *Main Selections for Continuous Shooting and Self-timer*

There are four options in the upper row of choices: A single frame, representing single shooting; a stack of frames, representing burst shooting; a plus-or-minus sign with a number from 1/3 to 3, representing bracketing options; and a timer dial with the number 2 or 10, representing the self-timer. Use the left and right buttons or the rear dial to move through this group of four icons, and select the one you want.

If you choose single shooting, just highlight the icon on the left of the top row and press the Menu/Set button or half-press the shutter button to exit back to the shooting screen. Selecting single shooting is equivalent to turning off all burst shooting, bracketing, and self-timer options. The camera will record a single image whenever you press the shutter button.

If you move the highlight to the second block from the left, with the stack of frames, you will see a broad range of icons appear on the row below the four icons, with the label of Burst Shooting at the top of the screen, as shown in Figure 5-40.

241

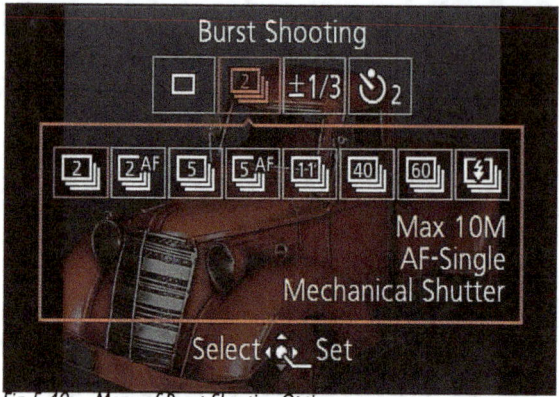

Fig. 5-40:   Menu of Burst Shooting Options

Now you need to move the red highlight frame into the lower row in order to select one of the eight options that appear. (There will be fewer options with some shooting settings, such as Snapshot mode.) Here again, as with the top row of icons, move the highlight to the option you want to select, then press Menu/Set or just half-press the shutter button to move back to the shooting screen with that option selected. You will then see its icon on the screen, in the upper right corner. For example, Figure 5-41 shows the icon for the third option from the left, which provides burst shooting at a rate of 5 frames per second.

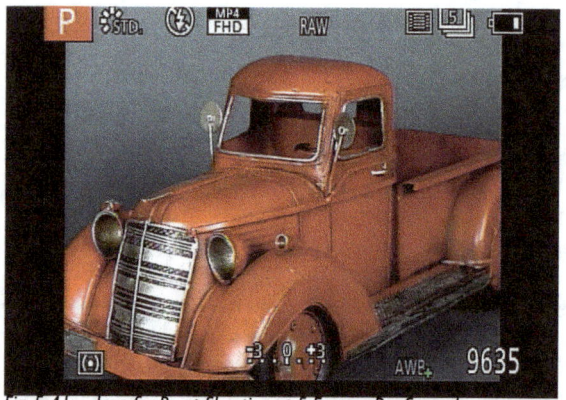

Fig. 5-41:   Icon for Burst Shooting at 5 Frames Per Second

Following are details about each of the eight burst-shooting options that are available. For each of these settings, after it is selected, just hold down the shutter button for as long as you want to keep taking pictures, or until the continuous shooting stops of its own accord. I will assume you have the camera's autofocus switch set to autofocus rather than manual focus in each case.

The first option on the left, whose icon is labeled with the number 2, provides continuous shooting at a rate of about 2 frames per second. The focus will be fixed with the focus setting for the first image in the stream of shots, but exposure and white balance will be adjusted as needed for subsequent images. The camera can take a maximum of 100 images in a steady sequence with this setting. However, as noted above, if you are using RAW quality, the camera will not take as many images; in my tests, it could take only about 17 RAW images before stopping or slowing down dramatically. Other factors will also affect the speed of shooting. For example, if the lighting is dim, the camera may have to use a slow shutter speed, which will require the shooting rate to be reduced.

The next option, whose icon has the number 2 and the letters AF, is similar to the previous one, except that the camera will adjust autofocus as well as exposure and white balance.

The third option, with the number 5 on the stack-of-frames icon, is similar to the previous ones, except that the shooting rate speeds up to about 5 frames per second; the focus is fixed to the setting of the first shot in the series, but exposure and white balance are adjusted as needed. The maximum number of shots is 100, in ideal conditions. In my tests, this setting could handle only about 13 shots before slowing down drastically. With Quality set to Fine, the camera managed a few more shots, up to about 17, before slowing its pace considerably. Even with Quality set to Standard and image size reduced to 5 MP, the D-Lux 6 slowed down its shooting rate after about 20 shots. I was using a fast SDHC card, rated at 45 MB/second.

So, at least in my experience, the 5 frames-per-second shooting rate is not a practical reality for a long series of images. You can capture maybe 15 or 20 shots at that rate, which is not bad, but don't count on taking a string of 100 images at that speed.

The fourth option's icon has the number 5 with the AF designation, meaning the camera will adjust autofocus as well as exposure and white balance for each shot. When I tested this setting, I found, not surprisingly, that it was no better in terms of speed than the previous setting.

The fifth icon, with the number 11, offers a maximum of 12 shots in a sequence, at 11 frames per second, but with no adjustments of focus, exposure, or white balance after the first shot. With this setting, which does not require the camera to make any adjustments between shots, the camera lived up to expectations, and managed to fire off an impressive-sounding barrage of shots in rapid fire, even using RAW quality.

The sixth icon, marked with the number 40, is similar to the previous one, except that the camera promises 40 shots in a single burst of one second, again with no adjustments to the images. In this case, the camera uses its electronic shutter, rather than the mechanical shutter it uses for the settings described above. The camera will not shoot with RAW quality using this setting; if RAW is selected, the camera will automatically reset it to Fine. In addition, the maximum image size with this setting is 5 MP. When I tested this setting, it performed as specified, shooting 40 images in about one second.

There is one other aspect of this setting that you need to be aware of. When you go to view the images, the camera places them all into a single, collapsed frame for viewing purposes. As shown in Figure 5-42, the camera displays only the first image in the series, with an icon in the lower right corner saying to press the down button to "open up" the series so that you can view the individual images, and an icon in the lower left corner saying to press the up button for "burst play."

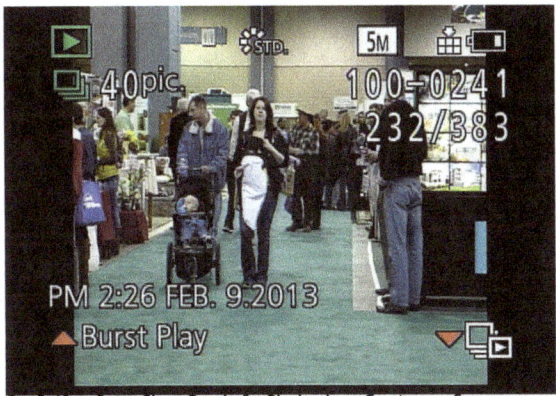

Fig. 5-42:   Burst Shots Ready for Playback as Continuous Sequence

If you press the up button, the camera will play back all of the images rapidly in a continuous sequence, similar to playing a movie. If, instead, you press the down button, the icons on the screen will change, as shown in Figure 5-43, indicating that you can now use the ordinary methods (rear dial or cursor buttons) to browse through the entire series of images. To collapse the series back into a group, press the down button again.

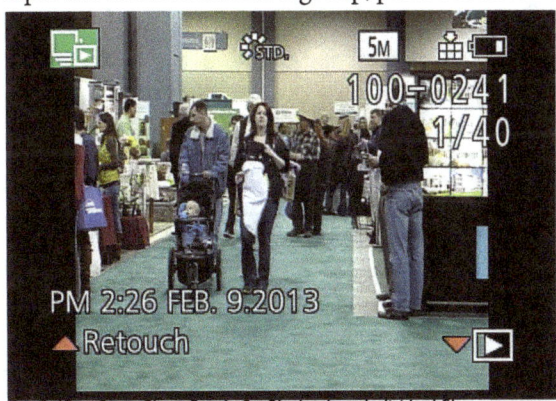

Fig. 5-43:   Burst Shots Ready for Playback as Individual Shots

The seventh icon is similar to the last one discussed, but with the number 60 rather than 40, meaning the camera will take 60 images in about one second, with no settings adjusted for the images after the first one. The Quality will be JPEG, and the image size will be no larger than 2.5 MP. When I tested this setting, the camera buzzed into action, with a sound like a constant whirring rather than a series of clicks, and it took exactly 60 images, as promised. With this setting, like the previous one, you can "open up" the series of images for playback by pressing the down button, or you can use "burst play."

The eighth and final icon represents the D-Lux 6's capability for taking a burst of images while firing its built-in flash unit. With this setting, the Quality is limited to Fine, the image size is limited to 3 MP, and the camera will not adjust exposure, focus, or white balance after the first image. The string of images is limited to a total of 5, taken at a rate of roughly one per second. It is fairly remarkable that the camera can take any burst of images using flash; many cameras disable their burst shooting when the flash is activated. This feature can be quite useful when an occasion arises at a party or elsewhere to take a short burst of frames while firing the flash.

To sum up the situation with burst shooting, which of the eight settings you choose depends a great deal on what situation you are faced with. You need to decide what are the most important factors for any given shooting session—such as speed, quality, focus, and image size. For example, if you are taking portraits of a family member and you want to capture a range of expressions, you might want to use the first setting, which lets you shoot with RAW quality and the largest image size, at a moderate rate of speed. It shouldn't matter that the focus will not be adjusted, because the subject will be at a constant distance. On the other hand, if you are analyzing a golf swing or some other quick action, you could use the 40 or 60 setting, which gives you a very rapid burst of shots at a lower quality; with this situation, the emphasis likely is on speed rather than on the quality of the images.

Note that, after shooting with any of the burst options, you are likely to see for at least a few seconds the red icon indicating that the camera is writing images to the memory card; while that icon is displayed, you should not try to take any more pictures, and you should not open the battery compartment cover or otherwise interfere with the camera's operation.

Auto Bracket

Next, I will discuss the Auto Bracket option. This feature lets you take three shots with one press of the shutter button at three different exposures, thereby giving you an added chance of getting a good, usable image. If you're shooting with RAW quality, exposure is not so much of an issue, because you can adjust it later with your software, but it's always a good idea to start with an exposure that's as accurate as possible.

Also, you can use this feature to take three differently exposed shots that you can merge into a single High Dynamic Range (HDR) image, in which the three images combine to cover a wider range of lights and darks than any single image could. This merging can be accomplished using software such as Photoshop (use the command File-Automate-Merge to HDR) or a more specialized program such as PhotoAcute or Photomatix. For HDR shooting, I suggest you set the interval between the exposures to the full range available. Of course, you should use a tripod if possible, so all three images will include the same area of the subject and can be easily merged in the software.

You get access to the Auto Bracket option through the third icon from the left on the top row of the burst menu, as shown in Figure 5-44. After you highlight that icon, press the down button to move the highlight down to the bracketing scale, shown in Figure 5-45, which extends from -3 EV (exposure value) to +3 EV. Then use the left and right buttons or turn the rear dial to set up the range of the three bracketing exposures that will be taken. You spread the interval further apart with the right button, and narrow it with the left button. The first picture taken is always at the metered level, or 0 change in EV; the second is at the lower EV (darker), and the third is at the higher EV (brighter).

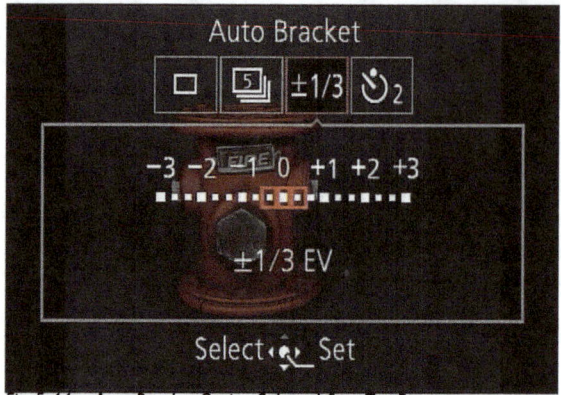

Fig. 5-44: Auto Bracket Option Selected from Top Row

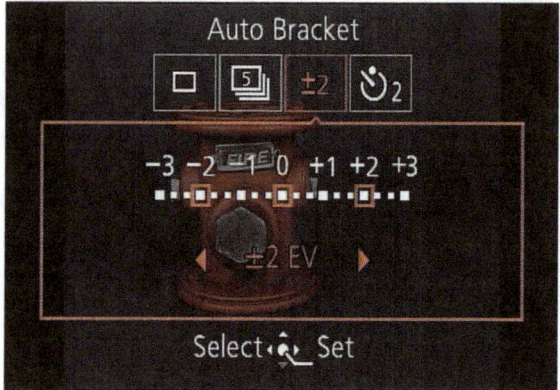

Fig. 5-45: Auto Bracket Setting Screen

The Auto Bracket procedure cannot be used with flash (either built-in or external); the flash will be forced off and cannot be activated. Auto Bracket is not available with Snapshot mode or when shooting movies, nor with several of the Scene mode and Creative Control mode categories. (Details are at page 126 of the Leica user's guide.) Auto Bracket is canceled when the camera is turned off.

Self-timer

The final icon on the main row of the burst options represents the self-timer, as shown in Figure 5-46.

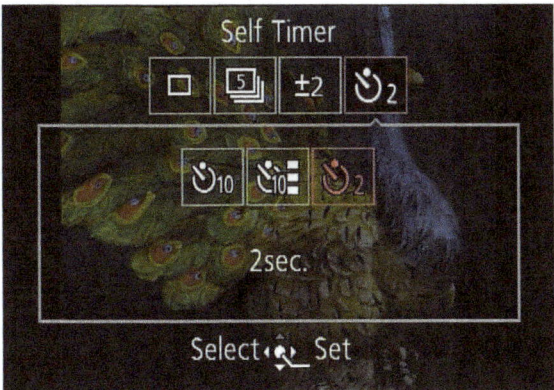

Fig. 5-46: Self-timer Selected from Top Row

When you activate the self-timer, the camera delays for the specified number of seconds (10 or 2) after you press the shutter button before taking a picture. The 10-second setting is of great use when you need to place the camera on a tripod and press the shutter button, and then run around to join a group of people the camera is aimed at. The 2-second setting is very helpful when you need to avoid jiggling the camera by pressing the shutter button as the exposure is taken. This is the case when taking extreme close-ups or other shots in which focus is very sensitive.

The self-timer is very easy to use on the D-Lux 6. Just press the down cursor button, move the highlight to the self-timer icon, and press the down button one more time to move to the bottom row of icons, which holds the three options for setting the self timer, as shown in Figure 5-47. These three selections are, from left to right, 10-second self timer; 10-second self-timer with 3 images taken; and 2-second self-timer. (In Snapshot mode, there are only the basic 10-second and 2-second choices; there is no option for multiple shots.) Select the setting you want with the left and right buttons or by turning the rear dial. Note: If you set the self-timer to take 3 shots, you can turn on the flash, and the flash will fire for each of the 3 shots.

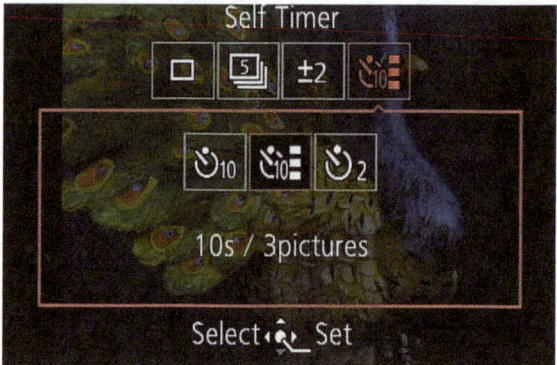

Fig. 5-47:   Self-timer Setting Screen

You can press Menu/Set or half-press the shutter button to exit back to the shooting screen. The LCD display will then have an icon on it showing the self-timer with the chosen number of seconds beside it, as shown in Figure 5-48.

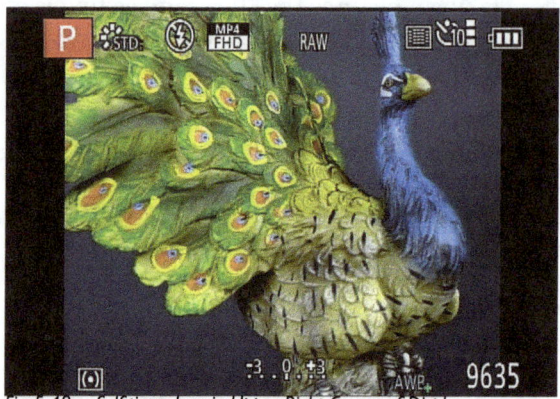

Fig. 5-48:   Self-timer Icon in Upper Right Corner of Display

Now you can wait as long as you want before actually taking the picture (unless the camera times out by entering Sleep Mode or you take certain other actions, such as changing the shooting mode). Compose the picture, then press the shutter button. The AF assist lamp, which does double duty as the self-timer lamp, will blink and the camera will beep, until the shutter is automatically tripped at the end of the specified time. The beeps and blinks speed up for the last second as a warning, when the timer is set to ten seconds. For the two-second operation, the camera just beeps four times and blinks five times as it counts down. You can cancel the shot while the self-timer is running by pressing the center button (Menu/Set).

It's not a bad idea also to use the option that sets the camera to take a burst of 3 pictures, so you'll have several choices after the self-timer has done its work.

When you are playing a slide show or a movie in playback mode, the down button acts as a Stop button on a VCR to stop the playback completely. When you use the Video Divide function from the Playback menu, the down button is used to "cut" a movie at your chosen dividing point.

Center Button: Menu/Set

The last button to discuss among those in the five-button array is the button in the center of the arrangement, labeled Menu/Set. You use this button to enter and exit the menu system, and to make or confirm selections of menu items or other settings. In addition, when you are playing a motion picture and have paused it, you can press the Menu/Set button to select a still image to be saved from the motion picture recording. The button also has some other uses, such as taking images using the Multi Exposure option on the Recording menu.

Display Button

The Display button is the round button at the bottom right of the camera's back, below the five-button array. It has several functions, depending on the context. If you have the D-Lux 6 set for still recording in any mode other than Snapshot, here is the progression you get from repeated presses of the Display button: (1) as shown in Figure 5-49, full display, showing information including battery life, Picture Size, Quality, Photo Style, flash status, ISO (if set to a specific value), motion picture quality and format, recording mode, metering mode, and number of pictures that can be shot with the remaining storage, as well as the histogram (discussed later), if that option is turned on through the Setup menu; (2) as shown in Figure 5-50, blank display except for the focus area (if in 1-Area AF or AF Tracking mode); (3) focus area (if in 1-Area AF or AF Tracking mode) and level gauge; and (4) as shown in Figure 5-51, full information with focus area, if applicable, and level gauge. If you have the Optional Viewfinder menu item turned on in the Recording menu, then a blank LCD is added as a fifth screen in the cycle.

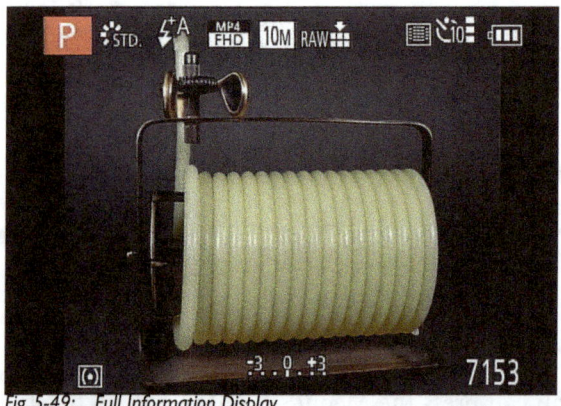

Fig. 5-49: Full Information Display

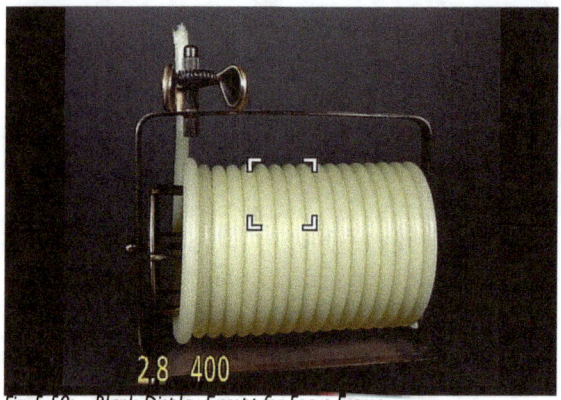

Fig. 5-50: Blank Display Except for Focus Frame

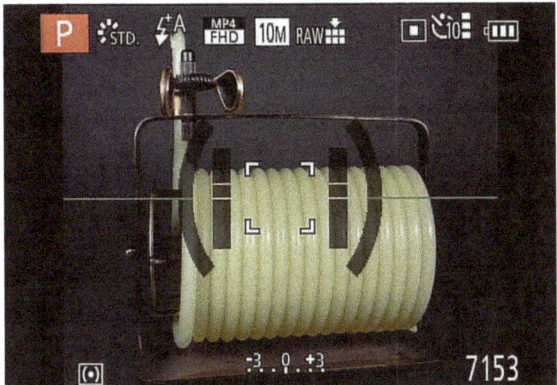
Fig. 5-51: Full Information with Focus Frame and Level Gauge

If the camera is set to Snapshot mode or Creative Video Mode, the Display button produces the screens listed above, but the histogram does not appear, even if it was turned on in the Setup menu. There also are other items that will appear on the information screens, such as Guide Lines, if that option is selected on the Setup menu, and icons for items such as the self-timer when they are activated.

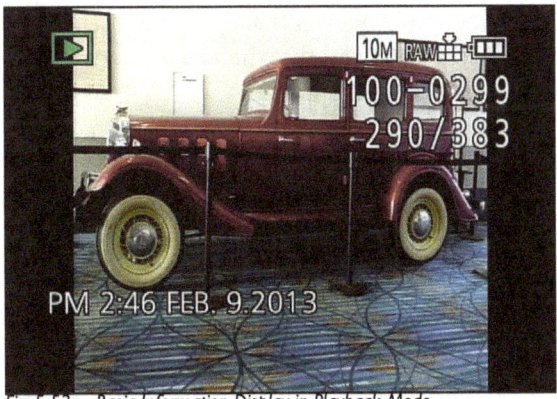
Fig. 5-52: Basic Information Display in Playback Mode

If the camera is set for playback, repeated presses of the Display button produce the following screens: (1) as shown in Figure 5-52, recorded image with time, date, image number,

253

and basic information including Picture Size and Quality; (2) as shown in Figure 5-53, the same information, with the addition of the shutter speed, aperture, ISO, white balance, flash status, and recording mode, as well as the histogram if that option is turned on through the Setup menu; and (3) just the recorded image, with no other information.

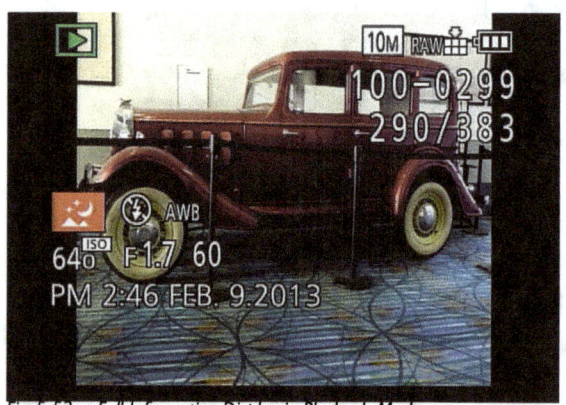

Fig. 5-53:   Full Information Display in Playback Mode

If you are playing back a motion picture, the display is similar, except for some added information that applies to that mode, including a brief display showing that the zoom lever controls the audio volume.

The Display button also has several other functions: You can press it to move the focus area back to the center of the screen after you have moved it off center when 1-Area focus mode is in effect. Also, as I'll discuss in Chapter 6, the Display button is used to select or de-select pictures you are marking for deletion after pressing the Trash button and selecting Delete Multi. During a slide show, the Display button toggles the display of image numbers and slide show controls on and off. In Title Edit mode, the button toggles between displays of various types of characters. Pressing the button displays information about each of the scene types when you are viewing them in the Scene menu. It also provides information about the Photo Style settings and the Creative Control settings. Finally, if you need a reminder of the current date and time, with the camera in recording mode, press the Display button enough times to cycle back to the screen with the most recording information, and the date and time will appear on the lower left of the screen for about 5 seconds.

Status Indicator

The status indicator is the small green light on the camera's back just to the lower left of the AF/AE Lock button. This little light turns on for about one second when the camera is powered on or off. It stays on when the LCD goes black, either because you have turned off the display using the Optional Viewfinder option on the Recording menu, or because the display has turned off because of the Auto LCD Off option of the Economy item on the Setup menu. In addition, the little light flashes to indicate certain problems, such as a dying battery or a failure of communication between the camera and a computer.

Chapter 6: Playback

If you're like me, you take the images you've created and import them into your computer, where you manipulate them with software, then post them on the web, print them out, e-mail them, or do whatever else the occasion calls for. In other words, I don't spend a lot of time viewing my pictures in the camera. But that doesn't mean it's not a good thing to know about. Depending on your needs, there may be plenty of times when you take a picture and then need to examine it closely in the camera. Also, the camera can serve as a viewing device like an iPod or other gadget that is designed, at least in part, for storing and viewing photos, and you can connect it to a TV set (HD or standard) to view a slide show or just a selection of images or movies. So it's worth taking a good look at the playback functions of the D-Lux 6.

I'll start with a brief rundown of the basic playback techniques. To quickly review a recently taken still picture, press the Play button—the one below the small gray triangle, at the upper right of the camera's back. Then scroll through your images with the left and right cursor buttons or by turning the rear dial or the ND/Focus lever to the right and left.

That's playback reduced to the very basics, and that's really enough to let you view your still images and show them to others with no problems. But there are considerably more options to choose from, so I will provide some further details in the rest of this chapter.

The Playback Menus

If you spotted the "s" at the end of "Menus" in the above heading, you are observant. And that is not a mistake. There is only one Recording menu (as well as one Motion Picture and one Setup menu), but there are two Playback menus. This situation could lead to some confusion, so I will try to sort through it clearly.

As you know, when the camera is in recording mode and you press the Menu/Set button, you enter the menu system. Once in that system, you can navigate to either the Recording menu or the Setup menu, or, if you have selected the Snapshot, Scene, Creative Video, or Creative Control mode with the mode dial, the camera displays a specialized menu for that shooting mode.

But if the camera is in playback mode when you press Menu/Set, you encounter a slightly different situation. Here you can navigate to the Playback Mode menu, the Playback menu, or the Setup menu. Figure 6-1 illustrates the menu screen when the camera is in playback mode, with the icon for the Playback Mode menu selected.

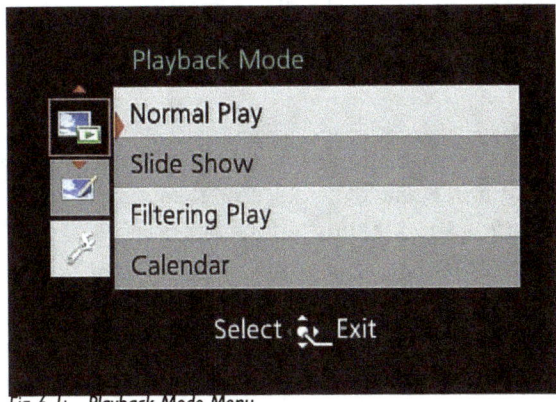

Fig. 6-1: Playback Mode Menu

The icon below that one represents the Playback menu, and the familiar wrench icon at the bottom of the column of icons stands for the Setup menu.

The first option, the Playback Mode menu, is akin to the mode dial on the top of the camera. In other words, this menu lets you select the playback mode (Normal Play, Slide Show, Filtering Play, or Calendar), just as the mode dial selects the recording mode. There was no room for another mode dial, and its existence probably would have been confusing, so the playback mode selection is done through this separate branch of the menu system.

The second option in the menu system is the actual Playback menu, which is similar to the Recording menu, letting you set various options for how playback works.

Let's look at these two menus one at a time. (I will discuss the Setup menu in Chapter 7.)

The Playback Mode Menu

The first option once you enter the menu system when the camera is in playback mode, as shown in Figure 6-1, offers four choices: Normal Play, Slide Show, Filtering Play, and Calendar. You use the Playback Mode menu like any other menu; just highlight the choice you want, such as Normal Play, and press the Menu/Set button to select it.

Here are the details for each of the four choices.

Normal Play

Normal Play is the playback mode for ordinary display of your images. With this mode selected, you scroll through the images individually using the left and right cursor buttons or ND/ Focus lever, or by turning the rear dial left and right. Whenever an image is displayed on the screen, you can press the Trash button to initiate the deletion process, and choose to delete either a single image, multiple ones, or all images. You can press and hold the left or right cursor button to speed through the images at a steady pace.

You can enlarge an image by pressing the zoom lever repeatedly to the right, with magnification ranging from 2X up to 16X, as shown in Figure 6-2.

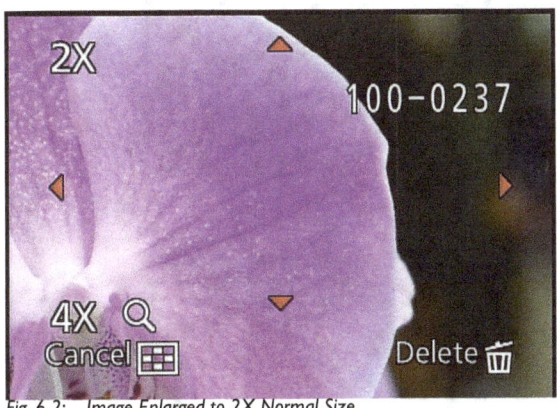

Fig. 6-2: *Image Enlarged to 2X Normal Size*

Reverse the process by moving the lever to the left. If you then keep pressing the lever to the left, you will reach screens, shown in Figures 6-3 and 6-4, that display 12 images, then 30 images. With one more press, you reach the Calendar display, shown in Figure 6-5, from which you can select images from any given date on which images were taken.

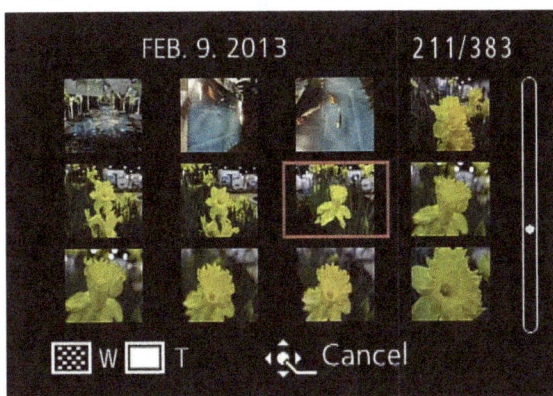

Fig. 6-3: *Index Screen with 12 Images*

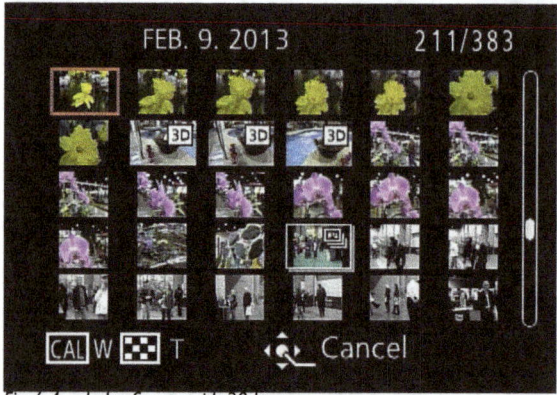

Fig. 6-4:   Index Screen with 30 Images

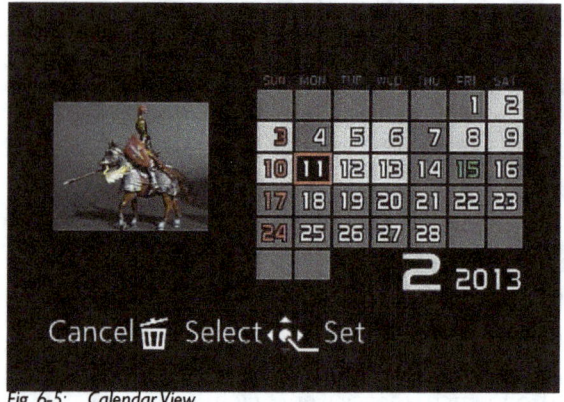

Fig. 6-5:   Calendar View

You also can enlarge an image, centered on its focus point, by pressing the ND/Focus lever while the image is displayed.

Slide Show

The second option on the Playback Mode menu is Slide Show. Navigate to this option, then press Menu/Set, and you are presented with the choices All, Picture Only, Video Only, 3D Play, Category Selection, and Favorite, as shown in Figure 6-6. (The Favorite option is on the second screen of this menu item, if any images have been marked as Favorites. If none have been marked, that selection does not appear in this list of choices.)

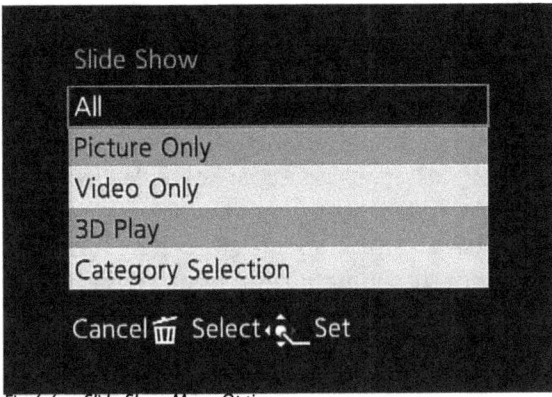

Fig. 6-6: Slide Show Menu Option

Following are details about each of these choices.

[Play] All

If you choose All from the Slide Show menu, you are taken to a menu with the choices Start, Effect, and Setup, shown in Figure 6-7.

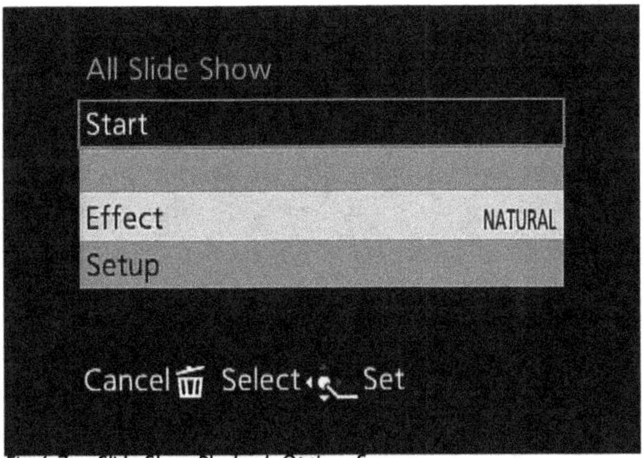

Fig. 6-7: Slide Show Playback Options Screen

You can choose Start to begin the slide show, or you can select Effect or Setup first and make some selections. Setup lets you choose a duration of 1, 2, 3, or 5 seconds for each still image, but you can only set the duration if Effect is set to Off. If you

261

select any effect, the camera will automatically set the duration to 2 seconds per still image.

You can also choose to set Sound to Off, Auto, Music, or Audio, but only if some effect is selected. If no effect is selected, the Sound option can be set only to Audio or Off. With Off, no sound is played. With the Auto setting, the camera's music is played for still images, and the motion pictures have their own audio played. The Music setting plays music as background for all images and movies, and the Audio setting plays only the movies' audio tracks.

Also, you can set Repeat On or Off. Note that you can set a duration even when there are videos included along with still images; the duration value will apply for the still pictures, but not for the videos, which will play at their normal, full length.

For effects, you have the following choice of styles: Natural, Slow, Swing, Urban, or turning effects off altogether. If you choose Urban, the camera not only plays "urban" music, it uses a somewhat more dramatic visual style with a variety of transitions, including converting some color images to black and white. So choose Urban only if you're a free-spirited type who doesn't mind a slide show with altered slides. If you use Category Selection as your choice for images and videos to play, then the camera gives you another choice of effect: Auto, in which the camera chooses an appropriate effect according to the category of each given image or video.

Once the slide show has begun, you can control it using the five-button array as a set of playback controls, the same as with playing back motion pictures. The up button controls play/pause; the left and right buttons move back or forward one slide when the show has been paused; and the down button is like a stop button—pressing it ends the slide show. A small display showing these controls stays on the screen during the show, along with image numbers, as shown in Figure 6-8, unless you press the Display button to switch to a screen showing the images only.

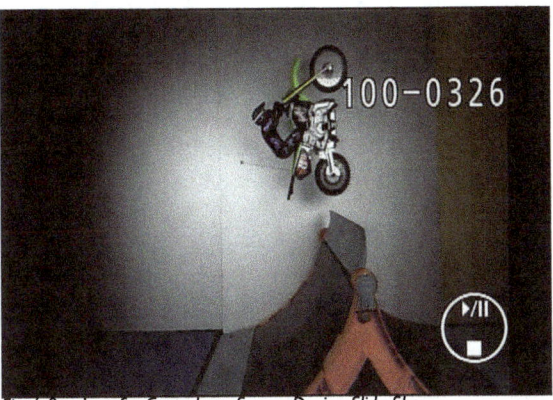

Fig. 6-8: Icon for Controls on Screen During Slide Show

[Play] Picture Only/Video Only

These next two options for playing the slide show are self-explanatory; instead of playing all images and videos, you can play either just still images or just videos. The only difference between the options for these two choices is that, as you might expect, you cannot select an effect or a duration setting for a slide show of only videos; the slide show will just play all of the videos on the memory card, one after the other. You can use the Effect setting to choose whether to play the videos with their sound tracks audible or with the sound turned off.

3D Play

The fourth item on the Slide Show menu screen gives you the option of choosing to play only 3D images that were recorded using the 3D option of Scene mode.

Category Selection

Besides having the slide show play all of the pictures and/or videos available, with the Category Selection option you can select the items to be played in the show by category. You can't place your pictures and videos in categories of your own making; the camera has a pre-defined list of eleven groups that it considers "categories," and it plays all of the images or videos in whichever single category you select. Note that some of the categories overlap with others—that is, an image might be in more than one category. Here are the categories:

All images and videos that used Face Recognition; if you select this option, the camera will prompt you to select a particular person whose face was recognized

All images and videos from the following scene types: Portrait, Soft Skin, Night Portrait, and Baby 1 and 2

All images and videos from the following scene types: Scenery, Sunset, Panorama, and Glass Through

All images and videos from the following scene types: Night Portrait, Night Scenery, and Handheld Night Shot

All images and videos from the scene type Sport

All images from the scene types Baby 1 and 2

All images from the scene type Pet

All images from the scene type Food

All images with a Travel Date

All images taken with the burst shooting settings of 40 or 60 frames per second

All images taken with the Time Lapse Shot feature

Favorite

The fourth and final option for selecting the images to play in a slide show is to play all of the images that you have marked as Favorites. In order to use this option, you have to have first used the Favorite setting in the Playback menu (not the Playback Mode menu) to mark one or more images as Favorites. I will discuss that process later in this chapter, in the discussion of the Playback menu.

Other Playback Modes

This next part could be confusing, so I'll try to explain care-fully. I have just finished talking about the Slide Show mode of playback, which includes within its own options the choices of playing the slides by Category or by Favorites. We now move on to the remaining modes of play other than Slide Show. (Earlier, I discussed the first mode: Normal Play.) The remain-ing two modes are Filtering Play and Calendar.

Filtering Play

The first of these modes, Filtering Play, is the third option on the Playback Mode menu, as seen in Figure 6-9.

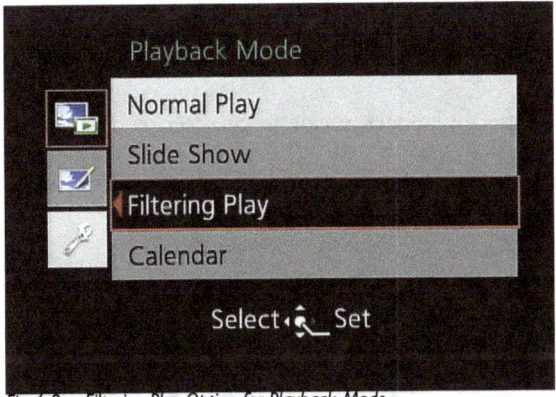

Fig. 6-9:   Filtering Play Option for Playback Mode

This option lets you select most of the same options that the Slide Show menu item does: Picture Only, Video Only, 3D Play, Category Selection, or Favorite, as shown in Figure 6-10. There is no selection of All, because that selection would de-feat the purpose of filtering. Another difference is that, in the Filtering Play mode, there is no slide show. That is, the images do not advance by themselves, there is no music playing along with them, and there are no transitions between them, as can be the case with a slide show. All you are doing if you select the Filtering Play mode is telling the camera which images to dis-play, so you can browse through them. The process of selecting the images to be played is the same as for the Slide Show option, as discussed above.

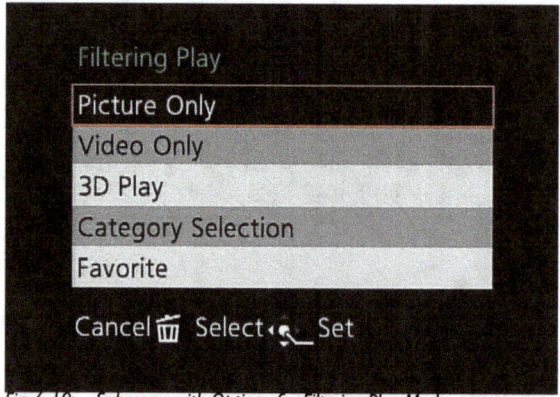

Fig. 6-10: Submenu with Options for Filtering Play Mode

Calendar

The fourth and final playback mode to be discussed is Calendar, as shown in Figure 6-11.

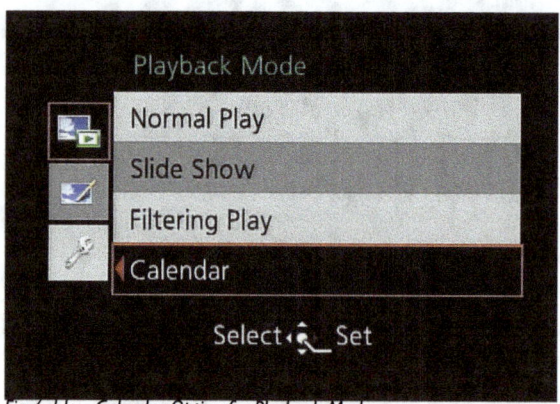

Fig. 6-11: Calendar Option for Playback Mode

When you select this option, the camera displays a screen like that shown in Figure 6-12. This is the same display that you can reach by pressing the zoom lever to the left in playback mode; after the index screens of 12 and 30 images, you will reach the Calendar screen.

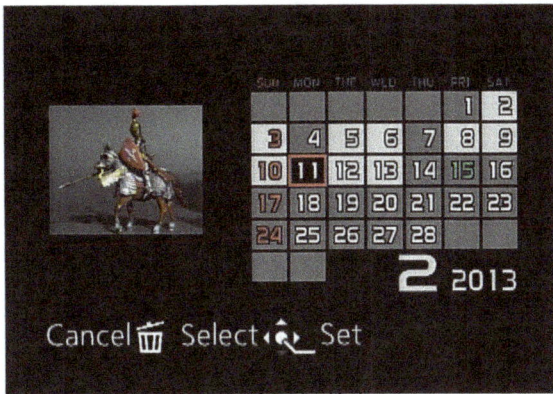

Fig. 6-12: Selection Screen for Calendar Mode

On this screen, the dates on which images were taken are displayed with light gray backgrounds. You can use the cursor buttons or the rear dial to navigate to any of those dates. Press Menu/Set when one of those dates is highlighted in black to move to a screen like that in Figure 6-13, which shows thumbnail images for that date. You can tell which thumbnails represent special types of images such as panoramas, high-speed burst shots, 3D shots, or videos, because an icon of a panorama, a movie camera, or other appropriate item displays in the upper right corner of the thumbnail.

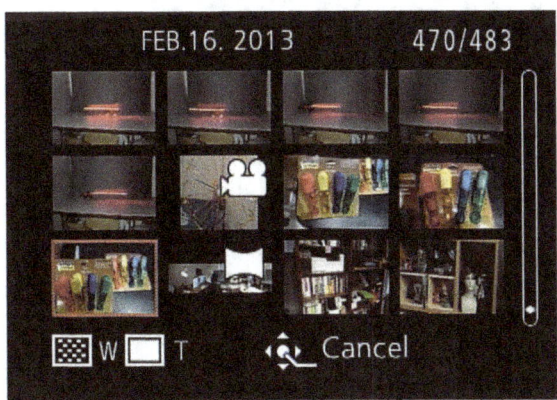

Fig. 6-13: Thumbnail Images Showing Movie and Panorama Icons

267

The Playback Menu

Now I am going to discuss the other playback menu. I just finished describing the operation of the Playback Mode menu; this one is just the Playback menu. If you recall, this one is similar to the Recording menu, because it offers a collection of options for how playback works and for altering images.

To reach the Playback menu, you first have to put the camera into playback mode by pressing the Play button. Then press the Menu/Set button, which takes you into the menu system. Make sure the cursor is in the far left column of the menu display, then press the down button to highlight the second icon, which represents the Playback menu, as shown in Figure 6-14.

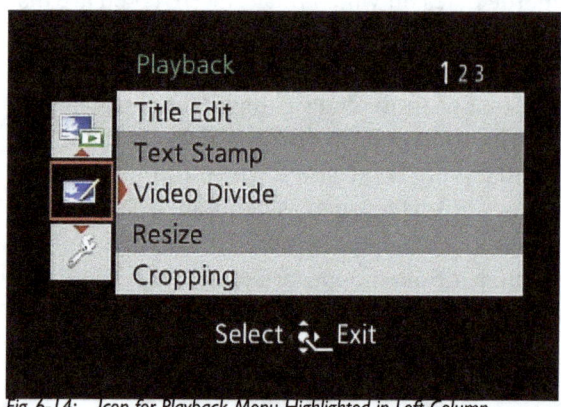

Fig. 6-14:   Icon for Playback Menu Highlighted in Left Column

Next, press the right button to place the black selection bar into the list of menu options as shown in Figure 6-15, and scroll down to the one you want. I'll talk about each one in order, from top to bottom. Note that not all 12 options are available in a given playback mode, depending on what images or videos are present in storage. They are all available for Normal and Calendar playback, but some may not be available for Filtering Play. For the following discussion, I will assume the camera is set for Normal Play.

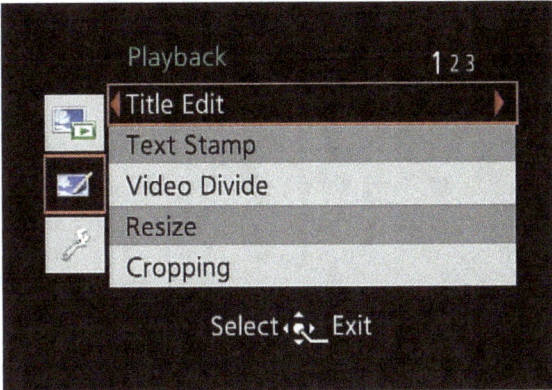

Fig. 6-15: First Screen of Playback Menu

Title Edit

The first option on the Playback menu lets you enter normal text, numerals, punctuation, and a fairly wide range of symbols and accented characters for a given image or group of images through a system of selecting characters from several rows. With this option, you select one or more images to have text added and then press Menu/Set to proceed to the screen with tools for entering text, shown in Figure 6-17.

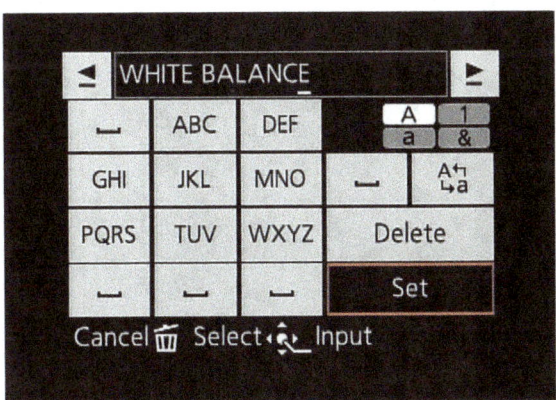

Fig. 6-16: Text Entry Screen for Title Edit Option

Navigate using the cursor buttons to the block that contains the character to be entered. You cycle through the choices in

269

each block, such as ABC, using the Menu/Set button, and advance to the next space using the rear dial. One point to be aware of is that you can toggle between three displays of capital letters, lower case letters, and numerals and symbols using the Display button. The maximum length for your caption or other information is 30 characters. You can use the Multi option to enter the same text for up to 50 images. You cannot enter titles for motion pictures, protected pictures (see discussion below), or RAW images.

Once you have entered the title or caption for a particular image, it does not show up unless you use the Text Stamp function, discussed below, or software such as the Adobe Lightroom software supplied with the camera. If you use Text Stamp, the title is attached to the image, and it will print out along with the image. There is no way to delete the title other than going back to the Title Edit function and using the Delete key from the table of characters, then deleting each character until the title disappears.

Text Stamp

The Text Stamp function, shown in Figure 6-17, takes information associated with a given image and attaches it to the image in a visible form.

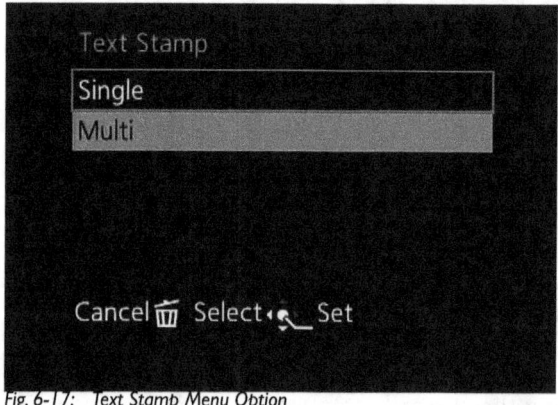

Fig. 6-17: Text Stamp Menu Option

For example, if you have entered a title or caption using the Title Edit function discussed above, it does not become visible until you use this Text Stamp function to "stamp" it onto the image, as shown in Figure 6-18. Once you have done this, the text or other characters in the title will print out if you send the picture to a printer. Besides the information entered with the Title Edit function, the Text Stamp function gives you the choice of making the following other information visible: year, month, and day; year, month, day, and time; age of subject (if set); travel date (if set); location (if set). Also, you can apply this function to information from pictures taken with scene types Baby 1 or 2 and Pet, if you have entered a name for your baby or pet, and to pictures that have names registered with the Face Recognition function.

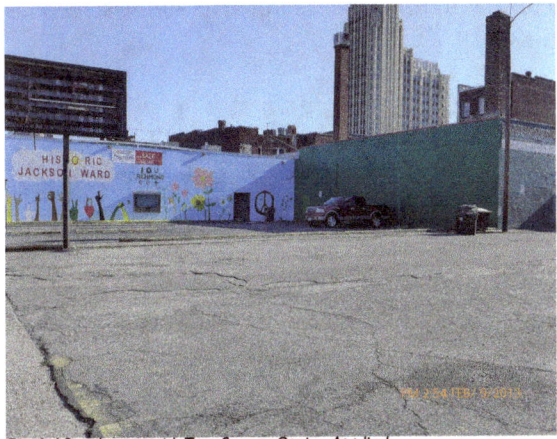

Fig. 6-18: Image with Text Stamp Option Applied

Using Text Stamp reduces the image size of higher-resolution images to the range of 2.5 – 3.0 MP. The function cannot be used at all with RAW images. The camera saves the text-stamped image to a new file, so you will still have the original. I have never found this function useful, but if you have an application that could benefit from it, it is available and ready to assist you.

Video Divide

The Video Divide function can be quite useful; it gives you a rudimentary editing or trimming function for videos using your camera. Using this procedure, you can, within limits, pause a video at any point and then cut it at that point, resulting in two segments of video rather than one. You can then, if you want, delete an unwanted segment.

Here is how to accomplish this: Choose the Video Divide function from the Playback menu. Then, press the right button to go to the playback screen. If the video you want to divide is not already displayed, scroll through your images using the left and right cursor buttons or the rear dial until you locate it. You can recognize videos because they will have an icon showing the video format in the upper left quarter of the screen, as shown in Figure 6-19.

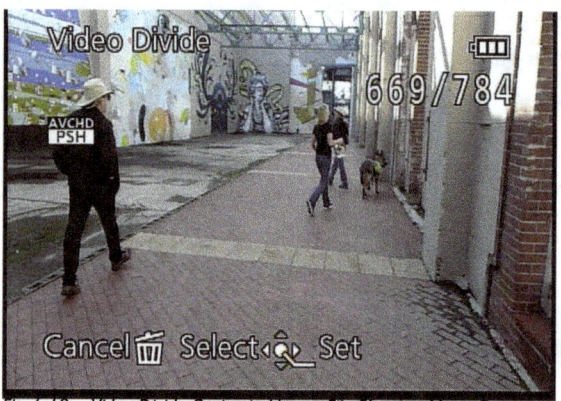

Fig. 6-19: *Video Divide Option in Use on File Showing Movie Format*

(Oddly, the camera displays all your images here, including stills, so you may have to scroll through many non-videos until you reach the video you want.) Once you have the desired movie on the screen, press the Menu/Set button to start it playing. When it reaches the point where you want to divide it, press the up cursor button, which pauses the video. At this point, while the video is paused, you can move through it a frame at a time using the left and right cursor buttons, until you find the exact point where you want to divide it.

Once you have reached that point, press the down cursor button to make the cut. You will see an icon of a pair of scissors in the little display of controls at the bottom of the screen, as shown in Figure 6-20. After you press the down button, the camera will display the message shown in Figure 6-21, asking you to confirm the cut. Highlight Yes and press Menu/Set to confirm. Now you have two new videos, divided at the point you chose.

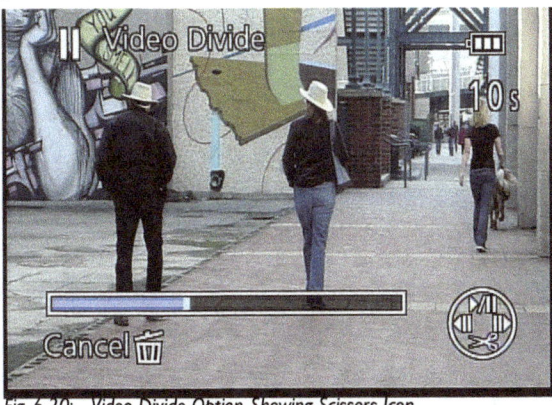

Fig. 6-20:   Video Divide Option, Showing Scissors Icon

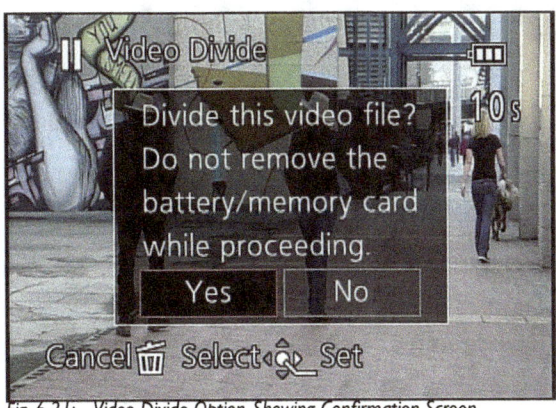

Fig. 6-21:   Video Divide Option, Showing Confirmation Screen

As I noted above, this is a rudimentary form of editing. It can't be used to trim a movie too close to its beginning or end, or to trim a very short movie at all. But it's better than nothing, and gives you some ability to trim away unwanted footage without having to edit the video on your computer.

Resize

This function from the Playback menu can be of use if you don't have access to software that can resize an image, and you need to generate a smaller file that you can attach to an e-mail message or upload to a web site. You activate the Resize function using the standard procedure with the cursor buttons, and select whether to resize a single image or multiple ones. Then, using the left and right cursor buttons, navigate to the image you want to resize, if it's not already displayed on the screen. You can use this function only on JPEG still images, not on RAW files or movies.

Once the image to be resized is on the screen, press the Menu/Set button to start the resizing process.

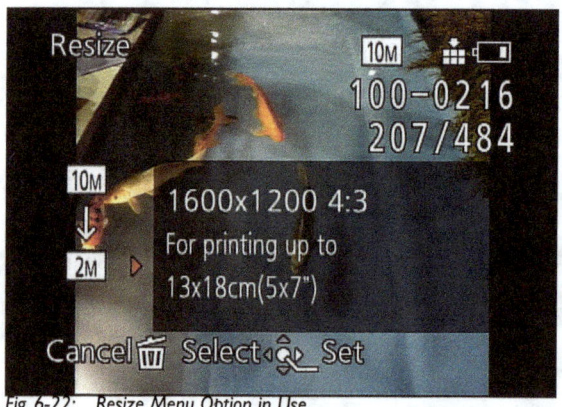

Fig. 6-22:   Resize Menu Option in Use

Then, following the prompts on the screen as shown in Figure 6-22, use the left and right cursor buttons to select what size to reduce the image to, down as far as 0.3 MP, depending on the aspect ratio of the image. The small red left and right arrows indicate what cursor button to press to see another option for the resizing. When the option you want to use is displayed, press Menu/Set to carry out the resizing process. The camera will ask you to confirm that you want to save a new picture at the reduced size.

As with the Text Stamp function, resizing does not overwrite the existing image; it saves a copy of it at a smaller size, so the original will still be available. The new image will be found at the end of the current set of recorded pictures. RAW images, protected images, and motion pictures cannot be resized, nor can 3D images, panoramas, or pictures stamped with Text Stamp.

Cropping

This function is similar to Resize, except that, instead of just resizing the image, the camera lets you crop it to show just part of the original image. To do this, select Cropping from the Playback menu and navigate with the left and right cursor buttons to the image to be cropped, if it isn't already displayed. Then use the zoom lever or the rear dial to enlarge the image, and use the cursor buttons to position the part of the image to be retained.

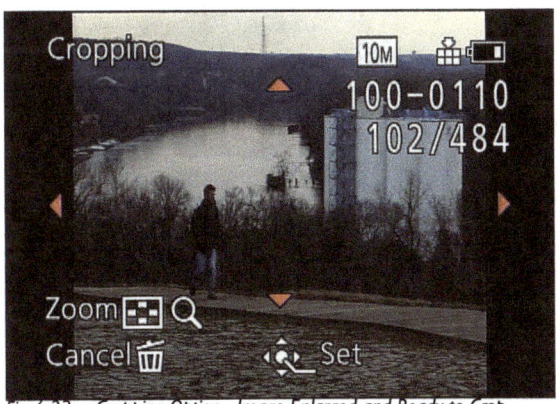

Fig. 6-23: Cropping Option - Image Enlarged and Ready to Crop

When the enlarged portion is displayed as you want, as shown in Figure 6-23, press Menu/Set to lock in the cropping, and

275

select Yes when the camera asks if you want to save the new picture. Again, as with Resize, the new image will be saved at the end of the current set of recorded images, and it will have a smaller size than the original image, because it will be cropped to include less information (fewer pixels) than the original image. The Cropping function cannot be used with RAW images, motion pictures, 3D images, panoramas, or pictures stamped with Text Stamp.

Leveling

This is an interesting function; it allows you to make minor corrections in the rotation of an image. For instance, if you have a straight object in your image that is slightly off-kilter, you can apply a small amount of clockwise or counter-clockwise rotation to correct the tilt.

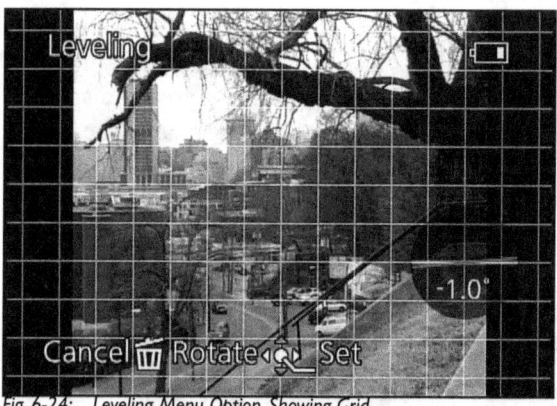

Fig. 6-24:   Leveling Menu Option, Showing Grid

When you select this function, the camera displays a framework of horizontal and vertical grid lines, as shown in Figure 6-24, to help you make fine adjustments. You then carry out the rotation using the left and right cursor buttons. As with other functions of this sort, the camera saves a new image with the new appearance.

Also, as with most of the modifications made through the Playback menu, there are several limitations. First, the cor-

276

rection is limited to two degrees of positive or negative rotation. Second, the process achieves the rotation effect in part by zooming in and cropping the image slightly, so a part of the image is lost and the size of the file and the resolution will decrease somewhat. Finally, as with the Resize and Cropping functions, this operation cannot be carried out with certain types of images, including RAW images, motion pictures, and pictures stamped with Text Stamp.

Favorite

I have mentioned this function a few times before, because you have the option of viewing just your Favorite pictures under some of the playback modes. Here is how to select images as Favorites. You select the Favorite option from the Playback menu, and then choose the images to mark as Favorites, either single or multiple images, using the same selection process as for other operations discussed above. The camera will display your images, either singly or as thumbnails, and you can mark any image as a Favorite by pressing the Menu/Set button when the image or its thumbnail is displayed.

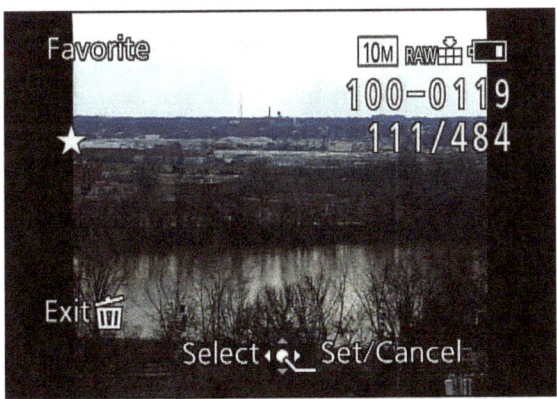

Fig. 6-25:   *Favorite Menu Option - Screen for Marking Favorite*

A star will appear on the marked image, as shown in Figure 6-25. Once the star appears, press the Trash button to exit from this screen. (Don't press Menu/Set on this screen; if you do, the star will be removed.)

When you later display an image that was marked as a Favorite, a star appears in its upper left corner, as shown in Figure 6-26, unless you are viewing the playback screen that displays no information. You cannot select RAW images as Favorites.

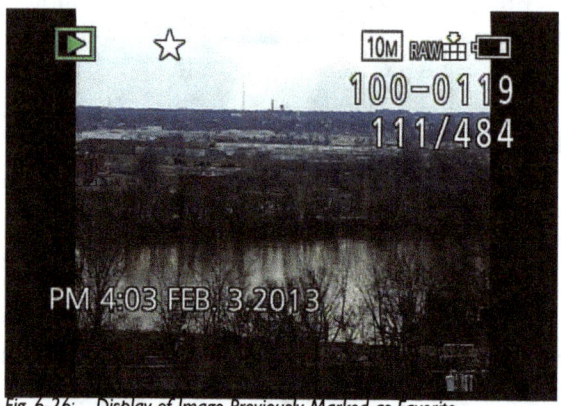

Fig. 6-26:   *Display of Image Previously Marked as Favorite*

Print Set

The next option on the Playback menu, Print Set, lets you select certain images for Digital Print Order Format (DPOF) printing. DPOF is a process that was developed by the digital photography industry to allow users of digital cameras to specify, on the camera's own memory card, which pictures to print and other details, then take the card to a commercial printing shop to have them printed according to those specifications.

With the D-Lux 6, you select this option from the Playback menu, and then select Single or Multi. If you select Multi, the camera gives you a display of six images at a time on the screen. Using the four cursor buttons or the rear dial, you navigate through the images. When you arrive at one you want to have printed, you press the Menu/Set button, and you then see a box with the word "Count" followed by a number and up and down arrows. You use the up and down cursor buttons to raise (or, later, lower, if you change your mind) the number of copies of that image you want to have printed, as shown in

Figure 6-27. In addition, if you press the Display button, the word "Date" is added to the small image for that picture, and the date will be printed on that picture. You can follow the above procedure for a single image by selecting "Single" when you first enter the DPOF option.

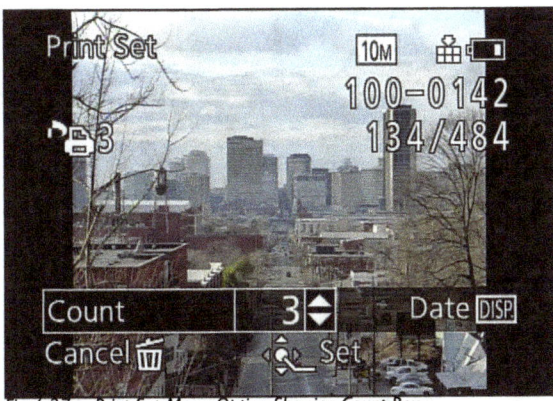

Fig. 6-27:   Print Set Menu Option Showing Count Box

If you want to use the DPOF system to print photos recorded in the camera's built-in memory, you need to copy them to a memory card and then take that card to the printing store, after setting the DPOF options. (See the Copy function, discussed later in connection with the Playback menu.)

The DPOF settings cannot be set for RAW images. Once you have set one or more images to print using this menu option, you can use the Cancel option from the Print Set menu to go back and cancel the printing setup.

Protect

The next Playback menu option is Protect, which is used to lock selected images against deletion. The process is essentially the same as that for the Favorite function; you enter the Playback menu system, select the Protect option, and then select Multi or Single. You can mark the images you want to protect using the Menu/Set button. When a picture is protected in this way, a key icon appears on the left side of the image, as shown

279

in Figure 6-28.

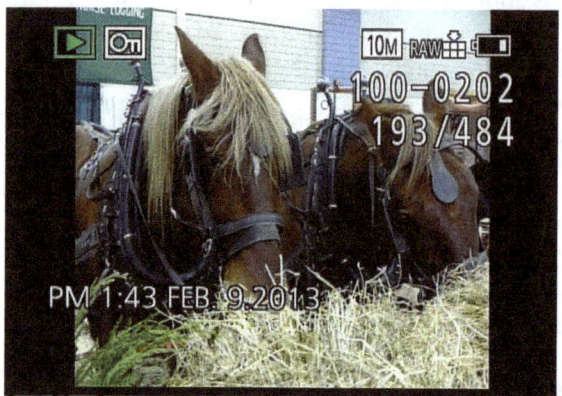

Fig. 6-28:   Protected Image with Key Icon in Upper Left Corner

The Protect function works for all types of images, including RAW files and motion pictures. Note, however, that all images, including protected ones, will be deleted if the memory card (or camera's built-in memory) is re-formatted.

Face Recognition Edit

This Playback menu option is of use only if you have previously registered one or more persons' faces in the camera for face recognition. If you have, use this option to select the picture in question, then follow the prompts to replace or delete the information for the person or persons you select. Once deleted, this information cannot be recovered.

Copy

The final option on the Playback menu, the Copy function, lets you copy images from the camera's built-in memory to an SD storage card, and vice-versa. After you select Copy from the Playback menu, press the right cursor button to pop up the little sub-menu, which provides two options, represented by two pairs of icons connected by a directional arrow, as shown in Figure 6-29. One icon has the label "In," showing that it represents the camera's built-in memory; the other icon is labeled

"SD," representing an SD card inserted into the camera. One pair of icons has an arrow going from the In icon to the SD icon, and the other pair has the arrow going from the SD icon to the In icon.

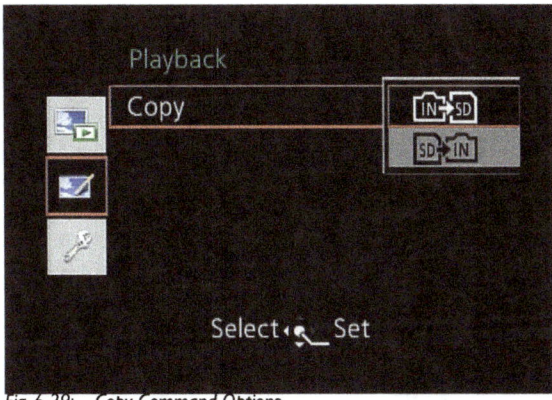

Fig. 6-29:   Copy Command Options

If you select the first icon, the camera will prompt you with a message asking you to confirm whether you want to copy the images from the built-in memory to the memory card. If you choose Yes to confirm, the process starts, if there are images to copy.

If you select the second pair of icons, the camera displays an image, and asks if you wish to copy it to the camera's built-in memory. If you select Yes, the camera copies that single image to the built-in memory. You can then move on to other images, or cancel out of the process with the Trash button.

Remember that the built-in memory has a capacity of only about 70 MB, so it does not hold very many high-quality images.

If you regularly copy your images to a computer, you probably won't have much need for this option, but it can be a handy procedure when a computer is not available. Also, if you have taken a few images with the internal memory, it can be quite

281

convenient to copy them to a memory card so you can save them, and then reformat the internal memory for future use.

Copying from an SD card to internal memory is not likely to be a function you need often, but it could be useful if you're at an event with another photographer who got some shots with another camera that you need copies of. You could copy a few shots from his or her SD card to your internal memory (and from there to your SD card) to take home with you.

Auto Retouch and Creative Retouch

There is one more operation that you can perform on your images in playback mode, which does not involve the Playback menu. When an individual image is displayed on a screen that includes at least basic information, the camera will display an icon representing the up cursor button along with the label Retouch, as shown in Figure 6-30.

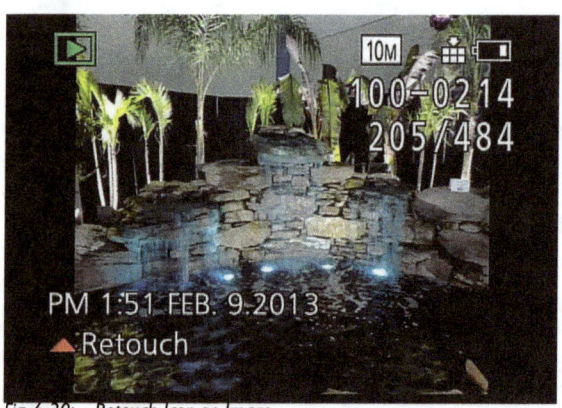

Fig. 6-30: Retouch Icon on Image

If you then press the up button, the camera displays a screen letting you select either Auto Retouch or Creative Retouch, as shown in Figure 6-31. With Auto Retouch, the camera will adjust the color and brightness of the image using its internal programming in an attempt to optimize its appearance. With Creative Retouch, the camera lets you select a special effect from a group of the same options that are available in the Creative Control shooting mode.

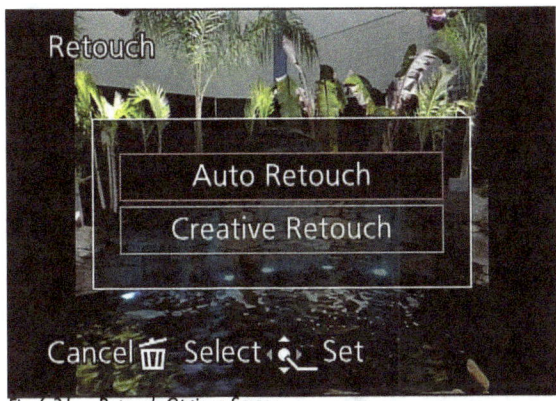

Fig. 6-31:   Retouch Options Screen

If you select Auto Retouch, the camera processes the image for a second or two, and then displays the screen shown in Figure 6-32, with the On/Off choices on a small menu.

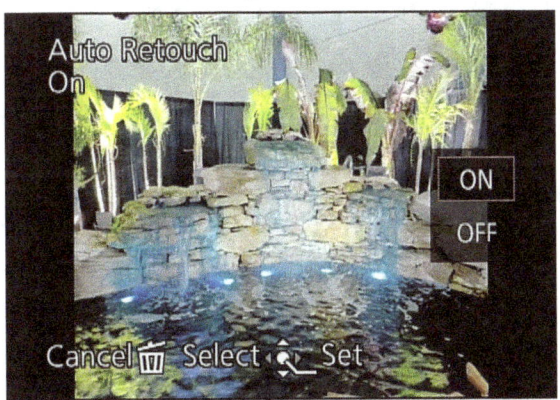

Fig. 6-32:   Auto Retouch Results Screen

You can select either On or Off using the rear dial or the up and down buttons, to see the image with and without the automatic processing. If you like the enhanced appearance, press Menu/Set while On is highlighted; otherwise, select Off to

283

cancel. If you keep the enhanced appearance, a new image is saved with that processing, so you will still have the original image.

If you select Creative Retouch, the camera presents the display shown in Figure 6-33, in which the image has a menu at the right with the list of Creative Control choices: Expressive, Retro, High Key, Low Key, Sepia, Dynamic Monochrome, Impressive Art, High Dynamic, Cross Process, Toy Camera, Miniature, Soft Focus, Star Filter, One Point Color, and Off.

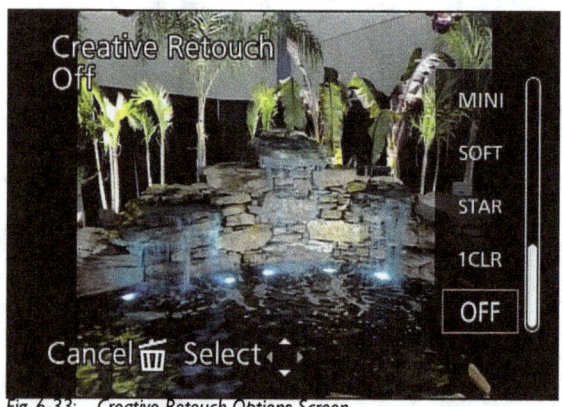

Fig. 6-33:   Creative Retouch Options Screen

Just as with the Auto Retouch option, you can scroll through these selections using the rear dial or the up and down buttons. As you highlight each choice, the camera alters the display to show how that selection would affect the image. When you find the effect you want to try, press Menu/Set. The camera will then take you to the next screen. In some cases, such as with the One Point Color option, you can then make adjustments specific to that setting, using the on-screen prompts. When you have finished, follow the camera's prompts to save a new image with the creative processing completed; the original image is preserved intact.

This is a great feature to use, not just for enhancing the appearance of your images, but for experimenting with the various

Creative Control settings in order to see how they would affect future shots.

Playback of Videos and Other Types of Files

Finally, I will include some reminders about the basic methods for playback of videos and other shots that are not ordinary still images. I have covered these playback techniques in earlier chapters, so I won't go into great detail here.

When a video is displayed on the camera's screen, you will see a message prompting you to press the up button to play the motion picture. Just press that button, and the video will start to play. You can then control playback using the cursor buttons as VCR controls, using the icon on the screen as a guide to those controls.

For most burst shooting, playback is just like it is for individual shots. However, when you use the 40 or 60 frames-per-second setting to take a burst of shots, the images are collapsed, so only the first in the series is displayed. You can press the up button to play back the whole series in a continuous playback mode. If you would prefer to be able to scroll through the images individually, you can press the down button, and then the series will be "opened up" so you can scroll through the images one at a time.

For shots taken with the Time Lapse option on the Recording menu, follow the same procedure as with the high-speed burst shots: Press the up button to play back the whole sequence quickly; press the down button to expand the sequence so you can browse through the individual images.

For panorama shots, the camera will display a message advising you to press the up button to play the panorama. When you press that button, the panorama will scroll across the screen. You can pause it and resume playback with the up button, scroll the image back and forth with the left and right buttons, or end the playback with the down button.

Chapter 7: The Setup Menu

I have discussed the options available to you in the Recording and Playback menu systems (including options in the Scene, Creative Control, and other branches of the menu system). The next menu system to discuss is the Setup menu. As a reminder, you enter the menu system by pressing the Menu/Set button (the center button in the five-button array on the right side of the camera's back). The available menus change depending on whether you're in recording mode, playback mode, or a special mode with a menu for the Scene or Snapshot settings, for example. However, no matter what other menus may be available, you can always enter into the Setup menu.

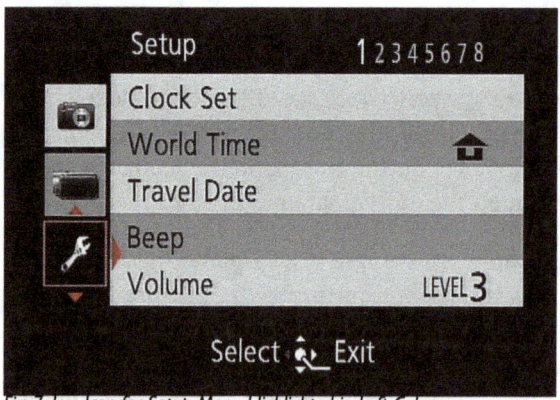

Fig. 7-1:   Icon for Setup Menu Highlighted in Left Column

After pressing Menu/Set, press the left cursor button to move the highlight into the left column of menu choices, then use the down button as many times as needed (up to three) to navigate to the wrench icon, indicating the Setup menu, as shown in Figure 7-1. Once the wrench is highlighted, press the right button to get back to the list of Setup menu options, which occupy 8 menu screens, discussed below. (All of these choices are available unless the camera is set to Snapshot mode, in which case only a limited number of options are available on the Setup menu.)

Clock Set

With the Clock Set option highlighted, press the right button to go to the settings screen, as shown in Figure 7-2, and follow the arrows.

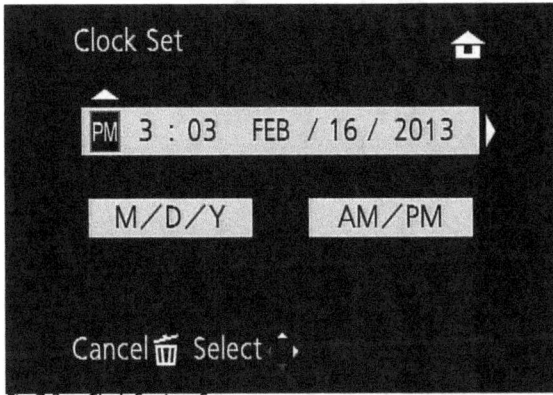

Fig. 7-2: Clock Settings Screen

Use the up and down arrows to adjust an item, then move to the next item with the right button or the rear dial. When the settings are done, press Menu/Set to exit and save. You can cancel with the Trash button.

World Time

This is a handy function when you're traveling to another time zone. Highlight World Time, and then press the right button to access the next screen. If you haven't used this menu item before, you'll be prompted to select your Home area. If so, just press Menu/Set and then use the left and right buttons or the rear dial to scroll through the world map as shown in Figure 7-3, and use the Menu/Set button to set your Home area.

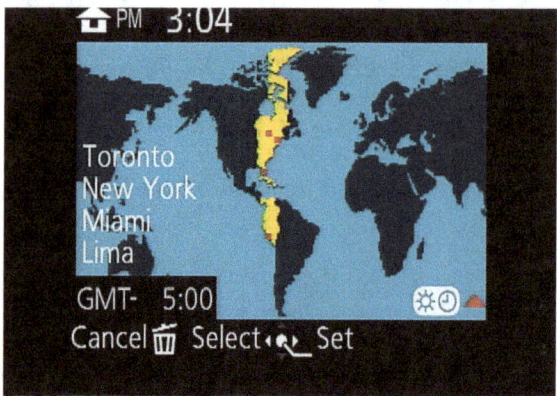

Fig. 7-3:   Map for World Time Menu Option

Then, on the World Time screen, shown in Figure 7-4, use the up button to highlight Destination, and use the left and right buttons to scroll through the world map to select the time zone you will be traveling to.

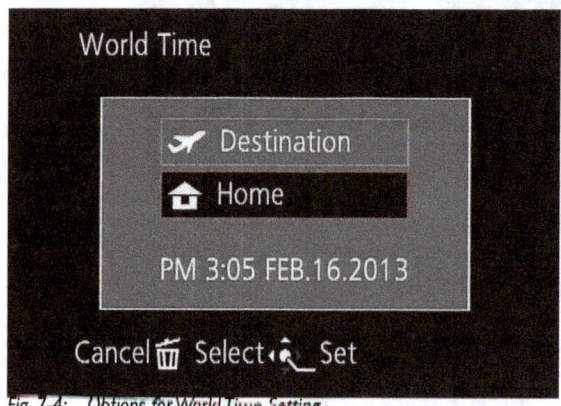

Fig. 7-4:   Options for World Time Setting

The map will show you the time difference from your home time. Press Menu/Set to select this zone for the camera's internal clock. Then, any images taken will reflect the correct time in the new time zone. When you return from your trip, go back into the World Time item and select Home to cancel the changed time zone setting.

Travel Date

This option lets you set a range of dates when you will be taking a trip, so you can record which day of the trip each image was taken. Then, when you return from your trip, if you use the Text Stamp function to "stamp" the recorded data on the images, the images will show they were taken on Day 1, Day 2, etc., of the trip. The entries are self-explanatory; just follow the arrows and the camera's prompts.

You also can set the location for your trip, and that will display along with the day number, if you set it. To do that, select Location from the Travel Date menu item, and then select SET from the sub-menu, as shown in Figure 7-5.

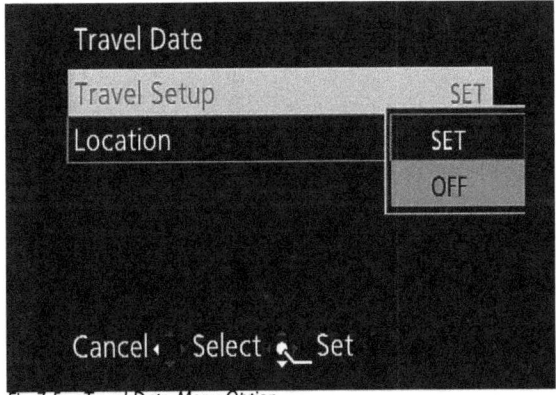

Fig. 7-5: Travel Date Menu Option

The camera will then display a screen where you can enter the name of the location using the same text-entry tools as are used for the Title Edit item, discussed in Chapter 6.

Beep

This menu option lets you adjust several sound items, as shown in Figure 7-6. First is the volume of the beeps the camera makes when you press a button, such as when navigating through the menu system. You can set the volume to off, normal, or loud. It's nice to be able to turn the beeps off if you're going to be in an environment where such noises are not welcome.

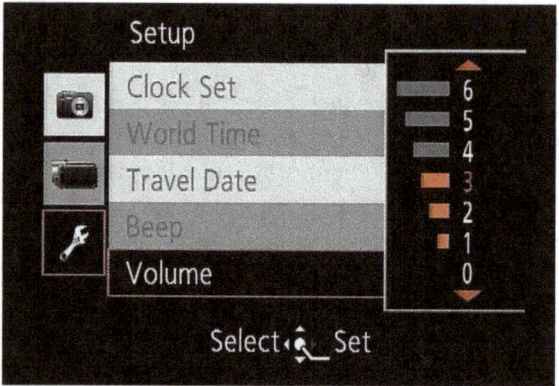

Fig. 7-6: Volume Menu Option

Second is the tone of the beeps. Check out the three possibilities and see which one you like best.

Third is the volume of the shutter operation sound. Again, it's good to be able to mute the shutter sound.

Finally, you can choose from three shutter sounds.

The Beep menu options are different when the camera is set to Snapshot mode. In that case, the only option available through this menu item is the volume level of the beeps; you cannot adjust the beep tone or the shutter volume or tone.

Volume

With this option, you can adjust the volume of the camera's speaker for playing back motion pictures and for slide shows that have audio turned on. There are 7 levels from 0 to 6, as shown in Figure 7-7. This setting does not affect the sound levels for beeps and shutter operations, which are controlled separately, as noted above. When you're playing a motion picture or a slide show, you can also use the zoom lever on top of the camera to adjust the volume, using the same 7 levels.

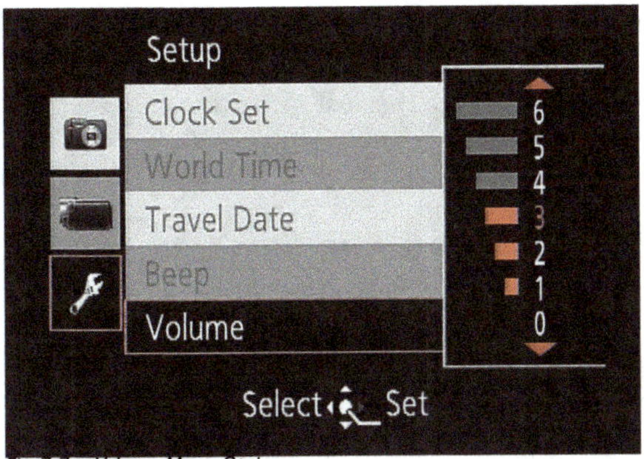

Fig. 7-7: Volume Menu Option

Custom Set Memory

I mentioned this feature in Chapter 3, in discussing the various selections on the mode dial—specifically C1 and C2, the two custom shooting modes. Custom Set Memory is the menu option you use to set up those custom modes.

This is a great feature for setting several shooting parameters without having to go into menus and fiddle with switches to set them for each shooting session. The camera lets you record four different groups of settings, each of which can be recalled quickly by turning the mode dial to C1 or C2. You can consider this function as a way to create four of your own custom-tailored shooting modes for use whenever you want them.

Here is how this works. First, you need to have the camera set to recording mode rather than playback mode, so if it's in playback mode, press the shutter button halfway or press the playback button to exit back to recording mode. Then, set the mode dial on top of the camera to the shooting mode you want to select as the base for your custom settings: Program, Aperture Priority, Shutter Priority, Manual, Creative Video, Creative Control, or Scene. (You can't use Snapshot mode in

291

a custom setting.) Next, make all of the settings that you want to have stored for quick recall, such as Photo Style, ISO, auto-focus method, exposure metering method, white balance, and the like. You can set most of the items on the Recording and Setup Menus for inclusion in the custom settings.

Once you have all of the settings as you want them, leave them that way and enter the Setup menu. Navigate to Custom Set Memory and press the right button, which gives you choices of C1, C2-1, C2-2, and C2-3, as shown in Figure 7-8.

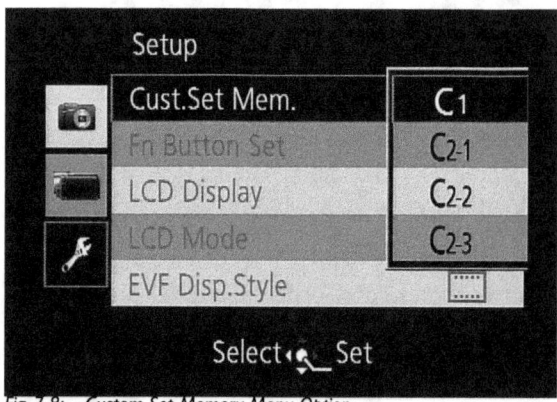

Fig. 7-8: Custom Set Memory Menu Option

For your most important group of settings, choose C1, be-cause that group of settings is the easiest to recall quickly. Press Menu/Set to select it, then select Yes on the confirma-tion screen that follows. Your group of settings is now saved.

When, at a later time, you want to use your group of saved settings, just turn the mode dial to C1 or C2. If you choose C1, you're done; the camera is now set as it was when you en-tered the C1 information. If you choose any of the other three groups of settings (C2-1, C2-2, or C2-3), you will also need to select the second part of the number (1, 2, or 3) from a short menu, as shown in Figure 7-9. Once you have selected the cus-tom mode you want, you are still free to change the camera's settings, but those changes will not be saved into the Custom Set Memory unless you enter the Setup menu again and save the changes there with the Custom Set Memory option.

292

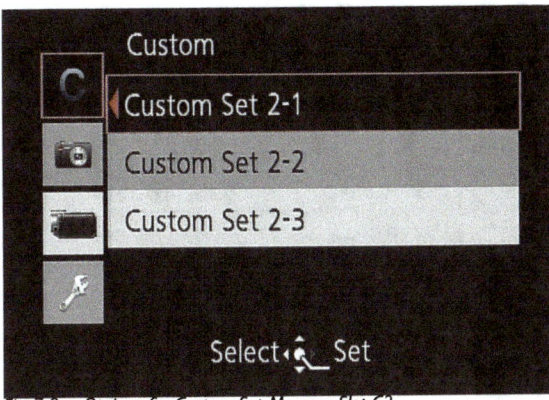

Fig. 7-9: Options for Custom Set Memory Slot C2

Following are listings of the more useful items that are saved to the Custom Memory slots for shooting still images. Note that the items will change somewhat according to what recording mode is selected. For example, if Creative Video is the selected recording mode for the Custom Memory slot, then the saved values include Recording Quality, but not Picture Size.

The table below provides a listing of items that are saved from the Recording menu, the Setup menu, and from other settings that are not made through the menu system.

Settings Saved to Custom Memory Slots		
Recording Menu	Setup Menu	Other
Photo Style	Fn Button Set	Shooting mode
Picture Size	Guide Line	Scene setting
Quality	Histogram	Creative Control setting
ISO Limit Set	Video Recording Area	ISO
ISO Increments	Remaining Display	Exposure compensation
Extended ISO	Highlight	White balance

Settings Saved to Custom Memory Slots		
Program Diagram	Exposure Meter	White balance adjustment
Face Recognition	Lens Resume	Burst mode
AF Mode	MF Assist	Self-timer
Quick AF	Play on LCD	Display screen
AF/AE Lock	Menu Resume	ND Filter
Metering Mode		
i.Dynamic		
Minimum Shutter Speed		
i.Resolution		
i.Zoom		
Step Zoom		
Stabilizer		
AF Assist Lamp		
Flash		
Flash Synch		
Flash Adjustment		
Red-eye Removal		

From the Recording menu, the only items that are not saved are those that would not make sense for this type of recall, such as Multiple Exposure and Time Lapse, which are not really settings, but are types of shooting. All of the important settings that affect your images can be saved.

From the Setup menu, there are quite a few items that cannot be saved, including Beep, Volume, LCD Display, Economy, and Auto Review, among others. There still are many useful settings that can be saved to a memory slot, however.

As for other settings that are not made through the menus, several very useful settings can be saved, but you cannot save items such as aperture, shutter speed, zoom position, aspect ratio, or focus mode (autofocus versus manual focus).

In summary, although it clearly has some limitations, Custom Set Memory is a powerful capability, and anyone who has or develops a favorite group of settings would be well advised to experiment with this option and take advantage of its power.

Also, don't shy away from using this feature even if there are only one or two settings that you want to change. For example, if you're comfortable with standard values for the most part, such as Program mode and Standard Photo Style, but you like to dial in, say -1.5 EV of exposure compensation, go ahead and use one of the four slots of the Custom Memory Set feature for that setting. In other words, you don't have to have a long list of exotic parameters to justify using this option.

Fn Button Set

I discussed this option in Chapter 5, in describing the functions of the various buttons on the camera. The Function button, which is also the left cursor button, is initially set to bring up the Photo Style menu option. With that setting, you can press this button while in recording mode to quickly change the "look" for your images to Standard, Vivid, Natural, or any of the other Photo Style settings. Using the Fn Button Set menu option on the Setup menu, you can set this button to carry out instead any one of several other functions from the Recording menu, the first five of which are shown in Figure 7-10. The available functions besides Photo Style are: Quality, Metering Mode, AF Mode, Focus Area Set, 1 Shot AF, i.Dynamic, Level Gauge, Guide Line, Video Recording Area, Remaining Display, Flash, Flash Adjustment, and Aspect Bracket. For example, if you often have a need to change your Quality setting between RAW and Fine, you might want to assign the Quality menu option to the Function button for ease of access.

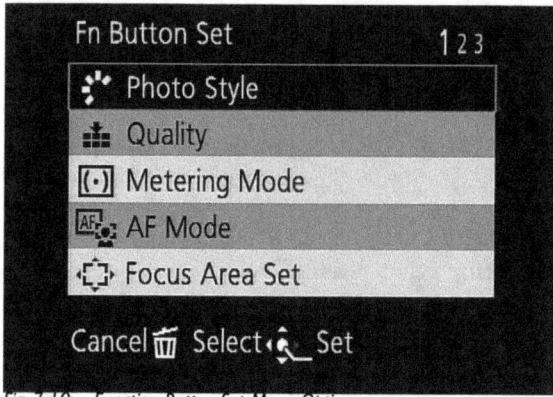

Fig. 7-10: Function Button Set Menu Option

Don't forget that several of these items, including Photo Style, Flash, Quality, AF Mode, and Metering Mode, also can be quickly adjusted using the Quick Menu system by just pressing the Q.Menu button and then navigating through the easy-access menu that appears.

Also, it's important to point out that, although most of the items that can be assigned to the Function button also can be reached through the menu system, there are two items that cannot be reached that way, or only with difficulty.

The first of these items is Focus Area Set, shown in Figure 7-11.

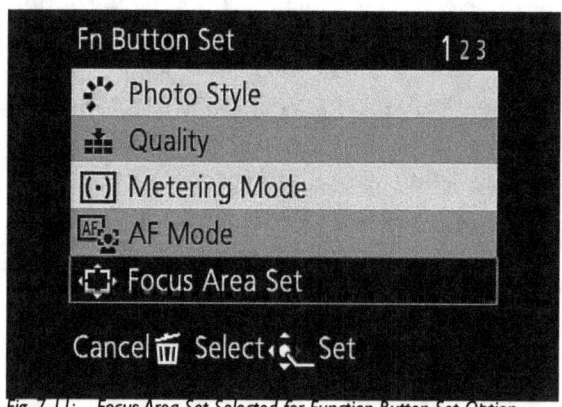

Fig. 7-11: Focus Area Set Selected for Function Button Set Option

This option gives you the ability to move the focus frame around the screen when AF Mode is set to 1-Area through the Recording menu. As was discussed in Chapter 4, when you first select that option, you can move the focus frame around the screen using the cursor buttons. However, if you want to move the frame around again later, you have to go through the whole process of entering the Recording menu, selecting 1-Area for the AF mode, and then moving to the screen that lets you move the frame to a new position. If you assign the Focus Area Set option to the Function button, you can just press this button, and you instantly see the focus frame adjustment screen, with the frame ready to be moved, resized using the rear dial, or both. I find this function to be a very helpful one, because of the several steps that it saves when I'm using this focus mode.

The other very useful option for the Function button that is not available otherwise is 1 Shot AF, shown in Figure 7-12.

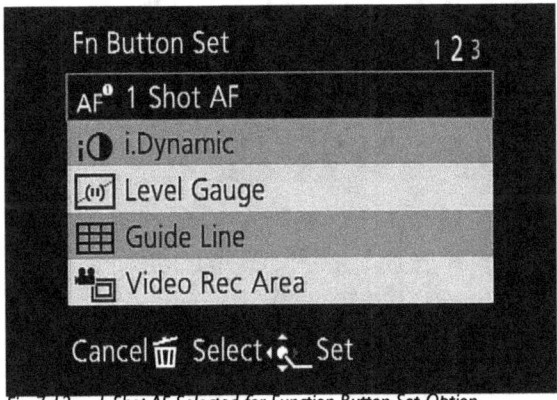

Fig. 7-12: 1 Shot AF Selected for Function Button Set Option

This option gives you an additional capability when you are using manual focus. You can press the Function button at any time, and the camera will use its autofocus mechanism to focus on the scene. You can then continue to make adjustments using the ND/Focus lever. Note, though, that the Function button will not carry out this autofocus operation while the manual focus scale remains on the screen; while that screen is visible, the Function button acts as the left cursor button, and makes fine adjustments to the manual focusing. After a few seconds, the manual focus scale will disappear, and then you can press the Function button to force an autofocus operation.

LCD Display

This menu option gives you four controls for adjusting the brightness and other aspects of the LCD display on the back of the camera. These settings also affect the optional electronic viewfinder, Model No. EVF3, if it is in use.

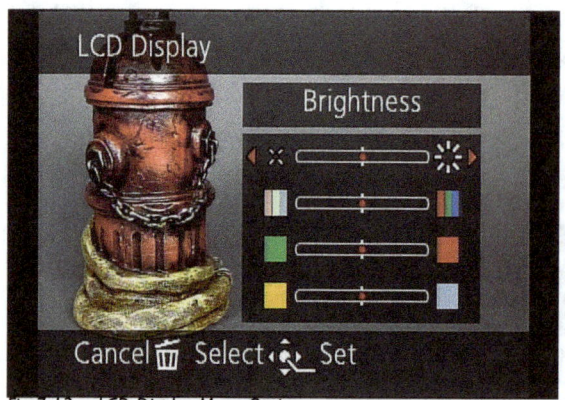

Fig. 7-13:   LCD Display Menu Option

As shown in Figure 7-13, This option has four linear scales for making adjustments. Use the up and down buttons to select a scale, and then use the left and right buttons or the rear dial to adjust the settings on the scale for each item. The normal settings are in the middle of the scale; move the red marker to the left of the scale to decrease a setting, or to the right to increase the value.

The top scale controls the brightness of the screen. Note that this setting works along with the next item on the Setup menu, LCD Mode, to control the overall brightness of the display. For example, you can dial down the brightness using this menu option, but then turn on the brightest option using the LCD Mode menu item; the camera will then reduce the brightness of the LCD Mode setting. It is unlikely you would want to do that, but you should be aware that both of these menu options will take effect, even if they cancel each other out to some extent.

The second scale controls contrast and saturation. Adjusting it to the left yields a subdued, softer appearance; the screen looks sharper and more vivid as the slider moves to the right. The third scale adjusts the tint from green on the left to red on the right, and the final scale adjusts from yellow on the left to blue on the right.

LCD Mode

This setting, like the previous one, also affects the brightness of the LCD display. This setting is different, in that it provides overall, on-or-off adjustments, rather than a sliding scale. As shown in Figure 7-14, this menu item has three settings: Off, Auto Power LCD (Icon with letter A and asterisk), and Power LCD (Icon with asterisk only).

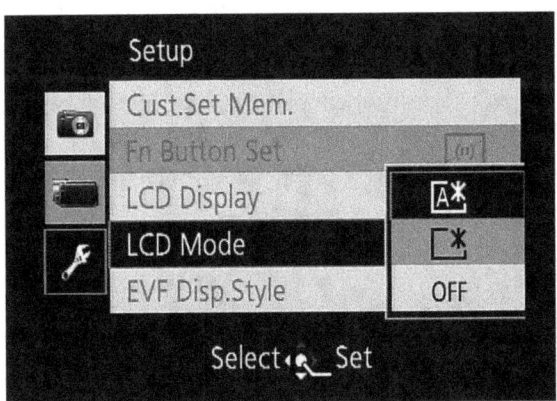

Fig. 7-14:   LCD Mode Menu Option

The Off setting does not turn off the LCD display; instead, it means that the Power LCD setting is off, and the LCD display is at its normal brightness (accounting for adjustments on the previous menu item, LCD Display). The Auto Power LCD setting means that the screen's brightness will adjust according to the ambient lighting conditions (again, taking into account the LCD Display setting). If you choose the Power LCD mode, the screen becomes extra-bright to compensate for sunlight or other lighting conditions that make it hard to see the screen. This mode dims back to normal after 30 seconds; you can press any button to make the screen turn bright again. An indicator appears at the left of the LCD display, toward the bottom, if Power LCD or Auto Power LCD mode is active. That indicator is an asterisk (*) for Power LCD and an asterisk with an A (A*) for Auto Power LCD.

You should note that using either Power LCD or Auto Power LCD mode decreases the battery's endurance, because of the use of extra power to make the screen brighter. If you find it hard to see the screen in bright sunlight and don't want to use an external viewfinder, you might want to try the Power LCD approach to see if the added brightness gives you enough visibility to compose your shots comfortably.

EVF Display Style

This menu option, shown in Figure 7-15, affects the appearance of the display screen when you have an optional electronic viewfinder attached, as discussed in Appendix A.

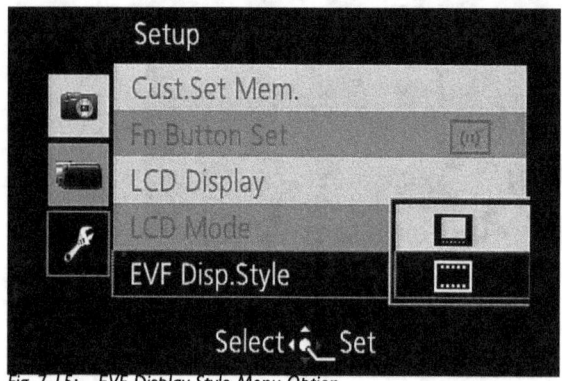

Fig. 7-15: EVF Display Style Menu Option

With the top option, the camera displays black bands at the bottom of the display and at the two sides. With the bottom option, the black bands are not displayed. The same information is displayed in either case. I prefer the top option with the black bands, because the band at the bottom of the screen makes it easier for me to see the recording information that is displayed. However, you might prefer the bottom option, which lets you see a bit more of the live view, so you can better see the context of the scene the camera is shooting.

LCD Display Style

This menu option, shown in Figure 7-16, has the same effect as the previous one, except that it applies when you are using the LCD display screen, rather than an electronic viewfinder.

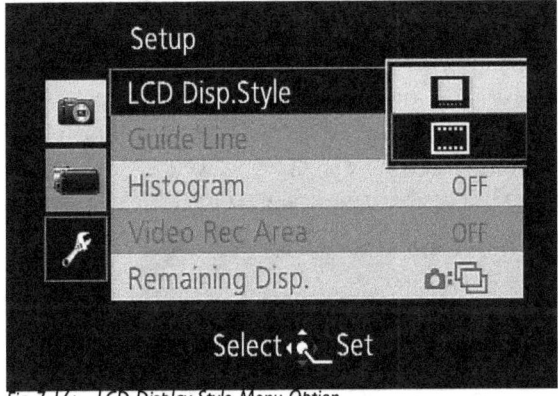

Fig. 7-16:   LCD Display Style Menu Option

Guide Line

This option gives you some control over the grid lines that can be displayed on the LCD screen (or in the electronic view-finder, if it is installed and in use) to assist you with the com-position of your pictures. Once you select Guide Line from the Setup menu, you get to a screen with four options: Off, and three patterns of lines, as shown in Figure 7-17.

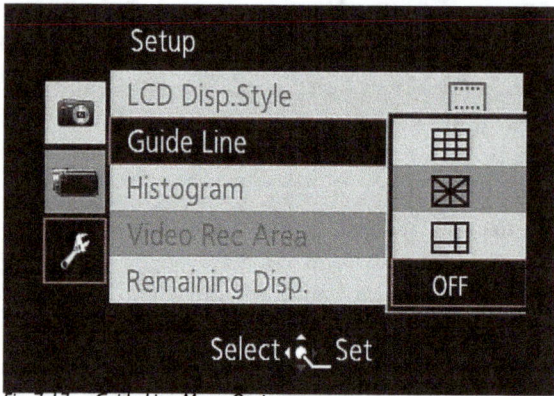

Fig. 7-17: Guide Line Menu Option

If you choose Off, no grid lines will be displayed. If you choose the top option, the camera will display a grid that forms nine equal rectangles on the screen. This choice can help you line up subjects, including the horizon, along straight lines. The second option for grid lines is a pattern of four rectangles along with a pair of intersecting diagonal lines, which can help you locate your subject along diagonals as well as along horizontal or vertical lines, as shown in Figure 7-18.

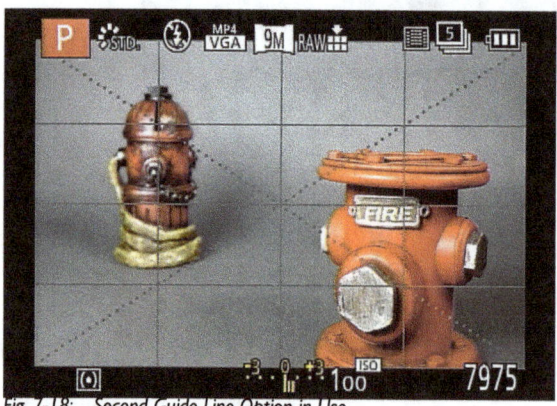

Fig. 7-18: Second Guide Line Option in Use

Finally, with the third option, the camera displays just two intersecting lines, one horizontal and one vertical, and lets you set their positions using the cursor buttons. This option can be useful if you need to compose your shot with an off-center subject.

When any of the Guide Line options is turned on, the grid lines will display whenever the camera is in recording mode, regardless of the shooting mode and regardless of the display screen that has been selected using the Display button.

Histogram

This option, which controls whether the histogram displays on the screen, has only two choices: On or Off. If you turn the histogram on, it will display on the right side of the LCD screen in both recording mode and playback mode for every image, if a detailed display screen has been selected using the Display button, as shown in Figure 7-19.

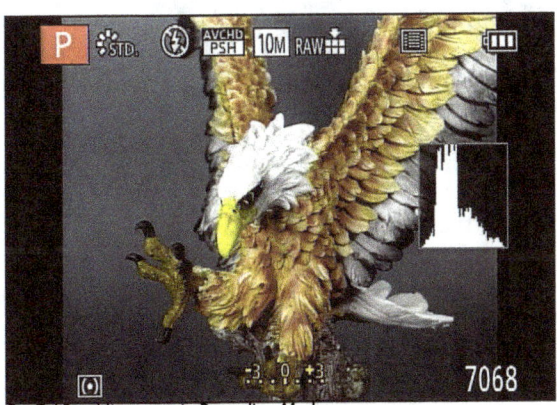

Fig. 7-19:   Histogram in Recording Mode

The histogram does not display in Snapshot mode or Creative Video mode, during the recording of a movie in any shooting mode, or when the HDMI cable is connected.

A histogram is a graph representing the distribution of dark and bright areas in the image that is being displayed on the screen. The darkest blacks are represented by vertical bars on the left, and the brightest whites by vertical bars on the right,

303

with continuous gradations in between.

If an image has a histogram in which the pattern looks like a tall ski slope coming from the left of the screen down to ground level in the middle of the screen, that means there is an excessive amount of black and dark areas (tall bars on the left side of the histogram), and very few bright and white areas (no tall bars on the right). Figure 7-20 illustrates this situation.

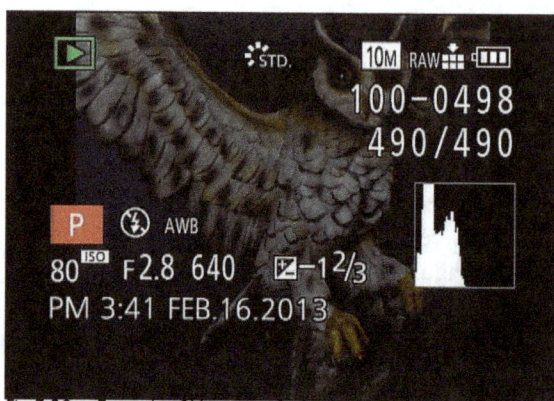

Fig. 7-20:   Example of Histogram for Underexposed Image

A ski slope moving from the middle of the screen up to the top of the right side of the screen would mean just the opposite; too many bright and white areas, as in the histogram shown in Figure 7-21.

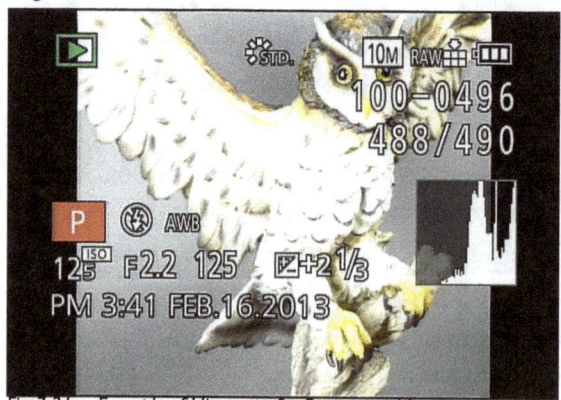

Fig. 7-21:   Example of Histogram for Overexposed Image

A histogram that is "just right" would be one that starts low on the left, gradually rises to a peak in the middle of the screen, then moves gradually back down to ground level at the right. That pattern indicates a good balance of whites, blacks, and medium tones. An example of this type of histogram is shown in Figure 7-22.

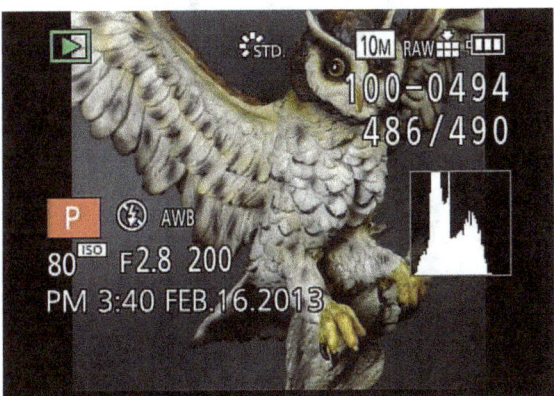

Fig. 7-22: Example of Histogram for Normally Exposed Image

The histogram is an approximation, and should not be relied on too heavily. It gives you some feedback as to how evenly exposed your image is likely to be. (Or, for playback, how well exposed it was.) If the histogram is displayed in orange, that means that the recording and playback versions of the histogram will not match for this image, because the flash was used, or in a few other situations.

Video Recording Area

This option can be set either Off or On. If you turn it on, the camera's screen in recording mode is shaded at the edges, as shown in Figure 7-23. The part of the screen that is left unshaded shows the area that will be viewed and recorded if you record a motion picture using the current settings. Motion pictures are recorded with aspect ratios that differ from the settings that are in effect for still images, so turning on this optional guide can give you an idea of what to expect, before you start recording a movie.

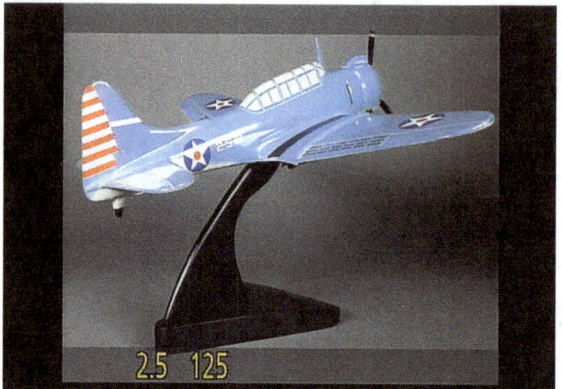

Fig. 7-23:   Video Recording Area Option in Use

Remaining Display

This feature lets you choose whether the camera's display shows how many still images can be taken with current settings, as shown in Figure 7-24, where the display in the lower right corner of the screen shows that 2077 still images can be recorded, or how much time is available for video recording, as shown in Figure 7-25, where the display shows that 29 minutes and 59 seconds of video can be recorded.

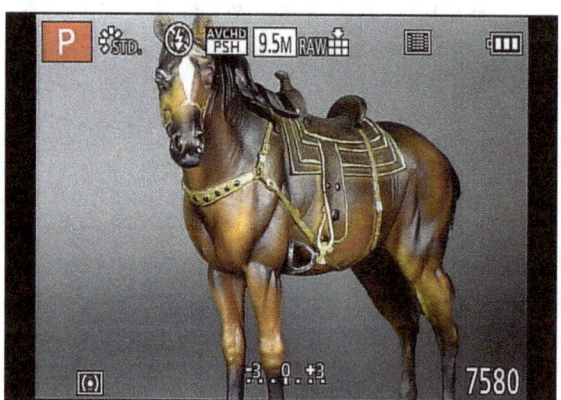

Fig. 7-24:   Remaining Display Option Showing 7580 Still Images

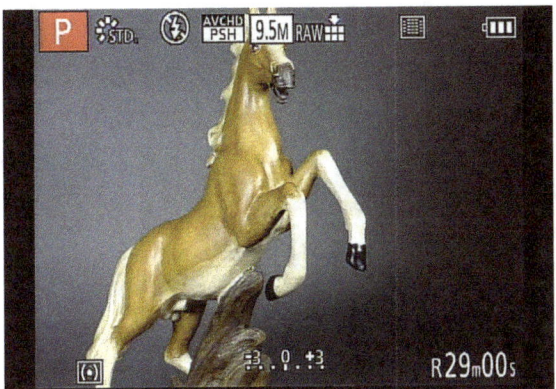

Fig. 7-25: Remaining Display Option Showing 29 Minutes of Video Recording

Highlight

This feature shows a flashing area of black and white on areas of the image that are over-saturated with white, indicating they may be too bright. The flashing effect takes place only when you are viewing the pictures in Auto Review or playback mode. That is, you will see the Highlight warning only when the image appears briefly on the screen after it has been recorded (Auto Review) or when you view the image in playback mode. The purpose of this feature is to alert you that your picture may be overexposed in some areas, and that you may want to reduce the exposure for the next shot. If you find that sort of warning distracting, just turn this feature off.

Exposure Meter

This feature gives you the option of having the camera display its Exposure Meter feature, which is a set of two graphical dials that appear when you are adjusting shutter speed, aperture, or exposure compensation, as shown in Figure 7-26. I find this display distracting and not all that helpful, so I leave it turned off, but you might find it instructive and useful, so you may want to try using it to see if it appeals to you.

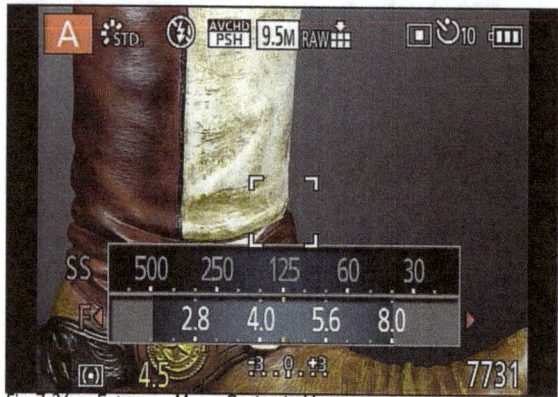

Fig. 7-26:   Exposure Meter Option in Use

Lens Resume

This setting has two sub-options: Zoom Resume and Manual Focus Resume, as shown in Figure 7-27, either of which can be turned on or off.

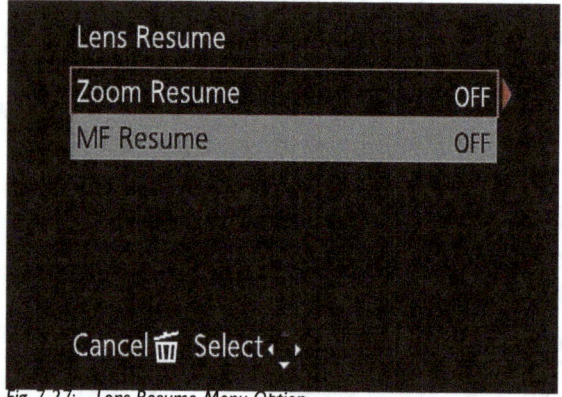

Fig. 7-27:   Lens Resume Menu Option

If you turn on Zoom Resume, then, after you turn the camera off and back on, the lens will return to its last zoom position. If you leave this setting turned off, the lens will zoom out to its widest angle when the power is turned back on.

If you turn Manual Focus Resume on, then the camera will

308

return to its previous manual focus position after the power has been turned off and back on, or after the camera has been switched off of manual focus and back, or has been switched to playback mode and then back to recording mode. If you leave this setting turned off, the manual focus will go to the infinity setting when the power is turned back on or one of the other conditions occurs.

Manual Focus (MF) Assist

I discussed this feature briefly earlier, in talking about how to use manual focus. This function lets you decide whether and how the screen display is magnified when you're using manual focus. With the MF Assist option highlighted, press the right cursor button to pop up the little sub-menu that lets you choose to set this feature On or Off, as shown in Figure 7-28.

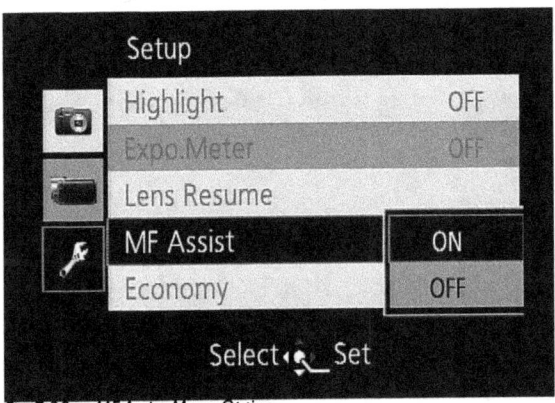

Fig. 7-28:   MF Assist Menu Option

If you choose Off, there is no magnification. If you choose On, then, when you press the ND/Focus lever left or right to focus, the screen will be magnified to about 5 times normal. Then, while it is magnified, if you press in on the ND/Focus lever (using it as a button), the display will be enlarged to 10 times normal. If you press it one more time, a small part of the center of the screen will be shown magnified 4 times normal.

If you want to select the part of the display that is magnified, press the Menu/Set button while the screen is magnified, and a white frame with red arrows will appear on the screen, as shown in Figure 7-29.

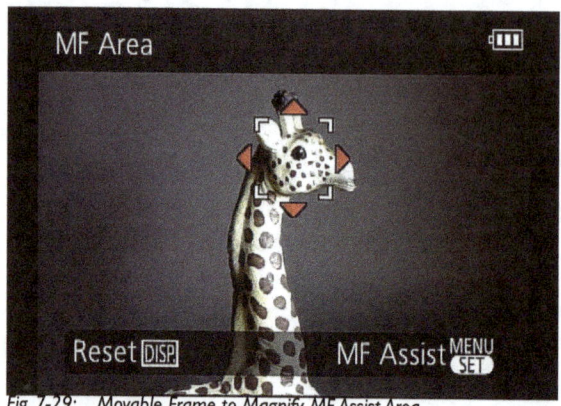

Fig. 7-29: Movable Frame to Magnify MF Assist Area

You can then move that frame around the screen using the cursor buttons. Press Menu/Set to lock it into place, and the part of the screen under that frame will be magnified. You can press the Display button to reset it to the center of the screen.

Economy

This menu option gives you access to three settings to help save battery power: Sleep Mode, Auto LCD Off, and Live View Mode, as shown in Figure 7-30.

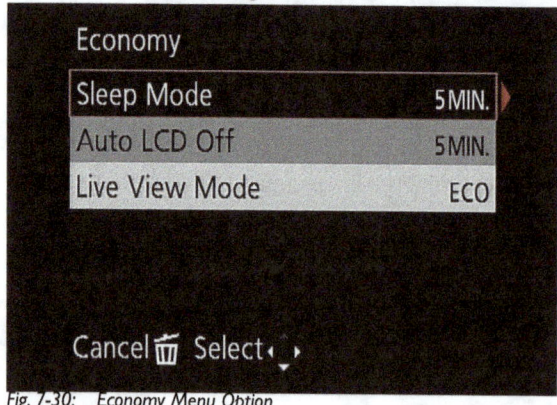

Fig. 7-30: Economy Menu Option

The first option, Sleep Mode, turns the camera off after a specified period of not using any of the camera's controls. The period can be set to one, two, five, or ten minutes, or the option can be turned off, in which case the camera never turns off automatically (unless it runs out of battery power). When Auto LCD Off is turned on, Sleep Mode is fixed to two minutes; in Snapshot mode, Sleep Mode is fixed to five minutes. To cancel Sleep Mode, press the shutter button halfway, and the camera will come back to life.

The second option, Auto LCD Off, which can be set to one, two, five, or thirty minutes, turns off the LCD after the specified time. If the screen is blanked through this feature, the small green status light to the left of the up cursor (ISO) button turns on to let you know the camera is still powered on and operating, even though the screen is dark. You can press any button to turn the screen back on.

The third option, Live View Mode, has two possible settings, Normal and ECO, as shown in Figure 7-31.

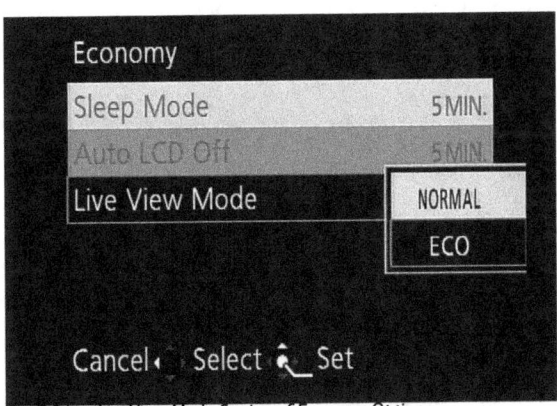

Fig. 7-31:   Live View Mode Setting of Economy Option

If you choose ECO, the screen uses less power and its display may be somewhat degraded. In my experience, the ECO setting does not interfere with my ability to use the camera effectively, and it can be a good way to preserve battery life.

Play on LCD

This option, as shown in Figure 7-32, is of use only if you have installed an optional electronic viewfinder, as discussed in Appendix A.

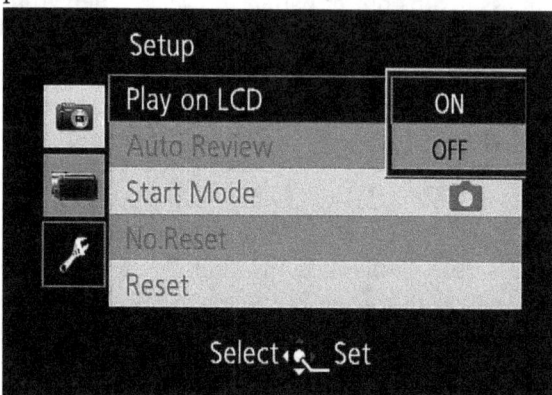

Fig. 7-32: *Play on LCD Menu Option*

When you attach an electronic viewfinder and turn it on, the LCD goes blank, because you will be viewing through the viewfinder. If you turn on the Play on LCD option through the Setup menu, then, when you enter playback mode, the LCD will automatically turn back on.

Auto Review

This option gives you control over how your pictures are reviewed immediately after they have been recorded by the camera. The possible settings are Off, 1 second, 2 seconds, and Hold, as shown in Figure 7-33. These choices are fairly self-explanatory; after the shutter button is pressed, the image appears on the screen (or not) according to how this option is set. If you set it to Hold, the image stays on the screen until you press a button. Auto Review does not work for movies or time lapse recordings, and this setting has no effect for bracketing or burst shots; those images are displayed regardless of the Auto Review setting. In Snapshot mode, this setting is fixed at 2 seconds.

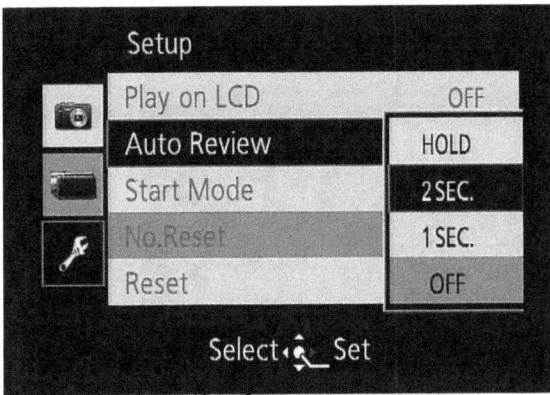

Fig. 7-33:   Auto Review Menu Option

One note: The user's manual says that Hold keeps the picture on the screen until you press any button, other than the Display button. That may be true, but if you press some buttons, such as the Burst/Self-timer or ISO button, you will be activating a new operation, so you're better off relying on the Menu/Set button for this purpose.

Start Mode

This function can be set to either recording mode (camera icon) or playback mode (playback triangle icon), as shown in Figure 7-34. This setting controls which mode the camera will be set to immediately after the power switch is turned on. One reason you might want to set the camera to start up in playback mode is that you can then turn it on without first removing the lens cap; if you start it up in recording mode without removing the lens cap, you will see an error message and will have to remove the lens cap before proceeding. So, if you know you will be viewing pictures or just using Playback menu or Setup menu options, you may want to set this option to start the camera up in playback mode. It won't hurt to do this, because you can then just tap lightly on the shutter button to go right into recording mode.

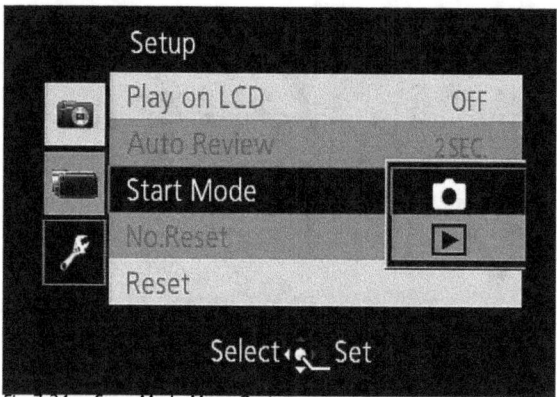

Fig. 7-34: Start Mode Menu Option

Note, though, that you don't really need to use this menu option if you just want to start up in playback mode occasionally; just hold down the Play button while turning on the camera, and it will start up in playback mode.

Number Reset

This function, as shown in Figure 7-35, lets you reset the folder and image number for the next image to be recorded in the camera. If you don't use this option, then the numbers of your images will keep increasing until they reach 999, even if you change to a different memory card. If you want each new memory card to start with images that are numbered from 1 up, use the Number Reset function each time you start using a new card, or when you start a project for which you would like to have freshly numbered images. I prefer not to reset the numbers, because I find it easier to keep track of my images if the numbers keep getting larger; I would find it confusing to have images with duplicate numbers on my various SD cards.

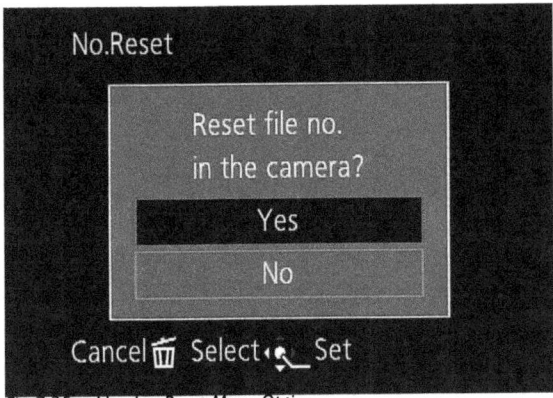

Fig. 7-35:   Number Reset Menu Option

Reset

This function, as shown in Figure 7-36, resets all Recording menu settings to their original states, and also resets all Setup menu settings to their original states.

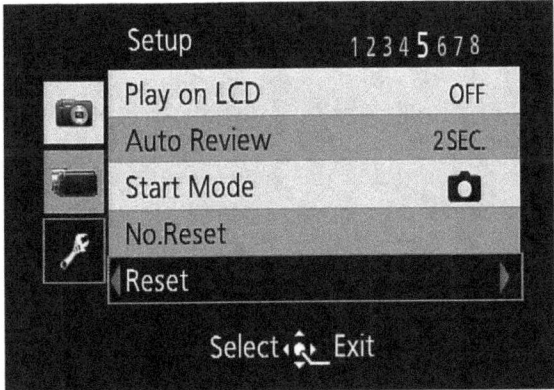

Fig. 7-36:   Reset Menu Option

This is a convenient way to get the camera back to its default mode, so you can start with fresh settings before you experiment with new ones. The camera prompts you twice, asking if you want to reset all Recording menu settings, and then all Setup menu parameters.

USB Mode

If you are going to connect the camera directly to a computer or printer, you need to go into this menu item and select the appropriate setting from the choices shown in Figure 7-37: Select on Connection, PictBridge (for connecting to a printer), or PC.

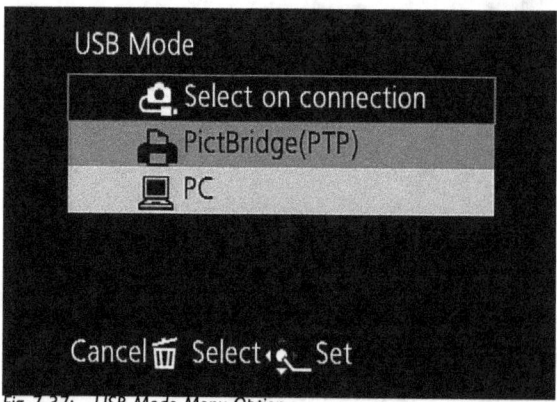

Fig. 7-37: USB Mode Menu Option

If you choose Select on Connection, you don't choose the setting until after you have plugged the USB cable into the device to which you are connecting the camera. The D-Lux 6 connects to a computer using the USB 2.0 connection standard, assuming your computer has a USB port of that speed. (If not, the camera will still connect at the slower speed of the computer's older USB port.)

Output

This menu option is available only when you have connected the camera to a TV by means of the standard audio-visual cable. The sub-setting, TV Aspect, provides only two choices—16:9 for widescreen or 4:3 for fullscreen. You can use this option to set the appropriate shape for the screen, depending on whether most of your images are full-screen (4:3 and similar settings) or widescreen (16:9). If you are playing videos, they will all be widescreen unless you recorded some using the MP4/VGA setting.

316

HDTV Link

This menu option is for use when you are connecting the D-Lux 6 to an HDTV set using a mini-HDMI cable. If you set this option to Off, then the operations of the camera are controlled by the camera's own controls. If you set it to On, then the TV's remote control can also control the operations of the camera, so you can play slide shows or review individual images and movies.

3D Playback

You can set this option to either 3D or 2D, as shown in Figure 7-38, to control how 3D images are displayed when the camera is connected to a 3D-capable TV set.

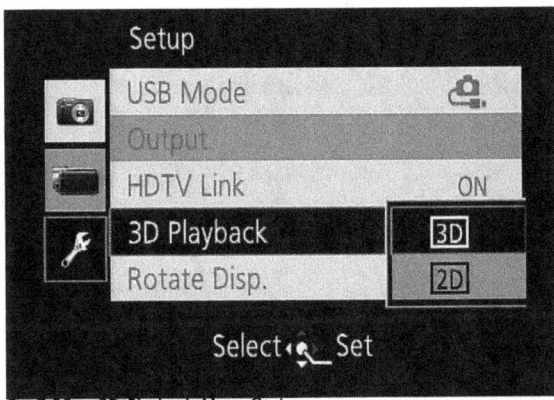

Fig. 7-38: 3D Playback Menu Option

Ordinarily, you would want to set this option to 3D, but, if you find that your eyes are straining from viewing the 3D images, you can set this option to 2D, and view the images as ordinary shots.

Rotate Display

This menu item does not modify your images. It can be set to one of three options, as shown in Figure 7-39, from top to bottom: rotate images when viewed on TV or in camera; rotate images only on TV; or don't rotate at all.

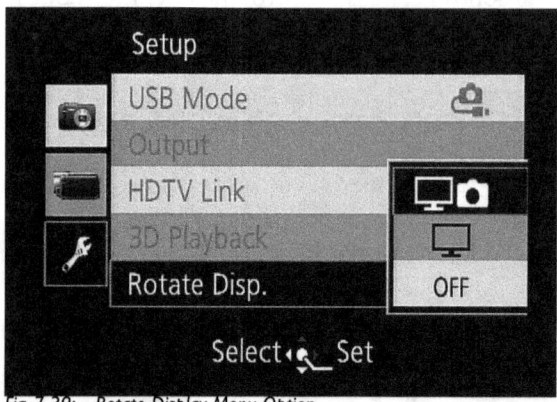

Fig. 7-39: Rotate Display Menu Option

This setting affects the way the camera (or TV, or both) displays images for which you held the camera in a vertical position when you recorded them. That is, images for which the top of the camera was rotated to be facing to the right or left when you took the picture. If you leave this option turned off, then those images will be displayed to look the way they were viewed when they were taken; that is, you will have to rotate the camera back to a vertical position to see such images properly. If you turn this option on, then the camera automatically displays those images in a vertical orientation when the camera is held horizontally. To do this, it has to shrink the image so the entire vertical image will fit within the horizontal screen, as shown in Figure 7-40.

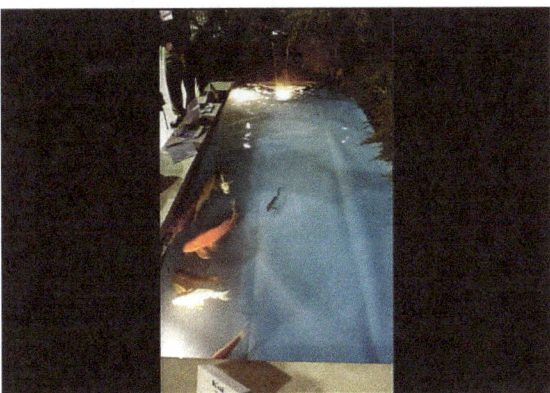

Fig. 7-40:   Example of Image Rotated for Vertical Display

The Rotate Display function does not work with movies or when you have pressed the zoom lever to the left (toward the W setting) to view images 12 or 30 at a time, or by date from the calendar.

Scene Menu

This option has two possible settings: Off or Auto, as shown in Figure 7-41.

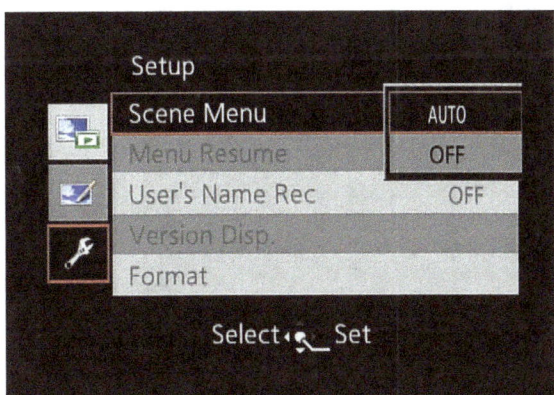

Fig. 7-41:   Scene Menu Menu Option

If you choose Auto, whenever you turn the mode dial on top of the camera to the SCN setting to select Scene mode, the

319

camera will immediately display the menu of scene types with one of them highlighted, so you can scroll through them and choose one. For example, it may start with Portrait highlighted, so you can press the Menu/Set button to select Portrait, or you can scroll through the other choices to find the one you want. This method saves you the step of entering the menu system and selecting the Scene menu.

If, instead, you turn the Scene Menu setting to Off, when you turn the mode dial and select Scene mode, the screen displays the live view image with the camera set to whatever scene type happens to be the last one used; if you want to select a different scene type, you need to press Menu/Set and navigate to the Scene menu to make a different selection.

I like the Auto setting, because chances are I will want a different scene type than the last one I used when I turn the Mode dial to SCN. But if you often choose the same scene type, you may prefer to leave this setting off, and go back to the same scene type each time you select SCN on the Mode dial. It's not hard to enter the menu system and choose a different scene type, if you need to.

Menu Resume

This menu item can be set either on or off, as shown in Figure 7-42.

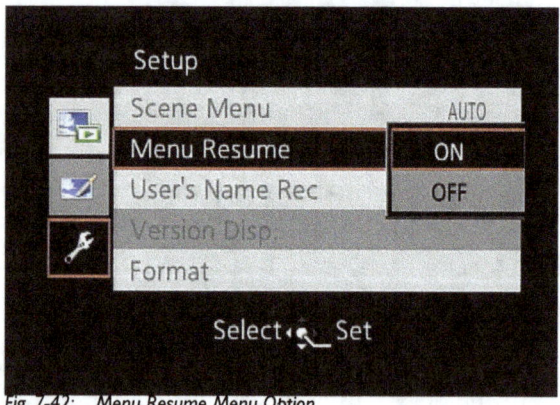

Fig. 7-42:   Menu Resume Menu Option

When it is turned on, whenever you enter the menu system, the camera displays the last menu item you had selected previously. When this option is turned off, the camera always starts back at the top of the first screen of the menu system, which may be the Recording menu, Playback menu, Setup menu, or the menu for a specialized mode such as Scene, Creative Video, or Creative Control, depending on what mode the camera is in (recording, playback, or specialized shooting mode). If there is a particular menu item you need to adjust often, this option can be of considerable use, because you can just press the Menu/Set button, and the item will appear, ready for you to make your setting.

For example, if you are in a situation where you need to change the metering mode frequently, turn on Menu Resume. Then, whenever you need to get back to the metering mode setting, just press Menu/Set, and the item will be there at your fingertips, as long as the camera is still in a mode in which that menu is available. (Of course, you also could set the Function button to bring up this option, or you could use the Quick Menu, but this is one other approach to consider.)

User's Name Recording

This menu item lets you enter your name (or any other name, word, or phrase), so that, if this option is turned on, that name will be recorded along with the image, giving you a record of who took the picture (or of something else, if you like). The name cannot be seen on the images in the camera; you can use the Adobe Lightroom software provided by Leica to make sure the name was recorded correctly. The name also will show up in other software that displays metadata (data recorded invisibly with an image), such as Adobe Bridge. If you try to turn this option on before having entered a name, the camera will prompt you to use the SET option on this menu to enter a name, using the standard text-entry screen. You can enter up to 30 characters. This function does not work with RAW files or movies in the AVCHD format.

Version Display

This menu item has no settings; when you select it, it displays the version of the camera's firmware that is currently installed. As I write this, my D-Lux 6 has version 1.0 of the firmware installed, as shown in Figure 7-43.

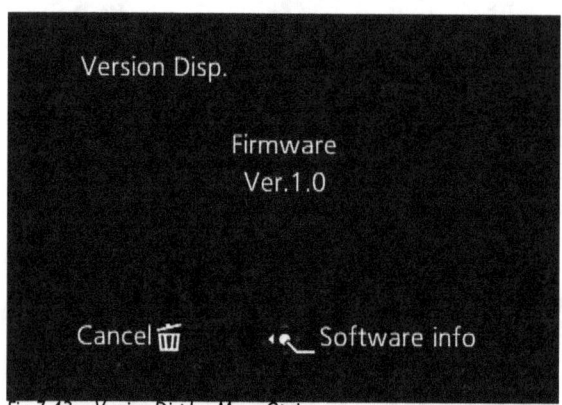

Fig. 7-43: Version Display Menu Option

Firmware is a term for something that is somewhat like both software and hardware; it is the programming for the camera's circuitry that is electronically recorded into the camera, either at the factory or through your computer if you upgrade the firmware with an update provided by Leica. A new version of the firmware can fix bugs and can even provide new features, so it's well worthwhile checking the Leica web site periodically for updates. Instructions for installing an update are provided on the web site. Essentially, the process usually involves downloading a file to your computer, saving that file to an SD card formatted for the camera, then placing that card in the camera so the firmware can be installed.

Format

This is one of the more important menu options. Choose this process only when you want or need to completely wipe all of the data from a memory storage card. When you select the

Format option, the camera will ask you if you want to delete all of the data on the card, as shown in Figure 7-44.

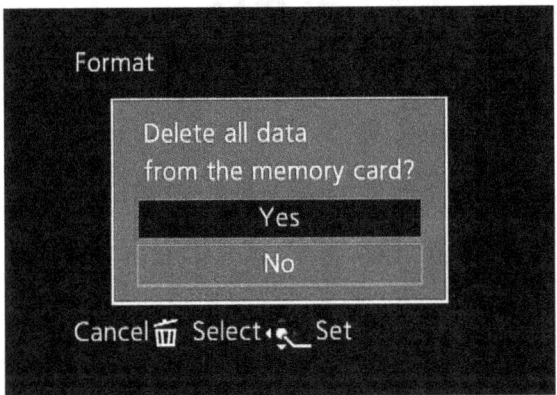

Fig. 7-44:   Confirmation Screen for Format Command

If you reply by selecting Yes, it will proceed to do so, and the result will be a card that is empty of images and is properly formatted to store new images from the camera. It's a good idea to use this command with any new memory card you use in the camera for the first time.

If you want to format the camera's built-in memory, you have to remove any card from the camera, so the built-in memory is the only possible memory to be formatted. Then, when you select the Format command, the internal memory will be wiped clean and formatted.

Language

This option gives you the choice of language for the display of commands and information on the LCD screen, as shown in Figure 7-45. If your camera happens to be set to a language that you don't read, you can find the language option by going into the Setup menu (look for the wrench icon), and then scrolling to this option, which is marked by a little icon showing a person's head with a word balloon. It also is the next-to-last option on the Setup menu.

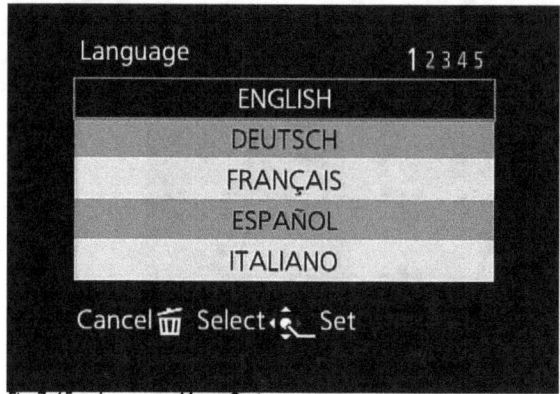

Fig. 7-45: Language Menu Option

Demo Mode

This last option on the Setup menu, shown in Figure 7-46, causes the camera to display an on-screen demonstration of the operation of its optical image stabilization system, abbreviated as O.I.S. on the menu screen.

Fig. 7-46: Optical Image Stabilization Demo Menu Option

When you select this option, the camera displays two camera icons, the top one with yellow lines, indicating the degree of shakiness as the camera is being held, and the bottom one with blue lines, indicating the degree to which the shakiness has been reduced by the stabilization system. An example of this display is shown in Figure 7-47.

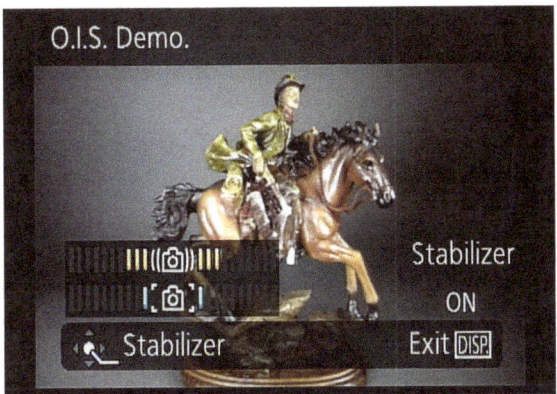

Fig. 7-47:   Optical Image Stabilization Demo in Operation

You can press the Menu/Set button while this display is on the screen to alternate between the results with the Stabilizer feature turned on and with the Stabilizer turned off.

Chapter 8: Motion Pictures

Until recently, most compact digital cameras had only quite basic video capabilities. They could record video sequences, but would not let you control the exposure or focus in some cases; in other cases, they could only record in standard-definition formats with moderate quality, or only for a few minutes.

The D-Lux 6 is part of a newer generation of video-capable compact cameras that are beginning to exhibit some features that rival those of dedicated camcorders. The D-Lux 6 is not sufficiently sophisticated to serve as the main camera for professional film-making, but its features in some areas are remarkably advanced. In fact, they are so sophisticated that video-making with the D-Lux 6 needs its own chapter just to cover the essentials. So let's get started.

Basics of D-Lux 6 Videography

In one sense, the fundamentals of making videos with the D-Lux 6 can be reduced to four words: "Push the red button." Having a dedicated motion picture recording button does make things very easy for the user of this camera, because anytime you see a reason to take some video footage, you can just press that easily accessible button while aiming at your subject, and you will get results that are likely to be quite acceptable. So, if you're more of a still photographer and not particularly interested in movie-making, you don't need to read any further. Be aware that the red button exists, and if a newsworthy event starts to unfold before your eyes, you can press the button and quickly get a serviceable record of the action.

But for those D-Lux 6 users who would like to delve further into their camera's motion picture capabilities, there is considerably more information to discuss.

Choosing the Shooting Mode and Other Settings

One aspect of motion picture recording with the D-Lux 6 that can be somewhat confusing is how to select the shooting mode. For still photography with this camera, when you choose a shooting mode by turning the mode dial on top of the camera, that is the mode that you will shoot your pictures in. That is not quite how it works with movie recording. In the motion picture arena, where you set the mode dial has some effect on your shooting, but not as direct an effect as for still photos.

Here is the situation. If you look at the mode dial, as shown in Figure 8-1, you will see icons for the various shooting modes for still photography: Snapshot, Program, Aperture Priority, Shutter Priority, Manual, Custom 1, Custom 2, Scene, and Creative Control.

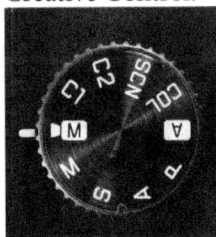

Fig. 8-1: Mode Dial

There is also one entry on the dial for movies, represented by the letter M with a movie camera icon: Creative Video mode. However, because of the red Movie button, you do not have to set the mode dial to Creative Video mode to record a movie (though you certainly can, as I'll discuss shortly). In fact, you can have the mode dial set to any of its settings and still record a movie. But, the results may not be what you might expect based on the name of the shooting mode.

For example, when the mode dial is set to M for Manual exposure mode, if you press the red button you will not be shooting a movie in Manual exposure mode. In fact, you'll be shooting a movie with the camera adjusting the exposure automatically by setting the aperture and shutter speed. This is the same result you'll get with any of the four PASM shooting modes on the mode dial (Program, Aperture Priority, Shutter Priority, and Manual).

Here is where the situation gets slightly complicated. As I just noted, when you set the mode dial to some of the major still-shooting modes, such as A, S, or M, the camera does not follow that mode's behavior for setting exposure when you press the red movie button. But the camera does use some (but not all) of the other settings that have been made in that shooting mode. For example, if you have the camera set to Aperture Priority mode on the mode dial, when you press the red button to make a movie, the camera does not let you set the aperture; instead, it chooses both aperture and shutter speed. However, the camera does use some of the settings that have been chosen through the Recording menu or physical controls while the camera was in Aperture Priority mode, such as metering mode and white balance. Of course, several options from the Recording menu and other controls make no sense for recording movies, and therefore have no effect when you press the red button, including Flash, Auto Bracket, and Aspect Bracket.

You also can set the mode dial to Snapshot mode, and the camera will take over even more of the settings for your movies, or you can set it to Scene mode and for movies it will use the basic settings for the type of scene you select, in many cases. For certain scene types, though, the camera will use its own versions of scene types, as follows: For the two Baby scene types, the camera will use the Portrait type. For Night Portrait, Night Scenery, and Handheld Night Shot, the camera will use what Leica calls the "Low Light" mode. And, for Sports, HDR, and

Pet, it will use its "Normal Motion Picture" mode. You cannot shoot a video using the 3D or Panorama setting.

Creative Video Mode

If you want to have more control over the camera's exposure settings while shooting your movie, that's the role of the movie-oriented setting on the mode dial, Creative Video.

When you turn the mode dial to that setting, the screen will display a menu of five exposure modes: Program, Aperture Priority, Shutter Priority, Manual, and High Speed, as shown in Figure 8-2.

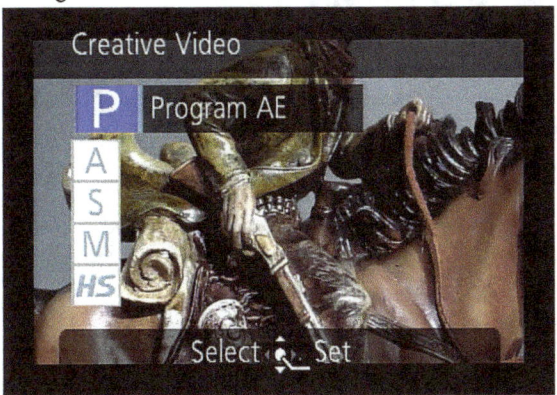

Fig. 8-2:   Display When Mode Dial Turned to Creative Video Slot

You have to select one of those five modes, which will then be in effect when you press the red button to record a movie. The first four of these modes work in ways similar to their still-photography counterparts, but they are distinctly separate, video-oriented shooting modes.

If you want to call up this screen to select a video exposure mode when the camera is already set to Creative Video mode, you have to use the menu system and select the top icon in the column at the left, which is marked with an M, for Motion Picture mode, as shown in Figure 8-3. This special menu, which is available only in Creative Video mode, lets you select one of the five available Creative Video exposure modes. Following are details on the first four of these modes. (I will discuss the High Speed mode later in this chapter.)

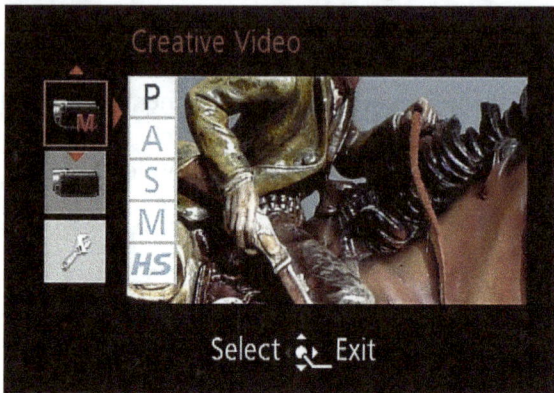

Fig. 8-3: Creative Video Menu - Exposure Mode Options

If you select Program, the camera chooses shutter speed and aperture, just as it does when the camera is set to one of the basic still-shooting modes on the mode dial (P, A, S, or M).

If you choose Aperture Priority, you use the aperture ring to select the aperture, and the camera will then adjust its shutter speed for the correct exposure, if possible. The D-Lux 6 has the same range of apertures available for setting in Creative Video mode as in Aperture Priority and Manual exposure mode: f/1.4 to f/8.0 when the lens is zoomed back to its full wide-angle position, and f/2.3 to f/8.0 when the lens is zoomed in fully.

If you choose Shutter Priority, you set the shutter speed and the camera sets the aperture. Because of the nature of video footage, which is recorded (in the United States) at about 30 frames per second, the slowest shutter speed you can normally choose is 1/30 second (but see the note below under Manual mode, for an exception). You can choose from a wide range of faster shutter speeds, though; in fact, for motion pictures in Creative Video mode, the camera has a special range of shutter speeds for video recording: 1/30 second to 1/20,000 second!

If you choose Manual Exposure, you set both shutter speed and aperture, in the same way as for still photography. Of

330

course, as with shooting stills, the camera will not make any changes in exposure on its own; it is up to you to you change one or both of the values, so, if the lighting changes, the exposure may be incorrect.

There is one more benefit in terms of creative options if you shoot your video in this Manual mode: If you also have the focus switch (on the lens barrel) set to manual focus, you can then set the shutter speed as slow as 1/8 second. This shutter speed setting results in a video frame rate of 8 frames per second, considerably slower than the normal (U.S.) frame rate of 30 frames per second. It lets you record usable footage in conditions of very low light and can result in interesting effects, such as ghost-like streakiness of your image if you pan the camera. You would not want to use this slow shutter speed for taking video of a sporting event, but if you're making a science-fiction or horror movie, this feature could present some promising possibilities.

Note, also, that you are completely free to change either shutter speed or aperture, or both, during your shot. So, for example, if you're shooting a movie in Creative Video mode using the Shutter Priority or Manual Exposure setting, you can gradually increase the shutter speed to a faster and faster value to make the picture fade gradually to black. In fact, I just did this, and was somewhat amazed to see the shutter speed value on the LCD eventually rise to 1/20,000 second! (Note that you have to be sure the rear dial is controlling shutter speed; if it is controlling exposure compensation, press in on the dial to switch its function.) This seems quite amazing in a camera whose fastest shutter speed for still photos is 1/4000 second. But it worked, and produced a nice fadeout. The only problem was that the motions of the rear dial could be heard on the audio track. But you can correct that problem in post-production by replacing or editing the audio track using video editing software such as Adobe Premiere Elements, if you are so inclined.

With the Program, Aperture Priority, and Shutter Priority settings of Creative Video mode, you can adjust exposure compensation, just as with still photography, by pressing in on the rear dial and then turning it left or right. Also, when the camera is set to Creative Video mode, you can use the shutter button to start and stop video recording. In all other modes, pressing the shutter button will take a still picture, but in this one situation, you can use either the red Movie button or the shutter button to control movie-making.

High Speed Video Recording

The last of the five exposure settings for Creative Video mode is represented on the main selection screen by the HS icon, which stands for High Speed video, as shown in Figure 8-4.

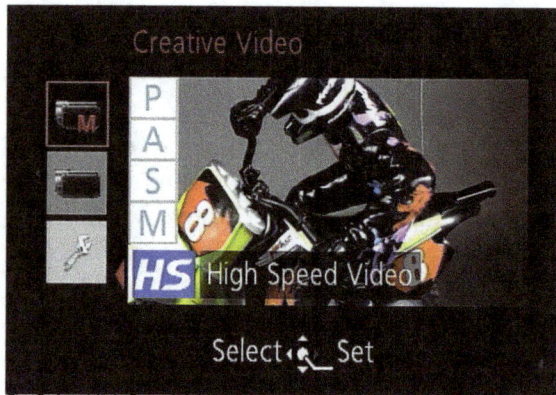

Fig. 8-4:   High Speed Video Menu Option

This mode, naturally, is quite different from the four others I have just discussed. It is a specialized setting for shooting movies at a higher speed than normal, so the action will appear to be in slow motion when the footage is played at normal speed.

Once you have selected the HS option, there are very few other settings that you can make for the motion pictures. They will be recorded at 120 frames per second, which is 4 times the normal speed for video recording (in the United States). Therefore, when the video is played back at the normal rate of 30 frames per second, the action will appear to be slowed down to one-fourth of the normal speed. You can use this option to analyze golf swings or other quick actions, or just to produce a dream-like aura for your scenes.

All High Speed video is recorded using the MP4 format with no sound. The AF Mode setting is fixed at 1-Area, but you can choose whether to turn Continuous AF on or off through the Motion Picture menu. You also can choose from the complete range of options for the Photo Style setting, so you can, for example, record a slow-motion sequence in black and white.

Making Other Settings When Recording Movies

I have just discussed the considerations for choosing a shooting mode for recording videos. Next, I will discuss the various other settings you can make with the camera's controls, and their effects on video recording.

First, when the camera is set to any of the still-shooting modes, you cannot set the ISO for motion picture recording; any setting you have made before starting the recording will have no effect; the camera uses Auto ISO at all times for video recording in those modes. In addition, the ISO Limit Set menu item is disabled for video recording. However, you can set the ISO if you use the Creative Video mode.

You can set the white balance for video recording using the WB button (right cursor button) when using a shooting mode that allows that setting. In addition, just as with still photography, after selecting a white balance preset, you can press the right button and then make further adjustments to the setting on the Amber-Blue and Magenta-Green axes. You cannot adjust white balance while a video is being recorded.

With respect to focus, the D-Lux 6 partially recognizes the focus mode that is selected on the Recording menu. If you have chosen AF Tracking or 23-Area for AF Mode, that setting will not be in effect if you press the red Movie button to record

333

a video. However, if you have selected Face Detection, that setting will function normally. If you have selected any of the other options, the camera will use 1-Area focusing.

As discussed below, the Continuous AF option on the Motion Picture menu controls whether the camera will continuously adjust its focus. If that option is turned on, the camera will focus on any object that comes within its focus frame. If Continuous AF is turned off, then the camera will not automatically adjust its focus. However, just as with still photography, you can half-press the shutter button during video recording to cause the camera to re-focus on the area under the focus frame. Also, if you have moved the focus frame away from the center of the display using the 1-Area AF Mode option on the Recording menu, the frame will be in the location you moved it to. If you have used the Function Button Set item on the Setup menu to assign the 1 Shot AF function to that button, you can press the button while the video is recording to cause the camera to re-focus.

When the camera is set to Snapshot mode, it will automatically adjust its focus; you cannot use manual focus or change the autofocus settings in that recording mode.

Finally, you can use manual focus when shooting movies (except in Snapshot mode), but there will be no enlarged focus area or distance scale displayed on the LCD to assist you in achieving sharp focus. If you have the 1 Shot AF function turned on, you can press the Function button to cause the camera to use its autofocus at any time. Using manual focus, you can produce a very nice "pull focus" effect, like the ones you occasionally see in feature films or TV commercials, when the camera's focus quickly changes from blurred to sharp, to bring a prominent subject quickly into focus.

The zoom lever functions normally to zoom the lens in or out while shooting a movie. Also, the Intelligent Zoom and Digital Zoom menu options work normally, if they have been activated through the Recording menu or the Motion Picture menu, depending on the shooting mode the camera is set to.

The ND filter operates normally during video recording, if it has been activated before you start recording the video.

The Motion Picture Menu

Next, I will discuss the one menu system I have not yet discussed in detail—the Motion Picture menu. This menu is available whenever the camera is in recording mode. The camera does not have to be in Creative Video mode, because, as we have seen, you can press the red Movie button at any time to record a movie. The Motion Picture menu changes according to what recording mode has been set with the mode dial on top of the camera. It's also important to note that many of the items that appear on the Motion Picture menu when the mode dial is set to Creative Video mode are similar to, or the same as, items that also appear on the Recording menu for still photos. This situation can be a little confusing to sort out. I find that the best way to approach the matter is to discuss each of the items on the Motion Picture menu, including those that have already been discussed in connection with the Recording menu, even if the discussion is very brief. Along the way, I'll note what modes the various items are applicable to.

With that introduction, following is the list of all items that can appear on the Motion Picture menu. Each item is accompanied by the list of mode dial positions in which it appears, abbreviated as follows: SS – Snapshot; P – Program; A – Aperture Priority; S – Shutter Priority; M – Manual; CV – Creative Video; C1 – Custom 1; C2 – Custom 2; SCN- Scene; CC – Creative Control.

Photo Style
(CV)

This setting lets you choose the "look" of your footage. It works the same as it does for still photos. The choices are Standard, Vivid, Natural, Monochrome, Scenery, Portrait, and Custom.

Recording Mode
(SS, P, A, S, M, CV, C1, C2, SCN, CC)

This setting gives you the basic choice of video format for any movies you make: AVCHD or MP4. If you want the highest-quality HD (high definition) footage to display directly on an HDTV, choose AVCHD. However, unless you are experienced in editing such footage, you may find it more difficult to work with on a computer than MP4, which produces the relatively familiar .mp4 files that can be used by Apple QuickTime and other commonly available software. In addition, if you want to produce smaller, lower-quality footage for e-mailing or web use, select MP4, which gives you the option of producing files that are easier to send via e-mail than AVCHD files.

AVCHD stands for Advanced Video Coding High Definition. This format, developed jointly by Sony and Panasonic, has become increasingly common in advanced digital cameras in recent years. As noted, it provides excellent quality, and movies recorded in this format on the D-Lux 6 can be used to create Blu-ray discs.

However, files recorded in the AVCHD format can be complicated to edit on a computer. In fact, just finding the AVCHD video files on a memory card can be a challenge. When you take a memory card from the D-Lux 6 camera and insert it into a memory card reader for viewing on your computer, you can find the still-image files and .mp4 videos within the folder labeled DCIM and then within sub-folders with names such as 100LEICA. The AVCHD files, however, are not in the DCIM folder; they are inside a different folder named PRIVATE. Inside that folder you will find another one called AVCHD, and within that one another one called BDMV. Open that folder and you will see more files or folders, including a folder called STREAM. With the card whose contents I am looking at now on my Macintosh, that folder contains numerous files with the extension .mts. Those .mts files are the actual AVCHD files that can be edited with compatible software packages, such as

Adobe Premiere Pro. (You don't have to worry about finding the file names if you connect your camera to the computer using the USB cable, only if you use an SD card reader, as I do.)

Recording Quality
(SS, P, A, S, M, CV, C1, C2, SCN, CC)

The choices for this next menu option depend on what you select for Recording Mode, above. If you choose AVCHD, the choices for Recording Quality are PSH, FSH, and SH, for progressive super-high, full super-high, and super-high. The first two selections produce videos of what is currently the maximum resolution for consumer high-definition video: 1920 X 1080 pixels, sometimes known as "Full HD." However, the PSH format involves "progressive" video with a bit rate of 28 megabits per second, or mbps, which is a high bit rate for consumer video, and yields excellent quality. The next level down in quality, FSH, is not progressive, but, instead, is "interlaced" video, with a bit rate of 17 mbps. This still yields excellent quality, but not quite as high as the PSH standard.

The first choice, PSH, is the only "progressive" video format available with the D-Lux 6. In the video context, "progressive" means the camera records 60 full frames per second, which yields higher quality than the alternative, which is "interlaced" video. The 60 frames are later translated into 30 frames for playback at the standard rate of 30 fps. However, if you want to, and your video editing software has this capability, you can play back your 60p footage in slow motion at one-half the normal speed and still maintain full HD quality. This possibility exists because, as noted above, the 60p footage is recorded with twice the number of full frames as 60i footage, so the quality of the video does not suffer if it is played back at one-half speed. (With other video formats, playback at half speed will appear choppy or jerky, because not enough frames were recorded to play back smoothly at that speed.) So, if you think you may want to slow down your footage significantly with a computer for playback, you should choose the 60p setting.

The next level down on the quality spectrum, SH, produces video at a resolution of 1280 X 720 pixels. This format, like all of the AVCHD formats, is recorded in the 16:9 widescreen format, regardless of how the aspect ratio switch is set.

There is one particularly important point to note about the SH setting. With the version of the D-Lux 6 that is sold in the United States, when you select the SH format, the camera can record for more than 30 minutes at a time, which is the limit for all other video formats. I will discuss this capability in more detail later in this chapter.

If you choose MP4 for Recording Mode, the Quality choices are the following, in descending order of quality: FHD (full high-definition)(1920 X 1080 pixels, 16:9 aspect ratio); HD (high-definition) (1280 X 720 pixels, 16:9 aspect ratio); and VGA (video graphics array, a standard for computer screens) (640 X 480 pixels, 4:3 aspect ratio). None of these formats provides the same quality as AVCHD formats, but the first two are HD formats that produce excellent results. The last format, VGA, is a low-resolution format that is suitable if you need to make an inventory of possessions or some other non-critical video recording. It also can be useful if you need a video recording with a small file size so it can be sent by e-mail.

ISO Limit Set
(CV)

As noted earlier, if the camera is set to any still-shooting mode, you cannot control the ISO in any way for shooting videos; the camera uses Auto ISO. However, in Creative Video mode, you can set the ISO to a value from 80 to 6400, or to Auto. The ISO Limit setting can be made only if ISO is set to Auto.

ISO Increments

(CV)
As with the Recording menu version of this setting, this option lets you set the ISO increment to 1/3 EV instead of 1 EV,

resulting in several interpolated values, including values such as 500, 640, 1000, 1250, 2000, 2500, 4000, and 5000.

AF Mode
(CV)

The AF Mode setting in Creative Video mode is limited to two choices: Face Detection or 1-Area AF. If you choose the latter, you can move the focus frame around the screen with the cursor buttons and resize it with the rear dial, just as with still image recording. The frame does not appear on the screen during video recording, but it still determines the focus point.

Continuous AF
(P, A, S, M, CV, C1, C2, SCN, CC)

This option has only two settings: On and Off. If you turn it on, the camera will attempt to keep its focus on the subject you first focus on. If you turn it off, focus will remain fixed where you first set it. However, if you assigned the Function button to have the 1 Shot AF option, you can press the Function button at any time to cause the camera to re-focus on a new subject within the focus frame.

AF/AE Lock
(CV)

This setting works in the same way as on the Recording menu.

Metering Mode
(CV)

This menu option gives you access to the same three metering methods found on the Recording menu: Multi, Center-weighted, and Spot. Note that, when you select the Spot metering mode from the Motion Picture menu, which you can do only when the camera is in the Creative Video mode, the camera displays a small cross to indicate that spot metering is in effect. You also can choose spot metering from the Recording menu, and it will take effect for video recording (when the camera is set to a mode that permits spot metering), but the camera will not display the cross in that case.

I recommend against using spot metering for video recording in most cases, because the exposure of the scene can vary widely as the spot covers areas of varying exposure. Of course, if your particular situation calls for using this metering method, it is available for use.

Intelligent Dynamic
(CV)

This setting works the same as on the Recording menu.

Exposure Mode
(CV)

This option lets you select one of the five special video-oriented exposure modes that are available in Creative Video mode: Program, Aperture Priority, Shutter Priority, Manual, or High Speed. You can select one of these modes when you turn the Mode dial to the CV setting, or you can use this menu option later to switch modes while you're still in the CV shooting mode.

Intelligent Resolution
(CV)

This setting also works the same as its still-photo counterpart.

Intelligent Zoom
(CV)

This setting is another one that is no different from the version on the Recording menu.

Digital Zoom
(CV)

Another setting that's the same as that on the Recording menu.

Stabilizer
(CV)

This setting works in the same way as the Stabilizer option on the Recording menu. I recommend leaving it turned on unless you are shooting your video with the D-Lux 6 attached to a tripod.

AF Assist Lamp
(CV)

This setting is the same as for still photography—off or on.

Wind Cut
(P, A, S, M, CV, C1, C2, SCN, CC)

This last setting on the Motion Picture menu is one of the few that appear only on that menu. It has two settings: Off or On. If it is turned on, the camera attempts to reduce the noise from wind while recording a video sequence. This processing may have an adverse effect on the quality of the audio, though. If you are recording casual scenes from a vacation, I would recommend turning this option on when recording in a windy area. If you will be using video-editing software, though, you may want to turn this setting off, because it can reduce some wanted sounds, and you can adjust the sound track with your software to minimize the unwanted sounds.

Finally, here is one more note about the Motion Picture menu. You also can take advantage of the Custom Set Memory option on the second screen of the Setup menu to save a group of menu options and other settings for motion picture recording. All of the settings from the Motion Picture menu can be saved to a Custom slot using the procedure discussed in Chapter 7. And, of course, many of the settings from the Recording menu can be saved as well, and many of them are applicable to video recording, as discussed in this chapter.

Recording Time

One other point about video-making with the D-Lux 6 is not related to the menu system: the length of recording time available. Although I understand that the version of the camera sold in Europe is limited to recording just under 30 minutes of video in one stretch, the version of the D-Lux 6 camera that is sold in the United States is capable of an amazing amount of continuous recording time—slightly more than 13 hours in the AVCHD format, but only when the camera is set to the SH setting for Quality. That figure is not for the total amount that can fit on a single SD card; it's for the total time you can record video in one uninterrupted shot! Figure 8-5 shows the camera's display of video recording time remaining under these conditions. That amount of recording requires a large memory card, with a capacity of at least 16 GB.

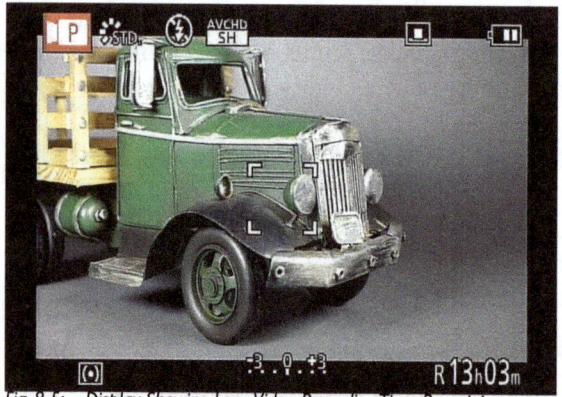

Fig. 8-5: Display Showing Long Video Recording Time Remaining

Although I don't expect to have much need for recording great lengths of video continuously, the need can arise, as I found when I recorded my daughter's high school play using two camcorders that each held only one hour's worth of tape; the juggling act to keep the recording going without any gaps was fairly hair-raising.

As an experiment, I loaded the D-Lux 6 with a 128 GB SDXC

card and plugged in an AC adapter (along with the required DC Coupler; see Appendix A). I set the camera on a tripod aimed at my computer with a video playing. With this setup, the camera recorded a single video file that lasted 3 hours and 7 minutes before I turned the camera off. The camera was still going strong when I turned it off. I played back the recording, and it showed no problems—that is, no gaps, pauses, or stutters. The audio was quite acceptable. The camera produced three .mts video files, two of them about 4.5 GB in size, and the third of them about 2.5 GB, for a total of about 11.5 GB. I joined the three files together in Adobe Premiere Pro software on my computer, and the entire sequence played back very well.

The results of this test showed me that the D-Lux 6 (U.S. version) is very capable of recording multiple hours of high-quality video and audio, as long as you have an AC adapter (with DC Coupler) and an SDXC card (or an SDHC card for shorter durations). I can imagine various situations in which the camera's ability to make super-long recordings could come in handy; besides school plays, there could be business conferences, speeches, graduations, concerts, and other long-running events that you might want to capture in HD quality video.

Shooting Still Images While Recording a Video

The D-Lux 6 has an excellent capability for capturing still images while you are recording a video, in any shooting mode other than Creative Video. (In that mode, pressing the shutter button will start or stop a video recording.)

In any of the still-shooting modes, while a video is being recorded, just press the shutter button, and a still picture will be captured using the same settings that are being used for recording the video, with some differences. The picture size of the still image will always be fixed at 3.5 megapixels, and the aspect ratio will be fixed at 16:9, which is the aspect ratio for HD video. You cannot take a still picture while the camera is recording a video using the low-quality VGA format.

Shooting still pictures should not cause any visual disruption on the video recording, but you are likely to hear the sound of the shutter being operated. Apart from that relatively small defect, this process is quite simple and powerful. So, for example, if you are photographing a graduation ceremony, you will be able to record the entire procession of the students, but still take some individual photographs of the one student you may be focusing on.

And, what is more remarkable, you can even take a burst of shots while recording a video. Just press the down cursor button and choose a setting from the burst menu. Here, again, there are some limitations on what sort of burst can be taken. The camera will not use a speed greater than 10 frames per second, even if you set it to a speed of 11, 40, or 60 frames per second. And, even with the slower modes that include continuous autofocus adjustment, the focus will be fixed when the first image is taken. Also, naturally, all shots will be at an image size no greater than 3.5 M, the maximum size for still shots taken during video recording.

Recommendations for Recording Video

Now that I have covered the essentials of recording video footage with the D-Lux 6, here are some recommendations for how to approach that process. I have to say that I am quite impressed by the wealth of features and capabilities of this camera in the movie-making arena. I don't pretend to have definitive answers as to how best to use the D-Lux 6 for making movies. The existence of such sophisticated video recording features in such a small digital camera is a fairly new phenomenon, and I expect filmmakers will develop a wide range of applications for those features. For now, I will just offer some general guidelines for how to use the D-Lux 6's motion picture functions.

For everyday use, such as for taking video clips of a vacation trip or a birthday party, it's probably a good idea to stick with the Snapshot setting on the mode dial, and, on the Motion Picture menu, set Recording Mode to MP4 and Recording Quality to FHD. In that way, the result should be excellent-quality videos, well exposed, and ready to show on an HDTV (or standard TV) or to edit in your favorite video-editing software. If you want the highest quality possible for viewing on an HDTV and don't care whether the video files are easy to edit, choose AVCHD with the maximum quality of PSH.

If you happen to be in a situation that clearly fits one of the scene settings, like a sunset or a night scene, you might want to switch the mode dial to the Scene position and select the appropriate scene type, to take advantage of the camera's programming for that environment.

If your inner Kathryn Bigelow or Quentin Tarantino is struggling to emerge, by all means turn the mode dial to the Creative Video position and start experimenting with the Manual Exposure setting using incredibly fast or quite slow shutter speeds, hours-long shots (using the SH setting of AVCHD video, if your camera permits it), custom Photo Style settings, pull-focus shots using manual focus, and maybe throw in some creative uses of white balance settings to boot.

If you aren't ready to deal with a whole host of manual settings, but still would like to add some flashy coloring to your movie scenes, consider shooting in Creative Control mode, choosing a style like Impressive Art or Cross Process. If you would like to produce slow-motion footage, use the High Speed setting of Creative Video mode to slow your video footage down to one-quarter normal speed.

My point is that the possibilities for creativity with the D-Lux 6's movie-making apparatus are, if not unlimited, at least sufficient to provide a framework for a great array of experimentation. So consider the options, and don't hesitate to press the red Movie button when inspiration strikes.

Chapter 9: Other Topics

Macro (Closeup) Shooting

Macro photography is the art or science of taking photographs when the subject is shown at actual size (1:1 ratio between size of subject and size of image) or slightly magnified (greater than 1:1 ratio). So if you photograph a flower using macro techniques, the image of the flower on the camera's sensor will be about the same size as the actual flower. You can get wonderful detail in your images using macro photography, and you may discover things about the subject that you had not noticed before taking the photograph. For example, I used the macro setting of the D-Lux 6 to take the picture shown in Figure 9-1, giving a detailed close-up view of a phalaeonopsis orchid.

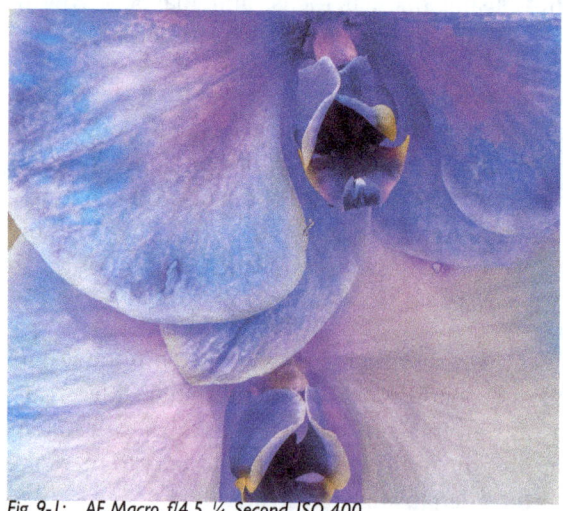

Fig. 9-1:   AF Macro, f/4.5, ¼ Second, ISO 400

346

The image of another orchid in Figure 9-2 shows how using a macro shot can blur the background to emphasize the subject in the foreground, because the depth of field is very limited when focusing this close to the subject.

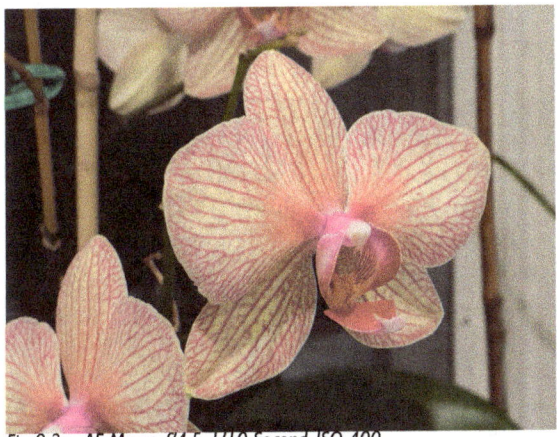

Fig. 9-2: AF Macro, f/4.5, 1/10 Second, ISO 400

The D-Lux 6, like many modern digital cameras, has a special capability for shooting in macro mode. To use this mode, you have only one basic setting to change: Move the focus switch on the left side of the lens barrel to its middle position, for Autofocus Macro, with the flower icon indicating macro, as shown in Figure 9-3.

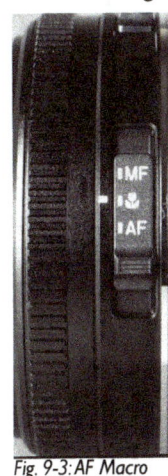

With the autofocus switch in the macro position, the camera can focus as close as 0.4 inch (1 cm) from the subject, when the zoom lever is pushed all the way to the wide-angle setting. With the lens zoomed in for its full optical zoom, the camera can focus as close as about 1 foot (30 cm) in macro mode. If the camera is not set to macro mode, then the closest focusing point is about 1.64 foot (50 cm) at either end of the zoom range.

Fig. 9-3: AF Macro

347

You don't have to use the AF Macro setting to take macro shots; if you use manual focus by moving the focus switch to its lowest position (MF), you can also focus on objects very close to the lens. You do, however, lose the benefit of automatic focus, and it can be tricky finding the correct focus manually.

When using the AF Macro setting, you should use a tripod when possible, because the depth of field is very shallow at close distances and you need to keep the camera steady to take a usable photograph. It's also a good idea to use the self-timer. If you do so, you will not be touching the camera when the shutter is activated, so the chance of camera shake is minimized. You normally should leave the built-in flash retracted, so it can't fire. Flash from the built-in unit at such a close range would likely be of no use in normal circumstances.

However, it may be possible to use the built-in flash for macro shots if you take a lightweight, translucent disk with a hole in its center and place it around the lens of the D-Lux 6. Then, when you fire the flash, it lights up the disk, which provides diffused light on the small subject you are photographing. For an excellent discussion of this and related issues, see *Closeup Shooting* by Cyrill Harnischmacher (published by Rocky Nook 2007).

One question you may have is: If the camera can focus down to one centimeter and out to infinity in macro mode, why not just leave it set in macro mode? The answer is that in macro mode, the focusing system is set to favor short distances, and it is not as responsive in focusing on farther objects. So in macro mode you may notice that it takes more time than usual to focus on subjects at greater distances. If you don't need the fastest possible focusing, you can just leave the camera set to AF Macro at all times, if you want the whole range of focusing distances to be available.

Using RAW Quality

I've discussed RAW several times before this. RAW is a Quality setting in the D-Lux 6's Recording menu. It applies only to still images, not to motion pictures. When you set the Quality to RAW, the camera records the image without as much in-camera processing as it performs for JPEG images; essentially, the camera takes in the "raw" data and records it, leaving you with a wide range of options for altering it through software.

There are both pros and cons to using RAW in this camera. First, the cons. A RAW file takes up a lot of space on your memory card, and, if you copy it to your computer, a lot of space on your hard drive. In addition, there are various functions of the D-Lux 6 that are incompatible with the RAW setting, including Snapshot mode, Intelligent Dynamic, Digital Zoom, Resize, Cropping, Leveling, Title Edit, Text Stamp, Favorite, Print Set (printing directly to a photo printer), Aspect Bracket, and White Balance Bracket. The bracketing settings will seem to work, but only one image will be recorded instead of the normal three or four. You will be able to go through the steps to set Aspect Bracket or White Balance Bracket, but the camera will display an X next to the icon for the setting on the screen, meaning you have set it, but it won't work.

You also cannot shoot in RAW quality with the Panorama, Handheld Night Shot, HDR, or 3D scene types, and you cannot shoot in RAW with the Extended ISO settings above ISO 6400. Also, you cannot use the fastest settings of burst shooting (40 or 60 frames per second) or the setting for burst shooting with flash when using RAW quality, and any burst shooting will be slowed down when shooting in RAW.

Finally, you may have problems working with RAW files on your computer because of incompatibility with editing software, though those problems can be overcome by getting updates to your software.

On the other hand, using RAW files has several very positive points. The main benefit is that RAW files give you an amazing amount of control and flexibility with your images. When you open up a RAW file in a compatible photo-editing program, the software gives you the opportunity to correct problems with exposure, white balance, color tints, and other settings. For example, the image in Figure 9-4 is shown as it is being opened in Adobe Camera Raw software, which gives you the opportunity to make basic adjustments to the image before performing other edits, such as cropping and retouching.

If you had the aperture of the camera too narrow when you took the picture, and it looks badly underexposed, you can manipulate the Exposure slider in the software and recover the image to a proper exposure level. Similarly, you can adjust the white balance after the fact, and remove unwanted color casts. You can adjust the highlights and shadows. In effect, you get a second chance at using optimal settings, rather than being stuck with an unusable image because of unfortunate settings when you pressed the shutter button.

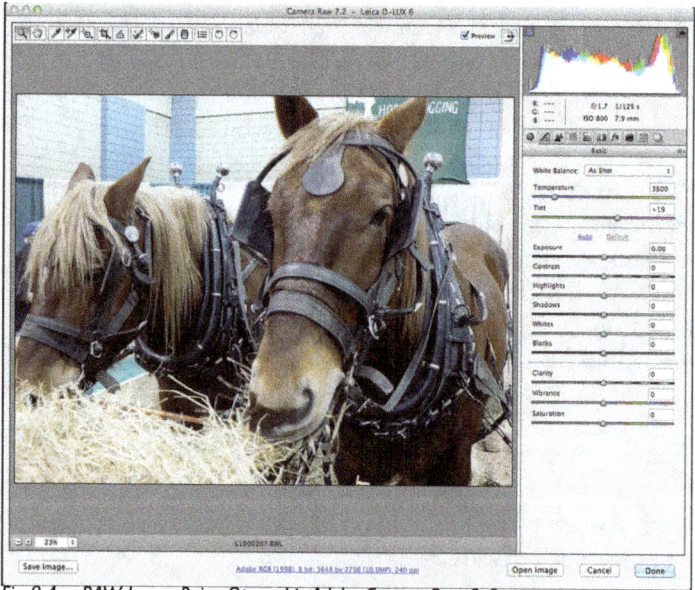

Fig. 9-4:   RAW Image Being Opened in Adobe Camera Raw Software

The drawbacks to using RAW files are either not too severe or they are counter-balanced by the great flexibility RAW gives you. The large size of the files may be an inconvenience, but the increasing size of hard drives and SD cards, with steadily dropping prices, makes file size much less of a concern than previously. I have heard some photographers grumble about the difficulties of having to process RAW files on the computer. That could be an issue if you don't regularly use a computer. I use my computer every day, so I don't notice. I have had problems with RAW files not loading when I didn't have the latest Adobe Camera Raw plug-in for Photoshop or Photoshop Elements, but with a little effort, you can download an updated plug-in and the software will then process and display your RAW images. The D-Lux 6 comes with a license for Adobe Lightroom, a program for processing RAW files, so you don't have to buy any additional software to work with your RAW images.

The bottom line is you certainly don't have to use RAW, but you may be missing some opportunities if you avoid it.

Using Flash

As I discussed earlier, the Flash setting, accessible through the Recording menu or the Quick Menu, controls the settings for flash: Auto, Auto with Red-eye Reduction, Forced On, Slow Sync/Red-eye, and (when using external flash) Forced Off.

These choices can be broken down as follows: First, decide if you want to allow the flash to fire at all. If you don't want to, then don't pop up the built-in unit and don't attach an external unit. (Remember, there are some cases in which you can't make that decision because the camera won't let you. The obvious one is the flash burst setting in burst mode. If you choose that setting without popping up the flash or attaching an external flash, the camera will not let you press the shutter button. If you choose the Night Portrait setting of Scene mode, the camera will remind you to pop up the flash, but will still let you take a picture without the flash.)

351

If you decide to allow the use of flash, you may have some further decisions to make, depending on what shooting mode you're using. If you're using Snapshot mode, once you've popped up the flash (or attached an external one), your flash decision-making is done. In that recording mode, the camera automatically selects Auto mode for the flash, will determine whether to fire it, and, if so, whether to use Slow Sync and/or Red-eye reduction.

With some scene types, the camera will also make flash decisions for you. For example, with the Scenery, Night Scenery, Handheld Night Shot, HDR, Sunset, Glass Through, and 3D settings, the flash is forced off, even if it's popped up. With the Portrait and Soft Skin settings, it's initially set to Auto with Red-eye Reduction, though you can use the Flash menu option to change it to Auto or Forced On. As noted earlier, with the Night Portrait setting, the flash is set to Slow Sync with Red-eye Reduction, and the camera displays a message asking you to pop up the flash; that flash setting cannot be changed.

To take back some of the decision-making authority from the camera, let's assume you're shooting in Program mode. Now you have to decide whether to choose Auto, Auto with Red-eye Reduction, Forced On, or Slow Sync with Red-eye Reduction.

Let's start with Forced On. Why would you want to force the flash to fire, when you could set it to Auto and let the camera decide whether it's needed? One case is when there is enough backlighting that the camera's exposure controls could be fooled into thinking the flash isn't needed. If, in your judgment, the subject will be too dark for that reason, you may want to force the flash to fire. Another such situation could be an outdoor portrait for which you need fill-in flash to highlight your subject's face adequately or reduce the shadows.

What about Slow Sync with Red-eye Reduction? Normally, the D-Lux 6's flash can synchronize ("sync") with the camera's shutter at any speed from 1/60 second to 1/4000 second. If you use the Slow Sync setting, the camera can sync at speeds as slow as one full second. With Slow Sync, the camera can set this relatively slow shutter speed so that the ambient (natural) lighting will have time to register on the image. In other words, if you're in a fairly dark environment and fire the flash normally, it will likely light up the subject (say a person), but because the exposure time is short, the surrounding scene may be black. If you use the Slow Sync setting, the slower shutter speed allows the surrounding scene to be visible also.

For example, Figures 9-5 and 9-6 were taken at the same time and in the same conditions; the only difference is that Figure 9-5 was taken with the shutter speed set at 1/160 second, in normal flash mode (Forced Flash). The background is quite dark, because the exposure was too short to light up the area beyond the vase. Figure 9-6 was taken in Slow Sync flash mode, which caused the camera to use a much slower shutter speed of 1/13 second, which allowed time for the ambient lighting in the room beyond the vase to illuminate the room so that it showed up more clearly.

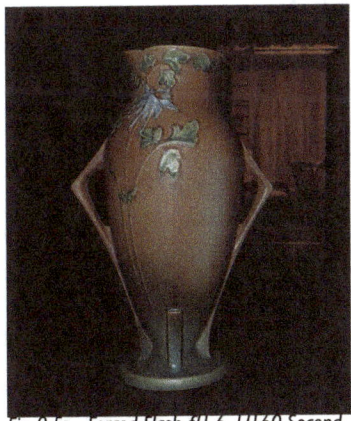
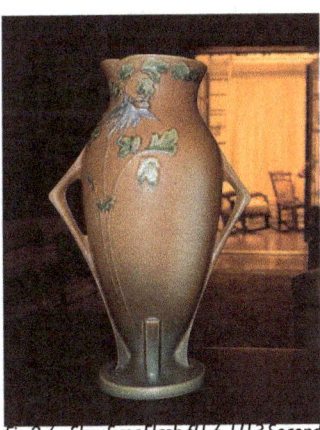

Fig. 9-5: Forced Flash, f/1.6, 1/160 Second   Fig. 9-6: Slow Sync Flash, f/1.6, 1/13 Second

The other aspect of this setting is Red-eye Reduction. Red-eye is a familiar problem in color photos of people taken with flash. If the subjects are sitting in a dark place, their pupils are likely dilated, and the sudden bright flash bounces off of the red blood vessels in their retinas, giving an unnatural red tint to their eyes. When Red-eye Reduction is set, the camera fires a quick pre-flash before the picture is taken. The idea is that the initial flash will cause the subjects' pupils to contract, reducing the chance of the red-eye effect.

The other choices in Program mode are Auto and Auto with Red-eye Reduction. Auto gives the camera a chance to use its programming to determine the best setting. It may set Red-eye Reduction and/or Slow Sync, depending on conditions. If you choose Auto with Red-eye Reduction, the flash will fire only if needed, but if it does, it will fire twice to reduce red-eye.

There are a great many considerations that go into the use of flash. The best advice I can give you is to consult an expert if you want to explore the subject further. An excellent book about the use of flash is *Mastering Digital Flash Photography*, by Chris George (Lark Books, 2008).

Infrared Photography

Infrared photography lets the camera record images that are illuminated by infrared light, which is invisible to the human eye. In some circumstances, cameras, unlike our eyes, can record images using this type of light. The resulting photographs can be quite dramatic, producing scenes in which green foliage appears white and blue skies appear eerily dark.

Shooting infrared pictures in the times before digital photography involved using infrared film and the appropriate filter to place on the lens. With the rise of digital imaging, you need to find a camera that is capable of "seeing" infrared light. Many cameras nowadays include internal filters that block infrared light. However, some cameras do not, or block it only to a relatively small extent. (You can do a quick test of any digital camera by aiming it at the light-emitting end of an infrared remote control and taking a photograph while pressing a button on the remote; if the remote's light shows up as bright white, the camera can "see" infrared light at least to some extent.)

The D-Lux 6 is capable of taking infrared photographs. In order to unleash this capability, you need to get a filter that blocks most visible light, but lets infrared light reach the camera's light sensor. (If you don't, the infrared light will be overwhelmed by the visible light, and you'll get an ordinary picture based on visible light.)

To accomplish this, you can purchase an infrared filter, such as an R72, along with an adapter that lets you attach the filter securely to the camera. Although Leica apparently does not sell an adapter as of this writing, there is a compatible adapter available from Panasonic, and other companies offer them also. I bought the Panasonic adapter, model no. DMW-FA1. To install the adapter, you have to unscrew the trim ring from the end of the D-Lux 6's lens and screw on the adapter in its place. You can then attach any filter or accessory lens with a 37mm diameter that screws on. Figure 9-7 shows an R72 filter attached to the D-Lux 6 using the Panasonic adapter. (Another adapter is discussed in Appendix A.)

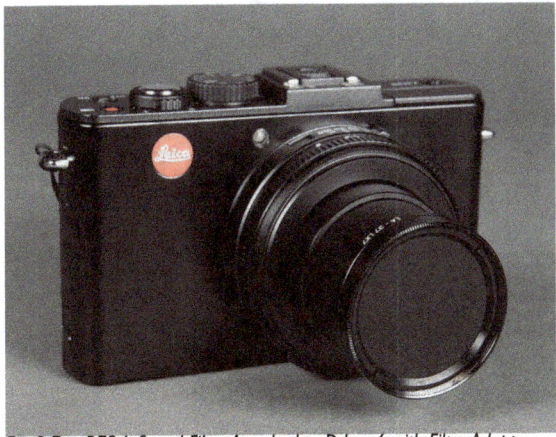

Fig. 9-7:   *R72 Infrared Filter Attached to D-Lux 6 with Filter Adapter*

To take the picture, I set a custom white balance, using brightly sunlit green foliage as the base. That is, I used the camera's White Balance setting and, in the screen for setting a custom white balance, I aimed the camera at the bright green foliage and pressed the Menu/Set button. I set the camera to shoot in Aperture Priority mode, set the camera on a tripod and the D-Lux 6 did the rest. The shot shown in Figure 9-8 was taken at f/1.4 with a shutter speed of 1/4 second, with an ISO setting of 640. I adjusted it somewhat in Photoshop. You can often get interesting results if you include a good amount of green grass and trees in the image, as well as blue sky and clouds.

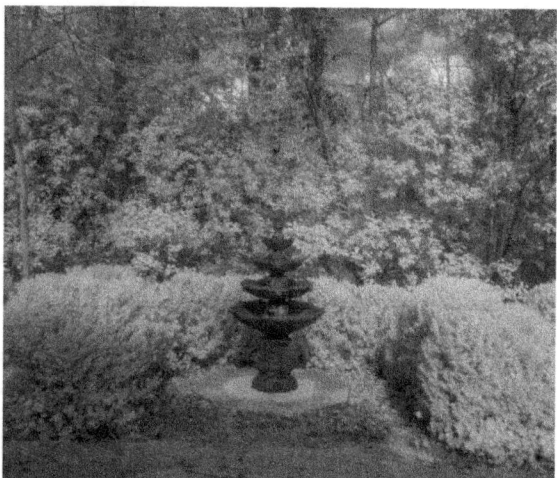

Fig. 9-8:   Infrared Image, f/1.4, ¼ Second, ISO 640

One problem that can arise with infrared photography using a camera like the D-Lux 6 is the presence of an unsightly bright "hot spot" in the middle of the image. One way around this problem is to use a wide aperture—f/2.0 or wider. In some cases, you can remove the spot in an editing program such as Photoshop or Photoshop Elements. Or, you may have to compose your shot so you can crop out the part with the hot spot. The image in Figure 9-8 did not contain a "hot spot," because I used a wide aperture.

Digiscoping and Astrophotography

Digiscoping is the specialized practice of attaching a digital camera to a spotting scope in order to get clear shots of remote objects, generally birds and other wildlife. Astrophotography involves photographing the stars, planets, and other celestial objects using a camera connected to (or aiming through) a telescope.

I can't say that using the D-Lux 6 is the best possible way to engage in either of these activities; if you want to take close-ups of animals, you might do better with a DSLR using a long telephoto lens, and for astrophotography you undoubtedly could do better with a special camera or imaging device that is designed for long exposures through a telescope. However, this book is about the D-Lux 6, and my goal here is to give you some suggestions about useful and enjoyable ways to use this camera, not to find the best possible methods for long-distance photography. That's not to say that the D-Lux 6 is a terrible camera for these types of photography; it does have several features that equip it nicely for taking pictures through a scope, including light weight, a high-quality lens, manual exposure, manual focus, RAW quality, and shutter speeds of up to 250 seconds.

One of the less-helpful features of the D-Lux 6 when it comes to astrophotography, however, is that it has a permanently attached lens. You cannot remove the lens and attach the camera's body directly to a telescope or spotting scope, as you can with a DSLR. So, you have to use the lens of the D-Lux 6 in conjunction with the eyepiece and main lens or mirror of the scope. There are many different types of scope and several different ways to align the scope with the D-Lux 6's lens. I will not discuss numerous combinations; I will talk mostly about the one combination I have recent experience with, and hope that it gives you enough general guidance to explore the area further if you want to pursue it.

For astrophotography, I used a Meade ETX-90/AT telescope, which has a diameter of 90mm (3.5 inches), an effective focal length of 1250mm, and a focal ratio of f/13.8. It is of the Maksutov-Cassegrain design, which uses both mirror and lens to focus light into a relatively small tube (small compared to the tube of a comparable reflector or refractor).

The challenge in using a camera like the D-Lux 6 to take photos through this telescope is to find a way to get the image that the eye can see through the scope's 1.25-inch (32mm) diameter eyepiece into the camera's lens. There are various possible approaches to using the D-Lux 6 for photography through a telescope or spotting scope, which is generally called "afocal" photography, meaning that both the camera and the telescope are focusing on the subject. One approach is to use a "universal" digiscoping adapter, such as one made by Zhumell. I tried that setup, but found it did not work well for me, because of the weight and bulk of the adapter and the fact that this adapter merely clamps the camera onto the telescope and does not provide a completely secure connection. It might be worth trying in some situations, though, and possibly might work better for terrestrial photography.

Another possibility is to use adapter rings to connect the camera directly to the telescope's eyepiece, providing a tight and continuous connection. For this approach, you need a filter adapter, such as Panasonic's Model No. DMW-FA1, as well as adapter rings that let you connect that adapter's 37mm ring to the telescope's eyepiece. You can get the proper adapter rings by purchasing the 37mm Digi-Kit, part number DKSR37T, from the online site www.telescopeadapters.com. That is the setup that is shown in Figure 9-9. The various connecting rings are shown in Figures 9-10 and 9-11, along with the telescope's eyepiece. You also might want to consider using the sturdier filter adapter that attaches to the camera by its bayonet mechanism, as discussed in Appendix A.

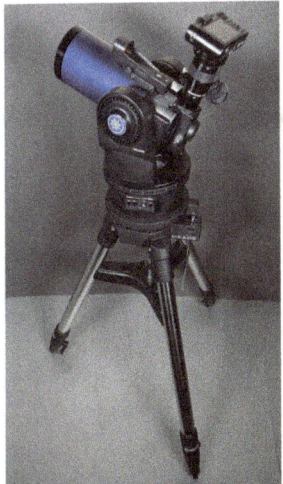

Fig. 9-9:   D-Lux 6 on Telescope

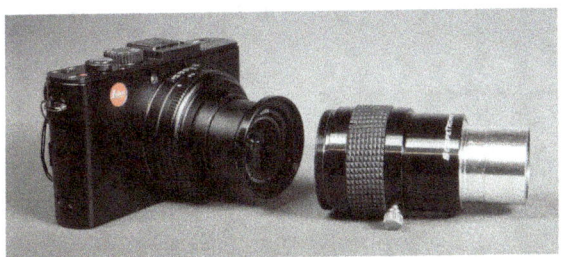

Fig. 9-10:   D-Lux 6 Next to Telescope Eyepiece

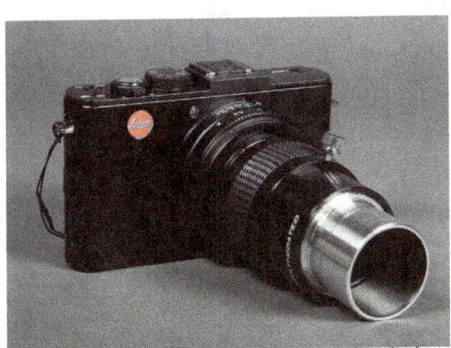

Fig. 9-11:   D-Lux 6 with Telescope Eyepiece Attached

359

When I used this setup to photograph the moon, I set the D-Lux 6 to Manual exposure mode and set the focus switch to manual focus. I initially set the camera's focus at infinity, and then used the telescope's focusing control to fine-tune the focus, using the MF Assist option with its enlarged view. I shot with RAW quality so I could adjust the exposure after the fact if necessary. It was hard to keep the telescope completely steady, so I used a fast shutter speed of 1/500 second to minimize the effect of the shaky image.

The most difficult aspect of this project was getting the focus accurate, because I found it hard to judge the focus on the screen, even with the enlarged image. I tried using the Clearviewer accessory (discussed in Appendix A) to get a magnified view of the LCD display, and I found that using that device helped me adjust the focus. After taking a series of shots I had several usable images, including the one shown in Figure 9-12.

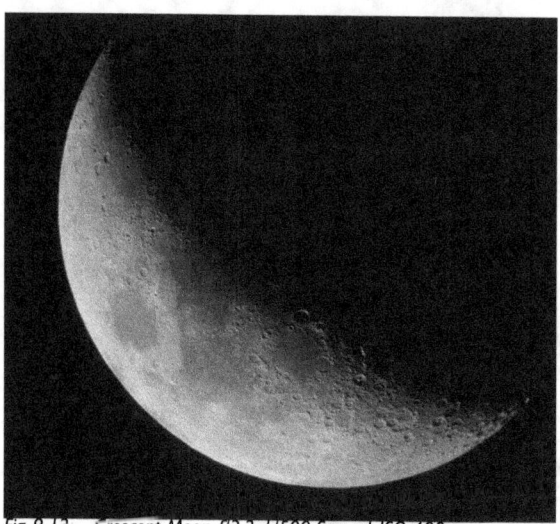

Fig. 9-12. Crescent Moon, f/3.2, 1/500 Second, ISO 400

To experiment with digiscoping, I used the same eyepiece to attach the D-Lux 6 to a Celestron Regal 80F-ED spotting scope, whose objective lens has a diameter of 80mm. This set-up in shown in Figure 9-13.

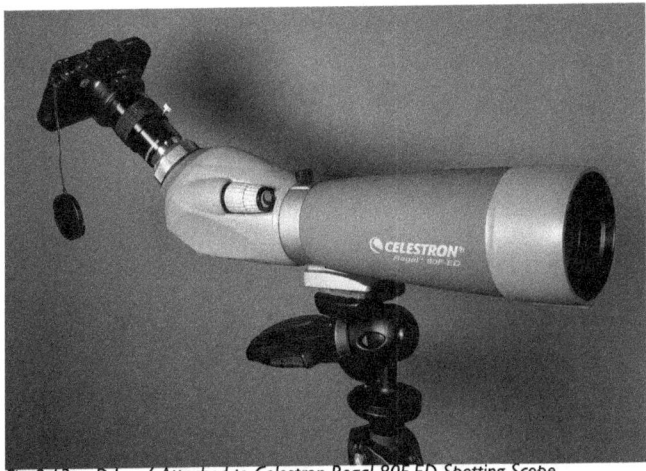

Fig. 9-13: D-Lux 6 Attached to Celestron Regal 80F-ED Spotting Scope

Using this scope with the D-Lux 6, I took a photo of a bird's nest high up in a tree, and it came out well. With this setup, I was able to use autofocus, and the camera managed to focus sharply on the nest, as shown in Figure 9-14.

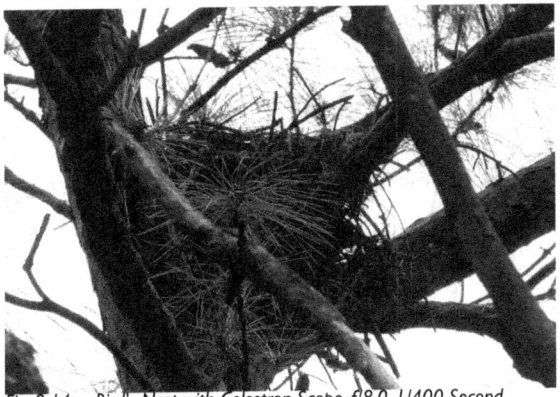

Fig. 9-14: Bird's Nest with Celestron Scope, f/8.0, 1/400 Second

361

For comparison, to show how much the scope magnified the nest, I took the shot seen in Figure 9-15, using the D-Lux 6's lens zoomed in to the limit of the optical zoom.

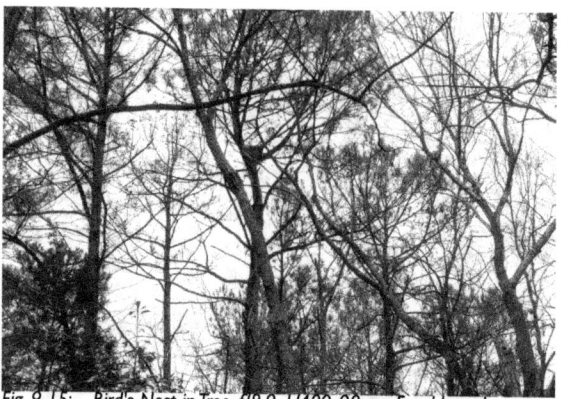

Fig. 9-15: Bird's Nest in Tree, f/8.0, 1/400, 90mm Focal Length

Overall, I was quite pleased with the ability of the D-Lux 6 to take photos through the Celestron spotting scope. This setup is not overly cumbersome, and the camera is able to capture sharp, well-exposed images while connected to the scope.

Street Photography

One of the reasons many users prize the D-Lux 6 is because it is very well suited for street photography—that is, for shooting candid pictures in public settings, often surreptitiously. The camera has several features that make it well-suited for this type of work—it is lightweight and unobtrusive in appearance, so it can easily be held casually or hidden in the photographer's hand. Its 24mm equivalent wide-angle lens is excellent for taking in a broad field of view, for times when you shoot from the hip without framing the image carefully on the screen. Its f/1.4 lens lets in plenty of light, and it performs well at high ISO settings, so you can use a relatively fast shutter speed to avoid motion blur. You can make the camera completely silent by turning off the beeps and shutter sounds.

What are the best settings for street shooting with the D-Lux 6? If you ask that question on one of the online forums, you are, naturally, likely to get many different responses. I'm going to give you some fairly broad guidelines as a starting point. The answer depends in part on your own personal style of shooting, such as whether you will talk to your subjects and get their agreement to being photographed before you start shooting, or whether you will fire away from across the street with a palmed camera and hope you are getting a usable image.

Here is one set of guidelines you can start with and modify as you see fit. To get the gritty "street" look, set Photo Style to Monochrome, but dial in -2 Noise Reduction and -1 Sharpening. Use RAW plus Fine JPEG to give you a good image straight out of the camera, but preserving your post-processing options. Set aspect ratio to 4:3. Set ISO to 800 for good image quality while boosting sensitivity enough to stop action with a fast shutter speed. Turn on burst mode at 5 frames per second, so you'll get several images to choose from for each shutter press.

When you're ready to start shooting, select manual focus mode and set the focus to approximately the distance you expect to shoot at, such as 6 feet (2 meters) on the MF scale. In the Setup menu, use the Function Button Set option to assign the 1 Shot AF option to the Function button. Then, when you're ready to snap a picture, use the Function button to make a quick fine-tuning of the focus. Some street photographers maintain that this method is faster and more efficient than relying on the autofocus system for the entire focusing process. For exposure, set the camera to Aperture Priority mode, with the aperture set to about f/4.5. When shooting at night, you may want to open the aperture a bit wider, and possibly boost the ISO to 1600. Of course, for this sort of shooting you will probably want to leave the lens zoomed back to its full wide-angle position, both to increase the depth of field and to take in a wide angle of view.

One of the main things I have found about street photography is that it is important to have your camera ready to shoot when an opportunity arises, and to be able to choose settings quickly. One way to do that is by storing a good group of street photography settings to the C1 or C2 slot of the mode dial, as discussed in Chapter 7. Another way is to find a Scene mode or other automatic setting that gives the kinds of results you are looking for.

One example is shown in Figure 9-16. In this case, I was taking photographs in a city park when I found an opportunity for a "street photograph" of runners doing warm-up exercises, even though this was not exactly a "street" shot.

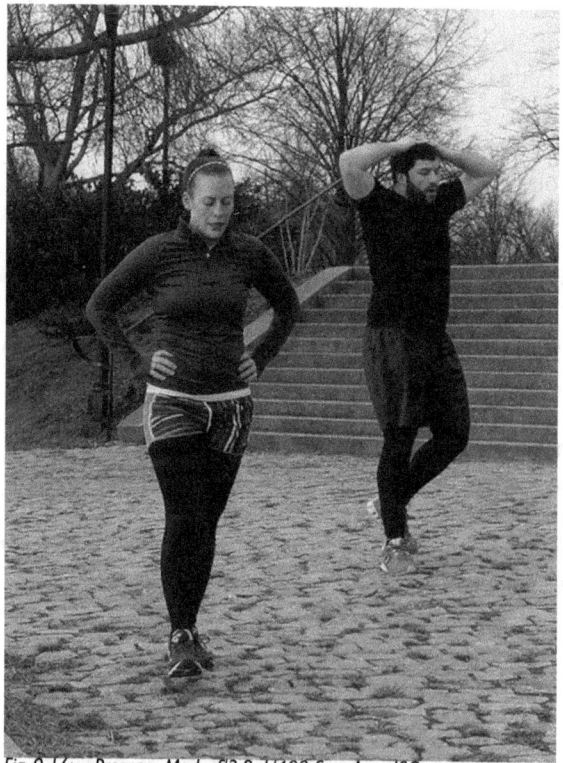

Fig. 9-16:   Program Mode, f/2.8, 1/400 Sec., Auto ISO

I took the photo in color because I did not have time to change to my "street photography" settings. I later converted the image to black and white in Photoshop, using the menu command Image-Adjustments-Black and White.

High Dynamic Range (HDR) Photography

I have mentioned High Dynamic Range (HDR) photography a few times earlier in this book, in connection with specific settings on the D-Lux 6 that use the HDR label: the iHDR menu option for Snapshot mode, the HDR setting in Scene mode, and the High Dynamic setting in Creative Control mode. Now I will discuss HDR photography more generally, and I will provide some advice about when to use these settings and offer an alternative approach when none of the in-camera options is sufficient to deal with a particular lighting situation.

HDR photography was developed to deal with the fact that cameras, whether using film or digital sensors, are not able to record images that retain clear details when the brightness of the scene includes wide variations. In other words, if part of the scene is in dark shadows and another part is brightly lighted, the scene has a "dynamic range" that may exceed the ability of the camera to deal with both the dark and the bright areas and still look presentable to the human eye.

A few years ago, the primary way to deal with this issue was to take multiple shots of the scene using different exposure settings, so the photographer would have a range of shots, some exposed to favor the dark areas, and some for the bright areas. The photographer would then merge these images using Photoshop or special HDR software to blend differently exposed portions from all of the shots. The end result is a composite HDR image that can exhibit clear details throughout all parts of the image.

More recently, many camera makers have incorporated some degree of HDR processing into their cameras in an attempt to help the cameras even out areas of excessive brightness and darkness to preserve details, without the need to use software to merge multiple shots. With the D-Lux 6, Leica has provided an HDR setting in Scene mode that is designed to deal with this sort of situation automatically. I will discuss the use of that setting and compare it to a more established way of processing HDR images—using special software to combine multiple images.

For this comparison, I found a location in the city where a red truck was parked in the shadow of a wall on a bright, sunny day. I first photographed the scene with the D-Lux 6 set to Program mode, with no special settings or adjustments. The result is shown in Figure 9-17.

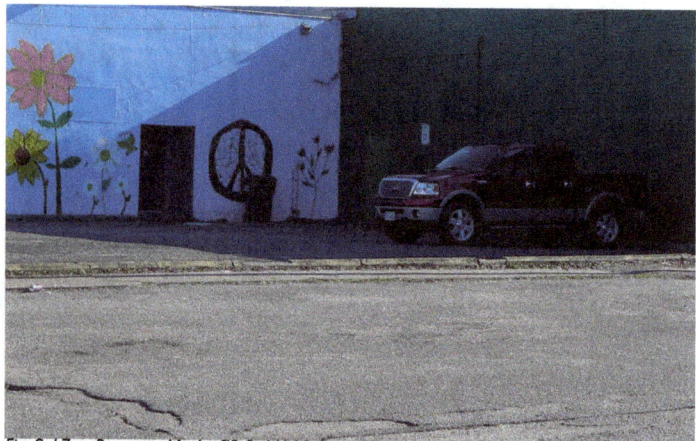

Fig. 9-17:   Program Mode, f/2.8, 1/160 Sec., ISO 80

As you can see, the truck is barely visible in the deep shadow cast by the wall on the right, and the wall at the left is also somewhat underexposed. The driveway and parking lot, being gray in color, appear to be exposed normally.

Next, using the Auto Bracket feature (discussed in Chapter 5), I took a series of three shots at the widest possible range of exposure settings. One of the shots looked like Figure 9-17, and one was much too dark to be of use. The third shot, shown in Figure 9-18, used settings that resulted in a definite overexposure.

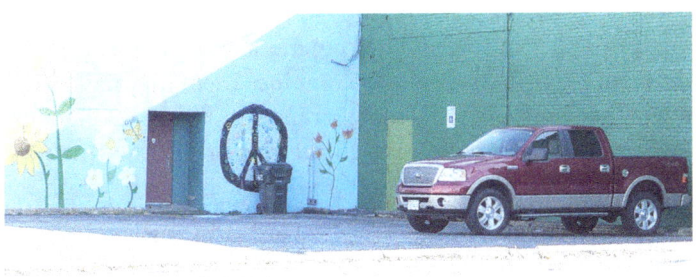

Fig. 9-18:   Program Mode, f/2.8, 1/160 Sec., ISO 80, +3.0 EV

In this image, the truck appears to be properly exposed, along with the wall on the right. The wall on the left and the parking lot and driveway are heavily overexposed.

I then used the D-Lux 6's special HDR setting in Scene mode to see how it would handle the wide dynamic range that is involved here. The result of using this setting is shown in Figure 9-19.

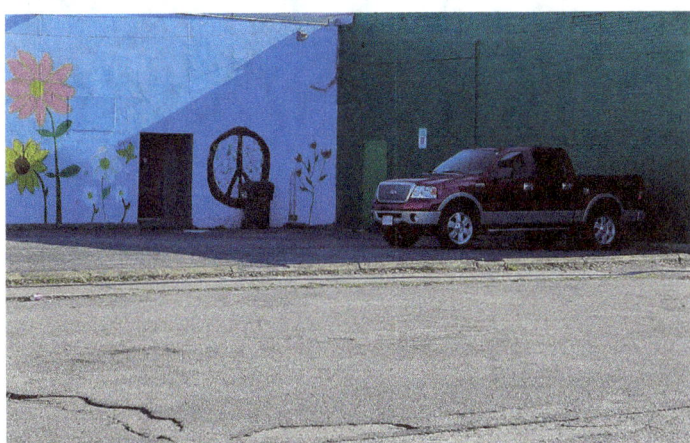

Fig. 9-19:   SCN Mode, HDR Setting

With this special setting, the camera takes several shots with different exposure values and combines them internally in an attempt to even out the dynamic range. In Figure 9-19, the D-Lux 6 produced a composite image that brings the truck out of the shadows to some extent and still keeps the wall on the left from becoming overexposed. However, the truck is still somewhat shrouded in darkness.

Next, I tried another approach. For Figure 9-20, I took one of the Program mode images that was shot with RAW quality. I opened it in Adobe Camera Raw software and moved the Highlights slider to the left, to a negative value, and move the Shadows slider to the right, to a positive value. I also moved the Exposure slider somewhat to the right, for increased over-all exposure. With these adjustments, the software pulled details out of the shadows and moderated the brightness of the highlights. This experiment helped to demonstrate the power of the RAW format for adjusting your images after they have been captured in the camera.

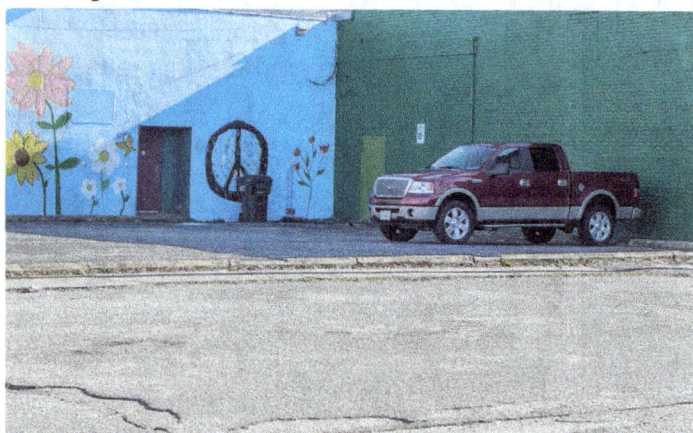

Fig. 9-20:   HDR Series - Image Adjusted in Adobe Camera Raw Software

Finally, for Figure 9-21, I took the images shown in Figures 9-17 and 9-18 and merged them in Photomatix Pro software, which is specially designed to create HDR images.

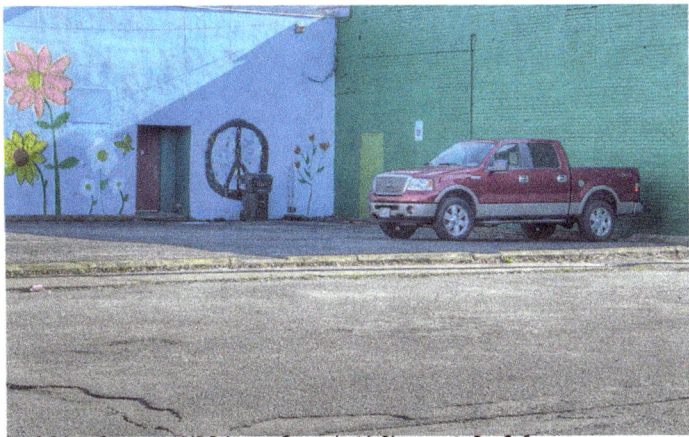

Fig. 9-21:   Composite HDR Image Created with Photomatix Pro Software

The final result produced by the HDR software did the best job of reproducing all areas with reasonable exposure values, in my opinion, because the truck is clearly visible and the other parts of the scene are displayed with a reasonable range of exposure values. However, the use of RAW processing came quite close to this result, at least in this particular case.

Of course, it can be time-consuming to produce an HDR image through post-processing with HDR software or a RAW processor like Lightroom, but this method of creating an HDR image has the advantage of letting you tweak the results to your satisfaction. If you want to produce reasonable results with a minimal expenditure of time and effort, though, the camera's built-in HDR settings can be of great value.

Connecting to a Television Set

The D-Lux 6 is quite capable when it comes to playing back its still images and videos on an external television set, though you have to purchase an optional HDMI cable in order to do this with an HDTV set.

If you want to get the best possible quality of audio and video, you should purchase an HDMI cable with a male mini-HDMI connector at one end and a standard male connector for an

HDTV input on the other end. Leica sells its own cable, part number 14491. However, you can use any cable with these connectors.

To connect the cable to the camera, you need to open the little door on the right edge of the camera (when held in shooting position) and plug the mini-HDMI connector into the larger (upper) of the two ports inside the door, as shown in Figure 9-22.

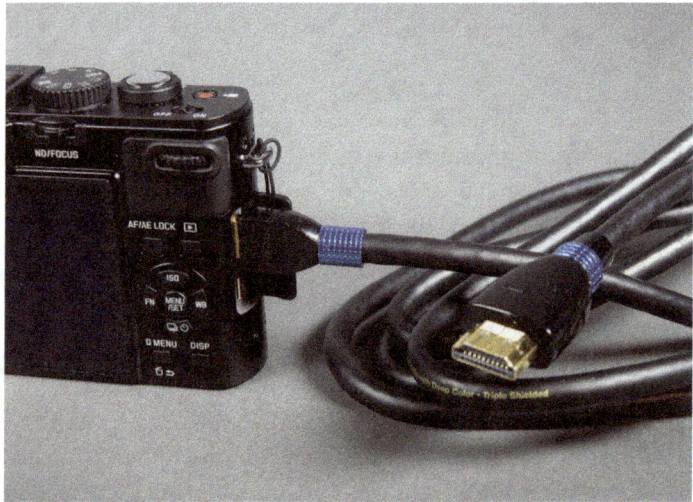

Fig. 9-22: HDMI Cable Connected to HDMI Port of D-Lux 6

Then connect the other end to an HDMI input on an HDTV, select that input with the TV's controls, and you should be able to enjoy your videos, images, and slide shows on the large screen with excellent quality, and stereo sound.

If you want to connect the camera to a standard TV set, you need to use the standard audio-video cable that ships with the D-Lux 6. This cable has a mini-USB connector at one end and two composite, or RCA, connectors at the other end. The white RCA plug is for audio; the yellow one is for composite video. The mini-USB connector plugs into the smaller port inside the door on the camera's right side, as shown in Figure 9-23.

370

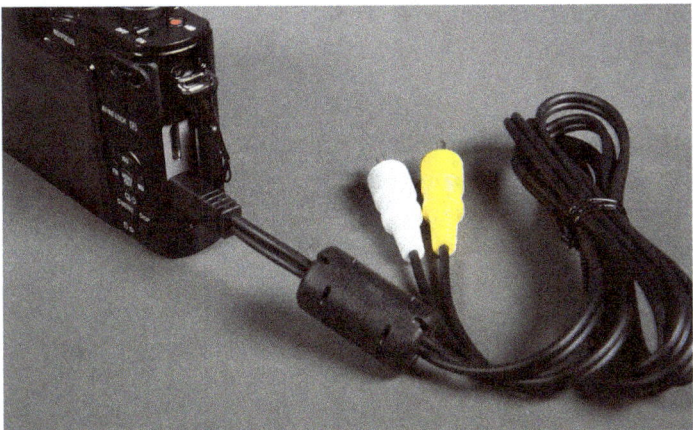

Fig. 9-23: Standard AV Cable Connected to AV Port of D-Lux 6

You then need to connect the yellow and white connectors to the composite video and audio inputs of a television set. You may then need to set the TV's input selector to Video 1, or AUX, or some other setting so it will switch to the input from the camera. Note that the camera outputs only monophonic (single-channel) sound through this cable; so, if you want stereo sound, you need to use the HDMI connection described above.

Once the connections are set and the TV is turned on with the correct input selected, turn on the camera in playback mode, and you can play back any images or video you have recorded. HD video will play back with no problems on a standard television set. You may need to switch the camera's aspect ratio to achieve the proper result on screen, using the Output-TV Aspect item on the Setup menu.

Once you have connected the camera to a TV set, the camera operates very much the same way it does on its own. Of course, depending on the size and quality of the TV set, you will likely get a much larger image, possibly better quality (on an HD set), and certainly better sound. This difference will be especially noticeable in the case of slide shows and videos; the

371

audio sounds much better through TV speakers than it does through the camera's minuscule speaker.

One side note: When the camera is connected to a TV with the standard audio-video cable, it not only can play back recorded images; it can also record as it normally does. Therefore, when the D-Lux 6 is hooked up to a TV while in recording mode, you can see on the TV screen the live image being seen by the camera. So you can use the TV screen as a large monitor to help you compose your photographs or video shots. (This setup does not work with the HDMI connection, only with the standard AV cable.)

Appendix A: Accessories

When people buy a new camera, especially a fairly sophisticated model like the D-Lux 6, they often ask what accessories they should buy to go with it. The D-Lux 6 community is fortunate in that there are quite a few options available. I will hit the highlights, sticking mostly with items I have experience with. For information about a wide range of other accessories, including underwater housings, cable releases, digiscoping adapters, and other items, see the web sites listed in the Resources list in Appendix C. Following is some information from my own experience.

Cases

There are endless types of camera case on the market. For those who like to get the case that is designed for their camera, there is the official Leica leather case, shown in Figures A-1 and A-2.

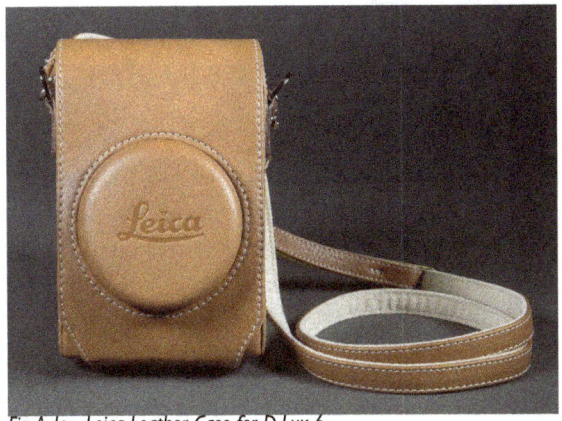

Fig. A-1: Leica Leather Case for D-Lux 6

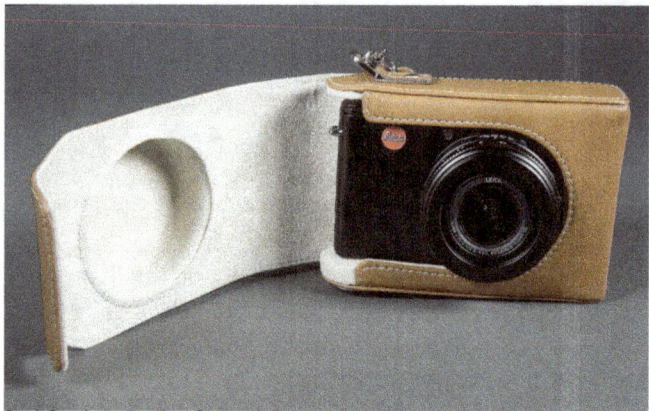

Fig. A-2:   Leica Leather Case with D-Lux 6 Inside

Actually, I really like this case, for several reasons. First, it is made of real leather, has an excellent feel, and protects the camera very well. Also, the case has a very nice appearance, and it comes with both a neck or shoulder strap, shown in Figure A-1, and a wrist strap, shown in Figure A-3.

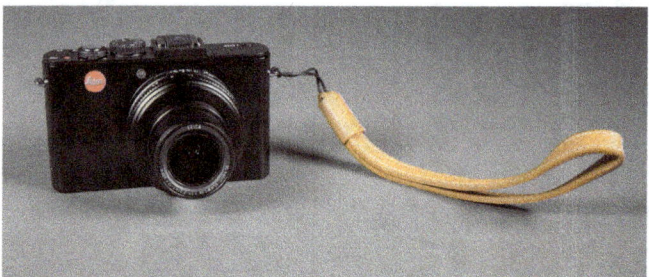

Fig. A-3:   Leica Wrist Strap for D-Lux 6

However, much as I like the official case, I usually like to keep my camera in a bag or case that has room for extra batteries, battery charger, connecting cables, the user's manual, flash, and other items, which the official case lacks.

With the D-Lux 6, I have been using the Tamrac Digital 2 camera bag, model number 5692, shown at the left in Figure A-4. It is compact and can be carried easily on a belt using a flap that fastens with both snaps and Velcro. It has a main compartment that easily accommodates the D-Lux 6 as well as a smaller, zippered compartment that can hold an extra battery or memory card. A similar model that also works well is the Lowepro Rezo 60, also shown in Figure A-4.

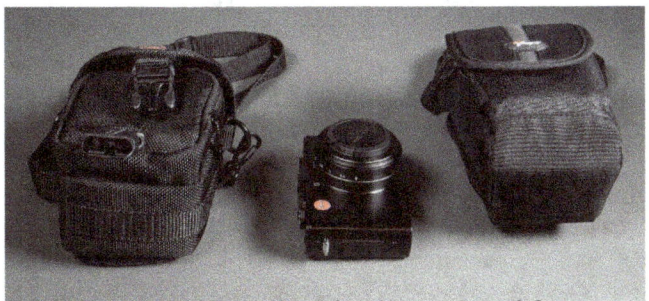

Fig. A-4:   Tamrac Digital 2 Camera Bag (left) and Lowepro Rezo 60 Case

When I need to carry more equipment, I often use a Lowepro Inverse 100 AW beltpack, shown in Figure A-5, which has plenty of room for the camera and accessories, as well as small water bottles and other items for a day trip.

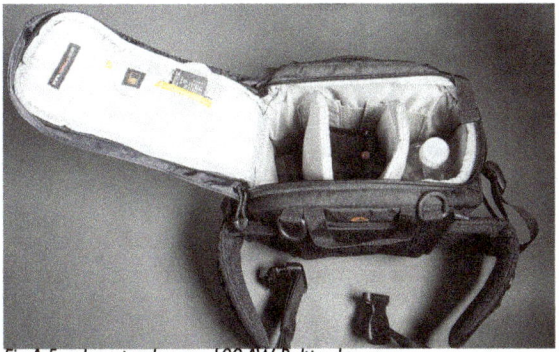

Fig. A-5:   Lowepro Inverse 100 AW Beltpack

Of course, there are countless other possibilities out there for carrying your D-Lux 6 and some accessories; these are a few items that have worked for me.

Batteries

This is one item you should get when you get the camera or soon after. I use the camera heavily and run through batteries quickly. You can't use disposable batteries, so if you're taking pictures and the battery dies, you're out of luck unless you have a spare (or an AC adapter and a place to plug it in; see below). The Leica battery used for the United States, model BP-DC10-U, costs about $70.00.

However, you also can use the battery sold by Panasonic for the Lumix DMC-LX7, which is very similar to the D-Lux 6. The battery used in that camera is the DMW-BCJ13, shown in Figure A-6, which costs about $40.00.

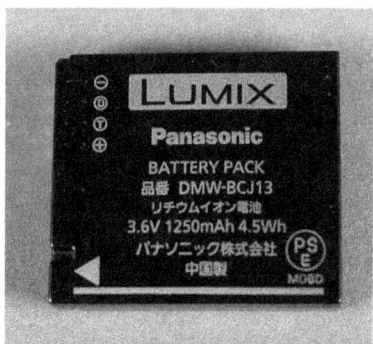

Fig.A-6:   Battery for Panasonic Lumix DMC-LX7

I have used the Panasonic battery in my D-Lux 6 for many hours with no problems; it appears to be functionally identical to the Leica battery. You also can find replacements from brands such as Wasabi for considerably less. I have not tried any third-party batteries in my D-Lux 6, but they should work well, as long as you are careful to check reviews and find a brand with a track record of reliability. Some brands do not have the chip that lets the camera show remaining battery power, though, so check the product description on that point.

AC Adapter

Another way to power the D-Lux 6 is with an AC adapter. Although Leica does not offer such an accessory, you can use the one made by Panasonic for the LX7 camera. This accessory works well in providing a constant source of power to the camera. However, it is inconvenient to use. You need to obtain not only the Panasonic AC adapter, model no. DMW-AC5, but a device called the "DC Coupler," model number DMW-DCC7, which looks like a battery, but has a connecting port in its side. Figure A-7 shows the AC adapter with the coupler at the right. Figure A-8 shows the DC Coupler separately, in a closer view.

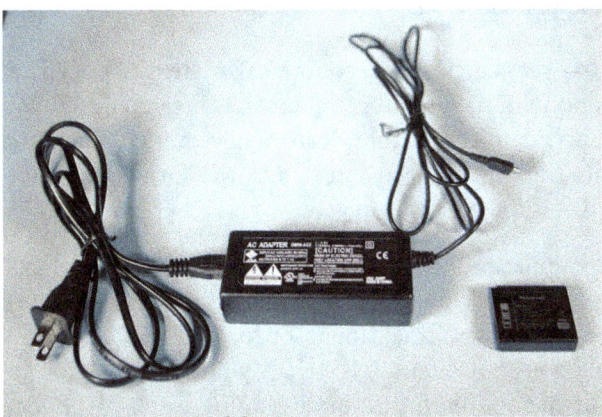

Fig. A-7: AC Adapter and DC Coupler

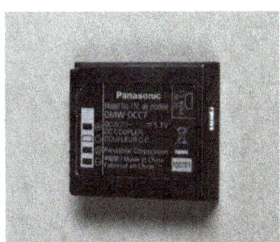

Fig. A-8: DC Coupler for AC Adapter

You have to insert the DC Coupler into the battery compartment of the camera, then close the battery door, open up a small flap in that door, and connect the cord from the AC adapter to the port in the DC Coupler, as shown in Figure A-9.

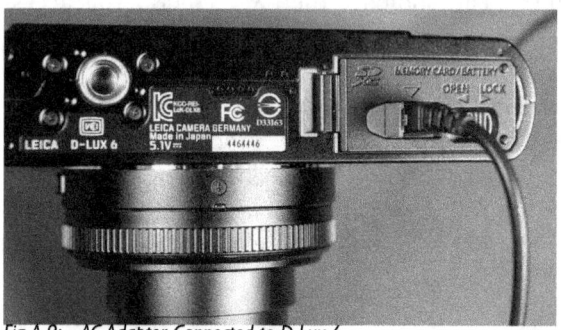

Fig. A-9: AC Adapter Connected to D-Lux 6

This is not a very efficient (or economical) system, at least from the standpoint of the user. It is a clunky arrangement, and you can't get access to the memory card while the AC adapter is plugged in. But, if you need constant power for a long period of time, this is the only way to get it.

I should emphasize that providing power to the camera is all this adapter does. It does not act as a battery charger, either for batteries outside of the camera or for batteries while they are installed in the camera. It is strictly a power source for the camera. It may be useful if you are doing extensive indoor work in a studio or laboratory setting, to eliminate the trouble of constantly charging batteries. Also, if you are taking advantage of the ability of the U.S. version of the D-Lux 6 to film very long videos, as discussed in Chapter 8, you will need the AC adapter; that is why I got one. It also could be useful for a lengthy series of time-lapse shots. For everyday applications and still shooting, though, the AC adapter should not be considered a high-priority purchase.

Viewfinders

The D-Lux 6 does not come equipped with a built-in viewfinder. There is no window for you to look through at eye level to compose your shot, as there is with a DSLR or with many rangefinder cameras. Nowadays you can find many small digital cameras that rely solely on the LCD screen for composition. Some photographers don't mind the lack of a viewfinder, and some find that lack unbearable.

Leica does not appear to offer an optical viewfinder for this model of camera. However, you can get an external optical viewfinder from Panasonic, model number DMW-VF1, that fits into the hot shoe of the D-Lux 6, as shown in Figure A-10. That viewfinder provides a 24mm field of view, the same as the wide-angle setting of the D-Lux 6's lens, so you can see the same view through the viewfinder as through the lens, provided the lens is zoomed all the way out. This viewfinder is very light and easy to install or remove. If you are going to be doing a good deal of shooting using the 24mm focal length and would like to compose your shots through a window rather than using the LCD screen, this accessory is an excellent addition to the camera.

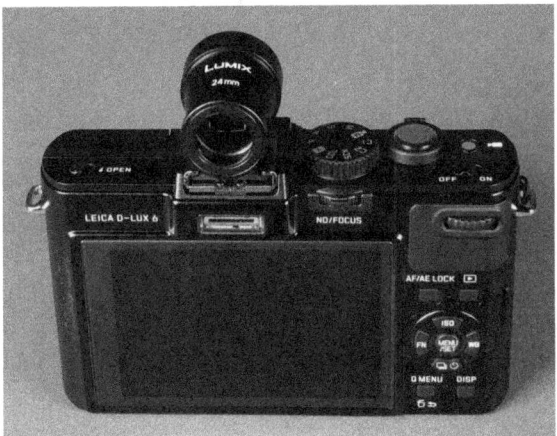

Fig. A-10:   Panasonic DMW-VF1 Viewfinder on D-Lux 6

You also can find many third-party optical viewfinders that will work well with the D-Lux 6. For example, Figure A-11 shows a Voigtlander 28mm viewfinder installed in the hot shoe of the D-Lux 6.

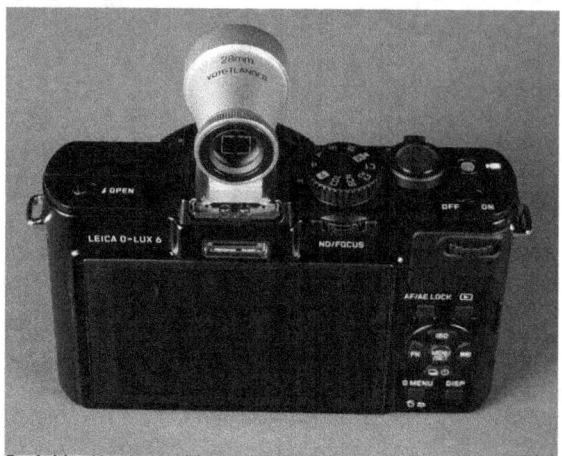

Fig. A-11: Voigtlander 28mm Viewfinder on D-Lux 6

When you use a viewfinder like this, you will probably want to use the Step Zoom feature of the D-Lux 6, discussed in Chapter 4, so that you can zoom the camera in precisely to the 28mm focal length. In that way, the viewfinder will be using the same angle of view as the camera's lens.

Another option with the D-Lux 6 is to use Leica's electronic viewfinder, Model No. EVF3. That viewfinder provides a clear, electronic view of what is seen by the camera's lens, along with all of the shooting information that ordinarily is displayed on the LCD screen. In effect, using this viewfinder gives the D-Lux 6 the functionality of a DSLR in the viewfinder arena. The view in the viewfinder is very clear and bright, and, of course, unlike the optical viewfinder, its view zooms in and out as you move the camera's zoom lever. You can flip the eyepiece up to a vertical position so it functions as a waist-level finder, also.

One drawback of the Leica electronic viewfinder is its cost. At this writing, it is selling for almost $400.00 in the United States. Because of that expense, I use the Panasonic version of the viewfinder, Model No. DMW-LVF2, which is functionally the same as the Leica version. The Panasonic viewfinder has a list price of about $250.00, and when I last checked at Amazon.com, it was available new for about $160.00. Figures A-12 and A-13 show the Panasonic LVF2 attached to the D-Lux 6, in standard position and in tilted-up position.

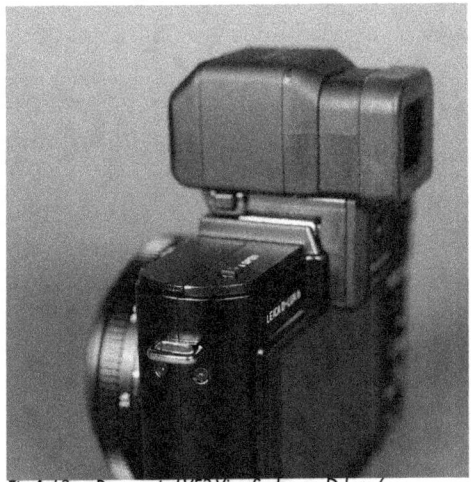

Fig. A-12:   Panasonic LVF2 Viewfinder on D-Lux 6

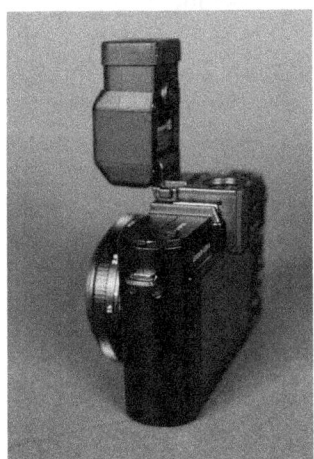

Fig. A-13:   LVF2 Viewfinder Tilted Up

Whether you need an external viewfinder with the D-Lux 6 is a matter of personal taste. Probably the main point in favor of having a viewfinder is that it lets you see clearly the scene the camera is aimed at, even in bad lighting conditions. For example, in bright sunlight, the LCD screen may be totally washed out, making it impossible to see the image on the screen well enough to compose the picture properly. Similarly, in dim light, it may be hard to make out the scene on the LCD.

Another point in favor of a viewfinder is comfort in your shooting position. Some photographers prefer to hold the camera up to their face and look through a little window when composing a shot. This may be from years of habit, or it may help them hold the camera steadier by bracing it against their forehead. The preference for a viewfinder also may have something to do with tradition; a person may feel more like a real photographer when using a viewfinder to evaluate the picture before pressing the shutter button. Finally, if you use an optical viewfinder rather than the LCD screen, you can turn off the D-Lux 6's screen, thereby saving battery power and extending the number of images you can record before changing batteries.

On the other side of the coin, the LCD screen provides a considerable amount of information, such as shutter speed, shooting mode, flash mode, etc., that the optical viewfinders available for the D-Lux 6 do not. (However, you could use the LCD screen to see that information and still use the viewfinder for composition.) Also, it may be possible to take candid pictures without detection more readily with the LCD screen, because you can casually aim the camera from waist level rather than holding it up to your eye. If you do get a viewfinder, one problem is that you cannot use any other accessory that uses the hot shoe, such as an external flash unit, at the same time. The viewfinder is light and easy to remove, though, so you can switch it out with the flash or other accessory.

Another option that is more expensive and bulky but works well for some photographers is the Hoodman Hoodloupe 3.0. This is a viewing device that you hold up against the LCD screen, shading the display and letting you view the screen through an eyepiece, as shown in Figure A-14.

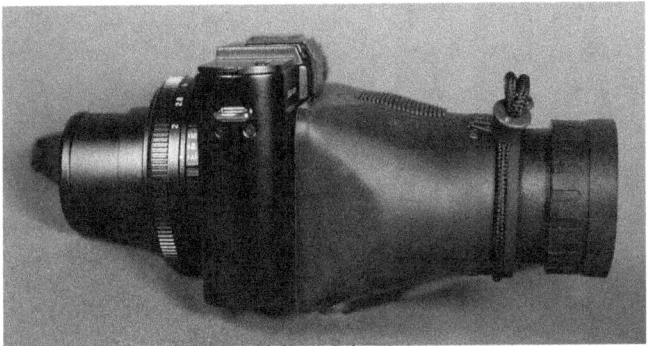

Fig. A-14:   Hoodman Hoodloupe 3.0 with D-Lux 6

With this setup, you can put the loupe's magnifying eyepiece up to your eye and see the camera's LCD screen very clearly without having it washed out by sunlight. Details are available at www.hoodmanusa.com.

Still another possibility for enhancing your view of the LCD in sunlight is the Clearviewer. This device attaches to the hot shoe of the D-Lux 6 and places a magnifying lens about two inches from the camera's display screen, as shown in Figure A-15.

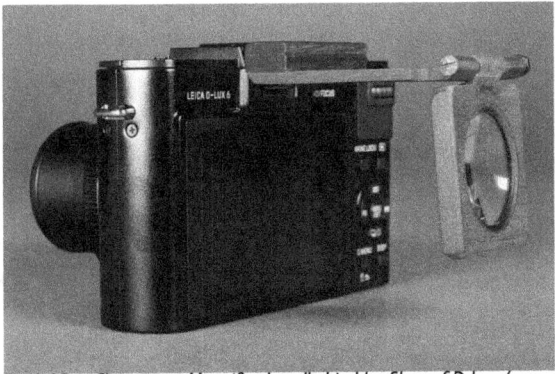

Fig. A-15:   Clearviewer Magnifier Installed in Hot Shoe of D-Lux 6

Some photographers are very happy with this system both because of its magnification and because it helps shield the screen from sunlight. Details about this option are available at www.clearviewer.com.

The ultimate decision in this area comes down to personal preference. Overall, I usually prefer to skip the viewfinders, the Clearviewer, and the Hoodman Hoodloupe, and just use the camera on its own, in order to keep down the bulk of the equipment and to leave the accessory shoe available for a flash if needed. But, if you're going to be using the camera in bright sunlight or if you prefer to hold it up to your face as you compose your photographs and videos, one of these external viewing devices can be a great plus.

Add-on Filters and Lenses

There is no way to attach a filter or other add-on item, such as a close-up lens, directly to the lens of the D-Lux 6. In order to add such accessory items, you need to get an adapter. As I discussed earlier in the Infrared section in Chapter 9, I have used the official adapter sold by Panasonic, model number DMW-FA1, as well as generic versions of the same item. In order to install the adapter, you first have to unscrew the thin trim ring from the end of the camera's lens, and set it aside in a safe place, as shown in Figure A-16. (The front ring is at the left in this image.)

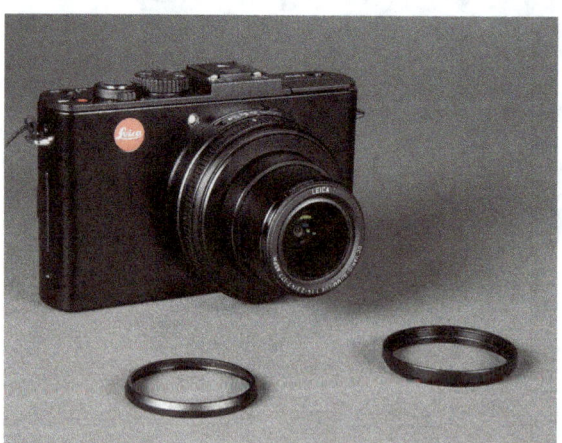

Fig.A-16: Panasonic-type Filter Adapter at Right, Camera's Front Ring at Left

The adapter, which looks very much like the trim ring that you just removed, screws onto the exposed threads of the D-Lux 6's lens assembly, and you can then screw any 37mm filter or similar accessory onto the end of the adapter. Figure A-17 shows the D-Lux 6 with a generic version of the DMW-FA1 adapter attached; a 37mm diameter filter or other accessory screws in to the adapter.

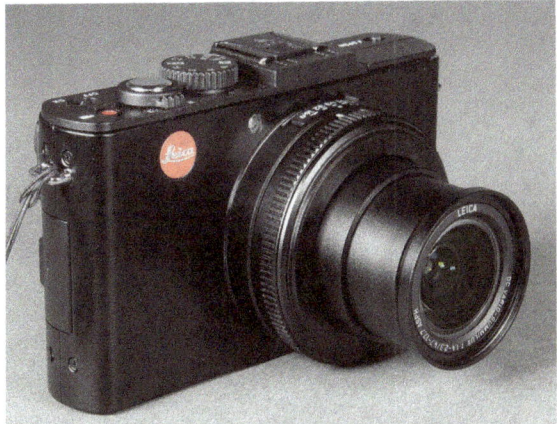

Fig. A-17:   Panasonic-type Filter Adapter Installed on D-Lux 6

Once you have the adapter, you may want to try attaching a UV (ultraviolet) filter, a neutral density filter, an infrared filter, a polarizer, or others, depending on your needs and interests. In addition, you might want to try attaching the D-Lux 6 to the eyepiece of a telescope or spotting scope using a suitable telescope adapter ring, as discussed in Chapter 9.

However, after I used the Panasonic filter adapter to connect my D-Lux 6 to the telescope, I became aware of a stronger adapter, made by a third-party company, Kiwi Fotos. This adapter, Model No. LA-52LX7, does not screw onto the front of the lens; instead, it attaches to a bayonet mechanism that is not mentioned in Leica's (or Panasonic's) official user manual. To get access to this mechanism, you have to grasp the thin ring located just in front of the camera's aperture ring. It can be difficult to get hold of, but, once you have grasped it, just turn it counter-clockwise and it comes off fairly easily. The

Kiwi adapter then attaches with its own bayonet mechanism, as shown in Figures A-18 and A-19.

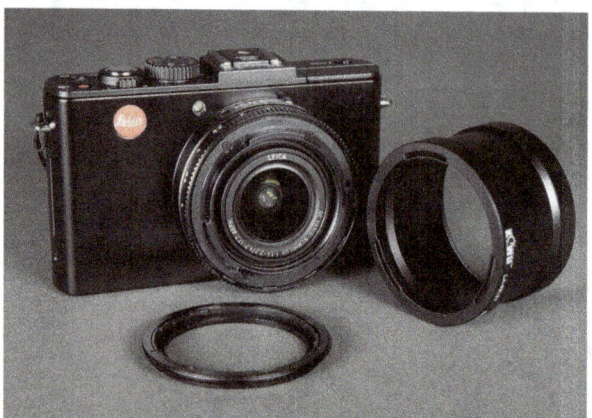

Fig. A-18:   Kiwi Fotos Filter Adapter, Bayonet Ring from D-Lux 6 is at Left

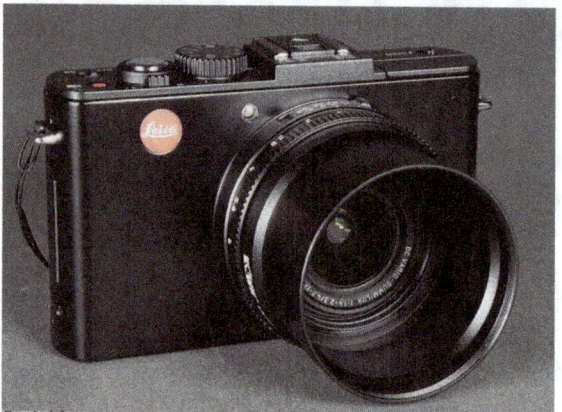

Fig. A-19:   Kiwi Fotos Filter Adapter Attached to D-Lux 6

This adapter system is, of course, not officially endorsed by Leica, but it has the advantage of using a strong metal tube that bayonets on to the lens, so it is capable of holding heavier objects, such as the Zeikos fish-eye lens shown in Figure A-20.

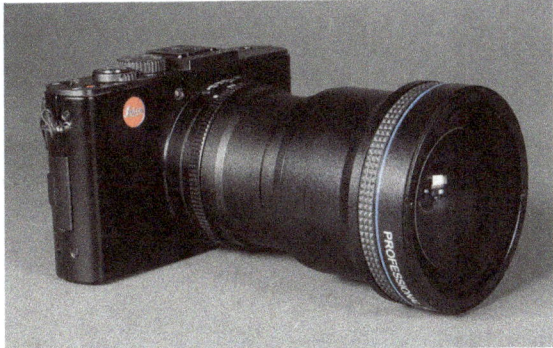

Fig. A-20: *Fish-eye Lens Attached to D-Lux 6*

That sort of lens produces images with a distorted, extreme wide-angle view, as shown in Figure A-18, which is useful for some applications and for creative effects.

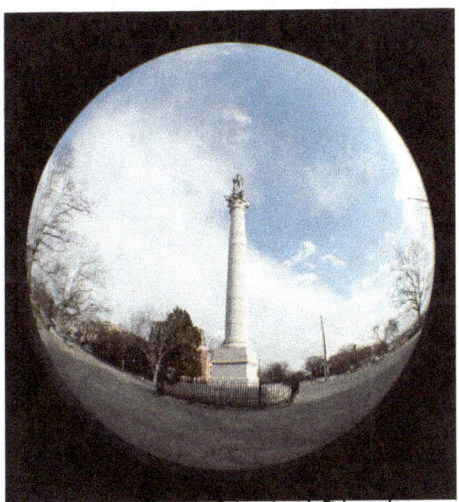

Fig. A-21: *Image Taken by D-Lux 6 with Fish-eye Lens*

It also may be preferable to use this sort of adapter when attaching the camera to a telescope, so the weight of the camera is not borne by the small plastic adapter sold by Panasonic. The Kiwi Fotos adapter accepts any filter or other accessory with a 52mm diameter. The company has a web site at www.kiwifotos.com.

External Flash Units

Whether to buy an external flash unit is going to be very much a question of how you will use the D-Lux 6. For everyday snapshots that are not taken at long distances, the built-in flash should suffice. It works automatically with the camera's exposure controls to expose the images well, and it is even capable of taking short bursts of flash exposures. It is limited by its low power, though. Using the Auto ISO setting at the wide-angle focal length, the range of the built-in flash is about 28 feet (8.5 meters), which is not bad, but, because this range is measured with Auto ISO, the ISO may have to rise to a level that introduces noise in the image, in order to expose the image properly.

If you need more flash power to take photos of groups of people in large spaces, or otherwise need more range or features, there are some options. One unit designated by Leica to work with the D-Lux 6 is the Leica CF22, shown in Figure A-22, a small unit that fits very well with the camera in terms of appearance and function.

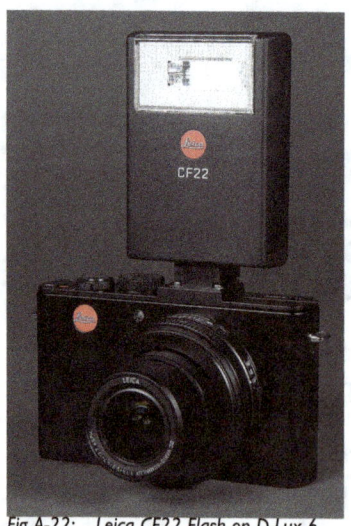

Fig. A-22:   Leica CF22 Flash on D-Lux 6

The CF22 fits into the camera's hot shoe and extends only about 3.75 inches (9.5 cm) above the camera. This flash unit weighs about 5.7 ounces (162 g) with batteries installed, provides more power than the built-in flash (its range at ISO 100 and f/2.0 is about 36 feet, or 11 meters), and communicates automatically with the camera in the same ways that the built-in flash does.

The main drawback with the CF22 is that it is a single unit with no rotating flash head, so there is no possibility of bouncing the flash off the ceiling or pointing it anywhere other than where the camera is pointing.

Other compatible external flash units are the Panasonic DMW-FL220, DMW-FL360 and similar models, including the Olympus FL-36R and the Metz Mecablitz 36 AF-4, which is shown in Figure A-23. (You need to purchase the version of the Metz flash that is compatible with Olympus and Panasonic cameras.)

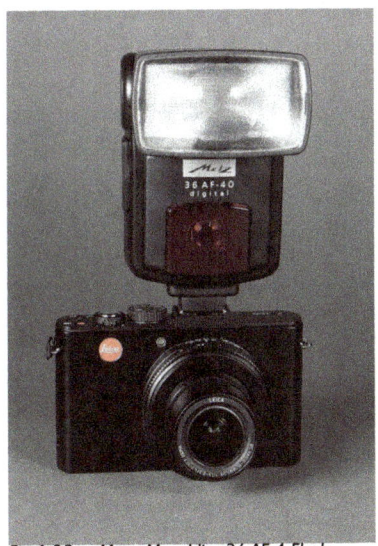

Fig. A-23:   Metz Mecablitz 36 AF-4 Flash

Like the CF22, these units function just like the built-in flash in terms of communicating with the camera for functions such as flash output and exposure control. The added benefit from the larger unit is that it provides features you probably would expect from an external flash: It has a flash head that rotates up to a vertical position, aiming at the ceiling, so you can bounce the flash at various angles. And, of course, it is considerably more powerful than the built-in flash.

The drawback to a flash unit such as this is its size. For example, the Metz Mecablitz 36 extends about 4.5 inches (10.8 cm) above the camera, as opposed to 3.75 inches (9.5 cm) for the CF22. The Metz flash with batteries installed weighs about 10.5 ounces (300 g), nearly twice as much as the CF22, and about the same as the camera itself. When I hold the camera with the Metz flash attached, the whole assembly feels a bit overbalanced by the flash. However, it is an excellent flash unit, and if you need the power and the flexibility that comes from having a rotating flash head, then this unit would be a good purchase.

Finally, here is one more area to explore in the flash arena: wireless triggers. Using a radio trigger on the D-Lux 6, you can control one or more flash units that are placed away from the camera, so you can have more options for the placement and effects of your flash illumination. I don't have a need to use this type of lighting very often, but in case your photography could benefit from this arrangement, here is information about a basic setup that I have used successfully with the D-Lux 6.

Figure A-24 shows a wireless trigger connected to the D-Lux 6's hot shoe, and Figure A-25 shows a matching wireless receiver connected by its hot shoe to a compatible flash unit, in this case the Leica CF22.

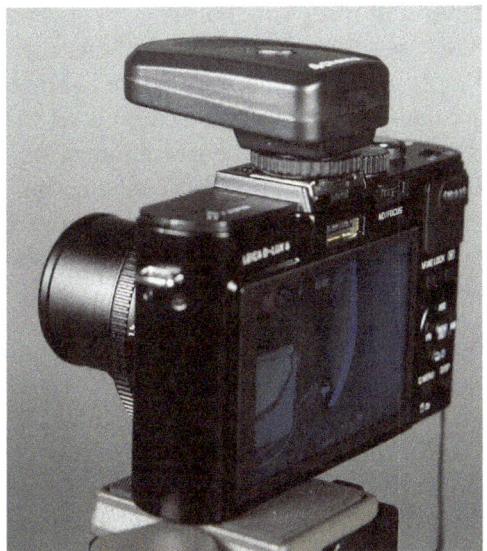

Fig.A-24:   Flash Radio Trigger on D-Lux 6

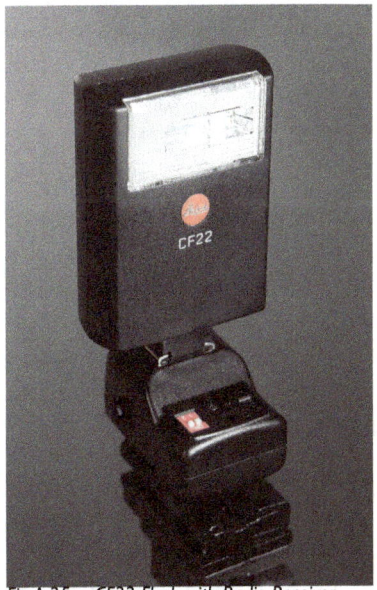

Fig.A-25:   CF22 Flash with Radio Receiver

I turned on the receiver and made sure both the trigger and receiver were set to the same channel using their DIP switches. Then I set the flash to its manual mode, and set the D-Lux 6 to Manual exposure mode with the flash forced on. I set the flash unit on a stand well away from the camera, aiming at my subject, and turned it on. Whenever I pressed the shutter button on the D-Lux 6, the flash fired. I had to adjust my exposure a few times until I had it right, because there is no automatic exposure with this setup.

One problem with this setup is that it only works with both the flash and the camera in Manual mode, and it won't work with a flash that has only TTL mode, such as the Metz Mecablitz 36 AF-4. But it worked well with the Leica CF22 flash. The particular set of trigger and receiver that I used is the NPT-04, sold by CowboyStudio through Amazon.com. The documentation is sparse, but the trigger and receiver worked as expected.

Another approach that has worked for some users is to use the built-in flash on the D-Lux 6 to control a remote flash that can be triggered by an optical slave unit, but I have not tried that setup with the D-Lux 6.

Cable Release Adapter

When you're taking long exposures with the camera on a tripod, or taking macro shots or engaging in astrophotography, it's critically important to avoid camera shake that can disturb the image. Using the self-timer is one way to minimize vibrations when the shutter is released. Another way is to use a cable release, so you can trigger the shutter remotely without exerting any force directly against the camera itself.

Of course, you may ask, where can you attach a cable release? With film cameras, it often is possible to screw a release into the shutter button. This is true even with some modern digital cameras such as the Fujifilm FinePix X100. It is not the case with the D-Lux 6, though; there is no place to screw in a cable release or even to attach an adapter that will fit over the shutter button, such as the adapter that fits into the flash shoe of some older Panasonic and Leica digital cameras.

I have tried one product that offers a possible solution to this problem—the Hama Cable Release for Digital Cameras. This item consists of a standard cable release that is attached to a round plastic plunger and a Velcro strap, seen in Figure A-26.

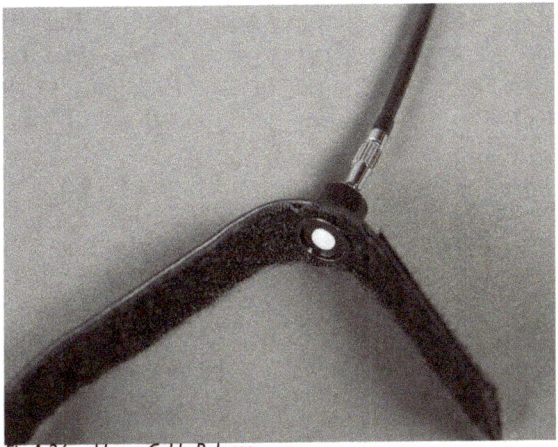

Fig. A-26:   Hama Cable Release

You wrap the strap around the camera with the plunger directly over the camera's shutter button, as shown in Figure A-27.

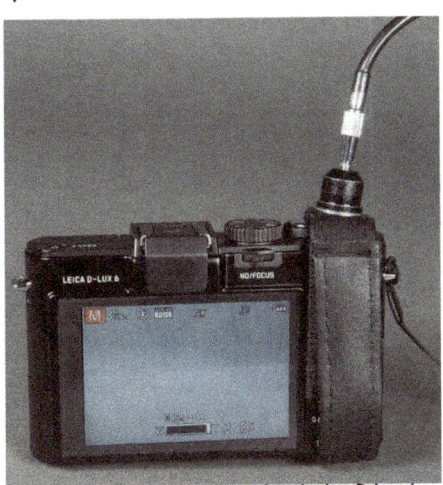

Fig. A-27:   Hama Cable Release Attached to D-Lux 6

Then, when you activate the cable release, the round plunger presses the camera's shutter button.

This device is designed to work with a variety of small cameras that do not have a way to screw in the standard connecting threads from a cable release. It takes some fiddling to get it properly situated so that it will activate the shutter button on the D-Lux 6. I had to shorten one side of the Velcro strap about one-half inch (1.2 cm) to get the strap to fit around the camera tightly. After a few attempts, though, I was able to get it to work. It does a good job, although I find that using the 2-second self-timer usually is just as effective.

If you have difficulty locating this item, as I did, a similar alternative is the Kaiser Strap-On Cable Release Adapter.

Automatic Lens Cap

Some photographers are unhappy that the lens cap of the D-Lux 6 is a separate item to keep track of. Although Leica provides a string to attach the cap to the camera, you still have to remember to remove the cap before turning on the camera, if you don't want to see the camera's warning message telling you to remove the cap and press a button to continue. You also may not like to have the lens cap dangling by its string, and possibly interfering with your actions while taking pictures.

One solution is the automatic lens cap seen in Figures A-28 and A-29. As you can see from the images, the automatic lens cap attaches to the camera's lens, and stays there whether the camera is turned on or off. When you turn the camera on, the three leaves of the cap open up automatically, allowing the lens to extend and operate freely. When you turn the camera off, the lens cap's leaves retract into place to protect the lens.

The automatic cap shown here is sold by a company called JJC and can be found online at Amazon.com and eBay. The company's web site is at www.jjc.cc. There may be similar items available from other companies.

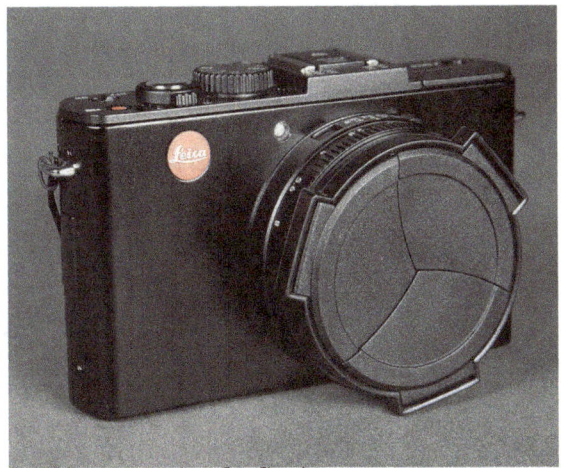

Fig. A-28:   Automatic Lens Cap Closed

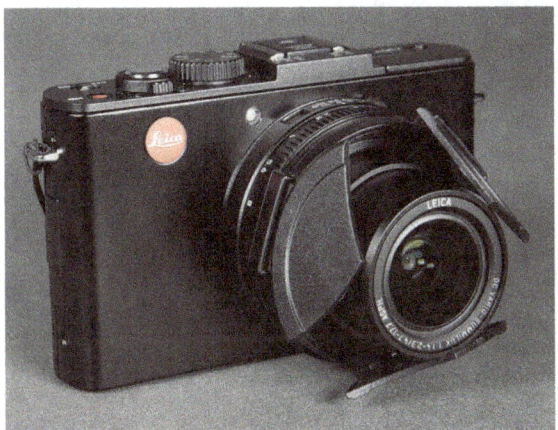

Fig. A-29:   Automatic Lens Cap Open

This lens cap uses the same bayonet mechanism used by the tube-style filter adapter shown in Figures A-18 and A-19. That is, to install the automatic lens cap, you have to remove the thin ring that covers the bayonet mechanism in front of the aperture ring.

Note that you may not be able to use this automatic cap if you have installed any other accessories on the lens using the Panasonic or other model of filter adapter.

Hand Grip

Some photographers find the D-Lux 6 a bit hard to grasp, because there is no raised area on the front of the camera that lets you get a firm grip with your right hand. The similar Panasonic Lumix LX7 has a curved area on the right side that is covered with a rubbery coating, giving you a firm handhold.

As a solution to the grip issue, Leica offers for sale a custom hand grip for the D-Lux 6, shown in Figures A-30 and A-31.

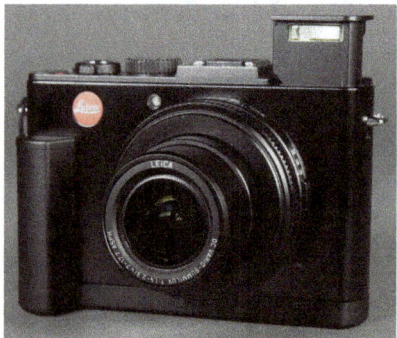

Fig.A-30:   Front View of Leica Hand Grip on D-Lux 6

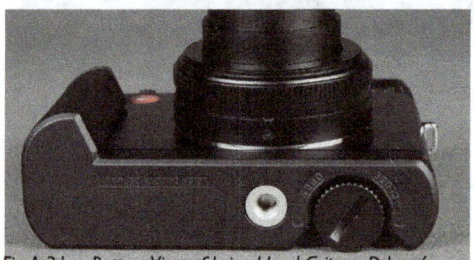

Fig.A-31:   Bottom View of Leica Hand Grip on D-Lux 6

This grip is solidly constructed and has a nice feel. Of course, when the grip is installed you cannot get access to the compartment where the battery and memory card are located. However, the grip does come with its own tripod socket, so you can still mount the camera on a tripod. I like the grip, but I do not consider it a high-priority purchase unless you find yourself having difficulty holding onto the camera without it.

Appendix B: Quick Tips

In this section, I'm going to list some tips and facts that might be useful as reminders, especially to those who are new to digital cameras like the D-Lux 6. My goal here is to give you small chunks of information that might help you in certain situations, or that might not be obvious to everyone. I have tried to include points that might be helpful but that you might not remember from day to day, especially if you don't use the D-Lux 6 constantly.

Use Burst shooting. The D-Lux 6 has excellent capabilities for shooting bursts of images. I recommend that you consider turning burst shooting on routinely for certain types of shooting sessions, unless you are running out of storage space or battery power, or have a particular reason not to use it. In the days of film, burst shooting was expensive and inconvenient, because you had to keep changing film, and you had to pay for film and processing. With digital cameras like the D-Lux 6, it just gives you more options. This type of shooting clearly works well for shooting sporting events and other scenes with fast-moving actions. It also is good for capturing shots of children at play or pets. Even with stationary portraits, you may get the perfect fleeting expression on your subject's face with the fourth or fifth shot. So, press the down cursor button, select one of the many burst options discussed in Chapter 5, and get multiple images with one press of the shutter button.

Avoid the Recording menu. You can't completely avoid it, but do your best to use the Quick Menu instead, because it gives you faster access to the settings you're most likely to need regularly, including Picture Size, Metering Mode, exposure compensation, Quality, Flash, and Photo Style. Also, set the Function button to call up an often-used option, such as

Photo Style, Quality, or AF Mode. When you do use the Recording Menu, speed through it by using the zoom lever to move a whole screen at a time, and wrap around to reach items that are far from your current position. And use the Custom Memory Set feature to set up your four most important groups of settings. For example, right now I have the C1 slot set up for my latest settings for street photography: Shooting mode = P; Photo Style = Monochrome; ISO = 800; AF Mode = 23-Area.

Use macro shooting for subjects other than nature. Many photographers create beautiful images using the macro capabilities of the D-Lux 6, shooting insects, flowers, and other natural items. But, with its focusing down to 1 cm (0.4 in), its wide-angle lens, and its excellent low-light performance, the D-Lux 6 can serve you in many other ways with its macro shooting. If you need a quick copy of a shopping list, memo, driving directions, receipt, or cancelled check, it might make sense to set the D-Lux 6's focus switch to AF Macro, maybe boost the ISO to 800 or so, and snap a quick image of the item. When you get to your destination, you can display the image on the LCD and enlarge it using the zoom lever, then scroll around in the document with the cursor buttons. The D-Lux 6 becomes a portable copy machine, if you want it to.

Explore the D-Lux 6's creative potential. The D-Lux 6 is a very sophisticated camera, with several advanced features that give you the ability to explore experimental photographic techniques. Here are a few suggestions: Use Manual exposure mode with its shutter speeds as long as 250 seconds to take night-time shots with trails of lights from automobiles, storefronts, and other sources. Use the shutter speeds as fast as 1/4000 second to freeze airplanes' propellers and other speedy objects in their tracks. Try "camera tossing," in which you toss the camera in the air, set to a multi-second shutter speed, to capture trails of light and color as the camera spins around. (But be sure to catch it on the way down!) Try zooming in or out during a multi-second exposure. Use long exposures (on a tripod) to turn night into day.

Adjust the camera's color settings. The D-Lux 6 has several settings that let you fine-tune them with further adjustments: White Balance, Photo Style, and several settings in Creative Control shooting mode. Try different settings for each of these until you find color combinations that convey what you would like to express with your images. Develop new settings, using the Custom option of Photo Style: Tweak the contrast, sharpness, saturation, and noise reduction settings until you find a combination that gives you the look you prefer. Some users like to use Standard Photo Style with sharpness at +1, noise reduction at -2, and the other settings at zero. You may want to try those settings and then experiment with variations. Once you have the settings the way you want them, save them to one of the four Custom slots on the Mode dial (C-1, C-2-1, C-2-2, or C-2-3), using the Custom Set Memory option on the Setup menu.

Take advantage of the RAW Quality setting. If you haven't previously used a camera that shoots RAW files, learn the benefits of RAW and use it to improve your images. Install and use the Adobe Lightroom software that comes with the D-Lux 6, or use other software, such as Adobe Photoshop or Photoshop Elements, to "develop" the RAW images. Learn how to fix problems with white balance, exposure, and other issues after the fact, using the flexibility of RAW shooting. Note, though, that if you shoot in the Scene or Creative Color mode using RAW only, your images will not have the special processing of those modes. I recommend you shoot with Quality set to Fine or RAW + Fine in those modes.

Take advantage of automatic and manual focus together. The D-Lux 6 offers a couple of ways to let you use the benefits of both automatic focus and manual focus at the same time. First, when the camera is set to manual focus mode, you can cause the camera to use its autofocus to check or correct your manual focusing. To do this, use the Setup menu to assign the 1 Shot AF option to the Function button. Then, just press the Function button to get the camera to use its autofocus after (or before) you have adjusted the focus manually. (Remember to wait until the MF scale has disappeared from the screen before pressing the Function button.) Also, if you have the camera set to autofocus mode, you can still use the ND/Focus lever to fine-tune the focus manually. To do this, make sure the AF/AE Lock button is assigned to lock focus. Then press that button to lock focus; at that point, you can move the ND/Focus lever left and right to adjust the focus manually.

Remember all the drawbacks of using High ISO settings. As you know, higher ISO settings (say, above 800) can introduce considerable visual "noise" into your images, and can detract from their appearance. What you may not always remember with the D-Lux 6, though, is that using any ISO setting above 6400 automatically reduces the resolution and Quality setting of the images. You could have a rude awakening if you someday forget this, and set out to take RAW images or 10 MP JPEG images at the best quality, but, after setting the ISO to 8000 or above, find that the images were reduced in resolution to 3 MP. (A similar issue arises with the fastest burst-mode settings of 40 and 60 frames per second.)

Use 1-Area autofocus in conjunction with Spot metering. When you do this, you can move the focus and metering area around the screen with the cursor buttons, so you can focus and meter a small, specific area of your scene. This procedure can make a big difference in the precision of your metering and focusing, and give you more control over your results.

Use the neutral density (ND) filter for some shots. There are some times when you want a slow shutter speed, but, in bright light, you can't achieve it, because the aperture can only go as narrow as f/8. One solution is to use the camera's built-in ND filter to reduce the light reaching the sensor, allowing slower shutter speeds. You might want to do this to slow down the rush of a waterfall to a smooth, blended look, or to achieve a motion blur in a shot of a passing runner or walker.

Diffuse your flash. If you find the built-in flash produces light that's too harsh for macro or other shots, some users have reported success with using translucent plastic pieces from milk jugs, other food containers, or broken ping-pong balls as home-made flash diffusers. Just hold the plastic up between the flash and the subject. Another approach you can try when using fill-flash outdoors is to use the Flash Adjustment menu option to reduce the intensity of the flash by -2/3 EV.

Use the self-timer to avoid camera shake. The D-Lux 6 has a solid self-timer capability that is very easy to use; just press the down cursor button and then choose your setting. This feature is not just for group portraits; you can use it whenever you'll be using a slow shutter speed and you need to avoid camera shake. It can be useful when you're doing macro photography, digiscoping, or astrophotography, also.

Always check your aspect ratio and autofocus switches. It's great to use the Custom Set Memory capability to store your favorite groups of settings in the four convenient slots. But remember that you can't store the settings for the aspect ratio or the focus mode, because they are controlled by physical switches. Whenever I turn my mode dial to C1 or C2 to activate a group of custom settings, I also quickly check to be sure the aspect ratio is where I want it and that the focus switch is set properly. Of course, you also need to open the flash if it might be needed, and set the zoom lever where you want it, but you're not as likely to forget those settings as the other two.

Set zone focusing. If you're doing street photography or are in any other situation in which you want to set the camera on manual focus for a specific zone or general distance, here is a quick way to do so. Set the focus switch to autofocus, then aim the camera at a subject that is approximately the distance you want to be able to focus on quickly. Once focus has been confirmed, slide the focus switch down to the manual focus position. Now you will have locked in the manual focus at your chosen distance, and you're ready to shoot any subject at that distance without the need to re-focus.

Appendix C: Resources for Further Information

Photography Books

A visit to any large general bookstore or library, or a search on Amazon.com or other sites, will reveal the vast assortment of currently available books about digital photography. Rather than trying to compile a long bibliography, I will list a few books that I consulted while writing this guide.

C. George, *Mastering Digital Flash Photography* (Lark Books, 2008)

C. Harnischmacher, *Closeup Shooting* (Rocky Nook, 2007)

D. Sandidge, *Digital Infrared Photography Photo Workshop* (Wiley, 2009)

S. Seip, *Digital Astrophotography* (Rocky Nook, 2008)

Web Sites

I will include below a list of some of the sites or links I have found to have useful information about the D-Lux 6, with the caveat that some of them may not be accessible by the time you read this.

Digital Photography Review

http://forums.dpreview.com/forums/1038

This is the current web address for the "LeicaTalk" forum within the dpreview.com site. Dpreview.com is one of the most established and authoritative sites for reviews, discussion forums, technical information, and other resources concerning digital cameras.

The Official Leica Site

http://us.leica-camera.com/photography/compact_cameras/d-lux_6/

The Leica company provides resources on its web site, including the downloadable version of the user's manual for the D-Lux 6 and other technical information.

Leica Rumors

http://leicarumors.com/category/leica-d-lux-6/

The "Leica Rumors" site provides posts and news reports about the D-Lux 6 and other Leica cameras. This is an excellent site to check for the latest news about the D-Lux 6.

Cambridge in Colour

http://www.cambridgeincolour.com

This is an excellent site with detailed tutorials about many topics in photography.

Infrared Photography

http://www.wrotniak.net/photo/infrared/

This site provides helpful information about infrared photography with digital cameras.

Digiscoping

http://www.birddigiscoper.com/

This site provides information about equipment and techniques for digiscoping in the form of a blog and a gallery of digiscoping images.

Reviews of the D-Lux 6

Following are links to reviews of the D-Lux 6 camera and of the very similar Panasonic LX7 camera:

http://www.ephotozine.com/article/leica-d-lux-6-review-21326

http://www.imaging-resource.com/PRODS/leica-d-lux-6/leica-d-lux-6A.HTM

http://www.reddotforum.com/content.php/299-Leica-D-Lux-6-Review-A-solid-improvement-over-the-D-Lux-5

http://www.dpreview.com/reviews/panasonic-lumix-dmc-lx7/

http://www.imaging-resource.com/PRODS/panasonic-lx7/panasonic-lx7A.HTM

http://www.cameralabs.com/reviews/Panasonic_Lumix_DMC_LX7/

http://www.steves-digicams.com/camera-reviews/panasonic/lumix-dmc-lx7/panasonic-lumix-dmc-lx7-review.html

http://www.adorama.com/alc/0013976/article/Panasonic-Lumix-DMC-LX7-Product-Review

http://www.photographyblog.com/reviews/panasonic_lumix_dmc_lx7_review/

http://www.whatdigitalcamera.com/equipment/reviews/compactcameras/129387/1/panasonic-lumix-lx7-review.html

Index

Symbols

A

C

D

S

Saturation
  adjusting with Photo Style menu option 135–136
Scene detection 63
Scene menu 95–97
Scene Menu menu option 319
Scene shooting mode 94–112
  getting information about scene types 97–115
  limitations on settings with 97
  selecting a scene type 95–97, 320
Scene types
  3D 110–112
  Baby 107
  Glass Through 109
  HDR 105
  Night Portrait 352
  Panorama Shot
    playback of panoramas 285
  Pet 108–109
  Portrait 97–98
  Scenery 98–99
  settings available with (table) 112
  Soft Skin 98
  Sports 103
  Sunset 109
SD card 22
SDHC card 22
SDXC card 22
  incompatibility issues 24
Sekonic Prodigi meter 228
Self-timer 76, 248–251
  icon displayed on screen 250
  limited options in Snapshot mode 249
  options 249
  setting for multiple shots 249
Setup menu
  in general 286–287
  using 32
Sharpness